I0815007

BORDEAUX

Liberté • Égalité • Fraternité
RÉPUBLIQUE FRANÇAISE
MINISTÈRE
DE LA CULTURE

BORDEAUX
MÉTROPOLE

GROUPE
Caisse
desDépôts

arc en rêve centre d'architecture

ACTES SUD

constellation.s

initiatives

Francine Fort
director, arc en rêve centre d'architecture

constellation.s is a major initiative designed by arc en rêve that explores new ways of living in the world. From 2 June to 2 October 2016, it took the form of a large exhibition with lectures and events focusing on particular themes. This book extends and augments that exhibition. More than just a catalogue, it is a way of continuing along the same path via discussions which, though by no means exhaustive, place a range of experiments and points of view in mutual perspective.

In response to the global upheavals that are transforming our living conditions, **constellation.s** identifies individual and collective initiatives that outline possible ways of building tomorrow's cities, taking into account the challenges we will face. In response to fear, inward-lookingness and extremism, constellation.s uses critical thought to help us to understand the world we live in. In response to the surfeit of images and words and omnipresent spectacle that characterise today's world, **constellation.s** fosters dialogue with people engaged in creative initiatives and ordinary people inventing new approaches to their daily lives.

constellation.s brings a range of different disciplines to bear—social sciences, philosophy, architecture and economics—all of which mirror the contemporary world.
constellation.s allows visitors to see and listen to experiments, testimonials, processes and situations from all over the world. These are like beacons pointing to possible new horizons that will help us live together in increasingly complex societies. In certain places we see practices emerging that challenge and undermine entrenched certainties. They are strategies that embrace instability and uncertainty, combine the tangible and the intangible, and open doors to new ways of using and producing architecture.

The aim of this book is to present and discuss this collection of micro-phenomena—this "constellation" of micro-initiatives.

As we know, the current crisis cannot be considered in economic and social terms alone. It is also, and above all, a political, ecological and cultural crisis whose solution can only lie in transforming civilisation itself. It is thus vital to place culture and knowledge at the heart of the matter as we explore challenges relating to civics and democracy and attempt to shed light on the future of our societies.

Because the primary aim of architecture is to give humans places to live in, it must be considered in relation to practical use and it must be carried out with the help of the residents themselves. To forge bonds and provide real "places" (in the strongest sense), it must reinvent the way it relates to the world.

constellation.s is intended to provide insights that make new conditions for human habitation intelligible; it highlights practices that take the risk of making the future meaningful; and it provides an opportunity to share innovative processes that help us to imagine new ways of inhabiting the world.

constellation.s, or how to change the World by inhabiting it

Michel Lussault

Prepared collectively over a three-year period, **constellation.s** was designed by the arc en rêve team as a kind of manifesto: a statement drawing on observations of the current state of our planet carried out by researchers in urban studies. Our approach was based on the premise that we have to recognise what makes the contemporary World so new. All too often, globalisation is reduced to an economic process and its derivative functions—such as the generalisation of tourism or access to information. But globalisation, which is generally considered as a primary cause (and indeed a final cause), is actually only an accompaniment to much more powerful changes.
This is only conceivable if we approach the contemporary World for what it is: a new way of using space for human societies and a paradigm shift in the order of human habitation on the planet. This is why it is useful to write "World" with a capital W, keeping the lower case presentation for what is "worldly"—i.e. social[1]. In a sense we are witnessing a revolution comparable in scale to that of the Neolithic period or the Industrial Revolution: two periods during which humans set up radically new frameworks for their existence. This time, it's an urban revolution: urbanisation, both globalised and globalising, is the principal force by which the World is instituted and imagined. By "instituted" I mean that urbanisation arranges new ways of seeing social, human and non-human realities; it "institutes" the spatial environments of societies. By "imagined", I mean that urbanisation sets up the ideologies, areas of knowledge, imagined scenarios and images that constitute globalised reality.
Some simple demographic data helps us to appreciate the scale of the phenomenon: urban populations underwent spectacular growth in the 20th century, rising from 220 million to 2.8 billion inhabitants—while world population grew from 1.7 à 6.1 billion. One in eight humans lived in cities in 1900, three out of ten in 1950 (the beginning of the new phase of global urbanisation), and five out of ten in 2008: for the first time since the beginning of humanity over 50 % of the world's population, at least 3.3-3.5 billion people, were living in urban areas. As the UN points out[2], by 2030 all of the world's regions will be more urban than rural, and in 2050 at least 70 % of the planet's expected population of 9.6 billion inhabitants (i.e. 6.7 billion people according to the UN's median hypothesis) will be living in cities. Asia will account for 50 % of the world's urban population

and Africa 20 %! In 150 years (1900-2050), the world's population will have grown six-fold, which is already considerable; but the world's population will have been multiplied by 30!
This is a major upheaval that changes all the conditions of our individual and collective existence. Urban growth is at least as rapid in medium-sized urban areas (500,000 - 1 million inhabitants) and small cities (less than 500,000 inhabitants) as in megacities (over 10 million). The latter focus our attention thanks to the "urban spectacle" they constantly offer and because of the part they play in structuring and polarising networks of flows and economic influences—but they only represent 9 % of the global population. Urbanisation is thus a phenomenon that occurs on all scales and, beyond statistics, primarily entails replacing modes of spatial organisation and long- prevalent lifestyles (those of the pre-industrial then industrial city, and their complementary "opposite", the countryside) with a new mode of existence: that of generalised urban development, which is rapidly imposing new geographical and temporal realities, new social and cultural structures, new economic frameworks, a new status for nature, new mindsets, and new dreamscapes. In a few generations, *Homo sapiens* really has become *Homo urbanus*[3], and an entire World has established itself via urbanisation: a World that constitutes the contemporary state of the terrestrial *ecumene* (the living space inhabited by humans)—which is different from everything that preceded it.

Starting with this approach to globalisation, we wanted to examine the current dynamic by presenting emerging modalities of human habitation and offering visitors another view of the local geography of the planet. The thesis we wanted to put forward was that the urbanised World faces new challenges relating to three global phenomena whose effects converge.

1. Even though poverty is on the decline, especially in the so-called "southern" countries, while working and middle classes in western states are being weakened by new forms of competition arising from the unbundling and delocalisation of systems of production, all societies are facing increased inequalities. This has put them under

all the more pressure because the dogma of neo-liberal economic regulation, applied continuously for almost fifty years, effectively considered this question to be irrelevant when compared to the perceived need for limitless growth. The latter would, thanks to the magical trickle-down effect (wealth trickling down from the rich to the poor), justify treating social problems as fringe issues.

2. Promoting connection and the free movement of people and goods as the supreme values of globalisation unquestionably leads to the constitution of a social and economic (and even political) space on a global scale, characterised by the constant circulation of everything and everyone and by the power of the agents and vectors that standardise landscapes, cultures and values. Some have inferred from this the idea of a so-called "flat" World[4]—an idea the exhibition actually rejected in its way (see below). But at the same time, the fears caused by such a redistribution of roles on a global scale and by the size of global migratory flows contribute to the re-emergence of aggressive ideologies of sovereign statehood and even xenophobic trends based on an exacerbated sense of national identity. This now poses a major political problem insofar as, more often than not, it involves calling into question the rights of individuals and groups on which the World has relied since the Second World War.

3. For several years now, people have increasingly found themselves facing a new force that is shaping the World in all its dimensions and challenging entrenched certainties and habits. We have entered the Anthropocene, and this is transforming everything. For us the Anthropocene has turned out to be not so much an exclusive interpretive tool as a meta-problem that informs and interrogates all aspects of society, on all scales. As for the question of widespread urbanisation, it prompts us to develop a systemic approach and to take into consideration all the activities of human and non-human agents. We are experiencing, and will be experiencing more and more intensely, a new state of the humanisation of the Earth directly linked to globalising urbanisation, which arises from the massive impact of certain activities on the planetary biophysical system and which is characterised, in particular, by global warming and its multiscale effects; by the exhaustion of non-renewable and even renewable

resources; by the reduction of biodiversity on a global scale; and by the increased vulnerability of spatial systems, including those that appear to be the most robust. This means we must develop a new understanding of global and local facts relating to the organisation of globalised spaces and the daily lives of Earth's inhabitants.

From the tension that exists between these three meta-changes we have inferred the following hypothesis, which we see as historically new: the generalised urbanisation of societies has produced conditions that bring us face to face with a paradoxical situation where the World—the particular organisation of human societies we are experiencing today—might disappear as a result of the very processes that brought it into existence. This paradox is at the heart of the intellectual adventure of **constellation.s**: it prompted us to look at the power that has brought our World into existence; the vulnerability that threatens that existence; and local attempts to find responses to problems of cohabitation.
At this juncture we should mention three further points that guided our approach.

1. We focused our attention on humans considered as "inhabitants" and on their "habitation activity", in other words the way each human organises the subtle combination of materials and ideas that constitutes his habitat: the spatial and temporal parameters of human life. A human's habitat goes far beyond his residence or his dwelling place; it involves the entire geographical environment of his individual and social existence. To be precise, what interests us is that all individuals constantly cohabit with all other humans (and indeed with non-humans too).

2. As a result we decided to focus on local experiments in cohabitation, as we felt that on this scale we could observe why and how these new ways of living in the world that we sought to document came to be invented—sometimes using very limited resources. We looked for concrete situations—where the people involved were facing the necessity to create a living environment—which might point to interesting current innovations that are unlike

the standard architectural and urban planning practices routinely implemented by public authorities and the architects and private firms that work for them.

3. For each case we selected, we tried to highlight a tension, which we feel is specifically contemporary, between standardisation (the increasingly uniform methods, forms, techniques, and financing that result from the global dissemination of more and more standardised urban projects) and differentiation (which arises from the increasing emergence of local initiatives). These initiatives, though they do not necessarily abandon the standard repertoire mentioned above, nevertheless represent new ways of approaching space and time that differ from the usual standards and rules of planning and urban design. They add variety to the World thanks to the relevant choices they make. The World cannot be considered as flat, smooth and even; instead it is characterised by a constant interplay between standardisation and differentiation, which produces geographical realities that are much more subtle and complex than some over-hasty analysts would have us believe.

Armed with this hypothesis, we patiently selected our examples and constructed the exhibition design and the visitor itinerary around them, thinking of each as a "bright star" in the "constellation" of initiatives whose aim is to change the concepts and forms of cohabitation. Our intention was not to produce a prescriptive catalogue of best practices or a set of "miracle cures" to be applied everywhere. On the contrary, we wanted to highlight special cases, without imposing particular interpretations and without ever ignoring their uniqueness—or indeed their strangeness.
Although **constellation.s** was characterised by a sense of profusion due to the wide variety of initiatives on show, this was conscious and deliberate: our intention was to present thought-provoking material without drawing conclusions or imposing a single, neat interpretation (that of the godlike curator). This is why it was possible to get lost in the exhibition, just as one might get lost in this book, which is also designed as an itinerary—a typographically transposed extension of the experience of Michel Jacques' exhibition design, in

the magnificent main hall of the converted warehouse that is home to arc en rêve.

As this book shows, it was the diversity of possible solutions that interested us, not handing out marks out of ten or discussing details of architectural doctrine. Indeed for us **constellation.s** was not an architecture exhibition but an *exhibition with architecture,* where we used architecture as a point of entry. By looking at architectural approaches and objects, and more precisely by looking at the procedures that make it possible to produce inhabitable space, we can understand what characterises this moment in time on our globalised journey.

One final remark, by way of conclusion: **constellation.s** is, in its way, an optimistic project. Of course it is based on the premise that we are facing considerable difficulties, but it also suggests that commitment and empowerment can help us invent solutions that will ensure that the planet remains inhabitable. It suggests that this can be achieved without sacrificing social justice, chasing the unicorns of geo-engineering, or adhering to proposals by technologists convinced that they can solve anything with the right technique, whatever the financial and environmental cost. Although the exhibition did not attempt to hide the vulnerability of the spaces we live in, nor the difficulties, failures and dead ends encountered by people experimenting locally by trial and error, we also wanted to find reasons to hope.

The new ways of inhabiting the World we have identified, although still uncertain and hesitant, open up perspectives that allow us to envision a future for human habitation that might not simply be the worst-case scenario.

1. Michel Lussault, *L'Avènement du Monde. Essai sur l'habitation humaine de la Terre,* Paris, Le Seuil, 2013.
2. In its 2010 report UN-HABITAT, *State of the World's Cities, 2010/2011. Cities for all : Bridging the Urban Divide,* London, Earthscan.
3. Thierry Paquot, *Homo urbanus. Essai sur l'urbanisation du monde et des mœurs,* Paris, Éditions du Félin, 1990.
4. Thomas L. Friedman, *The World is Flat. A Brief History of the Twenty-First Century,* New York, Picador/Farrar, Straus and Giroux, 2007 (première édition 2005).

Earth from the Moon:
The "Eathrise" photographed by William Anders
on 24 December 1968

constellation.s word cloud

this "cloud" brings together the key words relating to **constellation.s**. They refer to the issues and major themes of the exhibition and suggest what gives meaning to today's world: some shine like beacons to guide us, while others indicate dead ends and pitfalls.

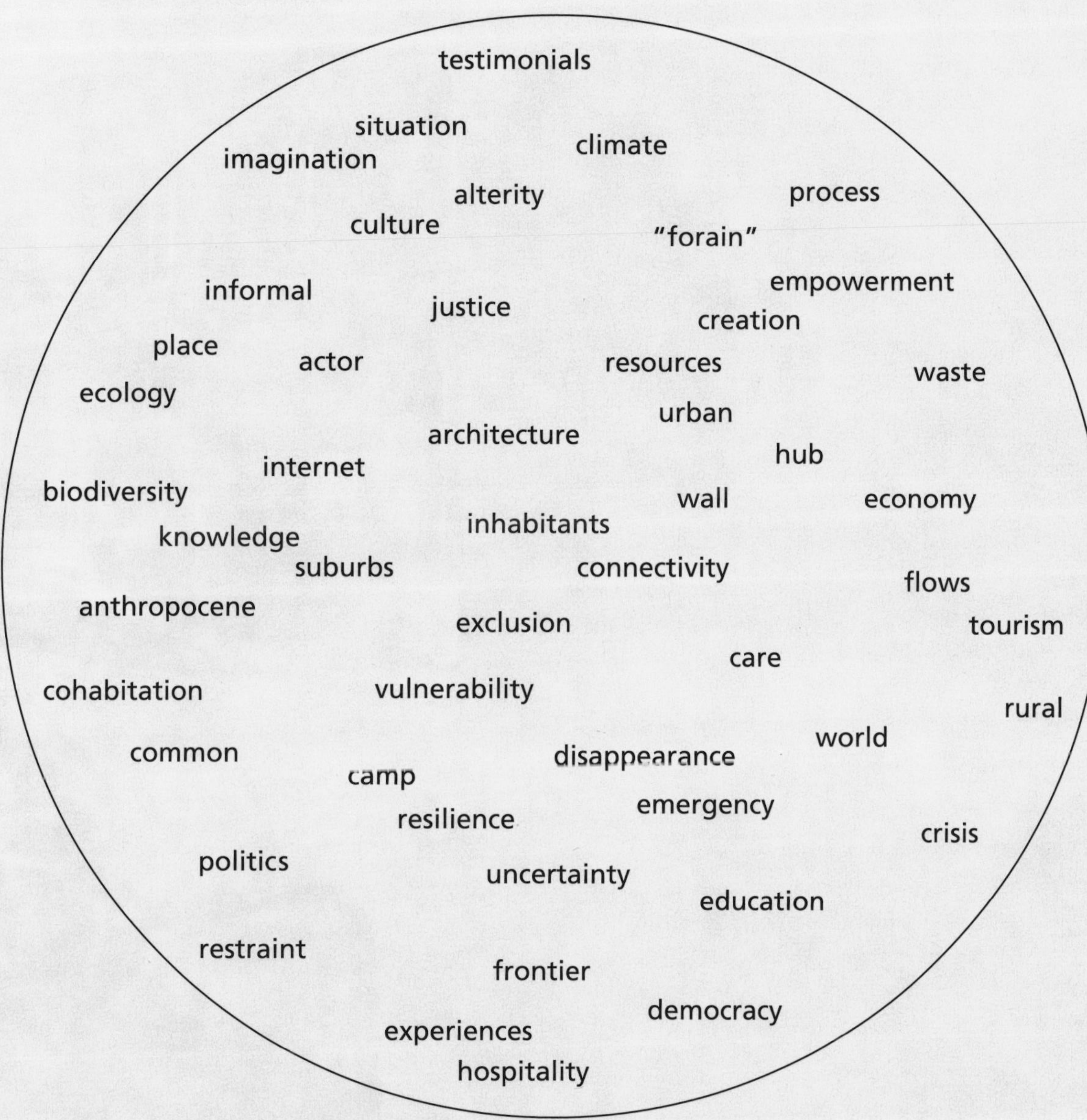
testimonials
situation
imagination
climate
alterity
process
culture
"forain"
empowerment
informal
justice
creation
place
actor
resources
waste
ecology
urban
architecture
hub
internet
biodiversity
wall
economy
inhabitants
knowledge
suburbs
connectivity
flows
anthropocene
exclusion
tourism
care
cohabitation
vulnerability
rural
world
common
disappearance
camp
emergency
resilience
crisis
politics
uncertainty
education
restraint
frontier
democracy
experiences
hospitality

GILERA

JCDecaux
ê
face
à la terreur
et à la folie
face
à la peur
et au repli
la culture
arc en rêve centre d'architecture bordeaux
arcenreve.com
constellation·s
habiter le monde

perspectives
by Michel Lussault

These "perspectives" take a theoretical look at what is at stake in terms of "inhabiting the world".

Humans, objects, materials, animals and plants all help us to understand the world and the way we build our living environment.

To "inhabit" means to settle somewhere, to meet other people, to move around, and to experience emotion in the spaces and timespans of our lives.

At a time when urban development is becoming ever more widespread and when movement takes place on a global scale, unique places are emerging, making us stop short and reflect upon new ways of experiencing and thinking about the world: new ways of living and behaving in it.

Tangible and intangible connections are everywhere, creating new cultures of space that are reshaping the places we live in. They are as diverse, multiform and shifting as sea foam.

Multiple anchor points, increased mobility, endless connections...
The Nation-State alone is no longer relevant. New ways of living in the world call for new political regulatory frameworks.

Doing as much as possible with as little as possible, without going too far. In response to illusions of omnipotence, a form of creative restraint is being invented every day, based on an awareness that endless possibilities exist.

Inequalities and vulnerabilities are increasing. Living environments, in all their diversity, welcome us and offer resources for action. Taking care of them is a requirement of spatial justice.

Economic parameters are part of the solution, not the problem. We must rethink the rules of the urban economy, opening up alternatives to a world all too often shaped by profit and speculation.

Climate change, declining biodiversity, scarce resources: the Anthropocene, the new geological era we are now entering, shows the influence of Man on the global bio-physical system. It calls for a radical transformation of the forms and processes of human habitation.

Imagination is a political force. It encourages people to act, and drives both feelings and values. It is a transformative force that highlights collective challenges and produces a narrative for our shared future.

We must take the words and actions of residents seriously. The challenge is to recognise the competence of individuals and their political right to take part in constructing living environments.

The notion of the individual asserts itself as the fundamental entity of urban societies. Though independent and unique, the individual is also connected in many different ways, and is eager to contribute to the common good.

philosophy

by Fabienne Brugère and Guillaume le Blanc

The point of view of philosophy creates perspectives that lie off the beaten track, helping to establish alternative approaches to inhabiting the world. By associating pairs of words that respond to each other more than they conflict with one another, these contributions give rise to questions that make **constellation.s** into a rhythmic series of points of view regarding the world.

ordinary / foreign

There is a worrying strangeness in ordinariness that relates not only to its ceaseless repetition, but also to its fleeting, shifting refrains that seem, at some point in reality, to throw the most regular arrangements out of line. The incorporation of routine is not the opposite of the transcendence of foreignness; it can give rise to it. Inhabiting means repeating a thread, a furrow; it also, in the same movement, means leaving intact the law of evaporation, the love of tangents. All "heres" are interwoven with "elsewhere", and, in a similar pattern, routines allow themselves to be carried away into the distance.

visible / invisible

The visible does not exist as a quality of the visual, an extension of sight. It is a selection of what deserves to be seen and lets a thousand appearances drop into the shadows, into invisibility. This means we have to challenge the way the visible is manufactured and wonder why the visible maintains doubtful forms in a state of invisibility: elements of the furniture of the world. But one can also inhabit the world by dodging the imperative of social visibility that performs lives. Becoming invisible is a law of social damnation, but not everybody can do it either. Many want to appear, but some strive to disappear.

humanity / nature

One might think that the unlimited extension of the area of human habitation had pushed nature back so far as to make it disappear. This is not the case. Nature is reinvented, on the contrary, as a quality of humanity, like a form of habitation. From communal gardens to green suburbs to forests suspended between two buildings, we really are "beyond nature and culture". Henceforth, each society creates areas of friction between them to build an ecological niche of a new kind, where the highest artifice competes with the most immediate naturalness.

resistance / resilience

Inhabiting means confronting a world that resists, a material that is already there, solid, intact, and which shatters hopes of transformation in advance. But it also means showing resilience, that ability to resurface despite crises, trauma or ordeals. Migrants, who leave a country where they can no longer live and move to another, show resilience. In more radical terms, resistance disturbs the most firmly established patterns, allows individuals to invent subtle new particles that scatter in the air and make the atmosphere less stifling. All life is a confrontation in space and time between resistance and resilience.

permanent / unstable

What if the unstable were more important than the permanent? What if the permanent were just a temporary instability that has not yet collapsed, for want of something better? Above all in our times, which we experience as uncertain? Of course, the permanence of materials seems to muzzle the energy of instability, but sustainability is a question that collides with the common unchallenged rules of consumer societies. All civilisations are still made of sand; and a habitation is an apparently permanent but deeply unstable form, prey to the folly of new beginnings which, far from being pathologies or ways of running away from existence, are often advanced signs of matchless creativity.

speeding up / slowing down

Inhabiting means finding the right pace: it means moving neither too slowly, nor too fast. The permanent acceleration we are promised in major global cities often ends up with deliberate deceleration processes: slowing down flows, taking one's time, and looking after oneself are not just breaks, but postures adopted by the athletes of daily life. Feeling the possibility of a change of pace is one of the great privileges of the city: running to escape acceleration, slowing down to get out of the flow, dreaming instead of sleeping, or on the contrary connecting oneself to global speed.

a glossary to help you on your journey through **constellation.s**
by Michel Lussault

this glossary explains the meanings of terms essential for describing and understanding new ways of inhabiting the world.

Anthropocene

We are living in a new "geological" era called the anthropocene because of the major role played by human activities in the global changes affecting the planet. Global warming, declining biodiversity, and increasing scarcity of resources will lead to radical transformations in the way humans inhabit the World. The recognition of this anthropocene represents a crucial point where individuals and societies become aware of their vulnerability and their direct involvement in that vulnerability. The change is both global and local, as are the analysis that has to be made and the action that must be taken.

Care

The word "care" is interesting for its multiple meanings: one can take care of something, and one can take care over an activity, for example. Joan Tronto defines it as an activity "that includes everything we do to maintain, perpetuate and repair our 'world' so that we can live in it as well as possible". Care is a basic principle of human life. It extends to what is around us: all the human and non-human realities that surround us. Creating relationships between the different components of individual and social life is at the heart of the development of spatial and environmental care.

Commonality/ common

"Commonality" results from what is pooled by key social operators in the framework of their activities. Because it requires the joint commitment of individuals, commonality is fundamentally political. It is also specific to each situation that gives rise to it: it arises in practice, including in activities that affect our daily lives. Commonality involves new forms of extended citizenship that are not restricted to taking part in elections.

Connectivity

"Connectivity" refers to the many possibilities for connections that are available to a given individual, group or space. Contemporary societies are influenced by a thriving culture of connectivity, which affects all areas of individual, social and family life, in particular via Internet. It is striking that the most emblematic global companies mostly base their business on an ability to connect people to each other and to the things that interest them. Microsoft, Apple, Facebook, Google, Twitter and many others sell and promote not so much instruments as intangible services expressing and magnifying a universal culture of apparently unrestricted, if not uncontrolled, contact.

Empowerment

"Empowerment" refers to a mobilisation process that is both political and educational and which makes it possible to enhance the actions of individuals who are initially on the margins of design and decision-making systems. Empowerment can allow a subordinate to become actively involved in a collective initiative, for example. Applied to urban planning, empowerment involves recognition of inhabitant expertise, and it is an instrument that can help us to respond to the requirements of spatial justice.

"Forain"

The French word "forain" refers, in this instance, to itinerant and non-permanent urban installations. The principle of non-permanence is essential to this way of inhabiting a space. Fragility and lightness hold the potential for creativity, and they also encourage people to take care of common spaces. The term "forain" also suggests spatial flexibility and fitout reversibility; developing a living environment thus appears as a necessarily unfinished process where what matters is the way people actually inhabit the space, however perfect or imperfect that space may be in formal terms.

Hub

"Hubs" are places that make it possible to connect several spaces of different scales and different kinds. Airports and stations are prime examples of hubs: they create a tangible and intangible connection between a very large variety of spaces that potentially intersect and interact. This is why this type of facility is so important in contemporary urban planning. The development of tangible and intangible flows explains this. But hubs also respond to a desire to control several spaces of different sizes at once—which is what a mobile phone allows you to do, for example.

Imagination

The way individuals and societies relate to living environments cannot be reduced to a functional or utilitarian relationship. It is also sensitive and emotional: it involves ideas, representations, and values. All this comes together as a form of geographical "imagination" that is both individual and social, and which is expressed and mediated via narratives, discourse, and images. This imagination makes it possible to describe and conceive the conditions for inhabiting space, and opens up a repertory of possible actions in situ for an individual or a group.

Inhabiting

The term "inhabiting" refers to all forms of experience and occupation of space by individuals and groups. To "inhabit" is not just to live somewhere; it also involves moving and connecting. Day by day, equipped with skills and driven by values and imagination, each inhabitant organises the subtle combination of materials and ideas that makes up his or her "habitat". What do humans do? They inhabit, constantly and on all scales—that of the body, that of housing, that of mobility, and that of the World. More precisely, they permanently co-habit with all other humans—and thus face the political challenge of how inhabited space can be shared.

Informal

An act or a spatial reality is considered "informal" when it escapes explicit public regulations and standards and lies outside the official market. In many situations, informality is omnipresent: it is even the normal regime for many urban processes, especially in economic and residential terms. Informality is often presented as the result of a need to survive when faced with poverty or corruption; however it often also arises from rational choices made because of the advantages it brings— even if such choices may lead to illegal practices.

Place

In the social sciences, a "place" is where a range of social realities (human and non-human realities and material constructions) are brought together in direct contact with one another and integrated into the limited space that contains them and gives them their meaning and function(s). "Places" manifest themselves via the explicit and tangible nature of their limits and the threshold and crossover effects that result from those limits. In a "place", the individual makes himself seen: he agrees to be looked at by others and to leave the family and domestic sphere. Globalisation restores the importance of "place", which constitute essential environments for communal life. "Places" are new magnets for globalised human life, and they both anchor and drive contemporary forms of cohabitation.

Restraint

Here, "restraint" refers to the optimum operation of inhabited spaces: it involves consuming as few resources as possible to meet the needs of the greatest number—including those needs that relate to celebrations, culture and excess, which are necessary for a society to breathe. Restraint is not the same as self-sufficiency, abstinence, or degrowth. It involves a successful combination of individual desire, efficiency, control of resources, and social justice. It opens up a way to reinvent democracy in the framework of a common political project that is both local and global.

Spatial justice

In the face of growing inequality, social justice promotes the principle of fairness in the way goods are divided up or in terms of access to resources. By analogy with John Rawls' Theory of Justice, "spatial justice" can be defined as a way of organising geographical space that allows us to provide maximum access to urban amenities and public assets to everyone, including the least privileged members of society. This principle, which has to be redefined to fit every situation, should be one of the main preoccupations of housing policies.

World

The World is the social space deployed by human habitation, which is now planetary. The advent of the World began a few decades ago, defining a new way of organising space that differs from all previous situations in terms of the modes of existence of human societies. Widespread urbanisation is the main constituent force of this World, via the spatial arrangements it produces and the imagination, knowledge and ideologies it cultivates.

The 42 contributions combine knowledge and expertise, convictions and a desire to pass knowledge on. They highlight ways of inhabiting the world via unusual initiatives or situations. Like beacons, they light our way and allow us to think and act in an urban world that is often hard to understand. They are reference points that allow us to move towards the implementation of concrete solutions, without predetermining the path to follow.

42 situations

Advanced Informality

01

Cairo

Disappearance of arable land to make way for new forms of urban speculation

Today almost 60% of the 20 million inhabitants of Cairo live in illegally constructed housing. Since the 1960s, this informal urbanisation has developed on farmland around the city, destroying hundreds of acres of arable land. Self-built housing has gradually turned into a semi-professional business, fuelled by the neo-liberal economy and the inadequacies of the State. The phenomenon, which accelerated after the Arab Spring in 2011, has now reached an almost industrial stage of development, where speculation is rife.
The Advanced Informality study reveals the damage wrought by the system on both people and land: standardised, poor-quality housing, residents owning illegal flats from which they can be evicted at any time, sacrificed farmland, and so on.

www.angelil.arch.ethz.ch

—

MAS Urban Design – ETH Zurich: Marc Angélil, Charlotte Malterre-Barthes and Something Fantastic in collaboration with CLUSTER Cairo and the American University of Cairo
photos: © Lorenz Bürgi ; © Julian Schubert
graphic design: Something Fantastic

Perfecting informal housing

In the light of rampant speculation concerning farmland around Cairo, the ETH Zurich team led by Marc Angélil and Charlotte Malterre-Barthes has worked on transforming the typology of these sets of buildings. By recombining architectural and structural elements, they seek to improve quality of life in the flats and create communal areas that will improve daily life across these districts.
To offer access to a view or to natural light, or to provide better ventilation in the flats, the architects proceed by removing materials from these hyper-dense residential towers. Other proposals for empty plots entail new ways of building under the same conditions: moving the circulation node, spreading out the structure, and so on. The idea is to improve housing quality through tactical interventions.

P3
P4

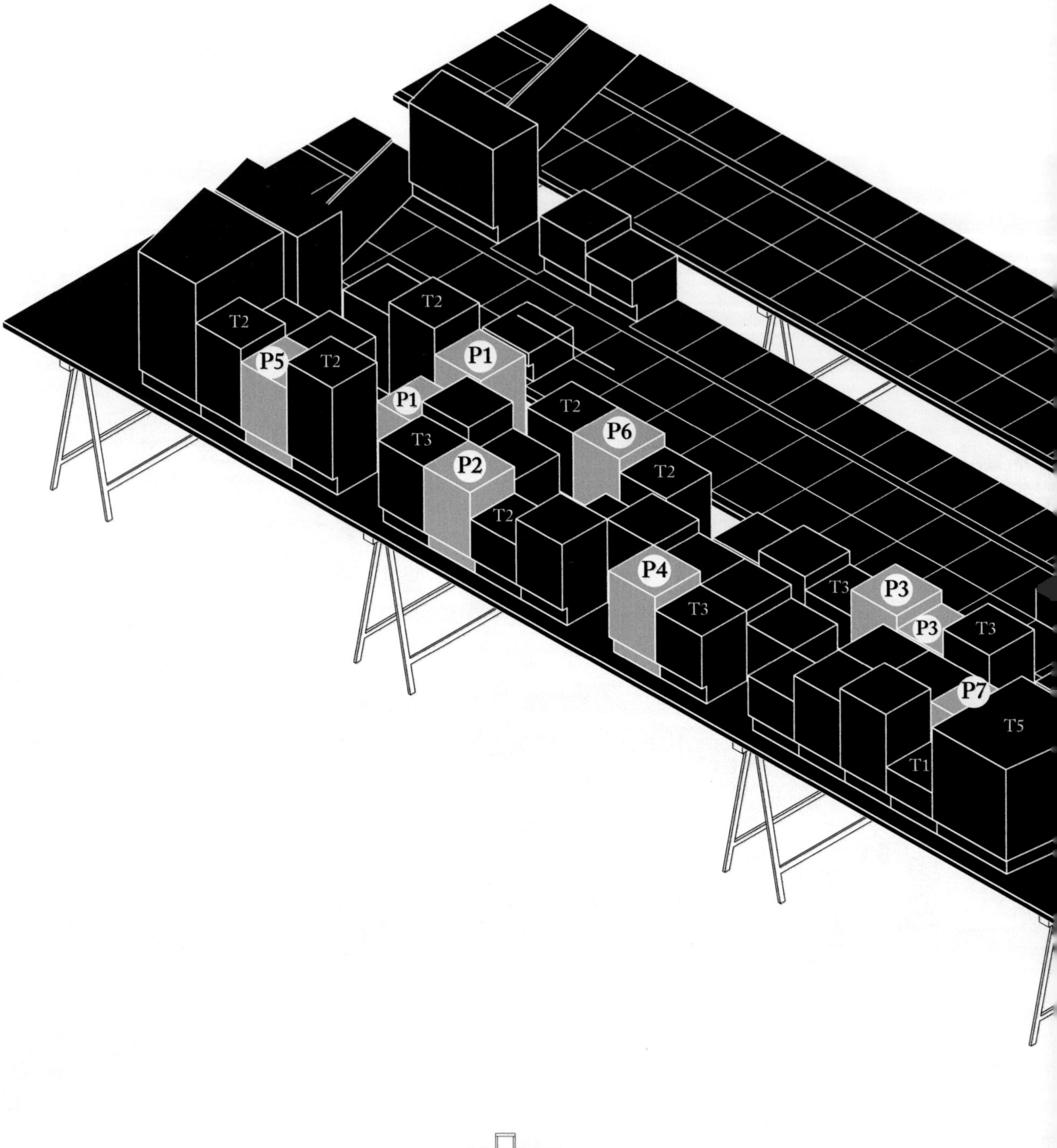

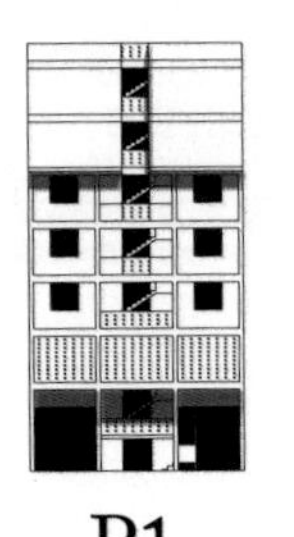

P1

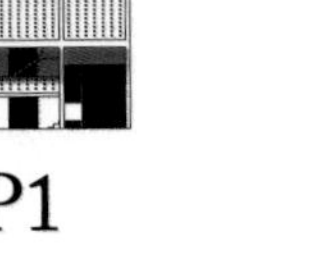

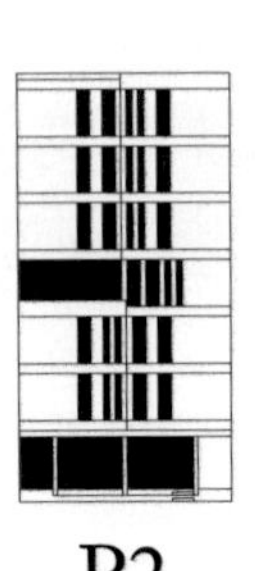

P2

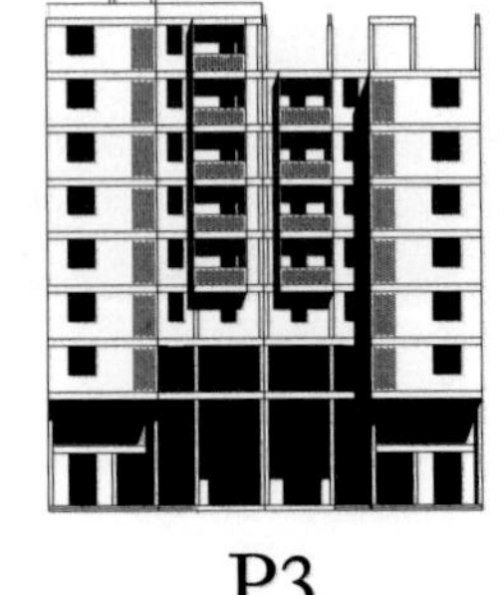

P3

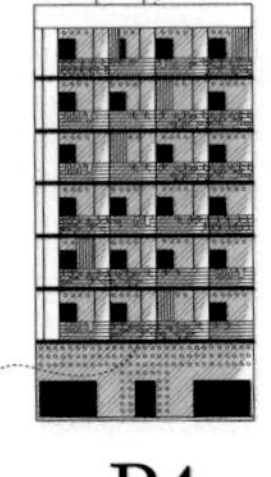

P4

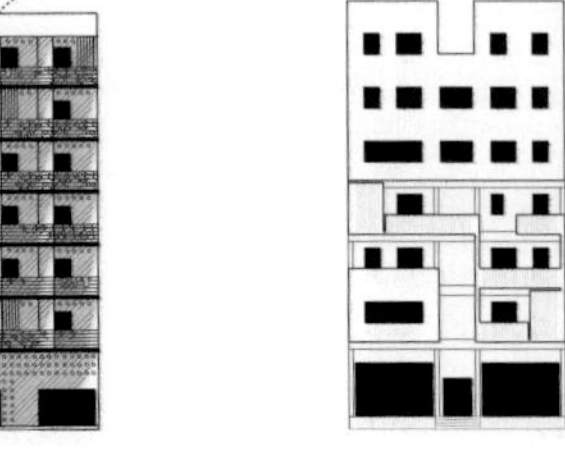

P5

1

2

3

Advanced Informality: From Agrarian Land to New Urban Forms in Cairo

MAS Urban Design ETH Zurich

TABLE 1

Pre-1970 / Agrarian land, pre-urban growth

Property lines and irrigation channels establish the primary territorial division and the base for later urbanisation.

TABLE 2

1970-2011 / Informal construction on arable land

Housing structures materialise, following an established typology of concrete frames and brick infill, with street patterns registering agrarian subdivisions, generating 'urban canyons'. The Ring Road is built.
Urban growth is relatively timid and buildings are at a distance from the main road as contractors aim to conceal illegal housing from the authorities' attention.

TABLE 3

2011-today / Post-revolution development

Contractors grow confident and engaged in speculative illegal construction, detectable via the change in building height. This phase shows the penetration of market forces operating in a neoliberal mode.
In this model, alternatives projects developed by MAS Urban Design for innovative architecture are positioned on site.

P6

P7

54

Resilience: The building is constructed
with local materials and construction knowledge.

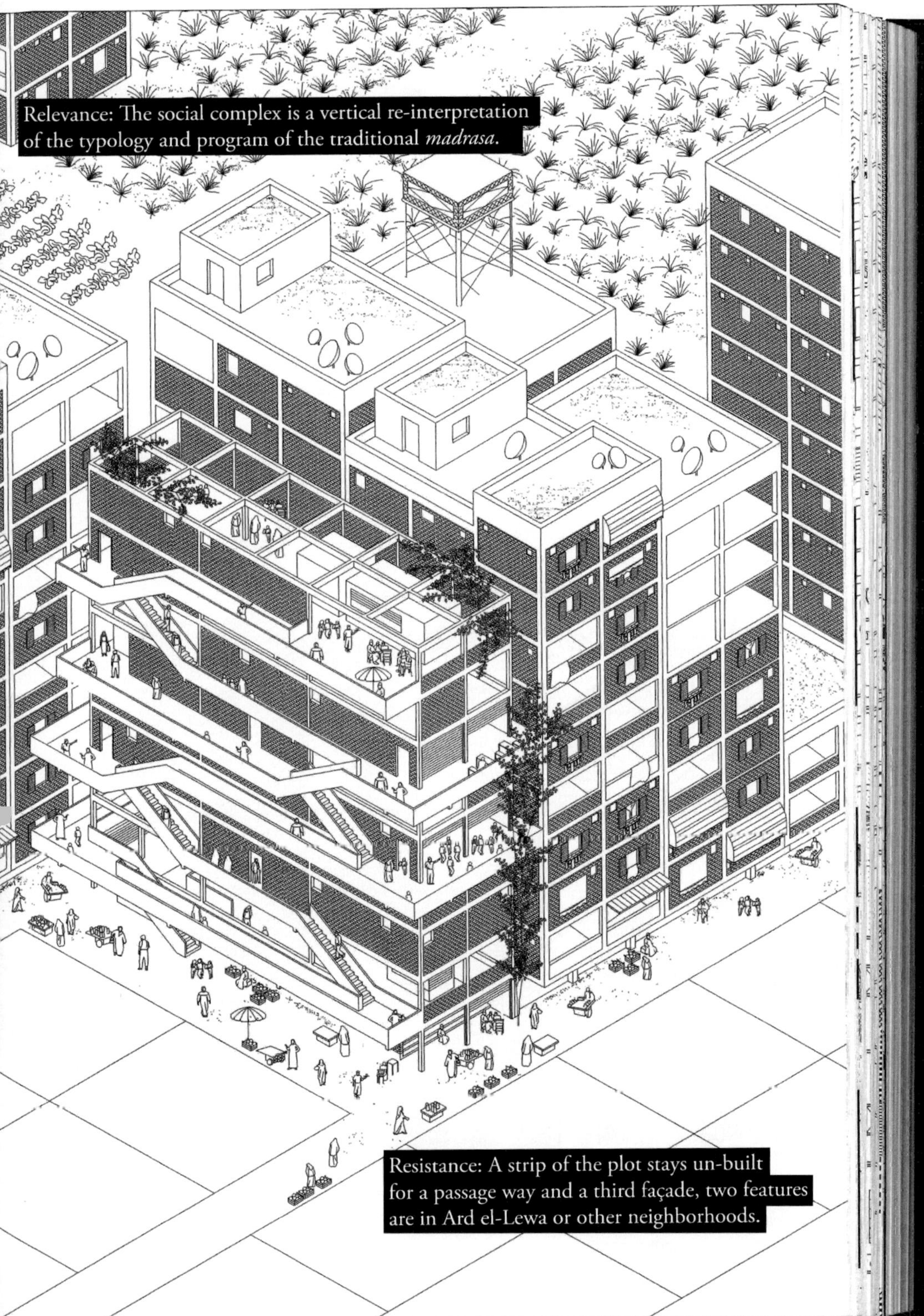

From: Marc Angélil and Charlotte Malterre-Barthes in collaboration with Something Fantastic and CLUSTER, *Housing Cairo – The Informal Response*, Ruby Press, 2016

0
1
5 m

The built fabric "breathes" thanks to the unbuilt space.

Based on existing elements
the combination of unit plans forms
a comprehensive building and creates social
spaces at all levels.

By designing the neighborhood's unbuilt spaces, the project gives room for common activities, generating urbanity.

Agricultural Printing and Altered Landscapes

02

Unterwaldhausen

A printed field to cultivate biodiversity

Agriculture in developed countries, as well as being highly mechanised, is increasingly robotised, with tractors steered remotely using GPS systems. With this in mind, designer Benedikt Groß has invented a system that makes it possible to print patterns in fields using a selection of seeds.
Still connected to GPS, the tractor and seed drill "scan" the field like a printer head, following a digitally defined path.
This is first and foremost a project concerning European policies that reduce agriculture to mere statistics. As well as its aesthetic effect, this technology would make it possible to develop the principle of mutually beneficial fences—a kind of metaphor for diversity that runs counter to the current trend for mono-specific crops.

www.benedikt-gross.de/log

—

photos: © Florian Vögtle

Benedikt Groß Stuttgart

Benedikt Groß is a speculative and computational designer who works in anti-disciplinary mode. His work deals with the fascination of relationships between people, their data, technology and environments. He is particularly interested in speculating about these relationships in the near future.

He uses design as a vehicle to visualise potential implications and scenarios. Benedikt's working mode can be described most of the time as 'thinking through making'; his preferred making material is software.

Atelier Gando

03

Gando

Learning to be independent

This is not the first time architect Diébédo Francis Kéré has carried out a project in his native village of Gando in Burkina Faso, which he left to pursue his studies in Europe: schools, a library, teachers' housing, a women's centre... all these buildings respond to the question of education. According to Kéré, who is the son of the former village chief, this is the first condition necessary for achieving autonomy.
He has now created Atelier Gando, a learning centre for building with local resources:
the materials and men and women of the area.
Atelier Gando is an amplifier of knowledge and expertise, which can then spread to even the remotest villages. It is also a bridge between Gando and the world that sparks interactions between Western and African craftsmen, labourers, architects, and students.

www.kere-architecture.com

—

photos: © Kéré Architecture

Kéré Architecture Berlin / Burkina Faso

Burkina Faso faces climate and energy problems that the North does not experience. Francis Kéré has understood that it is necessary to stop imitating others and invent an approach where African expertise is as essential as western know-how. The architect places all his expertise on the sands of Gando: local experience of climate and dwindling resources, European ecology and architecture, the solidarity economy, and African craftsmanship... Then he filters and balances them in each project, looking for just the right mix. This global critique of expertise is new: it produces architecture that is rooted in its microcosm and has a universal message.

Marie-Hélène Contal

We often think of earth as a building material for poor people. That's why people prefer expensive imported materials often used in entirely inappropriate ways.

Our architecture helps to eradicate illiteracy, because there can be no development without education.

This is architecture in rural areas of Burkina Faso: you get up and you build—there's no plan. The neighbours come and help.

You can't imagine how proud the people in my village are since they've found out that they're able to do all this

Diébédo Francis Kéré

Beyond Entropy, Angola

04

Luanda

Constructing a landscape for purifying water and producing energy

In Luanda, Angola, the Beyond Entropy project attempts to provide a response to the complex question of water purification. Planting Arundo Donax, a particular species of bamboo, in gaps in the houses may make it possible to naturally filter waste water and provide an income for the inhabitants, who would grow these plantations and produce biogas from the fibres of the cut plants. The project shows that by using simple technical solutions adapted to sustainability, new urban landscapes combining agriculture, infrastructures and human habitat can emerge. The project nonetheless came up against the economic and geopolitical power of major civil engineering firms. A system of buried networks, which is difficult to put in place and costly in terms of natural resources, was constructed instead…

www.beyondentropy.com

—

photos: © Beyond Entropy

Stefano Rabolli London
Paula Nascimento Luanda

Beyond Entropy is an architectural firm that uses the concept of energy as a poetic instrument for understanding, conceiving and producing new forms of architecture beyond the rhetoric of sustainability. Energy cannot be reduced solely to a technical issue; it is a mode of transformation that informs the concept of space. Beyond Entropy operates globally in situations of spatial crisis: from the urban sprawl of the most industrialised parts of the planet to the derelict infrastructures of deserted islands; from the overcrowded urban developments of emerging countries to the preserved areas of historical urban centres.

LD-15-85-CM
LD-15-85-CM

BUILTHEFIGHT 05

Building a space for resistance

In recent years there has been a significant growth in the number of protests in public spaces calling for more democracy and equality: Wall Street, Tahir Square, Gezi Park, Maidan Square, and more recently the Place de la République in various French cities. Although these resistance movements are maintained by social networks, they still need physical spaces in which to take shape.
Didier Faustino is interested in the conflict between fragile bodies and urban space; his installation provides a commentary on these events and continues with this work. These modules that look like parts of riot barriers can be moved to construct and deconstruct a compact circular area: an occupied space. The roughness of the barricade and the struggle taking place contrast with the delicate beauty of the neon lights bearing messages of hope.

www.didierfaustino.com

—

Courtesy of the artist, Michel Rein, Paris/Brussels and Parque Galeria, Mexico DF.
12 elements in galvanised laminated steel and neons.
Artwork created with the support of the Chicago Biennale.

Didier Faustino Paris

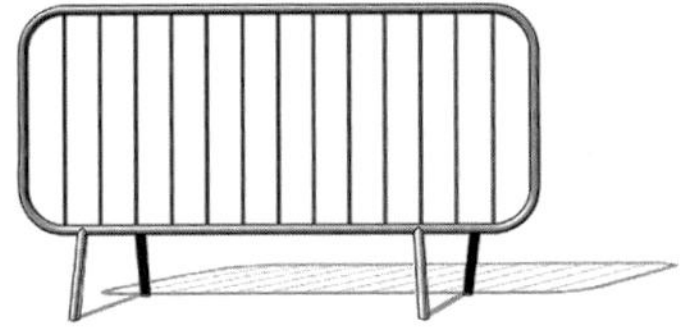

From: Didier Fiuza Faustino, *Vortex Populi*, it: editions, 2016

What appearance does this form take within the current social and political era and crisis? How does this idea of transversality help redefine the dynamic relation between form and content? The forms of *Vortex Populi* (2015), *Memories of Tomorrow* (2013), *BUILTHEFIGHT* (2015) are interventionist gestures that attempt to decolonize forms of conflict, security and surveillance present in current society and public space. Barriers are used, in a context of surveillance in the urban space, as a way to instrumentalize protesters, but also become the symbol of *Occupy* movements. The symbolic meaning of enclosure to ensure a form of security becomes today a hegemonic paradigm of civic space. The refugee crisis, riots and their effect on public spaces are not only a justification for expanding control over society but also for fostering the symbolic terrain for it. In that perspective, forms of enclosure such as barriers and fences play with a manipulated informed content. Faustino uses fences and barriers as exacerbated forms of security or defense, displaying transversal forms.

A space dominated by a state of exception, creates realities of confinement, such as camps, islands or *"spaciocides"*, where surveillance infrastructure and their network also lead to a definition of control or confinement of the hegemonic structures themselves. In *Love Song for Riots* (2013), as in *BUILTHEFIGHT*, fences become a transversal form that is performative in transforming the meanings of defense and security. The symbolic reality is questioned. The form and content are no longer dependent on each other.

Pelin Tan

PROTEST

RESIST

Camps as Laboratories

06

Western Sahara

Laboratories of urbanity

Refugee camps are becoming the urban environment for more and more people on this planet. Manuel Herz sees the camps as places for experimentation where inhabitants can trial new forms of territorial, political and economic organisation.
Refugees from the Western Sahara in Algeria have elected a government in exile. In Nairobi, Somali refugees supported financially by the diaspora have set up shopping centres that are now thriving. Other camps with infrastructures and health facilities become attractive to non-refugee populations and are undergoing urban growth. Could these camps be places where new ways of inhabiting the world and new models of urbanity are invented?

www.manuelherz.com/projects

—

Manuel Herz Basel

The refugee Camps of the Western Sahara – Camps as a tool for nation-building

The Western Sahara is a country located at the western edge of the African continent. Formerly a Spanish colonial territory, and since 1975 occupied by Morocco, it has been called the world's last remaining colony. Ith the beginning of a guerilla war against Morocco, most of the Western Saharan population (Sahrawis) had to flee across the border into Algeria where they settled in refugee camps, today housing approximately 160,000 Sahrawis. Even though the Sahrawis do not have control over their territory, they proclaimed independence from the Western Sahara on February 27, 1976. Its sovereignty is recognised today by 34 countries, though its status remains unresolved. Having lived for 40 years in refugee camps in the border zone of southwestern Algeria, the Sahrawi population has developed a unique set of urban and architectural tools and design methodologies to deal with conditions of transience and liminality.

Instead of seeing the camps as a place of limitation, the Sahrawis have used them proactively as a tool for nation-building. In fact, the camps have become the settings for novel architectural and urban conditions that test and question some of the underlying parameters of the discipline of planning. The design and constructions of the huts and houses in the Sahrawi camps always have to negotiate between the temporary and the permanent.

Even though the Sahrawis have lived for almost 40 years in the camps, the tent is still a central element in the range of residential typologies. Beyond its cultural significance and certain climatic benefits, the tent represents and materialises what is temporary. The tent is a physical representation of a political demand for a return to the home country of the Western Sahara.

Maybe the situation teaches us that the permanent and the temporary, are in fact maybe not a pair of opposites, nor categories of a binary dichotomy, but instead different means of expressing a political dilemma.

The exhibition presents contemporary Sahrawi architecture and urbanism. Instead of focusing on aspects of lack or poverty, its showcases the spaces of everyday life in the camps, and how architecture is consciously used as a tool for nation-building.

Les camps de réfugiés du Sahara occidental – Les camps comme outils de construction de la nation

The Refugee Camps of the Western Sahara – Camps as a tool of na

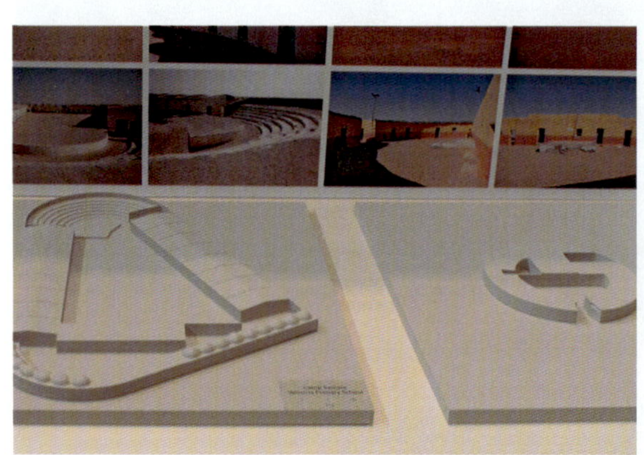

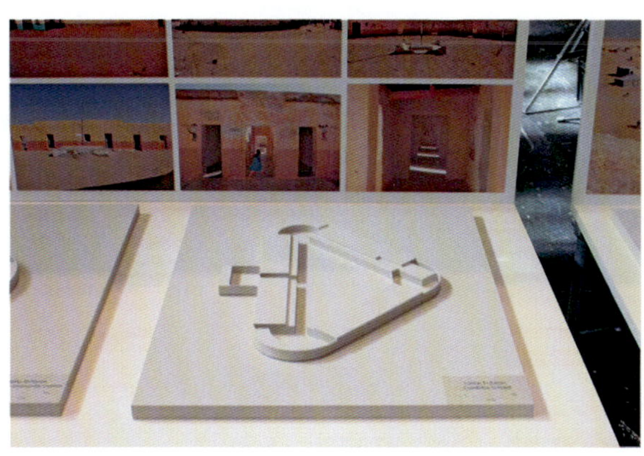

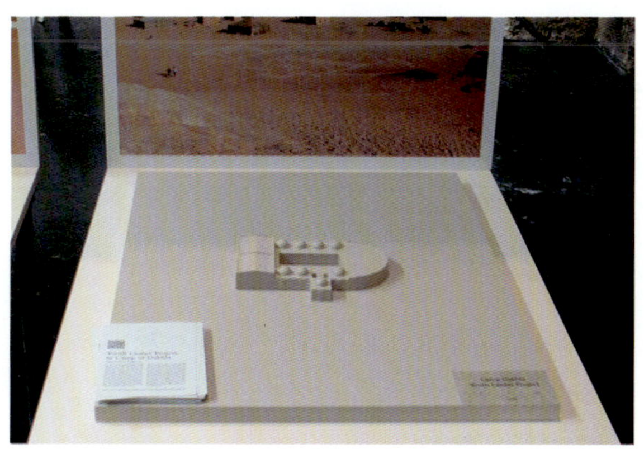

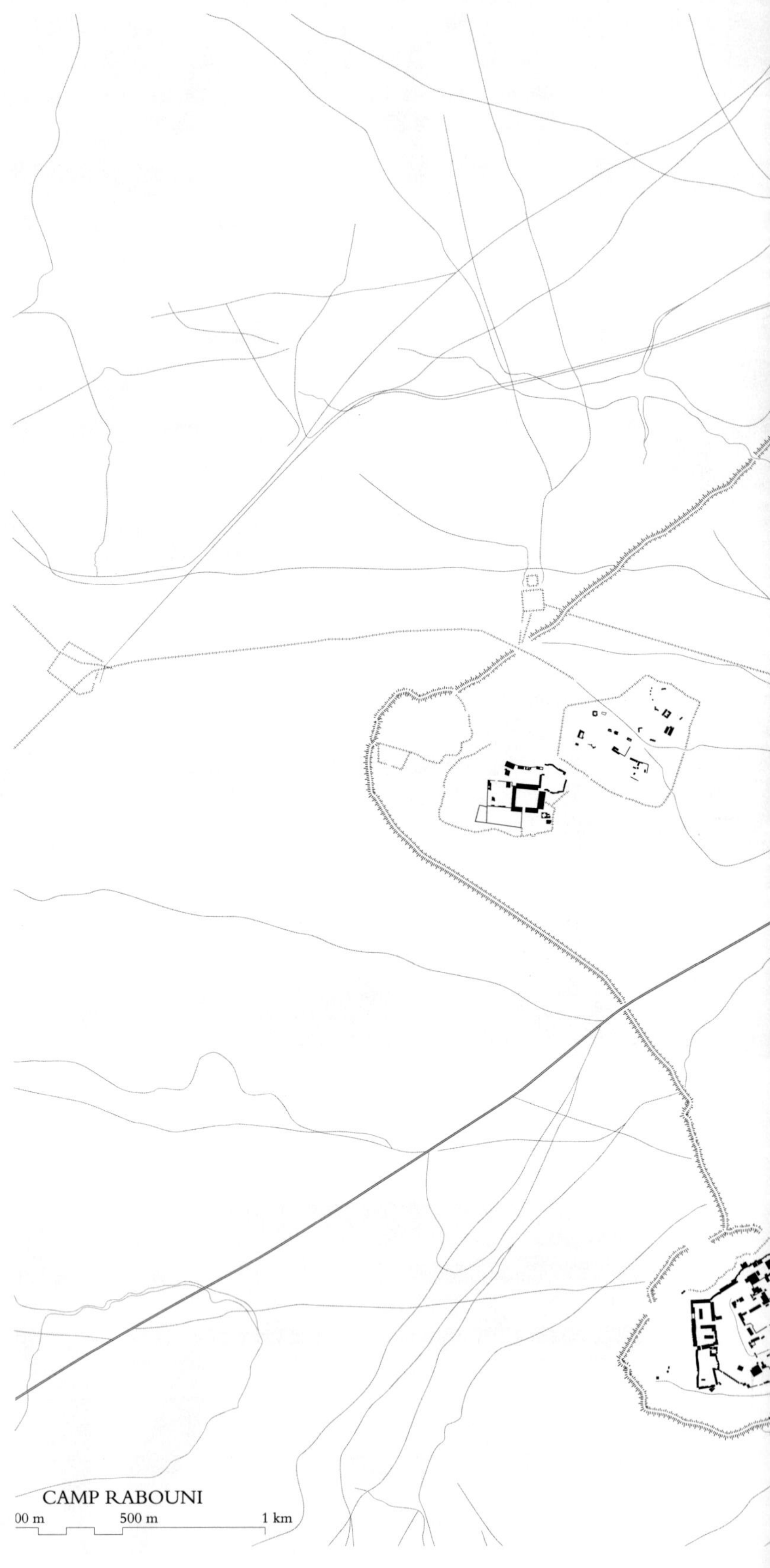
CAMP RABOUNI
00 m
500 m
1 km

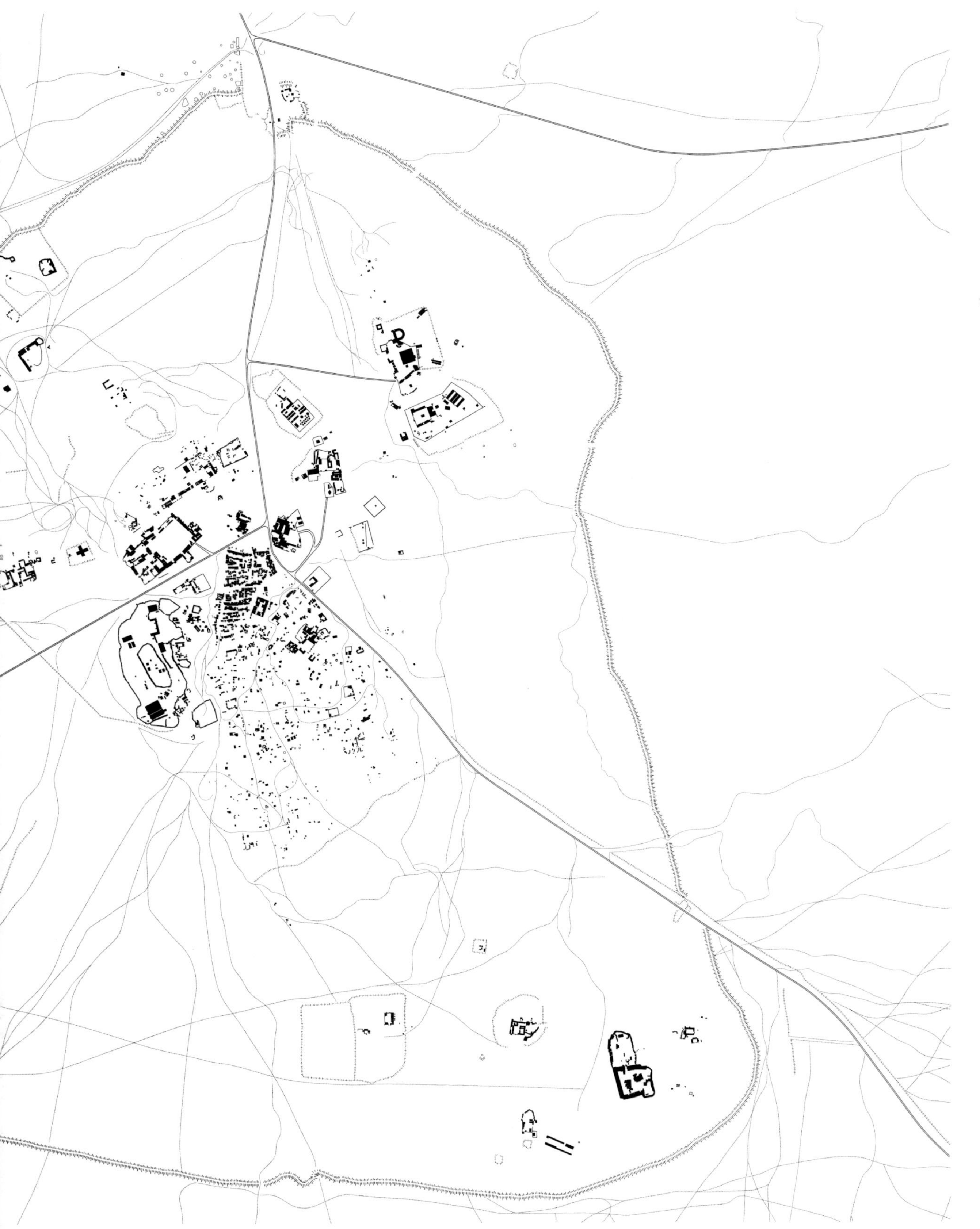

Chicoco Radio

07

Port Harcourt

A slum on air

By allowing the Port Harcourt community to set up and run its own radio station, the NGO CMAP, which works in the field of the media, offers inhabitants of this Nigerian slum the opportunity to express themselves in public space to tackle unsuccessful urban planning policies. It also trains people of all ages in audiovisual skills: recording, editing, broadcasting, etc.
For CMAP, working in informal neighbourhoods first involves re-establishing a feeling of belonging. A similar approach has been adopted for another initiative focusing on a process of participative cartography for the neighbourhood: naming things on a map is a way of formalising what is informal and starting to legitimise its existence. "Inhabiting" also means making one's voice heard.

www.chicoco.fm

—

photos: © CMAP

Chicoco Radio

480,000 people in the city's waterfronts live under the threat of forced eviction, and none feature on municipal maps, nor in the plans drawn up for the city's development. Thousands have already lost their homes. Informal waterfront communities are home to architects, hairdressers, teachers, footballers, shop owners, civil servants, engineers, lawyers, schoolchildren, welders, policewomen, musicians, bank clerks, marine biologists, house painters, pastors, plumbers and politicians—yet the stories of the many ordinary and extraordinary people that live here rarely feature in the local press.

Chicoco Radio is a radio station being built by residents of Port Harcourt's waterfront slums. It is part of The Human City Project's Communicating and Campaigning programmes that help marginalised communities gain a greater measure of control over how their communities are represented. We are building platforms for community voice and vision and sharing skills and technologies that allow people to describe the shapes of their city's future, helping people to speak up for their rights and detail new policy ideas.

GRAND-CANYON

CHICOCO
MAPS
OUR
CITY

PEOPLE
LIVE HERE
CAT
325B

CHICOCO RADIO
MODE

Circulatory Urbanism

08

Konkan Region, India

Back and forth between town and country

The urbanisation of lifestyles is a well-established phenomenon. Traditional farming has given way to a more mobile and complex world. Countryside areas have not disappeared, they still exist both quantitatively and culturally. Their interactions with big cities are changing, however, and call for new analytical frameworks.

In this perspective, by studying the train line in Konkan near Mumbai, Urbz highlights what can be seen as a new form of circulatory urbanism divided between the city, the countryside and the transport link that connects new city-dwellers with their village roots. Consequently, more than being a mere way of getting from A to B, the train, its carriages and its stations are "inhabited" locales forming part of a broader urban fabric embracing both village and city.

www.urbz.net/circulatoryurbanism

—

Circulatory urbanism

The Indian railway carries 9 billion passengers every year, four times more than China's network. The Indian diaspora spreads itself to all continents, yet maintains strong ties with its country of origin. Within the sub-continent itself, hundreds of millions of people live away from their ancestral regions and villages, while maintaining active links back home. The story of a mass exodus from rural parts of India to its booming megacities doesn't end in hyper-dense urban centres. The story stretches back to the villages, which are transforming just as rapidly as the cities.

Trains are indeed going back and forth, carrying an immeasurable flow of people and goods that seem to exist in a permanent state of flux. Home is here and there at the same time.

The ideal urban home is out of financial reach for 99.9% of Indians, while the village alone doesn't suffice to fulfil the economic and educational demands of an aspiring middle class. This is why an immense number of families from Mumbai, New Delhi, Bangalore or Chennai maintain two homes—a small crowded one in the city, besides the one they invest in, back in the village. The Indian village thus does not belong to the past as much as it belongs to the future—and this future is resolutely urban, networked and circulatory.

Over the last four years, we have looked at the Konkan region on India's western coast, from Mumbai to Mangalore. We have engaged with people from this region who have fuelled the city's workforce for at least a couple of centuries. This composition depicts the life journey of an urban family between the village and the city, reflecting their aspirations and diverse facets of their reality.

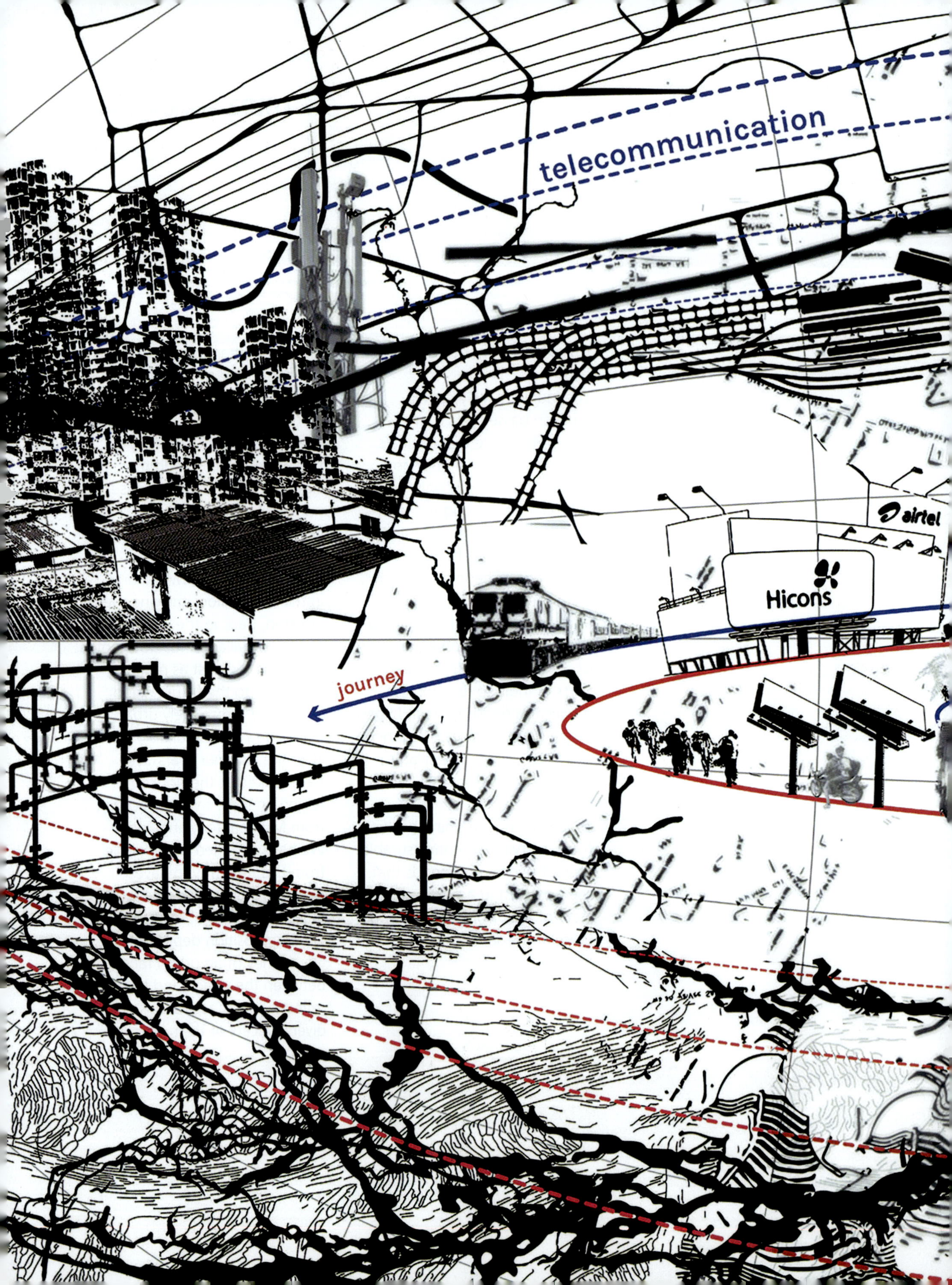

telecommunication
airtel
Hicons
journey

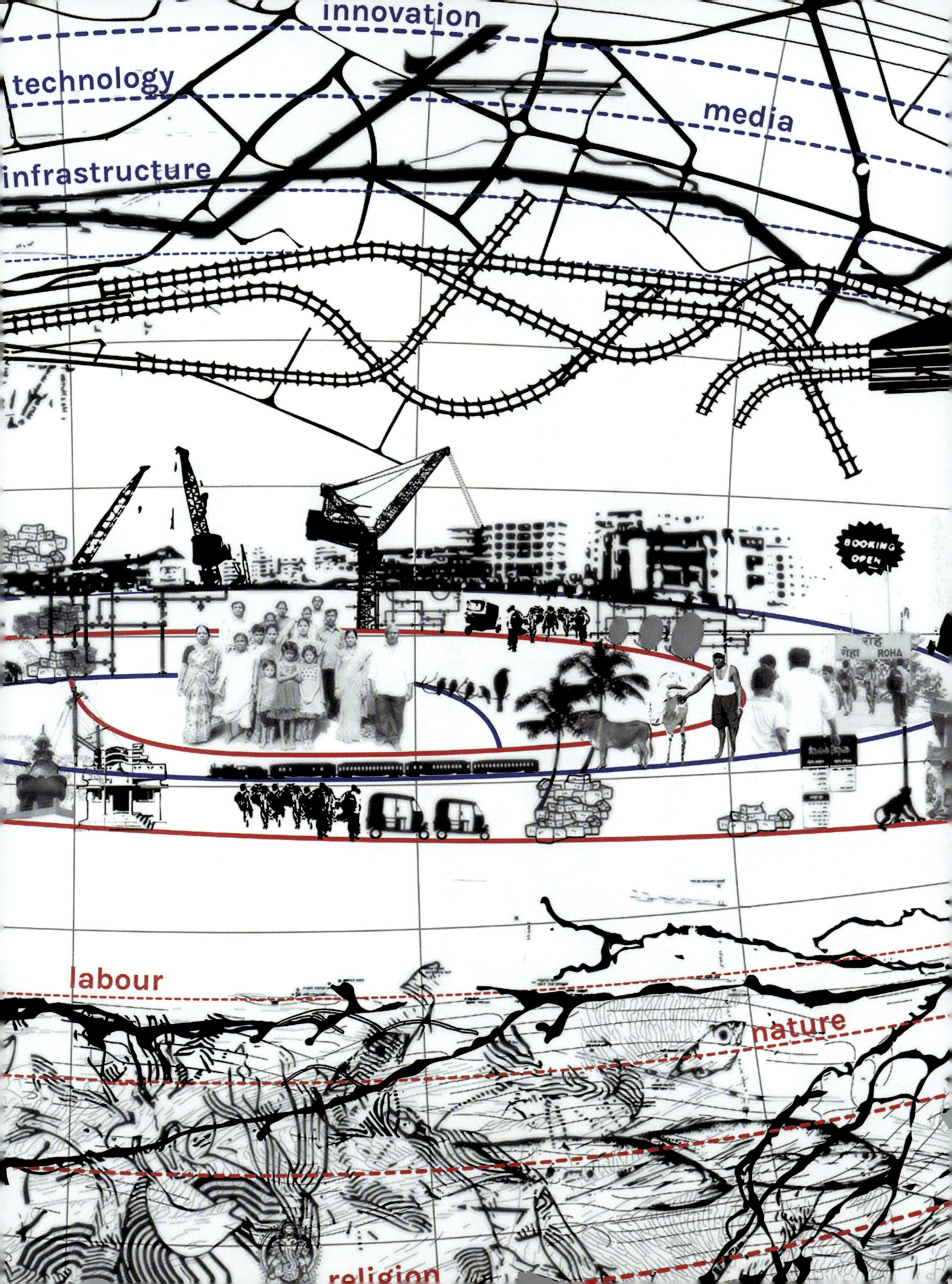
innovation
technology
media
infrastructure
BOOKING OPEN
ROHA
labour
nature
religion

Même quand le trajet par bateau

par bus nous prenait 24 heures –

...where I live now is
...use is ideal

This is my ideal house

BORDEAUX

1. Neighbourhood
a- present
Basal street (?)
HLM
Immigrants
Market Place
Residential + Commercial

SHATOU
CHINA

Not an...
presence...

"I can't remember where we lived"

I left when
I was ...

Home is within you

...ME

...Positive

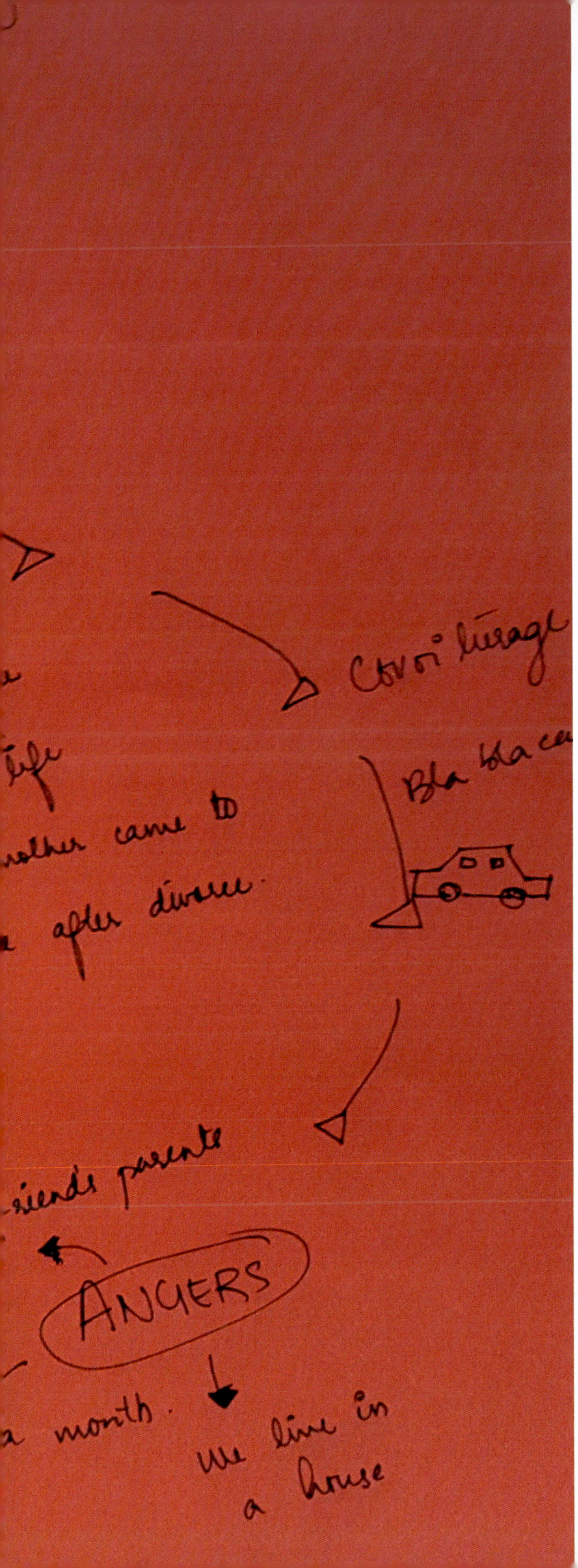

Covoiturage

life

mother came to

after divorce

Bla bla car

friends parents

ANGERS

a month.

we live in
a house

The urbz team conducting interactive sessions with constellation.s visitors and contributors

City Songs

09

Africa

A journey into Africa in sound and vision

Our ways of inhabiting the world are inseparable from culture. Florent Mazzoleni, a critic specialising in African music, takes us on a musical and visual journey based on a selection of songs linked to photographic fragments collected across the continent. Reflecting the varied experiences of a tireless globe-trotter, these exotic and evocative "haikus" make up a portrait that is necessarily incomplete and subjective, but which is nonetheless acutely sensitive to the African urban environment.

—

Florent Mazzoleni Bordeaux

The siren song of the African city

Acting as magnets in a magnetic twenty-first century, African cities are an inexhaustible source of inspiration.

A red record player refers to the discography we need to grasp an often spiritual quest for authentic emotion—the soundtrack of our tiny lives. From the corrugated iron roofs of big African markets to grand patrician houses, another world is indeed possible: *"Beter Negro City"* it says in sky-blue letters on an ochre wall in a Sahelian town. In search of more prosperous horizons, some travel towards new opportunities to be seized. Through the wide-open windows of a faded seaside hotel, they dream of real economic independence. Sometimes these are merely dreams of sustainable development and vital resources: water, fuel, and plastic containers found in a petrol station at nightfall to store these ingredients for a better life. "Soon"... Soon the long-awaited freedom will come, the consumer potential, the head-on collision between traditional mud dwellings and the quick-drying cement of new dreams. The impact sets them on a roller-coaster, careering up and down, their heads filled with Atlantic dreams. Urban paradises and tropical skyscrapers hang by a thread, with washing hung out to dry and satellite dishes turned towards an idealised elsewhere. A faded red epiphany greets us with a "pop" when we raise our heads. Or perhaps we can shield our eyes behind the goggles of a young welder in Bobo-Dioulasso, gazing towards an amazing future.
Between the power of architecture and powerlessness in a tough economic climate, these siren songs map out a set of feelings where the individual and the collective mingle. Dances, sounds, lyrics and colours speak not only of fragmentation and dispersion but also of distant inner migrations. African rhythms are now everywhere in our cities, through urban or electronic music that endlessly recycles the centuries-old vibes of the Dark Continent.
Often futuristic, sometimes turned towards the past but always authentic, African music forms the soundtrack of global cities such as Lagos, Dakar, Abidjan, Luanda and Kinshasa. Whether identified with particular places or without any particular home, these songs play the way to a stunning future.

Florent Mazzoleni
Bordeaux, May 2016

INDEPENDANCE

BETER
NEGRO
CITY
MONTANHA
RUSSA

POP

PLAYLIST

—

ET Mensah - Ghana Freedom (Ghana)
African Jazz - Independance Cha Cha (Congo Republic)
Franco & OK Jazz - Bazonzele Mama Ana (Congo Republic)
Belita Palma - Caminho do Mato (Angola)
Os Kiezos - Saudades de Luanda (Angola)
Bembeya Jazz - Armée Guinéenne (Guinea)
Sory Kandia Kouyaté - Conakry (Guinea)
Rail Band - Gansana (Mali)
Amadou Ballaké - Bobo-Dioulasso (Burkina Faso)
Pierre Sandwidi - Ouaga Affairs (Burkina Faso)
Tabu Ley Rochereau - Bel Abidjan (Congo Republic/Ivory Coast)
Alèmayèhu Eshètè - Addis Abeba Bètè (Ethiopia)
Fela & Africa 70 - Monday Morning in Lagos (Nigeria)
J.M Tim & Foty - Douala By Night (Cameroon)
Etoile 2000 - Boubou N'gary (Senegal)
Maitre Gazonga & International Challal - Jaloux Saboteurs (Chad/Ivory Coast)
Sandwidi Pierre et l'Orchestre Super Volta - Yamb Ney Capitale

Decentralised Neighbourhood Hotspot

10

Lagos

Self-powered local services

This project is part of a broader urban renewal programme for the Makoko/Iwaya slum in Lagos, Nigeria. This "village on the water", where 40,000 people live, is under threat from the elements and from the public authorities, who see it as an informal development that gets in the way of the growth of the city.
The deployment of heavy infrastructures would require the demolition of houses and the displacement of entire populations. As an alternative, in the perspective of an immediate improvements in living conditions, FABULOUS URBAN suggests centralising vital local services in small independent floating units: health care, waste, a space for the development of small-scale local economies, education, etc. The question of autonomy is central to the project: thanks to the production of biogas using local organic waste, the small scale of the facilities and their multi-functional nature, the regeneration of the district takes place with and for its inhabitants.

www.swiss-architects.com/en/fabulous-urban/?nonav=1

—

photos: © Isi Etomi / The MeMe Studio, Lagos
design, concept and implementation: FABULOUS URBAN
project partners: Heinrich Böll Stiftung Nigeria and SERAC, Lagos
structural engineering: Hermann Blumer
material consulting (solid wood): Robert Hüsler
funding: Embassy of Switzerland to Nigeria in Abuja

FABULOUS URBAN Zurich

Comprehensive, community-based concepts

FABULOUS URBAN is an urban design and planning practice for developing and emerging regions, established in Geneva and currently based in Zurich. Our design and planning approach is strongly research-led and radically hands-on. We stand for comprehensive, community-based concepts, preferably covering all scales in one project—from strategic planning to detailed construction design, with the human being in the centre of our thoughts. Empowering communities—and especially their women—is a key strategy in our projects, mainly through micro-entrepreneurial activities, micro-management and micro-urbanism, based on existing local traditions and embedded in local actor-networks. We operate from Switzerland, which offers excellent infrastructure, global networking and easy access to international as well as Swiss foundations and organisations.

Deconstruction

11

Belgium

The economics of reuse

The use of salvaged materials to build new buildings may have existed for a long time, but we still throw a huge amount away in contemporary society. Waste, the problem of managing waste, increasingly scarce resources..., our consumer habits are showing their limitations.
Working against regulatory and cultural norms that make it difficult to reuse materials in construction, Rotor has worked for about ten years with architects and political decision-makers, showing the ecological and economic relevance of reuse in the world of construction. By creating the company Rotor Déconstruction and its commercial website, the collective has managed to give value to materials from demolition sites in an economically viable way.

www.rotordb.org

—

photos: © Arne Baert
a project by Rotor for constellation.s
curated by: Lionel Devlieger and Andrea Ferreri
construction: Caroline De Decker and Andrea Ferreri
acknowledgments: Lionel Billiet, Tristan Boniver, Maarten Gielen, Benjamin Lasserre with the support of WBI (Wallonie Bruxelles International) and the Flemish Community (Vlaamse Gemeenschap)

The term DECONSTRUCTION, in the realm of building, refers to a form of reverse assembly: the careful dismantling of the constituents of a building. Contrary to traditional demolition, which is destructive, deconstruction aims at the re-use of components.

In earlier times, in other places, it was just plain common sense not to trash a sound material; most building components were re-used, sometimes more than once. Today, materials that leave a demolition or refurbishment site are doomed to more or less subtle forms of destruction. They will be dumped or incinerated, or transformed into secondary raw materials (re- or down-cycled). The procedures—logistic, administrative, legal—that would allow the non-violent extraction and reintegration of these materials in new buildings simply aren't ready yet, despite the goodwill of public authorities expressed in solemn pledges for a "circular economy".

The Brussels-based group Rotor has been engaged since 2006 in stimulating reuse practices in the building industry, through exemplary work, research and consultancy commissions and communication projects. Rotor has recently launched its own dismantling company, Rotor Deconstruction, which employs a team active in the dismantling, packaging, storing, treating, and reselling of second-hand building materials. The installation conceived for constellation.s presents six harvested materials, as well as the sites from which these were extracted, photographed after our teams did the job.

The term DECONSTRUCTION, in the realm of building, refers to a form of reverse assembly: the careful dismantling of the constituents of a building. Contrary to traditional demolition, which is destructive, deconstruction aims at the re-use of components.
In earlier times, in other places, it was just plain common sense not to trash a sound material; most building components were re-used, sometimes more than once. Today, materials that leave a demolition or refurbishment site are destined to more or less subtle forms of destruction. They will be dumped or incinerated, or transformed into secondary raw materials (re- or down-cycled). The procedures - logistic, administrative, legal - that would allow a non-violent extraction and reintegration of these materials in new buildings simply aren't ready yet, despite the goodwill of public authorities expressed in solemn pledges for a "circular economy".
The Brussels-based group Rotor is engaged since 2006 in stimulating reuse practices in the building industry, through exemplary realizations, research and consultancy missions and communication projects. Rotor has recently launched its own dismantling company, Rotor Deconstruction, which employs a team active in the dismantling, packaging, storing, treating, and reselling of second-hand building materials. The installation conceived for Constellation.s presents six harvested materials, as well as the sites from which these were extracted, photographed after our teams did the job.
The QR-codes next to each caption connect you to the corresponding webpage on the site rotordeconstruction.be

Laboratory of an Industrial Paper Mill, Nivelles (BE), 1960's

> p. 130

Arjowiggins is an international industrial group, leader in the production of paper for the arts. The group comprises, among other, the French brand Arches, which has been manufacturing paper since the 15th century. The factory in Nivelles, built and equipped in the 1960's, is now awaiting a new development. The laboratory of the old factory, responsible for fine-tuning the chemical treatment of the paper pulp, was equipped with elegant furniture produced by the Gettemans workshop from Braine-l'Alleud. Gettemans specialized in the production of laboratory furniture in wood and plastic materials. The high performance of these materials, skilfully assembled, gives these desks good resistance to aggressive substances. It makes them easily adaptable to a variety of reuses; in a workshop, a kitchen, or even a bathroom.

Solvay Office Building, Ixelles (BE), 1930-1950

> p. 131

From the 19th century on, a new technique for sealing parquet floor boards appeared: glueing the solid wooden slats in tar. The worker heats up the tar on site and spreads it, fuming, on the surface to be covered before pushing the wooden boards in place. The boards have a dovetailed profile that broadens to the bottom; once the tar cools down, the slats are firmly sealed. Until the 1950's, coal-based tar was used for this, to be gradually replaced by petroleum-based bitumen. We know now that coal-tar causes cancer; since 1990 it has been considered a dangerous waste-product in demolition operations. To the naked eye, though, both substances are impossible to tell apart. When we set out to extract a solid oak floor sealed in hydrocarbons, especially from a building dated 1960 or earlier, we systematically request a lab test of the glue, to check its content of PAH's (Polycyclic Aromatic Hydrocarbons), the carcinogenic molecules contained in coal tar. If PAH-content is safe, and the substance is confirmed bitumen, the boards are extracted and recalibrated by a subcontractor, who will mechanically sand the bottom surface to a pre-established point. While preserving the original surface patina, this treatment will guarantee a constant thickness of the salvaged slats, thus facilitating re-laying using contemporary (cold) glues.

Solvay Office Building, Ixelles (BE), 1930-1950

> p. 132

The corridor walls of this office building, which was fitted out in the 1950s, were covered with two types of natural stone: tiles in Solnhofen limestone and black Mazy marble, the latter used both as skirting and edging on top. These corridors, like the rest of the building, are currently undergoing thorough renovation. Our teams removed these wall coverings in the spring of 2016, using simple hand tools. Solnhofen limestone is famed for its extremely fine grain, which makes it one of the few stones in the world fit for lithography. The stone was quarried in the German state of Bavaria and is commonly known as 'Jura', referring to the geological age of the limestone deposit. These tiles are not sawn but cleaved, thus beautifully revealing the texture of the stone. The darker imprints are often mistaken for fossils, but are oxidations of manganese that have a characteristic tree-like or dendritic pattern. The black marble from Mazy (Belgium) is one of the only pitch-black and spotless marbles in the world. Already quarried in the Roman era, it is now only extracted from an underground, hardly accessible quarry, driving its cost to unknown heights.

Office building in Edegem (BE), 1960-2010

> p. 133

This building, part of an office campus in the Antwerp area, is owned by a large Belgian real estate company, specialising in rental property. A large proportion of their portfolio, amounting to a total of € 3,2 billion, is composed of office spaces. In the office rental business, it is customary to refurbish interiors entirely whenever there is a change of tenant. On average this will happen every 10 years, but it can happen much sooner. Elements such as glazed modular walls, doors, dropped ceilings, built-in lighting fixtures, raised service floors, carpet tiles etc., are usually removed using destructive methods, despite the fact that they are good candidates for reuse. These are exactly the kinds of materials Rotor Deconstruction specialises in. Every dismantling operation, nevertheless, requires carefully weighing the value of potentially salvageable materials against the cost of their dismantling in manpower and equipment. In the case of this project, we limited ourselves to the system walls in tempered glass; these are expensive materials if bought new, and are thus very much in demand on the second-hand market, if the dimensions are convenient enough.

Book Tower of the Ghent University Library, Ghent (BE), 1936

> p. 134

The Belgian architect Henry Van de Velde designed at the end of the 1930s, in uptown Ghent, a vast university complex in modernist style, comprising, among other things, the university library. The 3,000,000 books were brought together in a silo-like concrete tower rising up to 64 metres, meant to compete with the city's medieval church and belfry towers. All the spaces of this listed complex, including the 22 levels of the tower, are now undergoing thorough renovation. The university contacted us in 2015 regarding the metal bookshelves placed between the columns of the tower, which held the books. These shelves were to be removed in order to allow the refurbishment; the client was probing our interest for a take-over. We then discovered that part of the shelves were original, produced by a local contractor under licence from an American company, Snead, which has specialised since the early 1900s in the production of library equipment in lacquered steel plate. Snead had provided some of the biggest American libraries, including the Library of Congress, with its patented shelving system. We convinced the university to keep—at least on two floors—the original shelves. We carried out a careful cleaning, dismantling and packaging operation. The shelves are now stored away, until their reassembly after the renovation. A series of modules that will not be reintegrated in the building are available for sale.

Lobby of an office building in Brussels, 1960-2010

> p. 135

Lobbies are the ultimate show spaces. They often showcase the richest finishing materials in a property. In the case of this office building, located close to the European institutions in Brussels, a Carrara marble floor had been laid during the last refurbishment, despite the fact that it would probably not be a permanent fixture. A survey conducted on site allowed us to make out that the marble had been laid on a bed of plaster, an old technique which, unlike laying on cement mortar, enables easy dismantling without damage, while offering good stability. The joints between the marble slabs, though, had been filled with a cement-based mortar. To allow dismantling without damaging the slabs, we had to mill the joints with a thin, water-cooled diamond grinder. The fact that the marble was laid out in bands of constant width, hence with mostly continuous joints, made this job a lot easier. The splashes of cement slurry on the black walls caused by this grinding were clearly visible after we left.

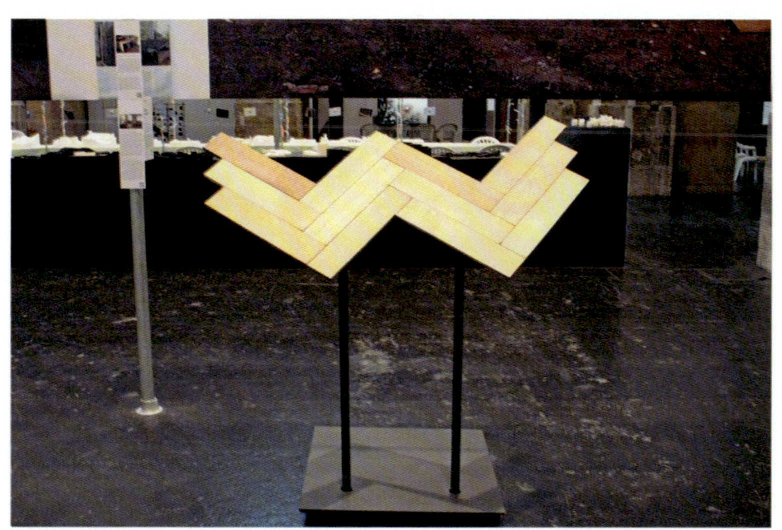

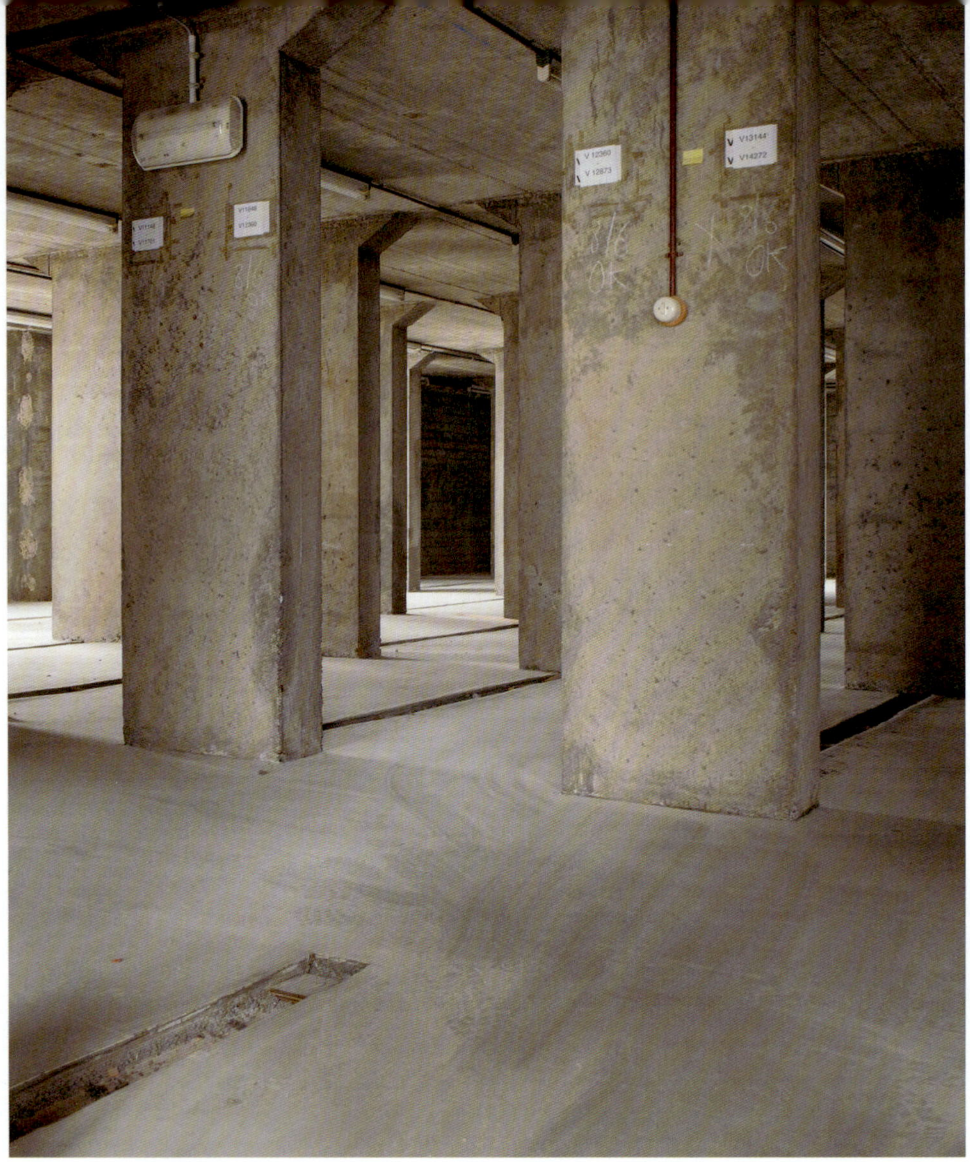
V 12360
V 12873
V13144
V14272

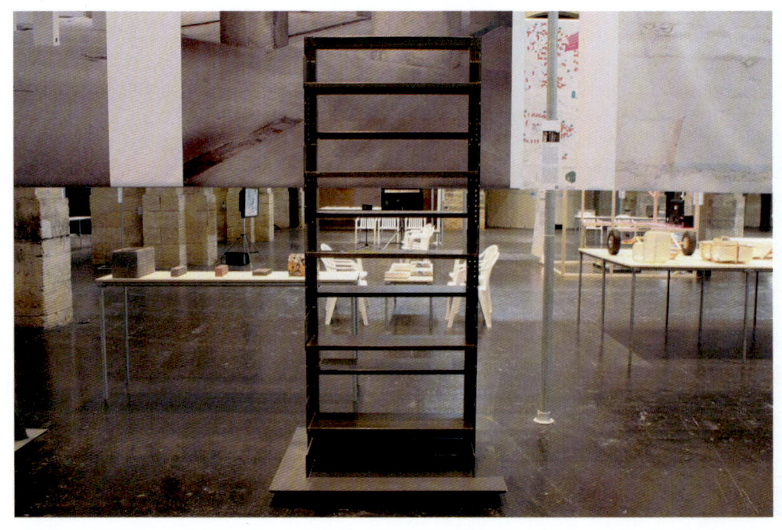

Design Build

12

Blacksburg

Designing and building as a single goal

In their practice as both architects and teachers, Marie and Keith Zawistowski seek to bring together the art of designing and the art of building. From a line drawn on a piece of paper to the assembly of a roof structure, they ensure perfect continuity between all the steps of the building process (from the brief and the budget to the actual build).
By taking a hands-on approach with their students, they face up to the physical conditions in which buildings are constructed, and are able to respond as well as possible to residents' needs.
When they work for private clients, they focus on one project at a time, involving themselves entirely and offering responses that are highly intelligent in economic terms and reflect great attention to user comfort.
In the framework of their teaching, with their group of students, they focus on projects with a social or humanitarian dimension, strongly anchored in their context.

www.onsitearchitecture.com

—

onSITE Blacksburg / Paris

onSITE is the design/build collaboration of husband and wife Keith and Marie Zawistowski. Marie and Keith's work has been driven by the desire to improve the lives of others through the making of architecture. Each one of their projects is deeply rooted in the unique identity of people and places. They only work on one project at a time, focusing on the art of building, often with their own hands. By working from within the context of their projects, onSITE strives to make buildings that are economically, culturally, and environmentally sensitive.

Initiated by onSITE, located at Virginia Tech until 2015 and now based in France, the design/buildLAB is a project-based experiential learning program focused on the research, development and implementation of innovative construction methods and architectural designs. Students collaborate with local communities and industry experts to conceive and build works of architecture that are both educational and charitable in nature. The aspirations of the programme are simultaneously to reinforce the capacity of young generations of architects, and to support development efforts in distressed communities by enriching the quality of their built environment. By framing the opportunity for architecture students to make a difference in the life of a community, the design/buildLAB shows students the positive impact Architecture can have and empowers them to pursue their vocation to the benefit of the common good.

design/buildLAB
Born To
Fuck Shit Up
FIX

CCD45

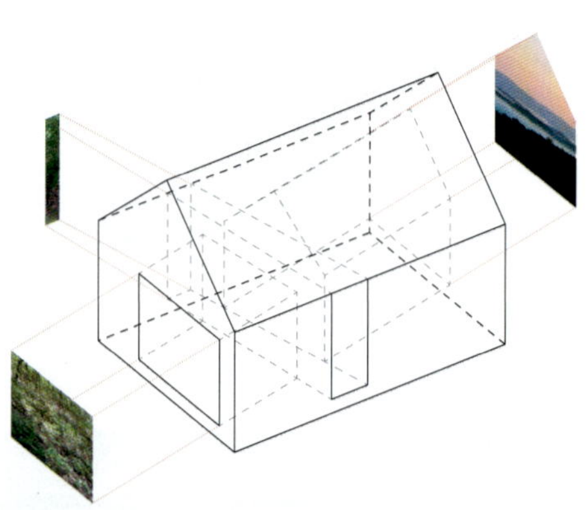

Housing Estate in Claveau

13

Bordeaux

Tact and sensitivity serving a neighbourhood

At the foot of the Pont d'Aquitaine bridge, the garden city of Claveau is going through a new stage in its history. Built between 1951 and 1959 on a site once used by the German army, the Cité Claveau is made up of small one-storey houses, each with its own garden. Over time they have gradually been remodelled, renovated and extended by their occupants, most of whom are rent-paying tenants.
The challenge today is to improve energy consumption and the overall quality of the buildings, while remaining sympathetic to the almost vernacular situations generated by decades of appropriation by residents. The renovation project for the Cité Claveau is careful to preserve what is already there whilst implementing case-by-case solutions with each resident, in order to develop and consolidate their autonomy.

www.construire.cc

—

Housing renovation in Claveau
Construire-Nicole Concordet
for Aquitanis, public housing development body for the Bordeaux metropolitan area, 2016-2020
photos: © Louise Cortella and Mathieu Baehr

Nicole Concordet / Construire Bordeaux
with aquitanis

The cité Claveau garden estate at Bacalan in the north of Bordeaux was built between 1952 and 1959. It comprises 350 two-level houses with gardens, each laid out on a plan offset at 28°. These dwellings have been thoroughly appropriated by their tenants, who have adapted them to needs according to their means, skills and tastes. Today, the entire estate needs to be refurbished. We propose an all-in experimental project based on re-use and appropriation, with added educational, economic and social value. Keeping residents in the flesh and bones of the project enables us to experiment with modes of production that are unusual and that highlight architecture.

The Maison Commune is where the project takes shape. It is a facility that houses the on-site architectural office, where the designers in charge of the project work. Nearness to inhabitants is the cornerstone of the upgrade. Our architects interview residents in their homes in order to get a proper understanding of their living habits by listening to them tell their own story. Residents guide the architects as they inspect and inventory, room by room, identifying needs so as to adapt their intervention to the arrangements that are already in place and make the best possible use of them. Adhering to a strict budget, the project will take place in two stages. First-phase 'systematic' work carried out by general contractors will be followed by detailed work carried out case by case, which will enable improvements and spaces to be added in collaboration with inhabitants.

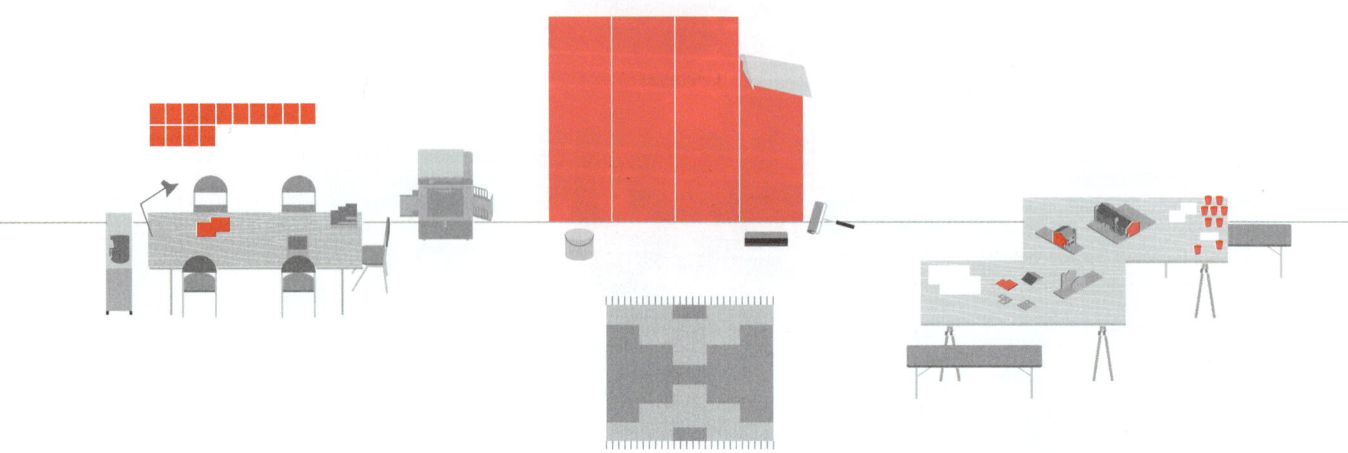

Drawings by Construire
for the "Housing Estate in Claveau"
project

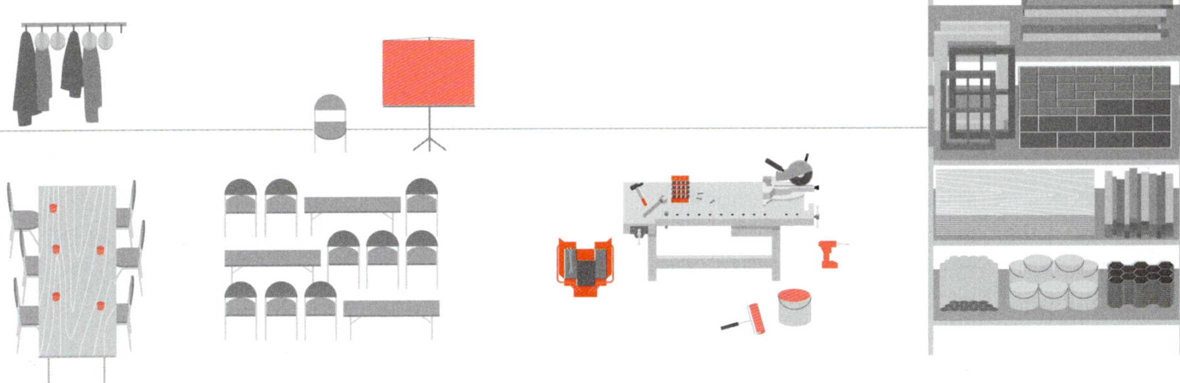

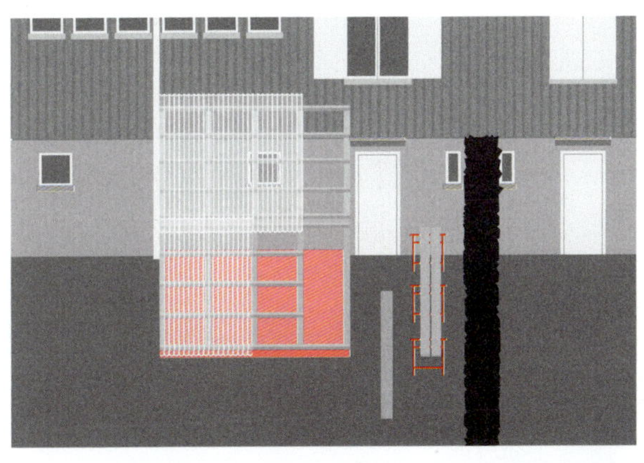

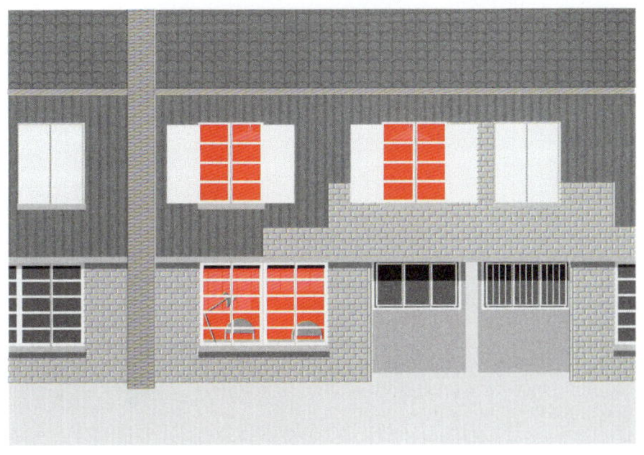

FireChat

14

Human digital chain

FireChat became famous during the "umbrella revolution", the name given to the pro-democracy demonstrations in Hong Kong in late 2014. When the authorities cut off access to the mobile network to attempt to sllence the protest, this application made it possible to connect together all the phones brandished by the protesters. Messages, alerts and slogans could continue to circulate.
The little mobile programme then appeared as the symbol of an alternative to the hyper-centralisation of telecommunications networks, a real power issue at a time when most people use their mobile phone as a personal communication centre. It can also be used in areas where the networks aren't working or simply don't exist, in concert halls and refugee camps, for instance.

—

photos: © Philippe Lopez / AFP

Hong Kong, last week of September, 2014. Joshua Wong, 17 years old, one of the leaders of the Occupy Central movement, launches an urgent appeal on social media: the authorities might cut off access to the Internet, but the protesters can stay connected, at least locally, if they install a messaging app called FireChat on their smartphones.

梁匪振英 + 功能組別 + 無恥政客 + 好人沉默 = 政府腐

政府墮落 議會失效
我衛我城 誓爭民主
今日佔中

Granby Four Streets

15

Liverpool

154

Getting back to doing things together

In Granby, an area of craftsman's houses in the suburbs of Liverpool abandoned for over 30 years, local residents have taken it into their hands to avoid its demolition, maintain it, and bring life into it despite everything. By using local dynamics, architectural value and cultural heritage, the Assemble collective works with them to renovate housing, build small facilities and public spaces, and create added value by developing a social, caring economy around specific crafts.
Carefully made, elegant objects are made from waste from demolition sites and sold on the spot, in the tradition of the Arts and Crafts movement of the nineteenth century. The value of making and the do-it-yourself spirit rooted in the identity of the district are thus reactivated.

www.assemblestudio.co.uk

—

photos: © assemble
illustrations: © Marie Jacotey

Assemble are a collective based in London who work across the fields of art, architecture and design. They began working together in 2010 and count 18 members. Assemble's working practice seeks to address the typical disconnection between the public and the process by which places are made. Assemble champion a working practice that is interdependent and collaborative, seeking to actively involve the public as both participant and collaborator in the on-going realisation of the work.

Turner Prize 2015

Granby Four Streets

Granby Four Streets is a strategic vision that seeks to build on the extraordinary efforts of the local residents by working with them toward the sustainable and incremental improvement of the area.
Granby Street was once a lively high street at the centre of Liverpool's most racially and ethnically diverse community. The demolition of all but four of Granby's streets of Victorian terraces during decades of 'regeneration' initiatives saw a once thriving community scattered, and left the remaining 'Granby Four Streets' sparsely populated and filled with tinned up houses. The resourceful and creative actions of a group of residents were fundamental to finally bringing these streets out of dereliction and back into use. Over two decades they cleared, planted, painted, and campaigned in order to reclaim the streets they lived on.

In 2011 they entered into an innovative form of community land ownership, the Granby Four Streets Community Land Trust (CLT) with the intention of bringing empty homes back into use as affordable housing. Assemble worked with the Granby Four Streets CLT and Steinbeck Studios to present a sustainable and incremental vision for the area that builds on the hard work already done by local residents and translates it into the refurbishment of housing, public space as well as the provision of new work and enterprise opportunities.
The approach is characterised by celebrating the value of the area's architectural and cultural heritage, supporting public involvement and collaborative partnerships, offering local training and employment opportunities and nurturing the resourcefulness and Do It Yourself spirit that defines the Four Streets.

E DICTUM SIT ALT

GW
GRANBY FOUR STREETS
10 MAISONS À CAIRNS STREET
LE JARDIN D'HIVER DE GRANBY
L'ATELIER DE GRANBY

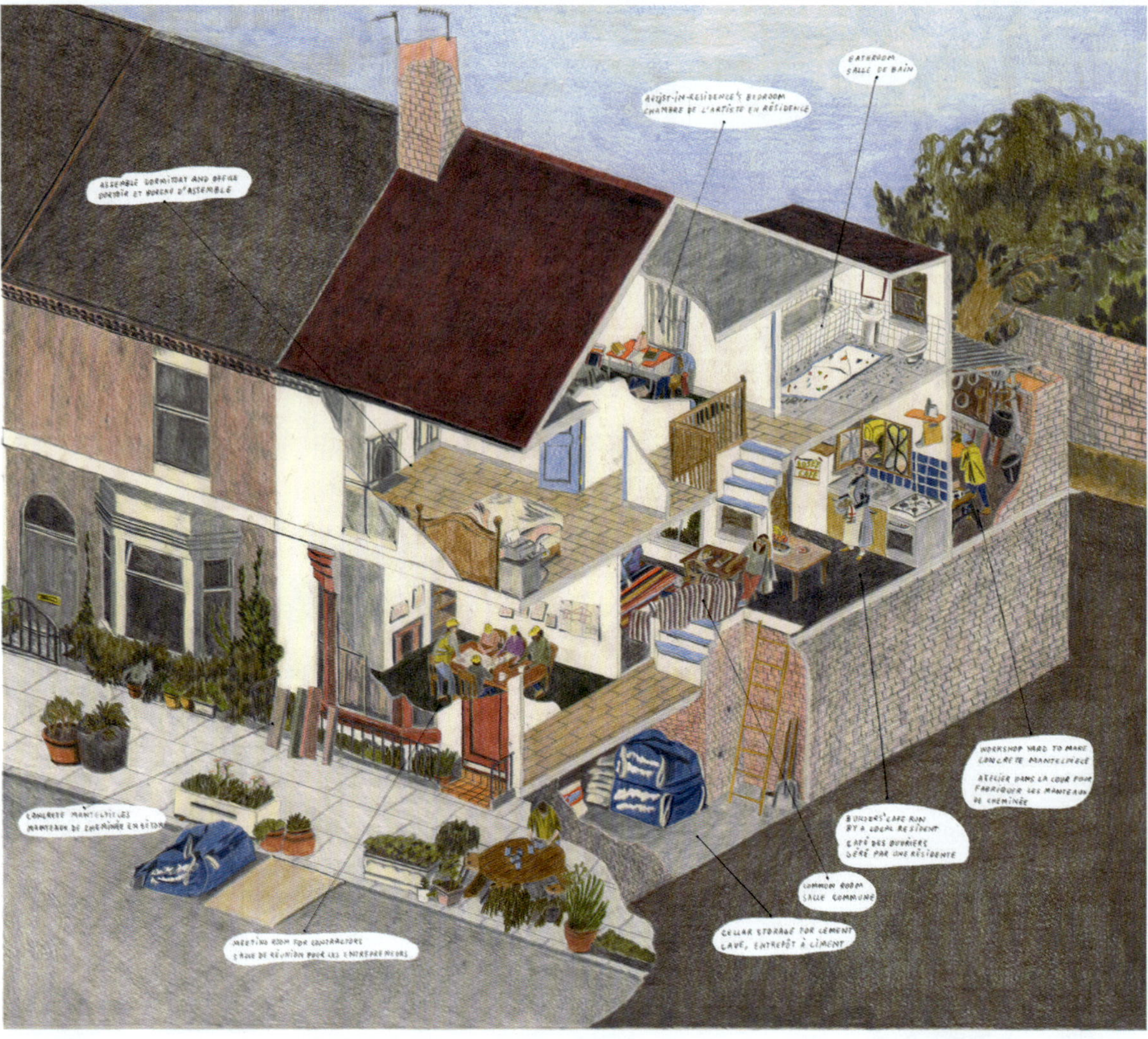

10 Houses on Cairns Street

ASSEMBLE ARE WORKING WITH THE GRANBY FOUR STREETS COMMUNITY LAND TRUST TO REFURBISH TEN DERELICT TERRACED HOUSES ON CAIRNS STREET IN LIVERPOOL.

The project is the result of a hard-won, twenty-year battle by local residents to save the terraced houses in Granby Four Streets from demolition. The residents have reclaimed and planted their streets, painted the empty houses and established a thriving monthly market. All of this has been consolidated by the foundation of a Community Land Trust (CLT). Assemble have worked closely with the CLT in order to incorporate ideas inspired by the residents' resourceful and Do-It-Yourself attitude into the refurbishment of the houses, and have worked to tight budgets so that the CLT can provide the houses at affordable rates for local residents that remain in community ownership.

The model for the houses is not one of restoration, but of repair and adaptation, responding to the specific condition of each house. Simple and low cost materials are used to provide light and open homes that usefully adopt elements or scars of previous damage to create enjoyable spaces to live.

As well as an otherwise economical palette, the houses include a number of bespoke handmade architectural elements, such as mantelpieces, tiles and doorknobs that help to characterise these simple houses as homes, replacing features stripped from the houses during decades of neglect. These elements are now being produced locally as part of the social enterprise set up by Assemble in collaboration with the CLT: Granby Workshop.

Granby Winter Garden

The Granby Winter Garden is a collaboration between the Granby Four Streets Community Land Trust and Assemble. Two derelict terraced properties on Cairns Street will be transformed into an internal garden and artist residency-space owned by and operated for the local community.

The project will be divided into two: the Winter Garden, and the Common House. The Winter Garden will be the garden itself; and the Common House will be a space for community meetings or gatherings, alongside an artist's residence comprised of a bedroom, bathroom and workspace. The Common House will aim to establish a resource for socially engaged artistic practice, that continues the history of creative action and engagement that has been a key driver for change in the area.

The artist residency programme is currently being developed by the Community Land Trust in partnership with local arts agencies and will feature a diverse range of artists, from the local to the international..

The Granby Winter Garden is a key part of the Granby Four Streets Community Land Trust's long-term plan to revitalise their neighbourhood. The CLT itself grew out of the residents' decades-long campaign to oppose the demolition of the area's terraces and to re-build their community through creative community action, growing and collaboration. The Winter Garden is key to ensuring that that spirit and those activities remain at the core of the area as it continues to develop and grow.

Granby Workshop

Granby Workshop is a new social enterprise that makes and sells handmade products for homes. Having grown out of the community-led rebuilding of its neighbourhood in Granby, the Workshop seeks to support and continue the hands-on, resourceful and creative cultures that were fundamental to bringing the streets back into use after years of deriliction.
The project was launched through the Turner Prize exhibition in 2015, where Assemble created a showroom to display the workshop's first collection. These were a set of handmade features, which ranged from mantelpieces to doorknobs, each of which had been designed in a collaborative method by Assemble and a group of accomplices. These features had been developed as part of the refurbishment process of the houses in the area, in order to replace the elements lost in their strip out by the council
Production of the objects started in early 2016: training and employing local designers and artists to make the products. Each product is manufactured using a process that embraces chance and encourages improvisation, so that each object is unique, developed in the hands of the people making it.
Profit from sales is funding a youth program that works with young people on creative, practical projects in order to help develop their capacity to enact change in their neighbourhood.

Green Steel

16

162

Bamboo v steel, a re-territorialisation of the economy

Developing countries are major consumers of reinforced concrete and rarely have the means to produce the necessary steel themselves; they find themselves dependent on a material whose price is determined by global markets. The Future Cities Lab suggests using bamboo as an alternative to this industrial product. Ecological and easy to grow, it has very interesting structural properties in terms of resistance to traction and could ideally replace steel. Bamboo-reinforced concrete already exists in certain tropical zones.

The researchers are now working on improving the product to as to solve the problems of rot and parasites that still limit its use. The innovation is promising in technical, social and economic terms. It offers southern countries the opportunity for greater geopolitical autonomy.

www.fcl.ethz.ch

—

photos: © Future Cities Lab, Singapore / Carlina Teteris

Alternative Construction Materials New Resources for Architecture and Construction

Assistant Professorship of Architecture and Construction
Dirk E. Hebel
ETH Zurich, Switzerland and Future Cities Laboratory, Singapore

The 21st century needs to introduce a radical paradigm shift in how to materialise our habitat. While the first age of industrialisation resulted in the conversion from regenerative to non-regenerative material sources, our time should address the reverse: a shift from a mining-based mentality towards an ideology of cultivating, recycling, recovering, breeding, raising, farming, or growing future construction materials.

As urban populations grow, so does the demand for materials and resources to support them. Where such resource demands were once satisfied by local and regional hinterlands, they are increasingly global in scale and reach. Our research at the ETH Zurich and the Future Cities Laboratory in Singapore concentrates on material alternatives and their application in specific contextual settings, taking into account the availability of materials, human resource capacities and skills. The 'alternative' aspect of this focus emerges from an exploration of innovative and entrepreneurial thinking.

A declared aim of the on-going research is to establish fibre composite materials as a future and alternative building material in developing areas of our planet. The research underway investigates the mechanical properties of natural fibres and how to control them in order to achieve desired characteristics for use as a construction material to replace steel and wood, and also to use it as a reinforcement system in concrete applications. The team established the 'Advanced Fiber Composite Laboratory' in Singapore, where they are able to produce and test new fibre reinforcement materials at the same time.

The exhibition shows a variety of necessary test samples taken from the FCL. Cylindrical concrete cones are needed in "pull-out-tests" in order to establish the bonding behaviour between concrete and the bamboo composite reinforcement, while the concrete beams are tested in bending to verify the qualities of the incorporated bamboo reinforcement in structural building components.

AFCL
Laboratory
mhe

EXIT

ETHzürich
DARCH

Halley VI Antarctic Research Station

17

Extreme habitat

The Halley VI scientific base replaces five earlier versions, all gradually swallowed up by the ice. Its eight coloured capsules standing on adjustable feet and equipped with skis are mobile and designed to withstand the extreme conditions of the South Pole. This latest version involved an international design competition so as to provide the researchers with optimum comfort: large windows overlooking the landscape, and an interior clad in fragrant cedarwood to make up for the lack of sensorial stimulation as a result of the environment.
Extreme environments call for exceptional solutions and lend themselves to innovation. Halley VI, which is like something out of science fiction, demonstrates this.

www.hbarchitects.co.uk

—

Hugh Broughton Architects London

The Antarctic is the coldest,most remote, and most difficult place in the world to live and work, and the British Antarctic survey's Halley research station is in a particularly difficult part of the continent. It sits on a shifting but featureless ice shelf and is subjected to high winds and annual build-ups of snow that have buried several previous stations. Working there throughout the year involves long months of darkness and, even with modern technology, isolation from family and friends. It is, however, a fantastic place for science, for looking both up above the earth and down into the ice, and for making discoveries that could affect all our futures.

MT02

Halley III emerging from the Brunt Ice Shelf (circa 1992)

Approximately 1.2 metres of snow accumulate each year on the Brunt Ice Shelf and in the past buildings constructed on the surface became covered and eventually crushed by snow, necessitating periodic rebuilding of the station. This part of the Brunt Ice Shelf is also moving westward by about 700 metres per year. Halley III was abandoned in 1984, and this picture was taken years later when its remains were spotted emerging from the ice shelf.

Île Derborence

18

Lille

A metropolitan plant sanctuary

In 1998, in the Parc Henri Matisse at Euralille, Gilles Clément erected a tumulus using landfill from the high-speed train station and planted a forest on it. The 2,500 sq.m. area, seven metres high, stands enigmatically at the centre of the park. Called the "Île Derborence", from the name of a place in Switzerland that is home to one of the last primeval forests in Europe, this strange monument is inaccessible to visitors. Only certain scientists are allowed to come and observe the gradual development of a variety of plant species. They find a rare environment, not modified by Man: a piece of what the designer calls the "third landscape". To the visitor walking in the park, l'Île Derborence appears as somewhere both close and very remote. It calls on the imagination and, in the heart of the city, encourages us to reflect upon our predatory relationship with nature.

www.gillesclement.com

—

photos: © Frédéric Delesalle

Gilles Clément Paris

The Third Landscape

The "Third Landscape"—an undecided fragment of the Plantetary Garden— refers to the totality of the areas where Man leaves the changing landscape to Nature alone. It concerns areas of urban or rural waste ground, transitional areas, brownfield sites, marshes, moors, peat bogs, and also roadsides, riverbanks, railway embankments, and so on. In addition to waste ground there are areas in reserve.
These may be de facto reserves: inaccessible places, mountaintops, uncultivated areas, deserts; or they may be institutional reserves: national and regional parks and "nature reserves".
Compared to the areas controlled and farmed by Man, the Third Landscape is the ideal setting for biological diversity. In cities, farms, managed forests, industrial sites, tourist areas and business districts, the control and decision-making process selects diversity and sometimes excludes it completely. The number of species identified in a farm field or an area of managed woodland is low in comparison to the number to be found in an adjacent area of waste ground.
Seen from this angle, the Third Landscape emerges as the gene pool of the planet and the space of the future.
Embracing the Third Landscape as a biological necessity that determines the future of living things changes the way we approach land and attaches value to places usually considered as being of scant interest. It is the politician's job to organise land use so that areas of indecision are created within the places under their control—which equates to planning for the future.
The Third Landscape is of interest to planning professionals and designers insofar as it encourages them to include non-developed areas in their projects, or to designate unused areas necessarily generated by any development initiative as spaces of special public interest.
The term Third Landscape (Tiers-Paysage) comes from an analysis of the landscape at the Vassivière site in the Limousin region commissioned by the Centre d'Art et du Paysage de Vassivière in 2003. The analysis shows the binary nature of the landscape: on the one hand there is shadow, with managed forests dominated by douglas fir: a landscape regulated by forestry agents; while on the other hand there is light, with farmland mainly given over to stockbreeding: a landscape regulated by agronomists. But although this blanket of light and shade seems to cover the entire area, it does not completely reveal it.
If we count the different species present in the area we notice that there are relatively few of them, and that species diversity is much lower than one would expect in such an area. A third set of areas at Vassivière—moorland, peat bogs, riversides, steep slopes and roadsides—accommodates all the species that have moved away from the farmland and that are capable of living in this climate and on this type of terrain.
The term Third Landscape alludes not to the Third World but to the Third Estate. It refers to the words of Abbé Siéyès: "What is the Third Estate? – It is everything – What has it been hitherto? – Nothing – What does it desire to be? – Something."

The only major project that deliberately highlights the Third Landscape is the Parc Matisse in Lille where the Island of Derborence, a central feature raised 7 metres above the surrounding area and covering 3,500 square metres, plays host to a naturally established "ideal forest". Inaccessible but observed, it acts as a template and a guide for managing the eight-hectare public park with the greatest possible economy of means.

"Le Manifeste du Tiers-Paysage" was published by Sujet/Objet in 2003.

Incremental Housing

19

Chile / Mexico

Half a good house is better than a bad house

The Chilean government offers each household a subsidy that allows it to buy a home. But the homes are of poor quality. To solve this problem, architect Alejandro Aravena and his team at Elemental offer housing "to be completed". Residents can carry on building gradually, depending on their means and their needs. The initial structure responds to all the local antiseismic requirements and includes the kitchen and bathroom. To allow people to extend the bedrooms or to create new ones without affecting the strength of the building, the size of the volumes to be completed is calculated with reference to standard construction elements. Each family can thus build the house it needs, at its own pace and to its own taste.

www.elementalchile.cl/en

—

photos: © Elemental; © Cristobal Palma; © Felipe Diaz; © Tadeuz Jalocha

Elemental Santiago
Alejandro Aravena

Out of the 3 billion people living in cities today, 1 billion are living under the poverty line. By 2030 out of the 5 billion people that will be living in cities, 2 billion are going to be under the poverty line. That means that we will have to build the equivalent of a city for one million people every week with 10,000 dollars per family. Given the magnitude of the housing shortage, we won't solve this problem unless we add people's own resources and building capacity to that of governments and the market. That is why we thought of putting in place an OPEN SYSTEM able to channel all the available forces at play. That way people will be part of the solution and not part of the problem.

On the other hand, it is a fact that available resources are not enough. To face such scarcity of means, the market tends to do two things: it reduces the size of the houses, threatening the quality of life of its inhabitants, and it displaces them to underserved peripheries where land costs nothing, segregating people from the opportunities that made them come to cities in the first place. In order to face scarcity we propose a principle we call INCREMENTALITY.

2142

2148

2127

Kumbh Mela: Mapping the Ephemeral Megacity

20

Allahabad

190

The ephemeral megacity as a resilient model of urban management

The religious festival of Purna Kumbh Mela, which takes place every 12 years on the banks of the Ganges, is the largest temporary gathering on the planet. Last time it was held, in 2013, it attracted over 100 million pilgrims over a period of three weeks.

The temporary megacity thus created demands very careful planning and construction—bridges and pontoons, tents, power cables and health services. Specific governance structures are also set up in cooperation with the religious authorities. Responding to these unusual conditions, this gigantic and well-managed temporary installation offers valuable lessons in efficiency and reversibility in the way we design contemporary cities.

www.rmaarchitects.com

—

photos: © Felipe Vera; © Dinesh Mehta; © Dhruv Kazi

Rahul Mehrotra and Felipe Vera Mumbai / Santiago

Learning from the pop-up megacity: reflections on reversibility and openness

The physical structure of cities around the globe is evolving, morphing, mutating and becoming more malleable, fluid and open to change than the technology and social institutions that generate it. Today, urban environments face ever-increasing flows of human movement, acceleration in the frequency of natural disasters, and iterative economic crises that modify streams of capital and their allocation as physical components of cities. In consequence, urban settings have to be more flexible in order to better respond to, organise, and resist internal and external pressures. At a time when change and the unexpected are the new norm, urban attributes like reversibility and openness are critical elements for thinking out and articulating a more sustainable type of urban development.

The lessons we can extract from the Kumbh Mela are clearly aligned with these attributes. This massive gathering, resulting in the biggest ephemeral megacity in the world, generates an extreme case that forces us to reflect deeply upon the way we think of cities. This essay examines the two key attributes of the ephemeral city of the Kumbh Mela and the lessons we can extrapolate from it for architecture, urban design and planning in the contemporary world.

Water

The Kumbh Mela, a Hindu festival held every twelve years, is an extreme example of a religious congregation that generates a temporary settlement. Approximately five million people gather for fifty-five days, with an additional flux often to twenty million people coming for twenty-four-hour cycles on six main bathing dates. The ephemeral city of the Kumbh Mela is not only framed by a strong cultural ecology, but also located in a highly dynamic physical geography, affected seasonally by the monsoon.

Unlike a more permanent city where the construction of the physical environment happens as the aggregation of relatively permanent parts that progressively materialise the space, the Kumbh Mela takes form like a choreographic process of temporal urbanisation, happening in coordination with environmental dynamics.

Governance

After the waters of the Ganges retreat, the riverbank becomes an interstitial space between three distinct locales-the city of Allahabad on one side, the small industrial village of Jhunsi on the other, and a still undeveloped span of rural land between. The coordination of these three settings [...] is resolved by the creation of a special regulatory framework that provides for the appointment of a Mela Adhikari (district magistrate) who has the power to administrate the site through an ephemeral jurisdictional framework that lasts for the duration of the event. Once the whole process is over, administrators are often promoted or reappointed in the pre-existing governmental structure. The institutional frameworks that supported such an enormous operation vanish like the traces of the city once the river washes over the terrain due to the flooding from the seasonal monsoon rains.

Deployment

One of the most interesting points about the construction process of the city is that unlike static and permanent cities- where the whole is comprised of the aggregation of smaller parts, constructed at different moments and tied together by pre-existing and connecting infrastructure- the city of the Kumbh Mela is planned and built in one go.

As the final form of the floodplain is unknown until the river actually recedes, most of the design is based on a certain level of structural flexibility and the ability to adapt to uncertain conditions. Other than the need for connecting with the pre-existing and more permanent infrastructures of Allahabad, there are no other constraints in the deployment of the network. Therefore, the final form of the city is the result of a progression of uncertainties, ranging from speculation about the possible physical forms that the flood plain might take once the river recedes, to the estimated duration of the monsoon.

Technology

The few building techniques implemented at the Kumbh are based on the repetition and recombination of a basic module with simple inter-connections. This is usually a stick (approximately 6 to 8 feet long) that by aggregation, generates diverse enclosures in a wide range of forms from small tents to complex buildings-providing expression to various social institutions such as theatres, monuments, temples, hospitals, etc. All of them are constructed out of the same elements, with bamboo sticks used as the framework and laminar materials such as corrugated metal and fabric. The simplicity of the building systems also facilitates the logistics and channels of distribution for each component and piece. One person or group provides the modulation of each material so that it can be carried and handled in the absence of heavy machinery. The strength of the method lies in its ability to achieve specific and determined forms with a couple of indeterminate solutions that are applicable in different contexts and adjustable at any moment.

Climax

The 2013 Kumbh Mela at Allahabad drew an estimated 100 million participants to the confluence of the Ganges and the Yamuna. Pictures of the festival testify to the immensity of the gathering, and they beg the question, what does it mean for a temporary city to actually house 100 million people? There is no other ecumenical event in the world, held on such a vast scale, where ascetics and lay people from theologically disparate traditions coexist and coalesce.

The Kumbh Mela pragmatically promotes the pluralism inherent in Indian civilization by creating the spatial and psychological conditions in which followers of disparate traditions live together, reflecting the spirit, "Whatever your faith, you will have to lose yourself in the one."

Deconstruction

It takes two months for total deconstruction of the Kumbh Mela. Some of the materials are put in storage in Uttar Pradesh, so they can be reused in future iterations. Each Kumbh Mela provides fresh ideas- always trying to rethink deficiencies. When it comes to decisions about the quantity, dimensions, and organization of key infrastructural elements, one of the most interesting strategies incorporated in the planning of the city is the implementation of resilience redundancy, instead of optimization. The seventeen pontoon bridges that connected both sides of the river are good examples of this, as they allowed the grid to operate effectively under extreme conditions of flux. The deconstruction stage starts after the last bathing day of the Kumbh Mela, which launches the reprogramming of space into agricultural fields until the Ganges floods again in the monsoon to erase the site of the city.

Next pages: from Roahul Mehotra and Felipe Vera, *Kumbh Mela, Mapping the Ephemeral Megacity*, Hatje Cantz.

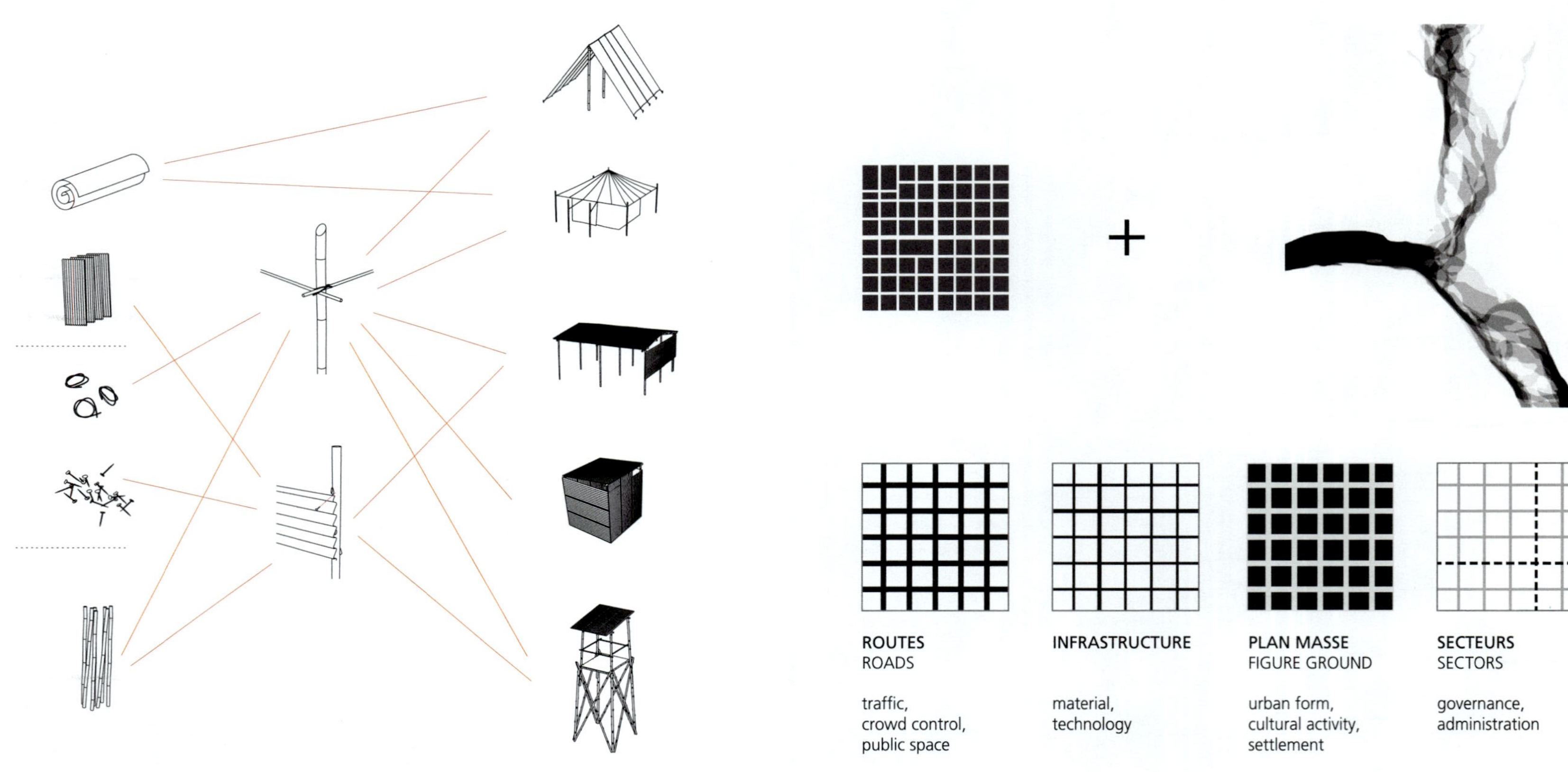
HORS SITE / OFF SITE
SUR SITE / ON SITE
ROUTES
ROADS
traffic,
crowd control,
public space
INFRASTRUCTURE
material,
technology
PLAN MASSE
FIGURE GROUND
urban form,
cultural activity,
settlement
SECTEURS
SECTORS
governance,
administration

→ **flux des personnes, longueur proportionnelle à la vitesse**
flow of people, lenght indicates speed

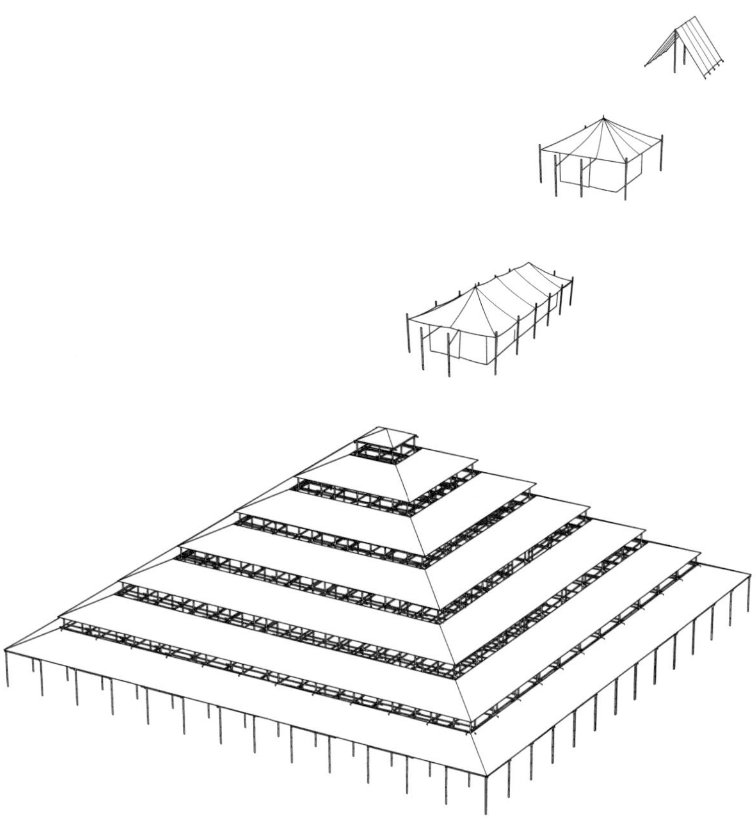

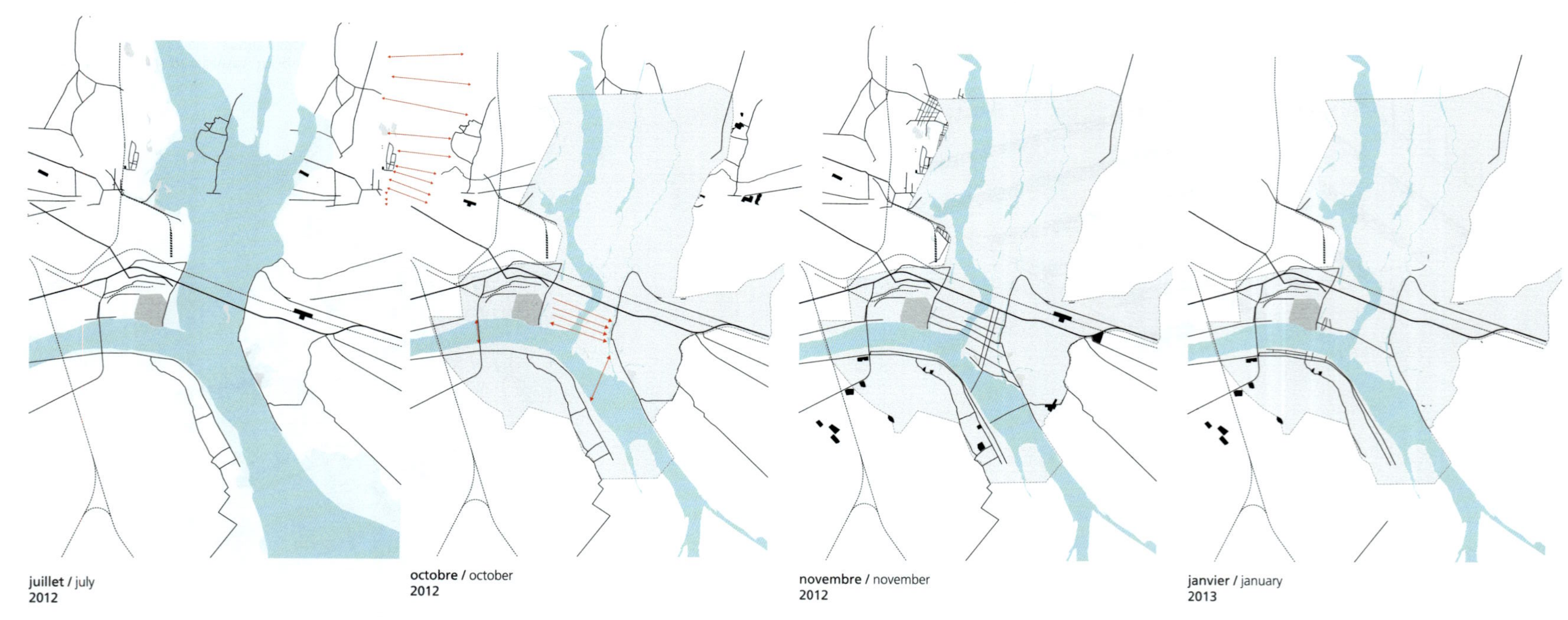
juillet / july
2012
octobre / october
2012
novembre / november
2012
janvier / january
2013

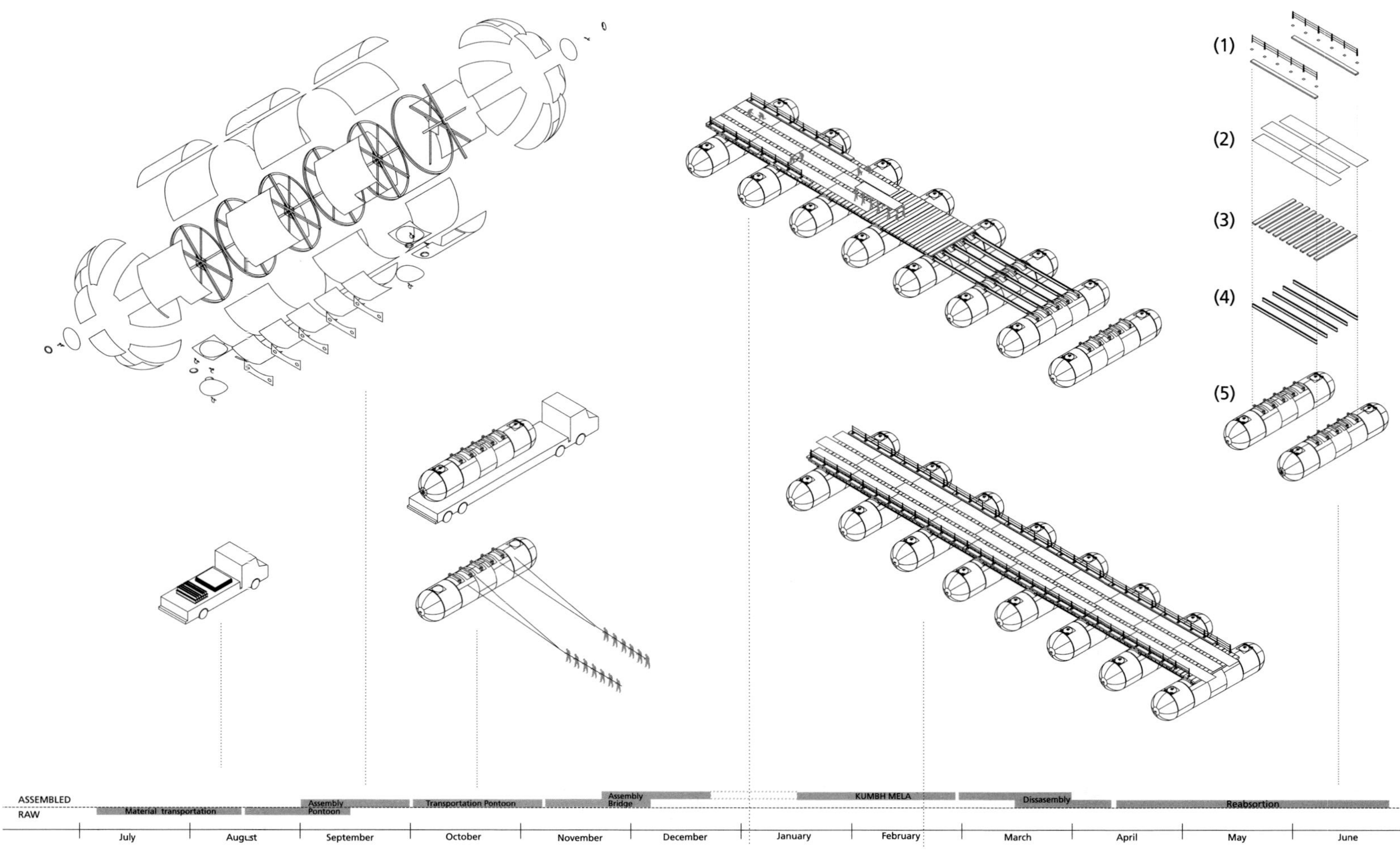
(1)
(2)
(3)
(4)
(5)
ASSEMBLED
RAW
Material transportation
Assembly Pontoon
Transportation Pontoon
Assembly Bridge
KUMBH MELA
Dissasembly
Reabsortion
July
August
September
October
November
December
January
February
March
April
May
June

Lali Gurans

21

Kathmandu

Protective structure

In the area around Kathmandu, Nepal, the Lali Guran was designed to become a small rural facility housing an orphanage, a day centre for women, a library and classrooms. But when a magnitude 7.8 earthquake shook the region in April 2015, the building turned out to be very useful for the local population even while it was still under construction.
Thanks to its reinforced concrete exoskeleton, it is one of the few structures to have survived the disaster intact. It could thus be used as a reception and first aid point, anticipating the central role it would play for the community when completed.

www.mos.nyc

—

photos: © MOS architects; © Sagar Chitrakar

MOS Architects New York

Lali Gurans is a semi-autonomous, sustainable community centre in rural Kathmandu, Nepal, containing a community library, meeting house, orphanage and classrooms for forty children and young adults. The design draws from the local building method of a 30cm reinforced concrete frame with block infill, but adds an extra layer of columns to eliminate the need for brick. This creates a more open framework that admits daylight to the interior. The form slopes inwards for structural and seismic stability, so the facade becomes closer to a roof than an elevation. Between the layers of exterior structure is a zone that oscillates between inside and outside, containing the primary vertical circulation as well as glazed solaria and planters. Stairs between the two layers of structure act as X-bracing for lateral stability, and connect various programmes together through a vertical picturesque landscape garden. In addition to its concentric exo-skeleton structure for seismic stability, the building also integrates low-energy and low-tech sustainable systems, including a brise-soleil, permaculture roof gardens, bio-gas, solar panels, rainwater collection, natural lighting, passive wastewater treatment, and passive heating and cooling. Built to withstand a seismic intensity of IX on the Mercalli scale, the structure withstood the Spring 2015 earthquake.

208

La Maddalena

22

Italy

Ethical questions

The island of La Maddalena north of Sardinia should have hosted the G8 in 2009. On the site of the former Arsenal, the brand new conference centre awaited the arrival of the heads of state. Prime Minister Silvio Berlusconi ultimately decided otherwise, and the G8 took place in Aquila, which had just been destroyed by an earthquake. The barely finished buildings on the island were abandoned, revealing fraud, corruption and pollution problems.

In the first of these two films that mirror one another, architect Stefano Boeri, who partially designed the site, bitterly describes the reasons for the disaster. Some miles away, on the island of Budelli, Mauro Morendi lives like Robinson Crusoe and has built his home using items deposited on the shore by the tide—for example making a chair from driftwood and Murano glass from the façade of the La Maddalena complex.

This simple, gratuitous act gives even greater resonance to the vanity of the La Maddalena project. These twin films highlight the disgraceful wastefulness of our times.

www.bekalemoine.com

Bêka & Lemoine Paris

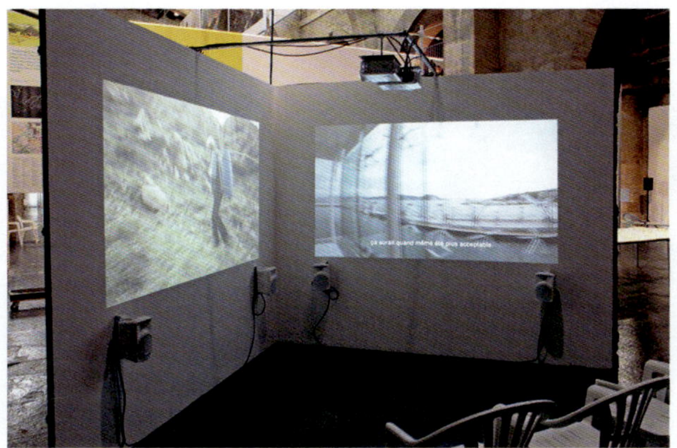

Our objective is not to offer an exhaustive view of a building. We only describe what we experience, and nothing is uniform: memory is not a continuous flow. Right from the first film, we decided to reproduce this piecemeal view via fragmented editing. Each fragment corresponds to what we saw and experienced during the day—which is why they are constructed with varying degrees of fluidity. We edited the film as we filmed it, working on the day's rushes in the evening. Our films are like ship's logs.

Ila Bêka, *Architecture d'Aujourd'hui,* 2014

La Maddalena Chair

La Maddalena

La Maddalena Chair

La Maddalena

Les Bogues du Blat

23

Beaumont, Ardèche

Building and living in a chestnut forest

In the heart of the Ardèche mountains, the village of Beaumont (population 232) comprises several hamlets scattered over a preserved landscape of chestnut groves and terraced farms. To welcome new families, the mayor has decided to offer an alternative form of ecological and affordable housing adapted to the rural context and to the needs of young families of modest means.
Thus the Bogues du Blat were born: hut-like houses perched on stilts on a slope, built using a budget usually allocated to social housing. To respond to changes in family structure and resources, the residents can gradually extend their home inside the arched roof, with the help of an instructor. The architects and the mayor have created the conditions for new ways of inhabiting a rural area.

www.construire.cc

—

A project for the Beumont community initiated as part of *l'action Nouveaux commanditaires* and the programme *Habitat, Développement social et Territoires* of the *Fondation de France*
mediation / production: Valérie Cudel / association A demeure
photos: © Loïc Julienne

Patrick Bouchain, Loïc Julienne and Sébastien Eymard / Construire Paris

Letter from Pascal Waldschmidt, Mayor of Beaumont:

From utopia to reality

Building for someone: dismantling the usual hierarchy of client / architect / builders / future inhabitants; replacing it with a synergy where everyone contributes something, combining artists with ordinary people: making the act of building into a founding cultural act.

Living with one's neighbours: before building, implementing a participative strategy where future inhabitants co-opt one another, together defining the rules of society, their rights and duties, the frontiers between private and public life, and the way they form part of village life, creating a form of "togetherness" where everyone both gives and receives.

Everyone should contribute: leaving room for, or even organising, a self-finishing process in so-called "social" housing, to reduce costs and give people the opportunity to make their home their own, thus fostering increased respect.

Building in an eco-friendly way: timber frames, dry toilets, lagoon-based sewage treatment, rainwater collection, etc. Buying one's home: why should home ownership be for the happy few when others throw money away paying rent all their lives?

A gradual home ownership mechanism must also be put in place for social housing.

Inhabiting and working: living in a rural area is a true life strategy. There have to be workshops, vegetable gardens and farm fields nearby.

Designing a group of eight homes. The first three houses were opened on 7 September 2013

These are, in brief, the founding principles of the housing plan for the town of Beaumont. They are the result of cooperation between local councillors, the mediator for Fondation de France and the Construire architecture firm.

222

living apart together

24

Belgium

Reinventing communal living

How can people live together and embrace individuality within a limited space? 51N4E, a Belgian architecture firm working in different areas of Europe, goes some way to answering this question, providing a response that is both architectural and urban. Their buildings—either completed or currently in progress—illustrate six key themes: fostering intelligent modes of use; offering shared spaces while preserving privacy; designing architecture in order to create urbanity; fostering interactions between living organisms and their environment to encourage the development of ecological systems; designing reversible architecture; practicing architecture collaboratively. All these themes reflect new ways of thinking about inhabited space in our complex societies.

www.51n4e.com

—

photos: © Harry Gruyaert / Magnum Photos; © Filip Dujardin; © Ruben Dario Kleimeer

51N4E Brussels

Europe today is experiencing a series of shifts: more and more people are living alone, new forms of families are emerging, and living units are losing square metres as the age of abundance reaches its limits. As a solution, shrinking what we currently have won't suffice. Our model must shift. Reflecting on what sharing can bring has become a necessity. An emergency, even. We must learn how to live apart together.

To organise this, architecture is a crucial tool and cannot just be a passive bystander: it must reflect on this open-ended question of living apart together as the 'new normal' and participate actively and collectively in its shaping and formulation. Architecture can do so step by step, carrying out projects and experiments that explore new possibilities. These will eventually change the meaning of sharing the same roof, and will gradually reshape buildings and even entire areas. Plenty of reconfigurations are possible, but few have been tested so far. Specialised residential projects are already providing valuable insights. Since they deal with the tension between privacy and sharing, they can be regarded as a kind of 'dress rehearsal', allowing us to imagine ways of living apart together within the society of the 21st century.

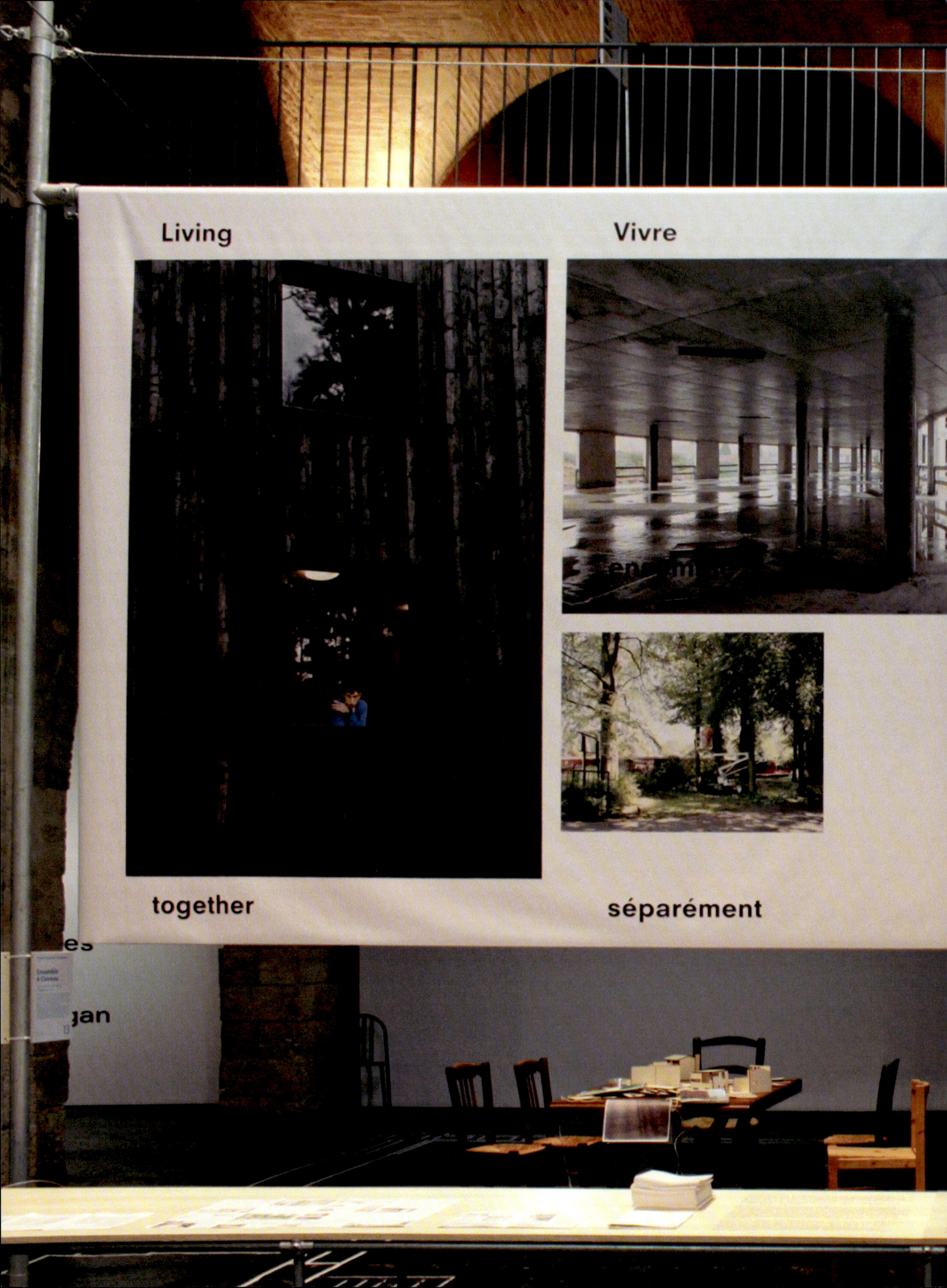
Living
Vivre
together
séparément

Living
Vivre
apart
ensemble
together
séparément

An affordable living environment is about more than just affordable housing. By designing the interaction between a building and the dynamics that surround it, a project can go beyond a brief in order to offer more, both to the users and to the city around them.
Through our work on the subject in the past years, we have identified several topics in which small shifts can together make a difference. Designing affordable living environments means considering how rethinking units, sharing, cities, habitats, structures & processes can have a highly significant impact once regarded as a whole.

Addressing all these shifts allows the project to become more than an object added to an urban field, and to rather become a constellation of interventions, tangible and intangible. Altogether, these create places one can really inhabit, share, and benefit from. As space producers, we strive to reconnect these topics (and their respective experts) to turn the design process into a moment for these specific shifts to be looked at in conjunction.

Manufactured Sites

25

San Diego / Tijuana

Custom strategies serving informal urban development

Teddy Cruz lives and works in San Diego, California, and has made the border with Mexico the subject of his work. Despite the apparent brutality of this administrative and political separation and the glaring inequalities it reveals, he shows that it works like an ecosystem, a place of friction and intense exchange where everyone tries to pursue their own interests. An example is the circuit of construction materials made in Mexico to be sold in the USA, but used to build slums housing candidates for immigration.
A careful observer of systems and the people involved, Teddy Cruz acts as a negotiator and mediator, elaborating support strategies for informal urban development, organising its economic systems, and improving life in these neighbourhoods.

www.estudioteddycruz.com

—

photos: © Estudio Teddy Cruz + Forman

Teddy Cruz and Fonna Forman San Diego

The informal districts of Tijuana are growing faster than the urban hubs surrounding them, transforming the rules of growth and erasing the distinctions between the urban, suburban and rural (...) Our approach began here by looking at the conflict that prevails in emergency housing, casual work and companies in free business zones ('maquiladoras'). While these factories occupy strategic positions on the edge of the favelas, which are a source of manpower, they give nothing back to these fragile communities in return. Our work focused on the factories themselves, suggesting that they make components that can be used by local residents to build homes. We are negotiating with the maquiladoras to create a portal that can act as a central hub bringing together materials collected in San Diego that can be reused in Tijuana.

Teddy Cruz

234

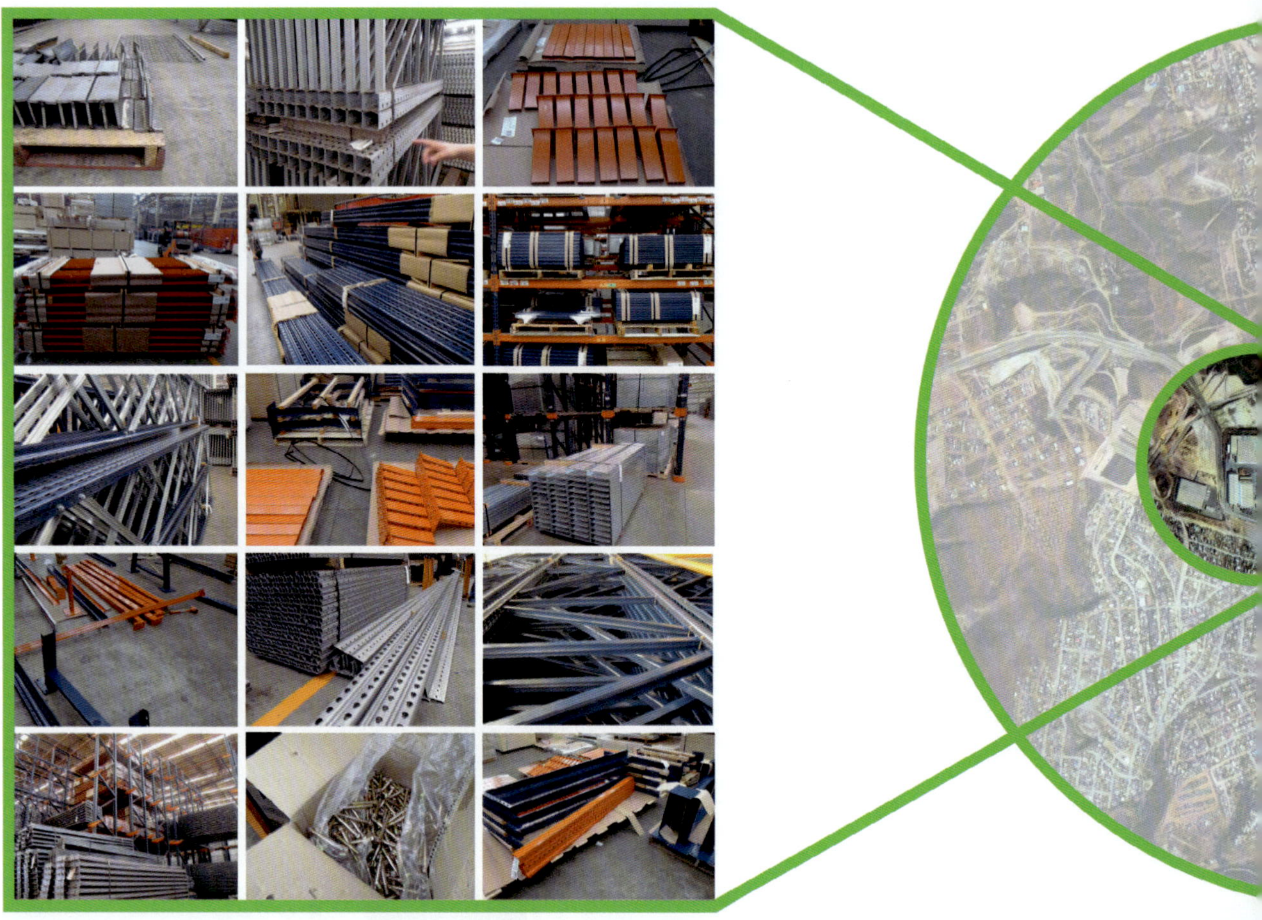

Maquiladoras:
Mecalux, a factory in Tijuana, produces light-weight metal shelving systems, distributed around the world.

Housing Made of Waste:
Tijuana slums recycle San Diego's urban left-overs: discarded houses, rubber tyres, garage doors.

Tijuana, A City of Factories:
Multinational “maquiladoras” in close proximity to slums, from which they get cheap labour.

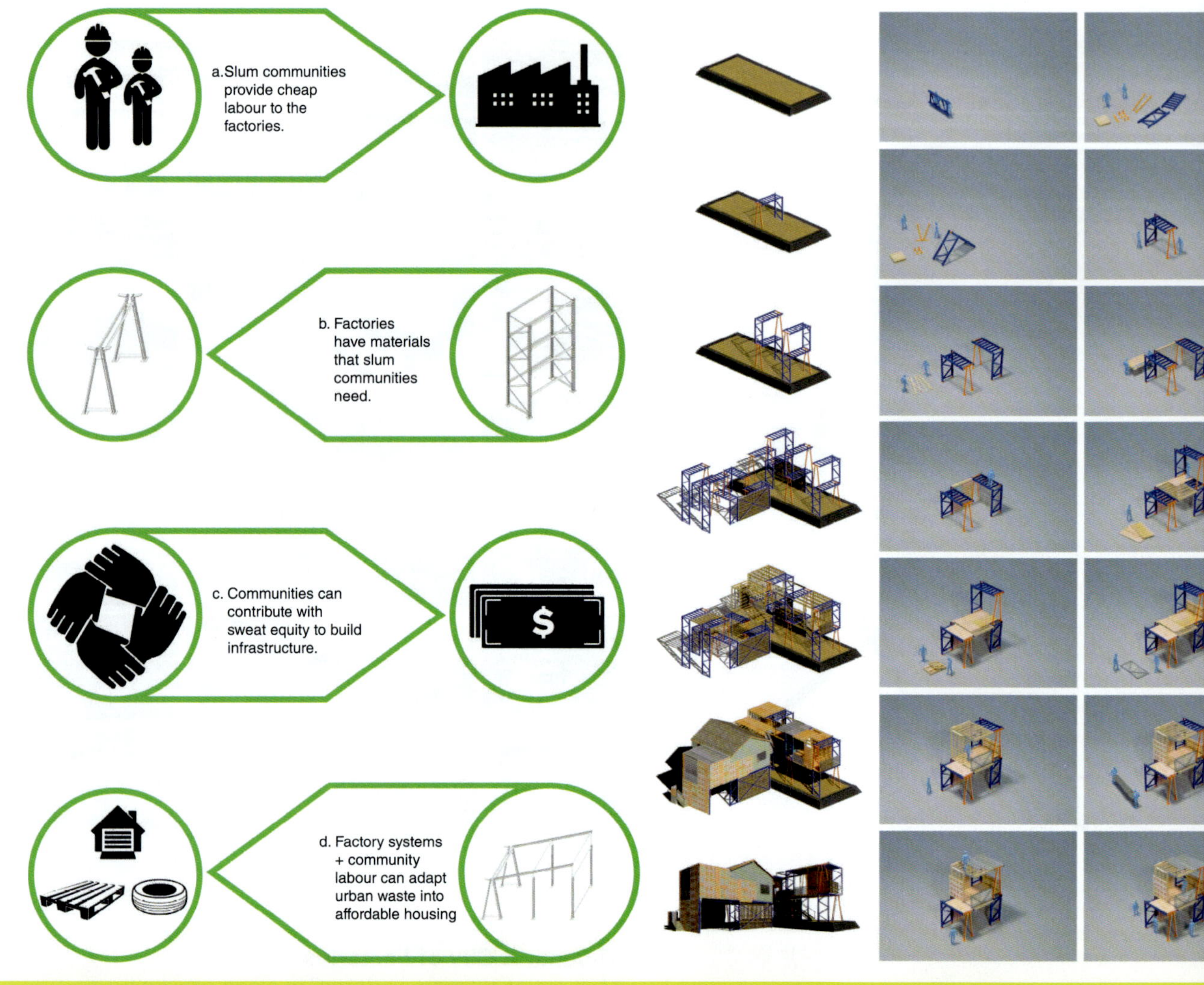

1. Community-factory ethical loops: holding maquiladoras accountable.

2. Adapting the Mecalux system into a framework for housing.

Gallery

Meeting place

Market

Protest

Housing

Cinema

School

3. The factory catalogue as a site of intervention.

4. The Mecalux structure becomes an infrastructural frame for informal urbanisation.

Monte Verità

26

Ascona

The lesson to be learned from a utopia

The little town of Ascona, in an area of Ticino famed for the beauty of its mountain landscapes and lakes, took part in its own way in major historic events of the twentieth century. Here on Monte Verita, a self-sufficient community was set up in around 1889, attracting dancers, artists and writers such as Isadora Duncan and Herman Hesse. Until the 1920s its members, who were strict vegetarians and nudists, experimented with new ways of living together close to nature.
Bureau A has reinterpreted the spaces left behind by the experiment, exploring the lessons provided by what has been called "the cradle of counter-culture". This utopia set up in the early part of the last century seems more relevant than ever today, at a time when, determinedly though not without difficulty, the question of habitat enters a new cooperative era.

www.a-bureau.com

—

photos: © Dylan Perrenoud
Vasca di sole from the book *90 objects from Monte Verità*

Bureau A Lisbon

The work done by BUREAU A is presented in three distinct forms within a single installation: an exploration of architectural objects and artefacts made by the community; a publication relating these objects to the landscape of Monte Verità as it exists today; and a fountain with a limited edition of furniture directly inspired by the archive of Monte Verità.

The installation aims to raise some profound questions—despite its playfulness—relating to the practice and participation of architects in a profoundly capitalistic society that increasingly blurs the challenges and objectives of creative undertakings.

The most lively thing that remains of Monte Verità today is not the most tangible part of the community's experience. Around the central buildings, symbolising the success of a contemporary economy of wellbeing, the ruins of more precarious constructions exist on the margins, like the discreet traces of a radical occupation, an "ethic" that its founders already saw as "doomed to failure". The part of the history of Monte Verità that resists probably lies in its most intangible dimension, its unique economy, and its impalpable ideology, which mirror our contemporary condition in an era of fluid reconfiguration of political identity. Ida Hoffmann's promise to create at Monte Verità "a school of superior life, a place to develop and bring together broader knowledge, a place of greater awareness," seems to have been constructed in opposition to "capitalism and all its evils using the materials of capitalism itself".

Monte Verità is thus not just the primitive model of ecological, sexual and educational revolutions in the 1960s. It can also be seen as that of their current reinterpretation, in all its "economic" complexity in both senses of the word: both in terms of its day-to-day organisation and in terms of its financial organisation, Monte Verità is admittedly a community, but it is also a network, an arrangement of multiple subjectivities, whose organic cohesion and non-uniform way of operating now appears as a possible matrix for the molecular revolutions that will follow, and seem destined to return nowadays."

Yann Chateigné

cueillent et offrent
ur l'action.
ulnerabilities are
environments,
y, welcome us
s for action.
m is a requirement

Nanogrid

27

246

Solar lamp and charger

Today in Africa, 900 million people have no access to electricity. Sunna Design, a startup founded in 2011 in Blanquefort, Bordeaux, wants to respond to this problem by launching the Nanogrid, an ecologically sound alternative to standard power networks. This system, which works on solar power, does not require heavy infrastructures and can be set up anywhere quickly. It takes the form of a street lamp to which four households can connect themselves, providing them with LED interior lighting and a mobile phone recharge service. People pre-pay for the service via their mobile phones according to their needs and resources.
Ecological, independent and flexible, the system could revolutionise the question of access to electricity in Africa and elsewhere in the world.

www.sunna-design.fr/nanogrid.html

—

photos: © Florian Coat

The Challenge

1. In Senegal, 56.5% of the population have access to electricity but the figure drops down to 25% in rural areas. Most villages have never had public lighting, as in the rural community as Cherif Lo.
In order to fight rural exodus and provide increased safety and development opportunities, the government has set up an emergency electrification program with the aim of providing 60% of the population with access to lighting by 2017.

2. The few communities that have access to electricity in the area struggle to pay their bills, and the Senelec, the national electricity company, has initiated a recovery programme for unpaid bills. Access to energy in the off-grid villages must therfore be accomplished without adding to the financial burden.

3. Senegal has heavy climate constraints: an average temperature of 32°C and a rainy season with high humidity and frequent heavy rainfall.

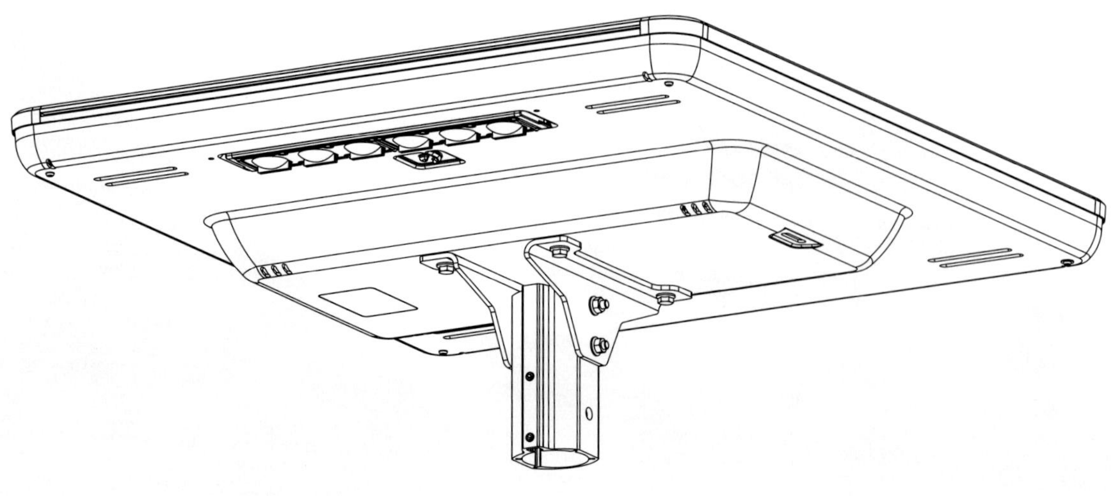

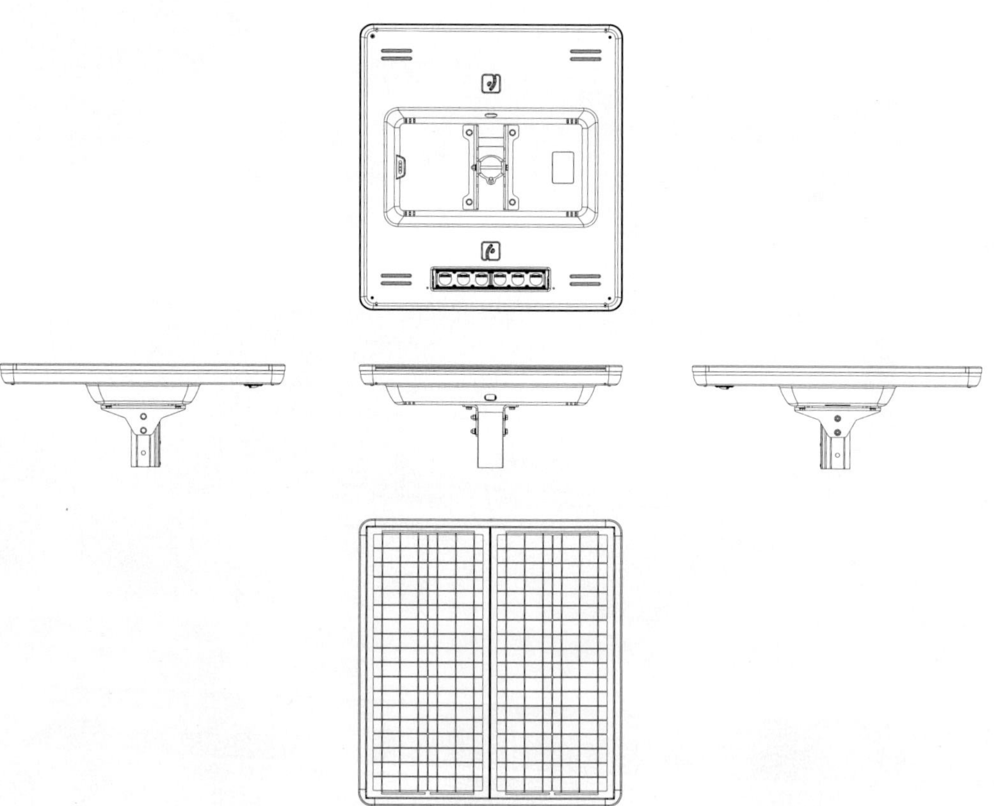

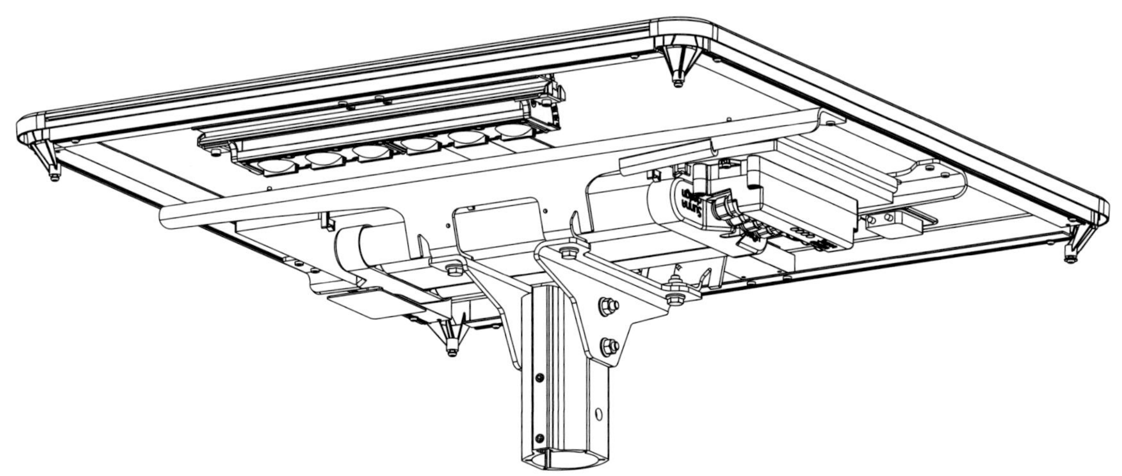

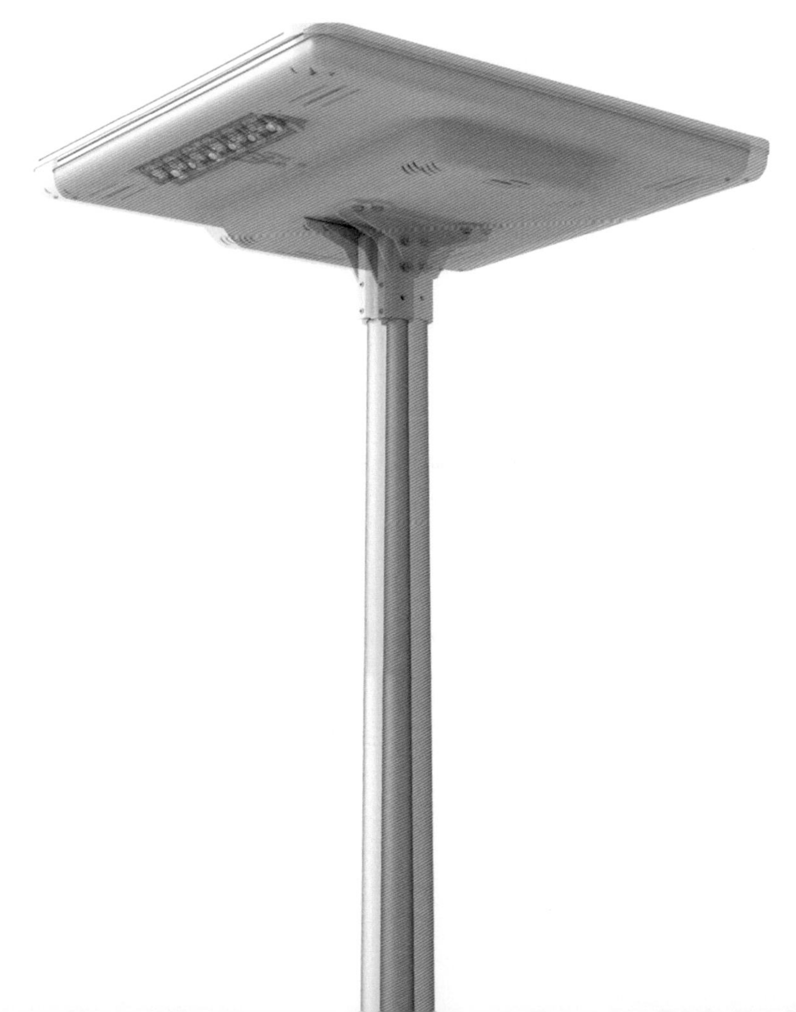

OpenStructures

28

Brussels

Responding to built-in obsolescence with a collaborative building set

The Open Structures project adopts an open-ended system (like Lego) instead of a closed system (like Playmobil), and seeks to bring the opensource IT philosophy into the material world. The system is based on a standard grid and standard joints, making it possible to come up with a form of universal language for objects that are infinitely adaptable, editable or recyclable, which makes the user into the co-creator of his own environment. This is an experiment that focuses on the on-going improvement of objects instead of built-in obsolescence. It's a good illustration of the zeitgeist, where everything seems to be "co-": collaboration, co-design, and co-manufacturing.

www.openstructures.net

—

photos: © Kristof Vrancken for Z33

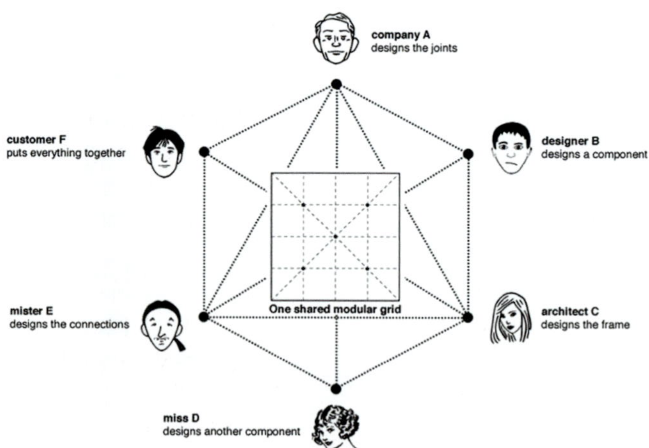

Thomas Lommée Brussels

The Openstructures project

OpenStructures {OS) explores the potential of a modular construction model where everyone designs for everyone on the basis of one shared geometrical grid. It initiates a universal and collaborative puzzle to which everybody—from do-it-yourselfers to multinationals—can add parts, components or more complex structures.
OS works according to the Wikipedia model, where different people contribute to one encyclopaedia. Instead of articles, everyone can upload or edit modular designs on the OpenStructures website, a growing database that allows the broadest range of people to design, build and exchange the broadest range of modular components.
It envisions a new standard for sustainable design that facilitates re-use and encourages the circular use of materials and objects. It allows us to build things together, introduces variety within modularity and results in a more flexible and scalable built environment for all.

The Openstructures grid

In order for new parts to be compatible with the existing ones they need to be designed from the OS grid. The OS grid is the centrepiece of the whole OS system. It's the common metrical tool that is shared among all participants which allows them to design interchangeable parts, components and objects, both independently and interdependently. The OS grid is built up out of 4x4cm squares. The borders of these squares mark the cutting lines, its diagonals mark the assembly points and its enclosed inner circles define common diameters.

The Openstructures design principles

All OpenStructures part designs are based on the OpenStructures design principles.
In practical terms, this means that:
For each part at least one of the following conditions should to be met (in order to be compatible with the OS grid):
> perforation centrepoints are 20mm from one another
> internal and/or external part diameters are a multiple of 20mm
> part dimensions are a multiple of 20mm.
For all parts the following principles apply (in order to be compatible with the OS values}:
> all objects should be designed for disassembly
> recyclable materials should be used for all parts whenever possible
> all part designs should be fully open and free for everybody to use at any moment.

OS part samples

> see how each of these parts relates to the OS grid by holding this paper against the light.
> discover when and where a part was designed and in which object(s) it has been used by surfing to openstructures.net (and giving in the name of its designer in the "search" section).
> edit and/or reproduce one or more parts yourself by downloading their dxf. files online (also available on openstructures.net).

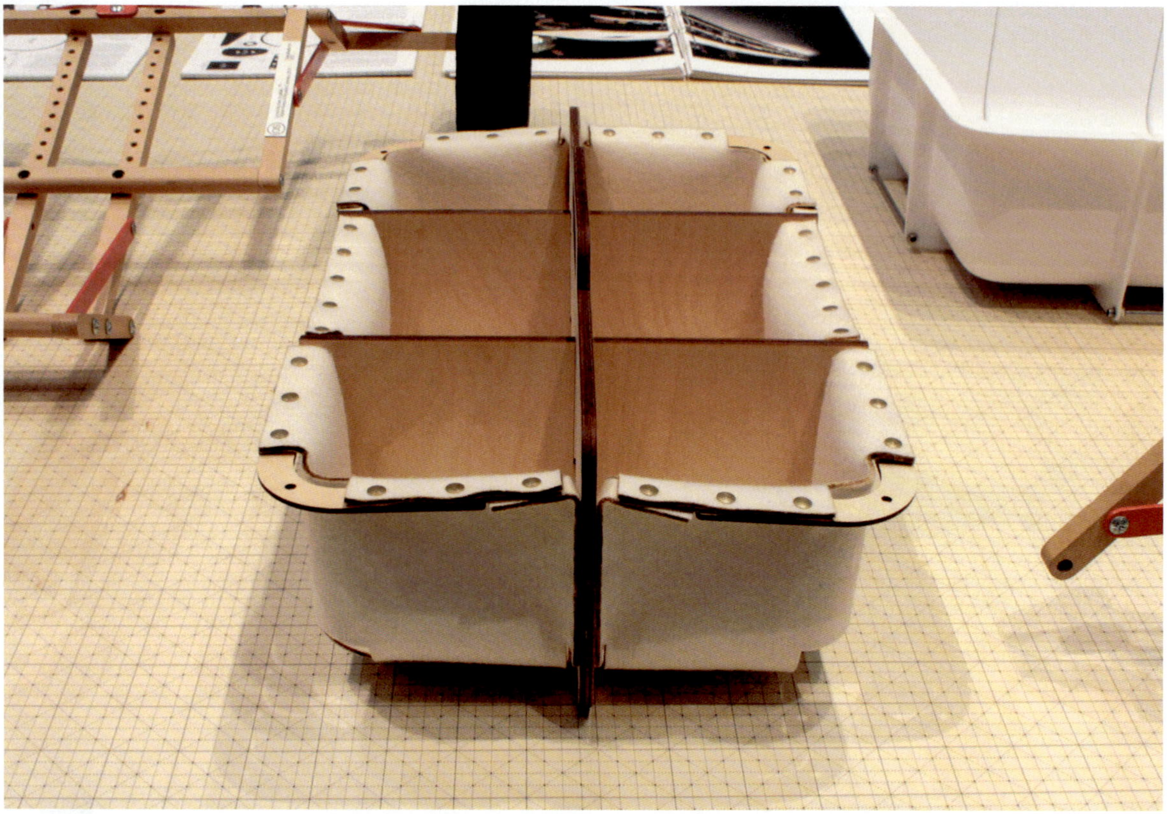

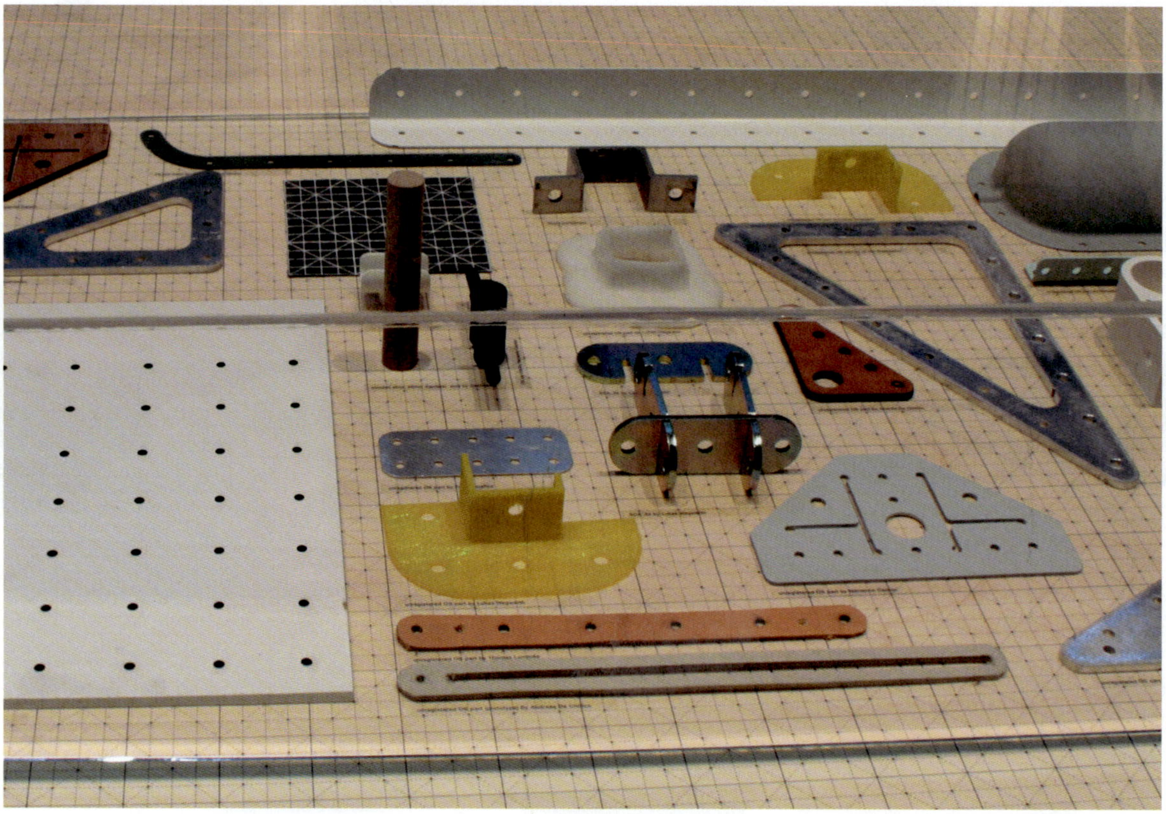

258

OS part samples
OS 2016
- see how each of these parts relates to the OS grid by holding this paper against the light.
- discover when and where a part was designed and in which object(s) it has been used by surfing to openstructurtes.net (and giving in the name of its designer in the 'search' section).
- edit and/or reproduce one or more parts yourself by downloading their dxf. files online (also available on openstructures.net).
perforation centerpoints are a multiple of 20mm from one another
OS PART 240
designed by Alexandre
part dimensions are a multiple of 20mm
perforation centerpoints are a multiple of 20mm from one another
perforation diameters are a multiple of 5mm
perforation diameters are 5mm
perforation centerpoints are a multiple of 20mm from one another
part dimensions are a multiple of 20mm
OS PART 016
designed by Jo
perforation centerpoints are a multiple of 20mm from one another
part dimensions are a multiple of 20mm
OS PART 127
designed by Lukas
perforation centerpoints are a multiple of 20mm from one another
OS PART (UNREGISTERED)
designed by Karen
External diameter is a multiple of 20mm
internal and / or external diameter is a multiple of 20mm
COMPATIBLE TUBE
found and purchased at the local DIY store
part dimensions are a multiple of 20mm
perforation centerpoints are a multiple of 20mm from one another
OS PART 229
designed by Tim
perforation diameters are 5mm
OS PART (UNREGISTERED)
designed by Thomas
perforation centerpoints are a multiple of 20mm from one another
40X40MM WOODEN BEAM
cut on measure
part dimensions are a multiple of 20mm
part dimensions are a multiple of 20mm

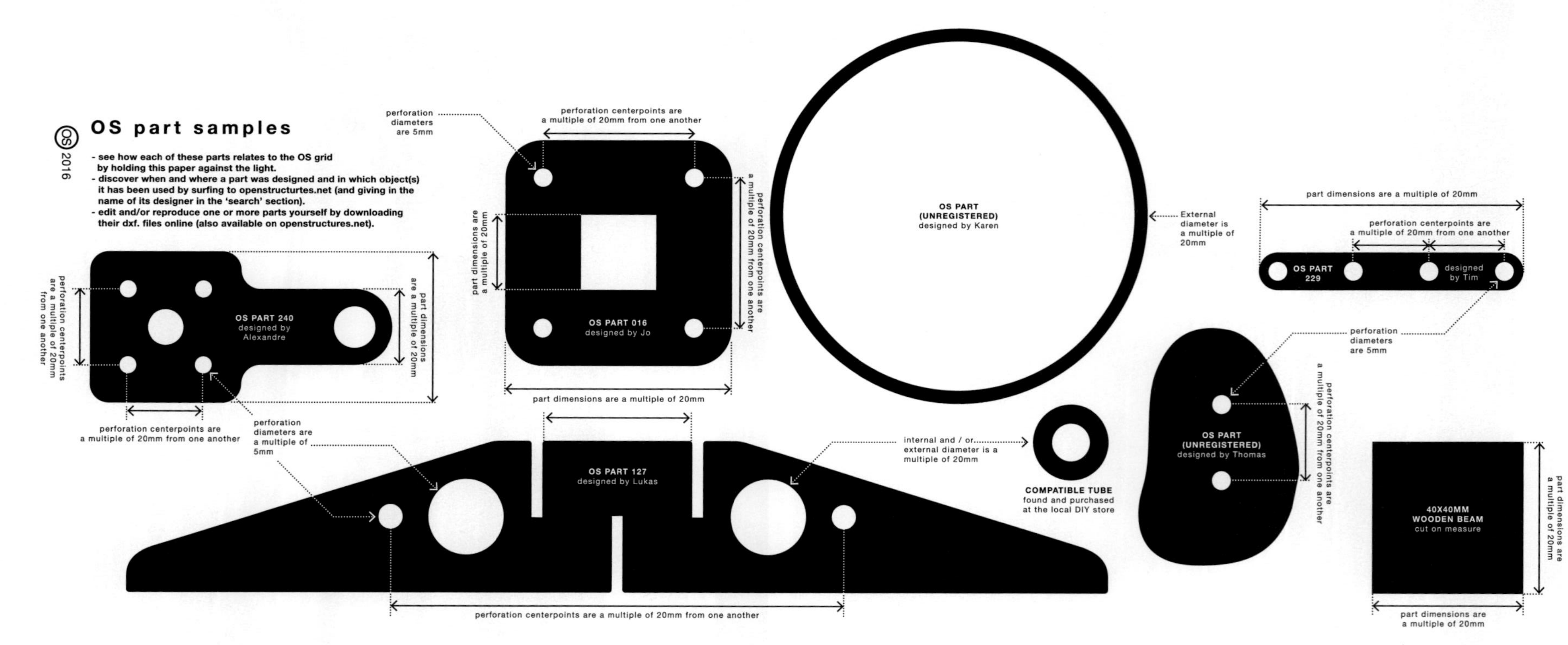

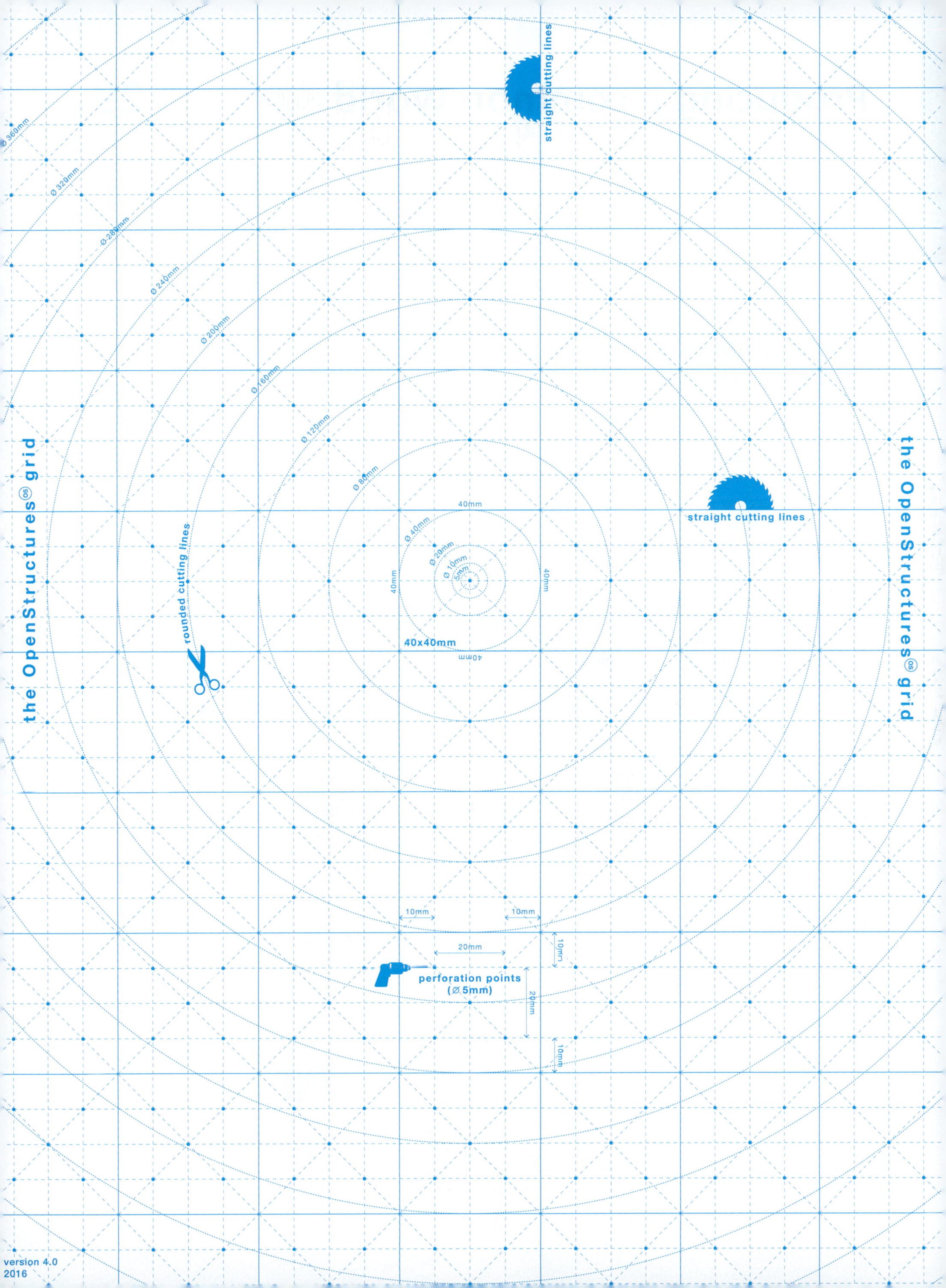

the OpenStructures grid
straight cutting lines
straight cutting lines
rounded cutting lines
Ø 360mm
Ø 320mm
Ø 280mm
Ø 240mm
Ø 200mm
Ø 160mm
Ø 120mm
Ø 80mm
Ø 40mm
Ø 20mm
Ø 10mm
5mm
40mm
40x40mm
10mm
20mm
perforation points
(Ø 5mm)
the OpenStructures grid
version 4.0
2016

Producing a common world 29

Neither public nor private: designing shared space

The question of the metropolitan area as a "condition" has always interested designers at AUC. This increasingly complex reality, which has blurred the clear distinctions between the urban, the peri-urban and the rural, or which makes local spaces overlap with major global networks, requires the invention of new analytical frameworks.

Instead of making big planning gestures, careful attention to everyday situations will allow the features of "commonality" to emerge. This "commonality" is designed as an alternative and more inclusive definition of what was formerly known as "public space", which is more characteristic of historic urban models. Commonality occurs in both private and public space. It involves everything that brings us closer to one another and makes us stay together. It's the main challenge of the contemporary metropolis we all live in.

www.laucparis.com

"The Effects of Good and Bad Government", an allegorical fresco painted by Ambrogio Lorenzetti between 1338 and 1340, "Sala della Pace" in the Palazzo Pubblico, Sienna, Italy

The tremors shaking our world question the sustainability of the economic and social model according to which our societies are organised.
Recession and environmental crisis are two sides of the same systemic crisis, calling our societies to reappraise the way they project themselves in time and space.
Architecture is currently facing major questions, flowing through professional practices within the city.

Questions that may seem disconnected at first, each opening onto new and unique opportunities, must allow us collectively to develop a new global approach and to roll back the limits of architecture.
This approach will allow us to rise to major contemporary challenges, in particular that of building a common world.
We believe that this remains the most important issue in an increasingly metropolitanised world.

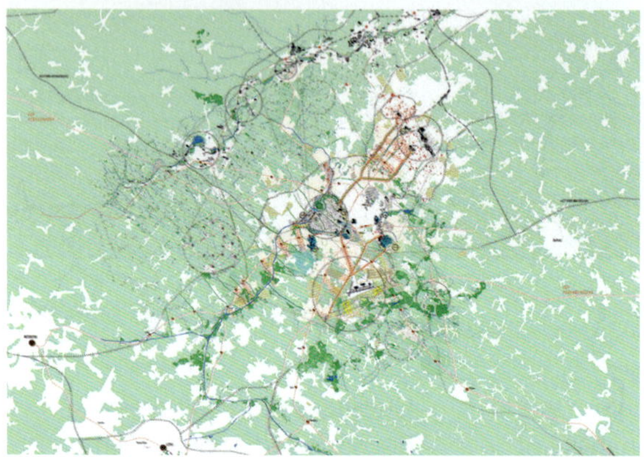

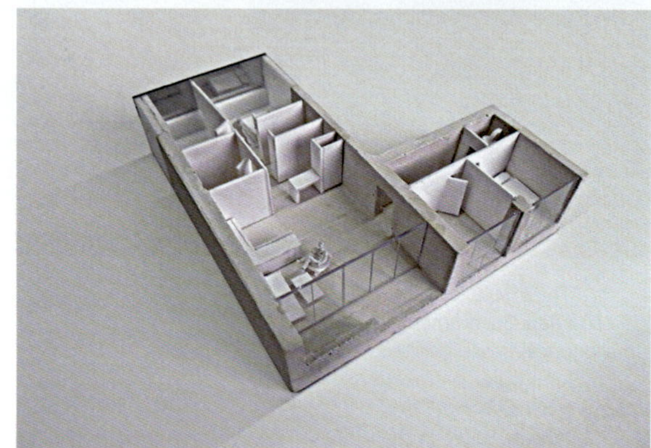

the metropolis

A metropolis is not a place that can be drawn. It is a condition that can be described.
All recent debates in France and Europe lead us to consider the metropolis as the most relevant scale to re-launch a virtuous cycle of land development.
Political debates remain focused on the construction of united, attractive and intensive metropolises, capable of generating new added value for the benefit of all; this would happen through appropriate governance, a more ambitious mobility policy, a more target-driven housing policy and, ultimately, the stimulation of hybrid ecosystems favourable to social and economic changes and innovations embedded in metropolitan area.
The contemporary metropolis remains a living thing, continuously shaped by contradictory forces; solidarity and competition, hyper-productivity and rational management of resources, immediacy and forward-lookingness
… an increasingly complex, unpredictable, entangled, irreducible reality, where ecology (land use sustainability) and equity (land use equality) themselves become issues of economic efficiency.

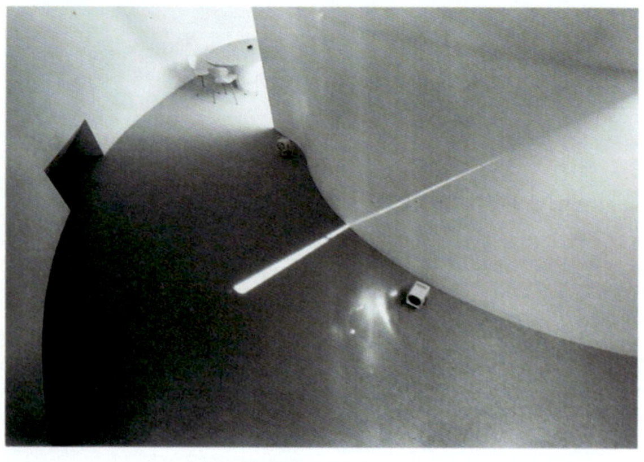

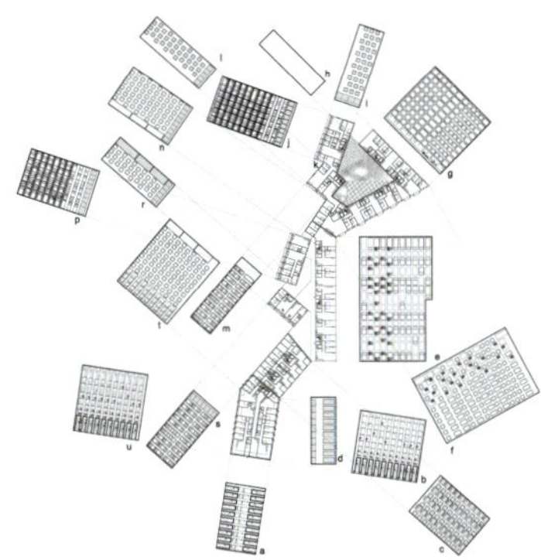

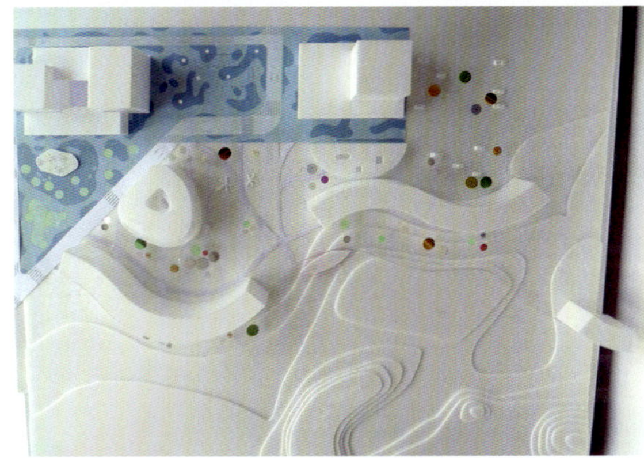

The autonomy of architecture

More and more, we see a return to the Plan as a means of space construction and also as an ethics marking the end of iconic architecture. The architectural and urban news convey this tendency, between a more relaxed and less academic re-appropriation of history and an orientation towards a more direct, more basic and always more honest architecture. The question is no longer the "generic" as posed by Rem Khoolaas, or the "specific", or the "specific within the generic", but the emergence of project figures informing a new synthesis between singularity and networking, between small and large scale, between situations of the inhabited and metropolitan extent, between architecture and the metropolis.

In this context, we want to raise the question of architecture's role in the contemporary world, resolutely urban if not metropolitan. And imagine how architecture, in its autonomy, with its capacity to establish relations, can be the vector of a singular form of metropolisation, which we think of as a "bottom up metropolisation".

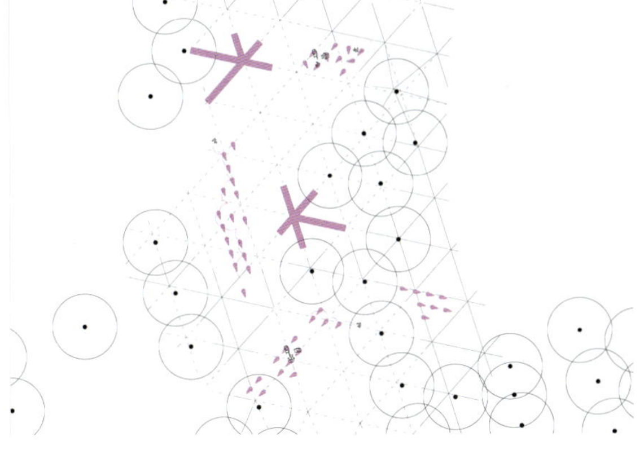

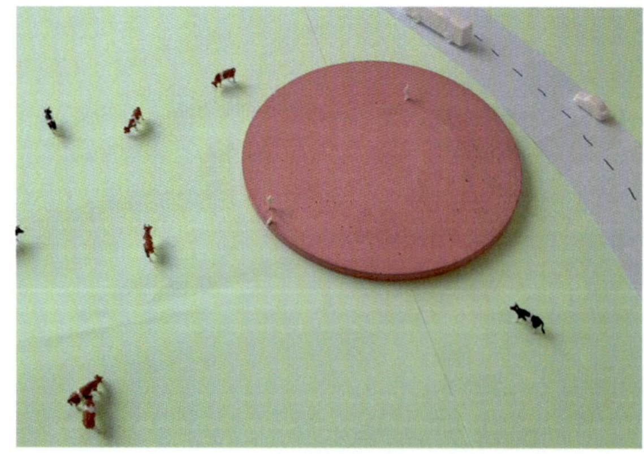

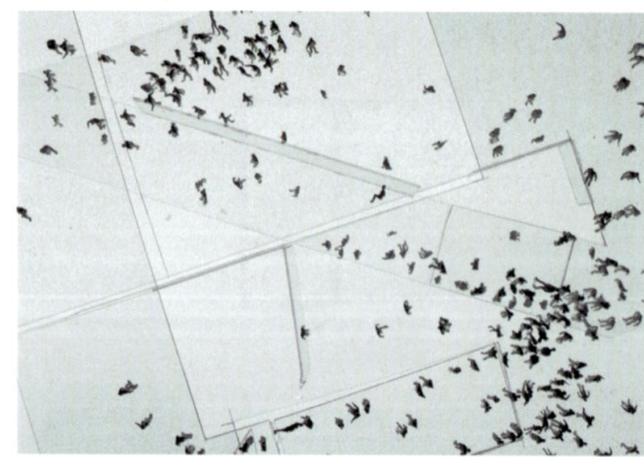

264

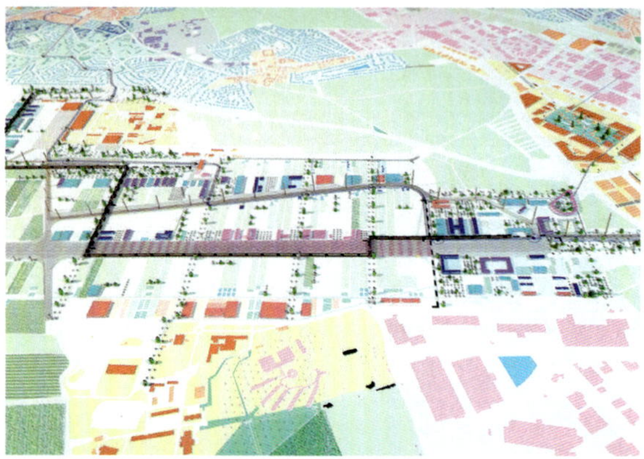

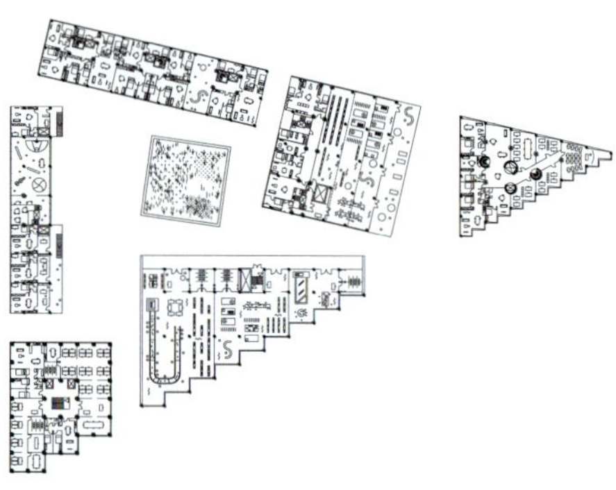

the project in the public sphere

The desired city, the contemporary city, is a territory that must be capable of offering singularities, which are not considered in a complete form of autonomy or self-sufficiency but are part of a set of metropolitan relations. The relational can be made tangible by a meta public space that reveal all scales at once; from domestic to metropolitan, from public to common, through shared determinisms of housing (between intimacy, compactness, publicity and flexibility) and through an architecture benevolent to existing territories; a pro-active benevolence seeking to transform a territory without damaging it.

If public space within the compact historic urban finds its place "between", in streets and squares, as an expression of a people and as a stage for a city of the spectacle, the space of metropolitan intensity is a space as such, without clear physical boundaries. Hence, we envision to leave the sphere of the public, with all its ideologies and related planning tools, and turn towards the more relevant notion of the "common". The "common" allows to conceive situations where the different scales of the inhabited articulate together. Situations where all specificities of inhabiting are, in a same movement, revealed and exceeded.

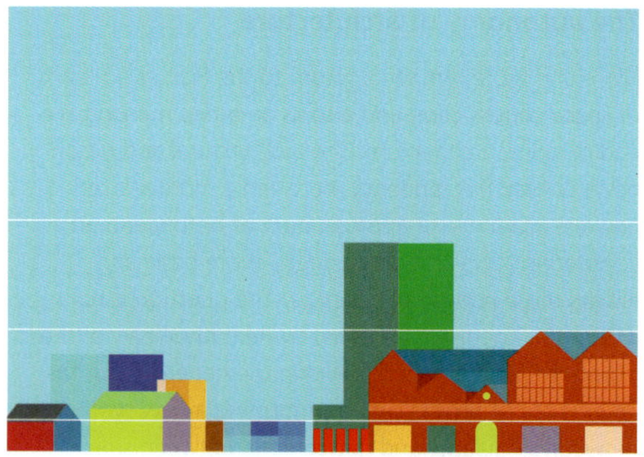

" Technology is the answer... but what was the question? Design must be concerned with mixing unknown emotions and responses – or at least enabling such unknows to work together happily "

Cedric Price
Technology is the Answer but what was the question ?, 1979
Coll, «Pidgeon Audio Visual

Virtuous proximity

From then on, how to re-think a city inclusive and for all; how to make happen a metropolis where housing and economic activity rebind a virtuous proximity; where the metropolis of the inhabited and the productive metropolis draw new spatial alliances embedded in innovative urban and architectural typologies, within which can be drawn positive benefits from short and circular circuits, from architectural experiments making social and functional mixity a necessary condition of togetherness; projects drawing new eo-productions between education, production and living; experiments bringing out co-operation between stakeholders for the production of exemplary metropolitan situations; etc.
In short, it is about seizing the virtuous process of bottom-up metropolisation, from the infinitesimal, in order to grasp the common within it, this is the programme.

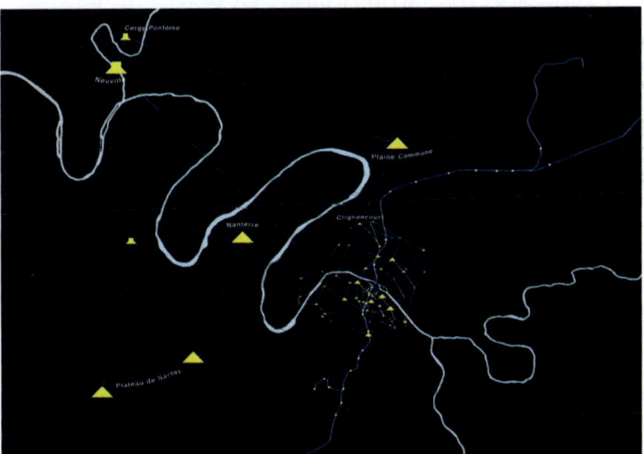

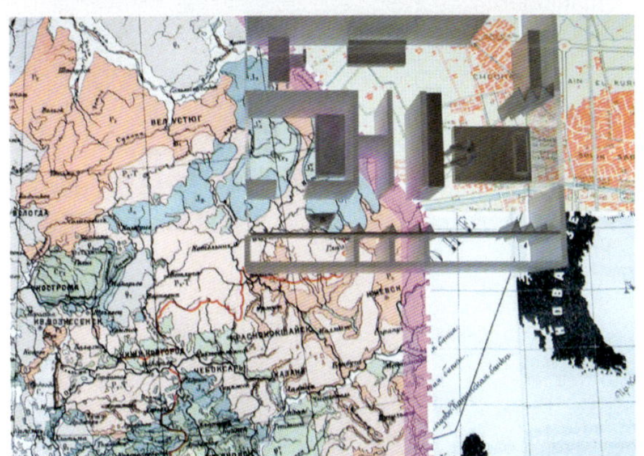

Rebirth Brick

30

China

Rebuilding life from rubble

To respond to the urgent situation following the Sichuan earthquake in 2008, architect Liu Jiakun invented a manual process that makes it possible to make bricks from rubble and wheat husks.
They have been dubbed "rebirth bricks" because in addition to responding to ecological and economic issues, they are able to incorporate the symbolic dimension of mourning and reconstruction.
This new material was first used to build housing and a museum devoted to the memory of the disaster. Adapted to the huge construction needs in China and the large quanity of waste generated by the demolition of entire districts, the process has now become almost industrial, which has allowed Liu Jiakun to use these bricks in several large-scale projects.

www.jiakun-architects.com

—

photos: © Jiakun architects

Jiakun architects Chengdu

Looking at / Building

31

274

A place in the sun

Bourbouze & Graindorge present here two types of practice - looking at and building - to try to throw footbridges between documentary and fiction, insofar as each project reflects what André Bazin described as an attempt to build a world closer to our own desires. Architectural process is indeed constantly inspired by built situations in which architecture is absent.
To identify in the clutter of generic settlements, situations where construction appear to be adequate, beautiful or simply in their place, requires a sustained act of selecting, to which they have subjected themselves during a field study (extra-normal architectures) along the Mediterranean coastline, from Gibraltar to the Dardanelles.
By the same token, in the real and imperfect world that is France today, to imagine, design and build projects in which the tremor of life is present, consists in bringing to bear memories and savoir-faire, in leaving aside certain reflexes, in laying claim to certain conventions and abandoning others, in mixing trivia and sophistication, to succeed in producing built artefacts that will resist the attrition of time and passing fashions.

www.bourbouze-graindorge.com

Bourbouze and Graindorge Nantes

private collection

Discovery and production form a catalogue of situations, of which each project is the expression, opening the way to countless transfers, re-uses and transformations.
The force of these constructions discovered in our peregrinations, and which we try to put back into our productions, lies in the belief that while each built artefact is informed by site, programme and building culture, it is autonomous and has the faculty to be born again elsewhere: transformed, re-worked, but still possessed of the essential qualities related to its *type*.

surfaces: mixing table

The mixing table brings together gathered and built situations, photographs and drawings that constitute epiphenomena of the projects presented. It establishes a parallel between reading and writing, laying claim to the idea of a *cover* in the musical sense, where each project refers to a matrix that others develop further.
This assemblage also presents the different time scales of projects, drawings, work sites and buildings that are new and clean, or deteriorated and aged, as possible representations of the potentials of any project, from inception to obsolescence, emphasizing the preponderant role of structure.

structures: typical floor plans

On the table, like a field of ruins, are assembled the typical floor plans of twenty projects. These relief maps at 1/100, shaped in volumes the height of a man, stage direct one our favourite tools (the plan and its *generating* nature) and describe different modes of residential grouping. This shadowscape also aims at illustrating the need for concision and rationality proper to the design of such groupings, which we feel should not be dissociated from the more obvious vitality presented on the mixing table.

the art of living

Above all, these various researches and their modes of representation, between ordering and organization of disorder, aim at revealing a sort of natural state of architecture (the native illusion of Modernism). This condition is not that of a virtuoso production nor is it perfect, but corresponds rather to an architecture capable of establishing coherence in construction, spaces and materials in the cultural and economic framework of its production. In this, it resembles one of those *great ailing films* that François Truffaut speaks of, insisting on their human imperfection more than their vain virtuosity.
In organizing the contradictory and violent influences at work in the production of the contemporary city, we are the militants of a paradoxical cause - bound like a cat in its basket to seek liberty in order.

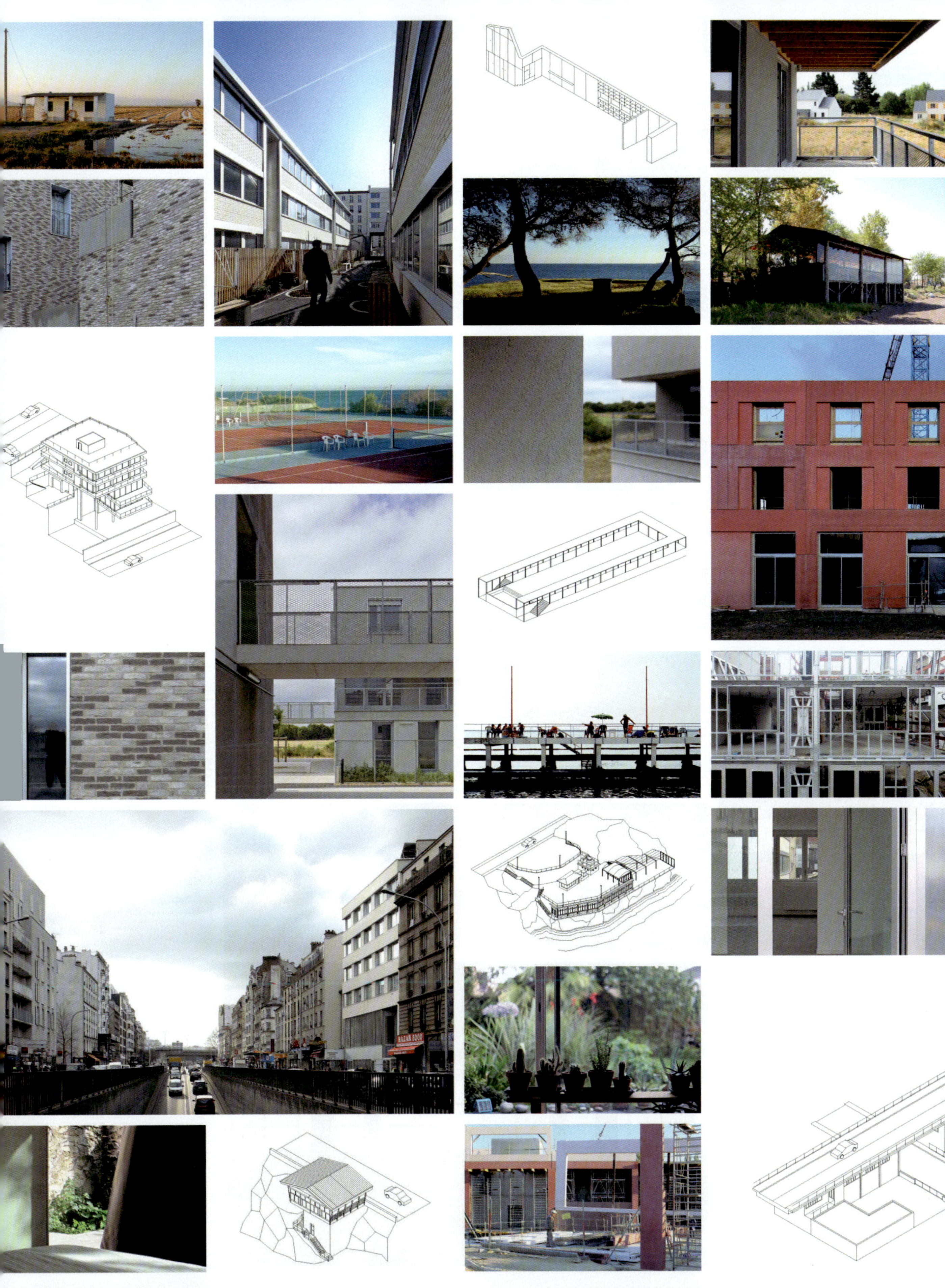

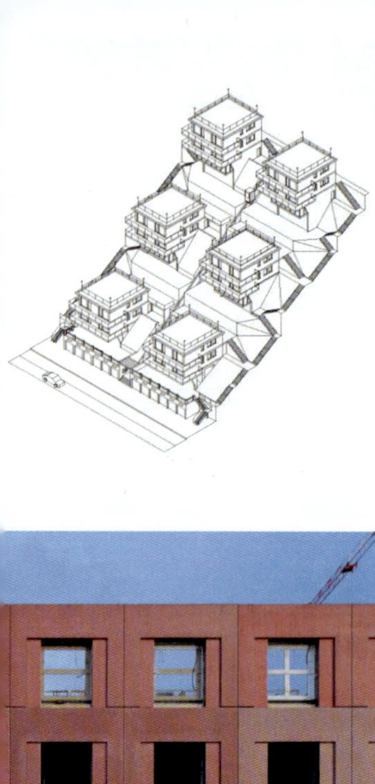

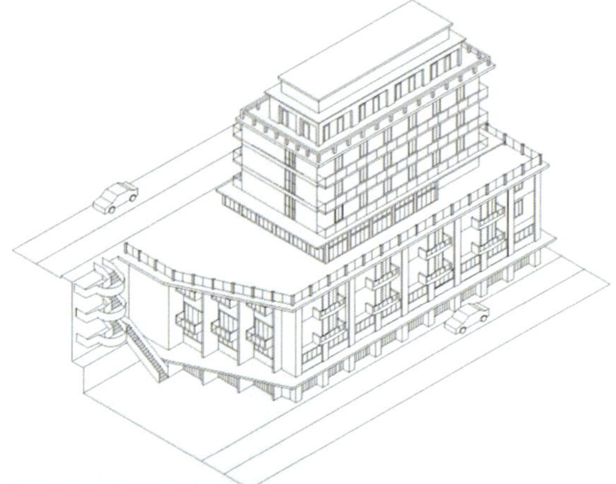

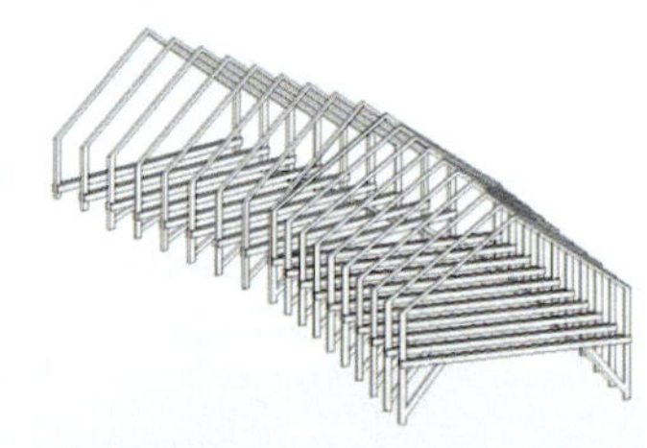

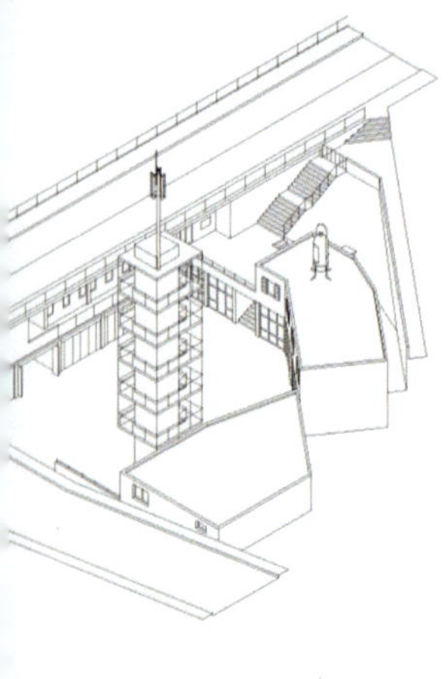

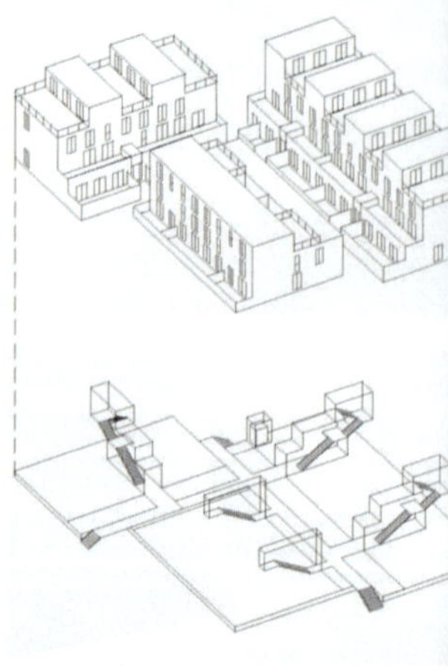

Reinventing Calais

32

Showing reality to counter xenophobic fantasies

What we call the "Jungle of Calais", and which politicians comment on abundantly without actually going there, is in fact an extraordinary globalised city. Driven by the energy of men and women who have fled horrific situations and who hope for a better future, the Jungle is a forum for intense and inventive activity: people live there, but they also invest their energy to come up with new ways of living together. Restaurants and shops spring up, and cultural facilities are created. PEROU is a collective of architects, artists, designers and researchers in the social sciences that has been working in the Jungle for two years. Via reportage work, analysis and project proposals, they show the reality of this spontaneously organised city, responding to gloomy views of the situation by highlighting its potential for adaptation.

www.perou-paris.org/index.html

—

photos: © André Merian
Graphic design: Malte Martin

PEROU Paris

A call for ideas by PEROU to give a future to what is invented, asserted and built today in and around the New Jungle in Calais.

> for an ephemeral city of the 21st century

> for a parliament of boundaries

> for signage in calais the world city

> for a house of the republic

> for a school of joyful knowledge

> for a european ressource centre in the dunes

> for an archipelago of care units

> for an artistic factory in the hauts-de-france region

> for a station in calais the world city

The hell of the living is not something that will be: if there is one, it is what is already here, the hell where we live every day, that we form by being together. There are two ways to escape suffering it. The first is easy for many: accept the hell and become such a part of it that you can no longer see it. The second is risky and demands constant vigilance and learning: seek and be able to recognize who and what, in the midst of the hell, are not hell, then make them endure, give them space.

Italo Calvino,
The Invisible Cities.

TER
es du
onner
ui
rme,
jourd'hui
de la
Calais.

Rural Urban Framework

33

China

Reinventing contemporary rurality in China

The exponential sprawling growth of Chinese megacities has caused profound changes in less dense areas which until recently might have been termed "rural" and which are now caught up in a series of contradictions. For about ten years, Joshua Bolchover and John Lin have been studying what has happened in several Chinese villages. From these studies have arisen several projects that attempt to respond to the specificities of contemporary rural life, which is largely dependent on the Hukou, a strict policy of distinction between the rural and the urban created under Mao and still applied today.
The micro-projects that have been carried out provide possible alternatives in response to the complex forces acting behind the scenes in the domain of urban development.

www.rufwork.org

—

Joshua Bolchover and John Lin Hong Kong

Rural Urban Framework (RUF) is a research and design collaboration between Joshua Bolchover and John Lin.
The objective of our work is to engage in the rural-urban transformation of China through built projects, research, exhibitions and writing.
We operate as a not-for-profit agency and collaborate with charities, private donors, Chinese governmental bureaux, and universities. The work is conducted within the Faculty of Architecture at the University of Hong Kong.

Our goals

To make buildings that actively contribute to the future transformation of the areas in which they are located.
To make architecture that influences policy makers in their approach to the design of schools, community facilities and other public buildings.
To find new models of rural development that enable the social, economic and spatial evolution of villages to resist the overwhelming process of urbanisation.

Tongjiang recycled brick school

Like many other areas of China, Tongjiang village in Jianxi Province is undergoing an urbanisation process. Here, buildings at various states of completion reflect the ebb and flow of incoming funds. Within this context of limited resources, the Tongjiang Primary School is a project that expands upon an existing school. Responding to the prevalence of demolition in rural areas, this project proposes a strategy for recycling old buildings into a new primary school. It demonstrates a way to recycle old material into a new prototype for a sustainable school building. It responds to the specific forces of transformation within its context yet also stakes a claim to an architecture that is not overly nostalgic or vernacular.

Angdong hospital project

Rural healthcare in China currently faces a multitude of challenges. Rural institutions are generally inadequate compared to those in urban locales. Working closely with charities and government in Angdong Village of Hunan Province, our task was to develop a model rural health care building capable of supporting the many progressive reforms relating to rural hospital management and care giving. This includes providing basic necessities absent in current establishments, some as simple as waiting rooms.

Additionally, given that most institutions in China, such as schools and hospitals, are walled off and managed as self-contained programmes, we were interested in recasting the hospital as a user-friendly facility. The design begins with a simple strategy to provide access to all floors via a continuous ramp. A wide ramp allows for seating and improves circulation. This also creates a large central courtyard space open for public use.

Taiping bridge renovation

The Taiping Bridge Project was a two-year reconstruction and surface renovation project of a historic 300-year-old bridge in Guizhou Province. Damaged by flooding in 2005, this Tang Dynasty bridge historically served as a junction between two neighbouring villages and as space for commercial activities to take place. However along with disrepair, the bridge faced another issue. Construction of a nearby highway pulled away not only traffic, but also local significance from the site. The project attempted to reconcile the long history of the existing masonry construction with modern techniques using pre-cast concrete. The latter was used to rebuild the arch and to pave the bridge. Bridge pavers were custom designed in collaboration with local industry in order to create planters of various sizes as well as seating. In this way the bridge was re-programmed as a public space. As village areas in China undergo dynamic changes, the question is whether it is possible to mediate between the sense of history and the sense of forward development.

Shichuang community centre

The project for the community centre responds to a growing social need in villages and the recognition of the importance of maintaining public space. As more and more people continue to migrate for work, the overall population of the village continues to grow. One important function in the village is that weddings and funerals are still commonly held there. This project, entirely self-funded by the villagers, was envisioned as an open and flexible space. Whereas in the traditional houses, the courtyard doubled as a public space for various events and reunions, the current density of the village fabric leaves no room for large gatherings. The centre stands on three functional core structures, leaving the ground free. After much discussion, doors were installed for security reasons. The community centre gradually began to look like a house, fully enclosed, with a flat roof with potential for the construction of additional floors. While villagers in the city remain disconnected from it, the village still retains an important role as the social anchor for this population.

Lingzidi bridge

The construction of a new highway in southern Shaanxi Province required the destruction of hundreds of local bridges. This project involves the design of a pedestrian bridge in Lingzidi Village to service the disrupted network. The bridge is a unique-looking loop linking two levels of the riverbank and an additional arm spanning the river. This produces a wide, direct path for small trucks and motorcycles and a pedestrian path that cuts under the bridge, allowing access to the river for purposes such as washing, cleaning, and fishing. Steps and shaded areas provide places to sit and relax.

With the construction of this bridge, villagers are once again able to commute freely across the river, meeting at the bridge for trade and commerce. Despite its small scale, this bridge is a critical link for the local village economy, emerging as a social hub and mitigating some of the many uprooting effects of large-scale infrastructure construction. It encourages villagers to maintain and improve their local economy rather than rely on sources sent back from family members working in factory towns.

Qinmo community centre

When Qinmo Primary School was built, the old courtyard school building in the village was left vacant and unused. This project is a part of the Qinmo Village Development. It involves renovating the school to create a community centre and demonstration eco-household. The new programme includes a meeting room, dormitory, large dining area, communal kitchen and office space. The centre is used by villagers as a place to host ecoworkshops and volunteers. This old school has now turned into an active community centre that not only provides physical space for the village's social activities, but also educational opportunities through its scholarship programmes. The old and new school are architectural settings that facilitate social engagement and knowledge exchange. By promoting sustainable and holistic agricultural practices, the village can incrementally renew an interest in rural productivity while at the same time offering educational opportunities for the younger generation, providing them alternatives to the mass exodus to cities.

Mulan school and educational landscape

In Mulan Village, Huaiji, Guangdong Province, the construction of the high speed railway created a huge cut in the landscape and a pile of earth at the back of an existing primary school. The slope was unstable and also led to flood damage to the old courtyard building. This school was designated for expansion and our commission was to design an educational landscape involving the creation of a new school block, complete with toilets and a playground. Our strategy was to organise the site as a series of sequential open spaces, linking the courtyards between the existing school, the new building and the playground. The loose earth of the slope was re-contoured and retained through the creation of a reed-bed filtration system and toilet on the edge of the basketball court. As the urbanisation of Huaiji begins to expand and encroach on the village, through the provision of these common, shared areas, the school can become a community focal point and a place for discussions, meetings, study, play or relaxation.

Qinmo school

In 2006, the Green Hope Foundation selected Qinmo Village, a poor and remote village in Guangdong Province, as the site for a new school with an emphasis on environmental education and good practice. As this village had not damaged its agricultural land with chemical fertilizers or pollutants, there was also an opportunity to help villagers grow organic products that could be sold in the Hong Kong market. The project began with the construction of a new school building and was followed by the conversion of the old school building into a hybrid community centre and demonstration eco-farm.

This project is a prototype for a village school that goes beyond mere building construction through integrating educational programmes and sustainable concepts.

Yongxin secondary school prototype

This design responds to the recent shifts in China's school policies. The Yongxin county schools consist of 4 secondary schools with a total of 3,300 students and 1,800 live-in students from nearby rural areas. Treating the school as a village community, our initial strategy creates a perimeter building that frames a large courtyard. This wall, much like a traditional old city wall, contains the inner public life of the school.

The challenge for us during this project lies in the objective to achieve flexibility without falling into the generic vernacular. As such, the resulting design is capable of adapting to different programme requirements and site conditions, including those specific to small villages or even developing town centres.

A unique range of social building types within the perimeter would complement specific surrounding landscapes. So while responsive to the specificity of its locality, this prototype also digresses from conventional school designs.

A house for all seasons

Development in rural areas such as Shijia typically abandons traditional styles in favour of more generic housing types. This is partly the result oft he area's gradual shift away from economic self-reliance. All the houses in the region around Shijia are constructed of mud brick and occupy land parcels of 10 metres by 30 metres. The design promotes a sustainable alternative within this framework by integrating rammed earth, biogas, rainwater storage, and reed bed cleansing systems. Understanding the courtyard as an important component of the home, our design includes four distinct courtyards to be the primary elements.
The final result is a house that integrates traditional technologies into contemporary rural life. Serving also as a centre for women's handicraft, the Shijia House bridges the individual and collective identity of the village. Construction of the house has initiated a new phase for the local economy, developing a new cooperative business in traditional straw weaving.

Jintai village reconstruction project

Jintai Village is located near Guangyuan, Sichuan Province- one of the places hardest hit by the Wenchuan Earthquake in 2008. The disaster left nearly 5 million people homeless and it is estimated that 80% of all buildings in the affected area were destroyed. A total of twenty-two houses are to be rebuilt including a community centre. The design strategy provides four different types of houses, differing in their roof sections. These demonstrate new use of local materials, a green stepped roof, biogas technologies, and places to keep for pigs and chickens. The design also invests in reed bed waste-water treatment and collective animal rearing. By relating various programmes in the village to an ecological cycle, environmental responsiveness is heightened, transforming the village into a model for nearby areas.
This is an investigation into modern rural livelihood.

Senior Recreational Vehicle Community of the US

34

The networked urbanism of contemporary nomads

An estimated 2-3 million Americans live in camper vans. Most are "young-at-heart seniors" belonging to a generation of healthy, retired, connected 60-75-year-olds who have chosen to turn their back on the traditional house and live their independent lives to the full. Thanks to the Internet and the social networks, these neo-nomads form temporary communities according to the seasons. They thus form more or less volatile and autonomous groups, from circular encampments to instant cities in the middle of the desert. These impermanent settlements, strongly marked by a need for social grouping, are above all the expression of a new form of urbanism that is more lightweight and adaptable.

—

Such examples spell out the lineage of *Young-Old*. But "old age is not a mere statistical fact". Reframing aging as a new field of urban research, Simpson's book goes beyond the lure of data, searching for potential in social and physical mutations while avoiding the trap of moral judgment. Urban innovations that respond to the needs and desires of newly ascendant elderly populations serve as timely case studies to trace present entanglements of demography and territory. In doing so, Simpson lays bare an entire repertoire of unexpected urban features that mirror deep-seated changes in the makeup of both people and place. Examples ranging from new infrastructure for golf cart cities, to commercial strips transformed into strings of roadside medical amenities, to instant cities formed by migratory RV communities, all serve to identify new strategies of spatial production, giving rise to "gerontopias" formed by a coming-toget of age and idyllic place. What these and other examples covered by Simpson present is an amended inventory of managed lifestyle products aimed at literally "teleporting" elderly cohorts—as with Cranach's painting—out of the everyday grind of getting old to modern-day utopias of rejuvenation and a world forever young.

Marc Angélil and Cary Siress

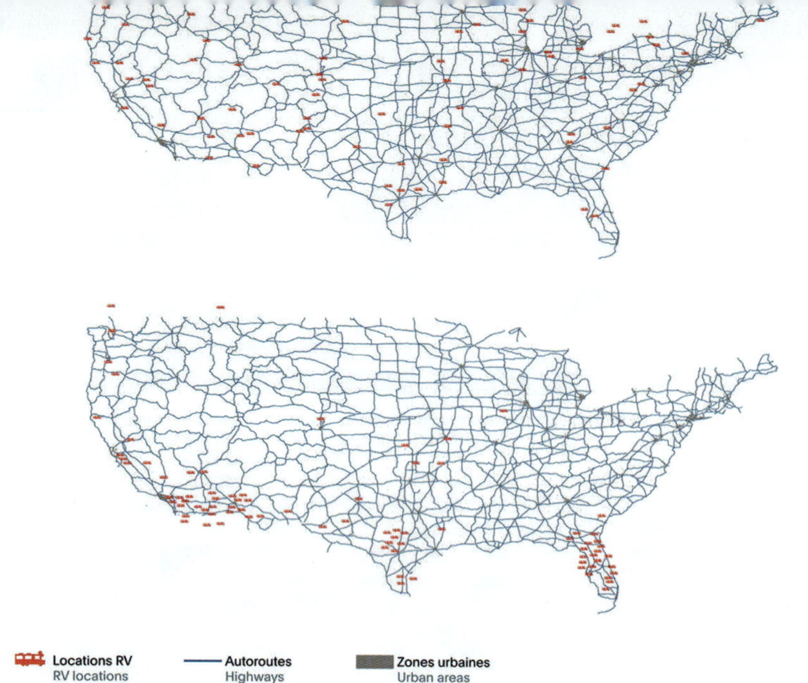

Locations RV
RV locations
Autoroutes
Highways
Zones urbaines
Urban areas

MIGRATION SAISONNIÈRE DES UTILISATEURS DU LOGICIEL DATASTORM ENTRE UNE JOURNÉE D'ÉTÉ ET UNE JOURNÉE D'HIVER / SEASONAL MIGRATION OF DATASTORM USERS BETWEEN SUMMER DAY EXAMPLE AND WINTER DAY EXAMPLE

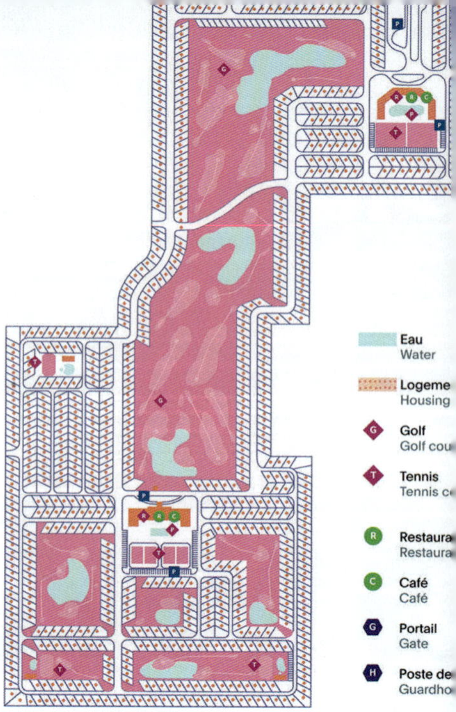

Eau
Water
Logeme
Housing
Golf
Golf cou
Tennis
Tennis c
Restaura
Restaura
Café
Café
Portail
Gate
Poste de
Guardho

STATION EN PLEIN AIR POUR LES RV, PALM SPRING
OUTDOOR RV RESORT, PALM SPRINGS, CALIFORNI

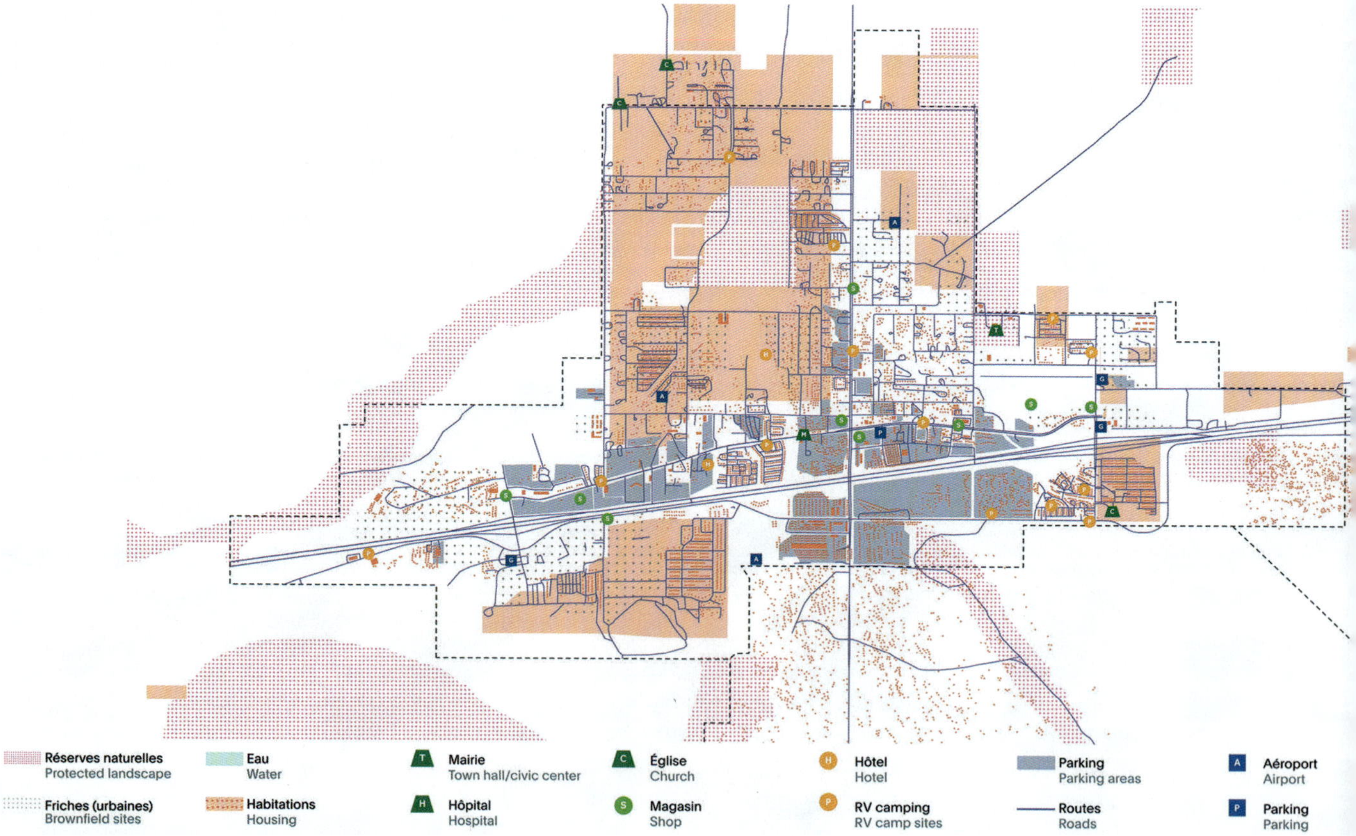

Réserves naturelles
Protected landscape
Friches (urbaines)
Brownfield sites
Eau
Water
Habitations
Housing
Mairie
Town hall/civic center
Hôpital
Hospital
Église
Church
Magasin
Shop
Hôtel
Hotel
RV camping
RV camp sites
Parking
Parking areas
Routes
Roads
Aéroport
Airport
Parking
Parking

QUARTZSITE, ARIZONA / PLAN D'ENSEMBLE / QUARTZSITE, ARIZONA / URBAN MAP

nformal campsites supporting
›pulated settings such as deserts
nformal parking sites in urban
lart parking lots. The latter, non-
ısed upon portable satellite In-
hich allow the internet based RV
as the dominant social staging
y. Collectively, these infrastruc-
le and socially coherent urban

SUPERFICIE LAND AREA

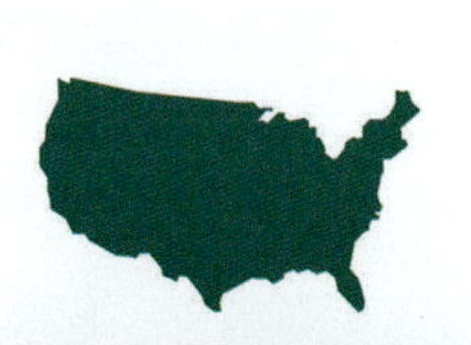

POPULATION

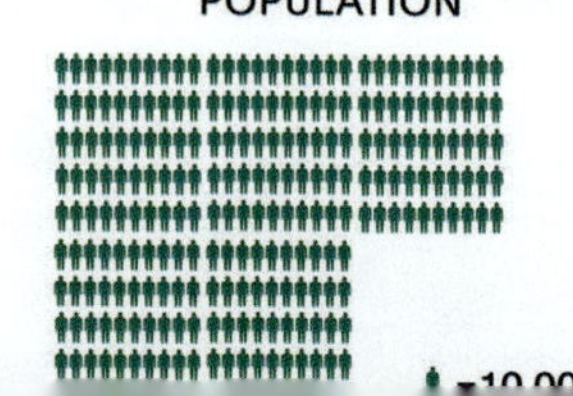

DENSITÉ DENSITY

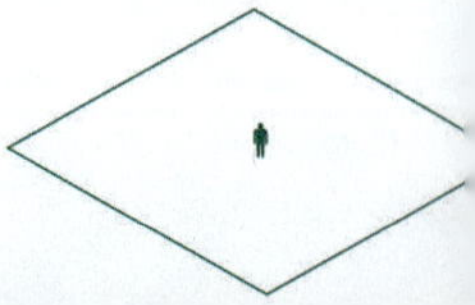

Parking area
Parking areas

Route
Road

Parking
Parking

0m
0.05 mi

NE

STATION EN PLEIN AIR POUR LES RV, PALM SPRINGS, CALIFORNIE / TISSU URBAIN
OUTDOOR RV RESORT, PALM SPRINGS, CALIFORNIA / URBAN TEXTURE

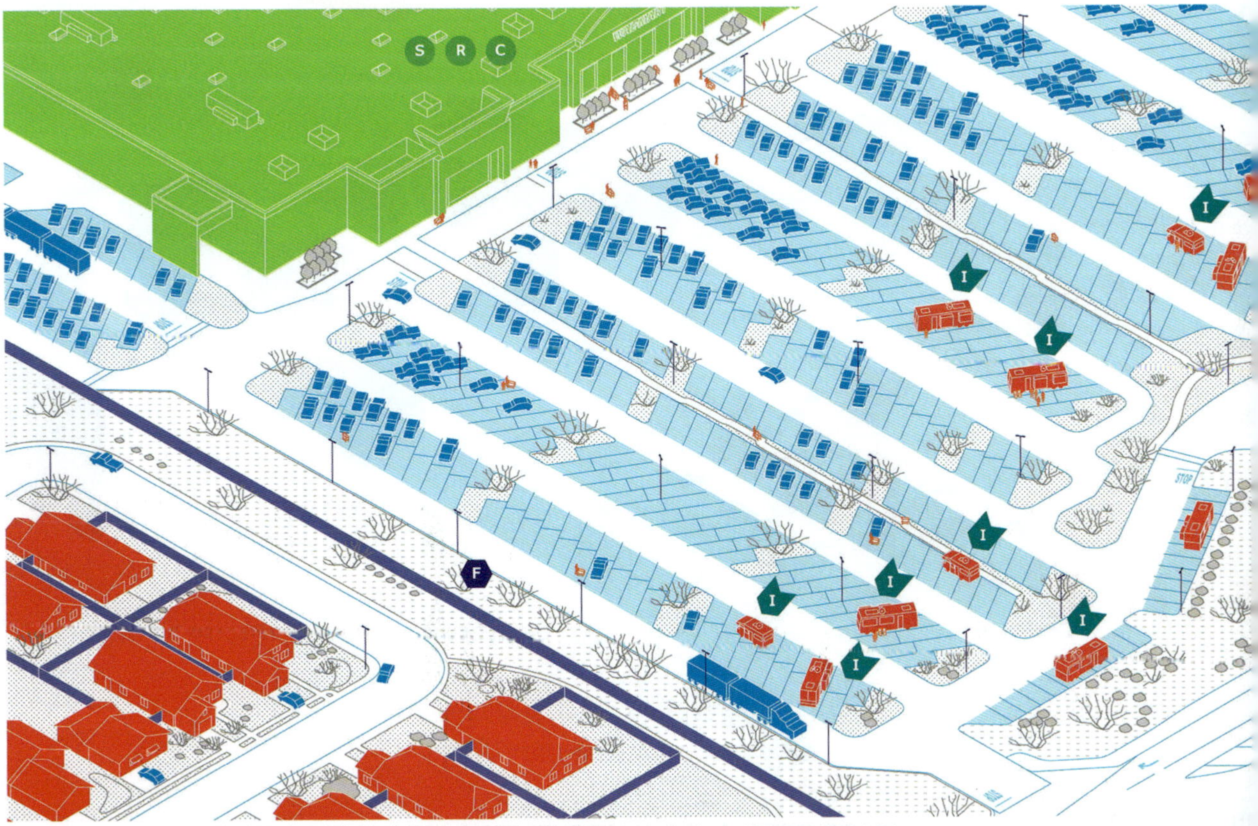

arage
arage

500m
0.5 mi

AIRE DE CAMPEMENT, SUPERMARCHÉ WAL-MART, PHOENIX, ARIZONA / TISSU URBAIN
DESTINATION BOONDOCKING, WAL-MART SUPERCENTER, PHOENIX, ARIZONA / URBAN TEXTURE

ÂGE MOYEN AVERAGE AGE

59

COMPOSITION ETHNIQUE
ETHNIC COMPOSITION

Local ethnic majority 98 %

REVENU MOYEN PAR MÈNAGE
AVERAGE HOUSEHOLD INCOME

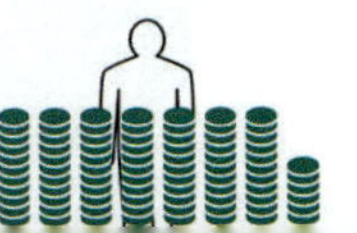

PRIX MOYEN D'UNE HA
AVERAGE HOUSE P

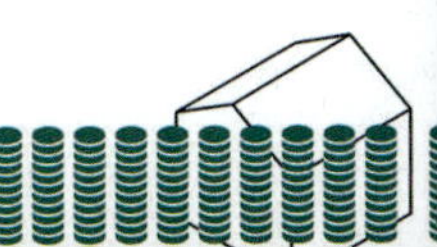

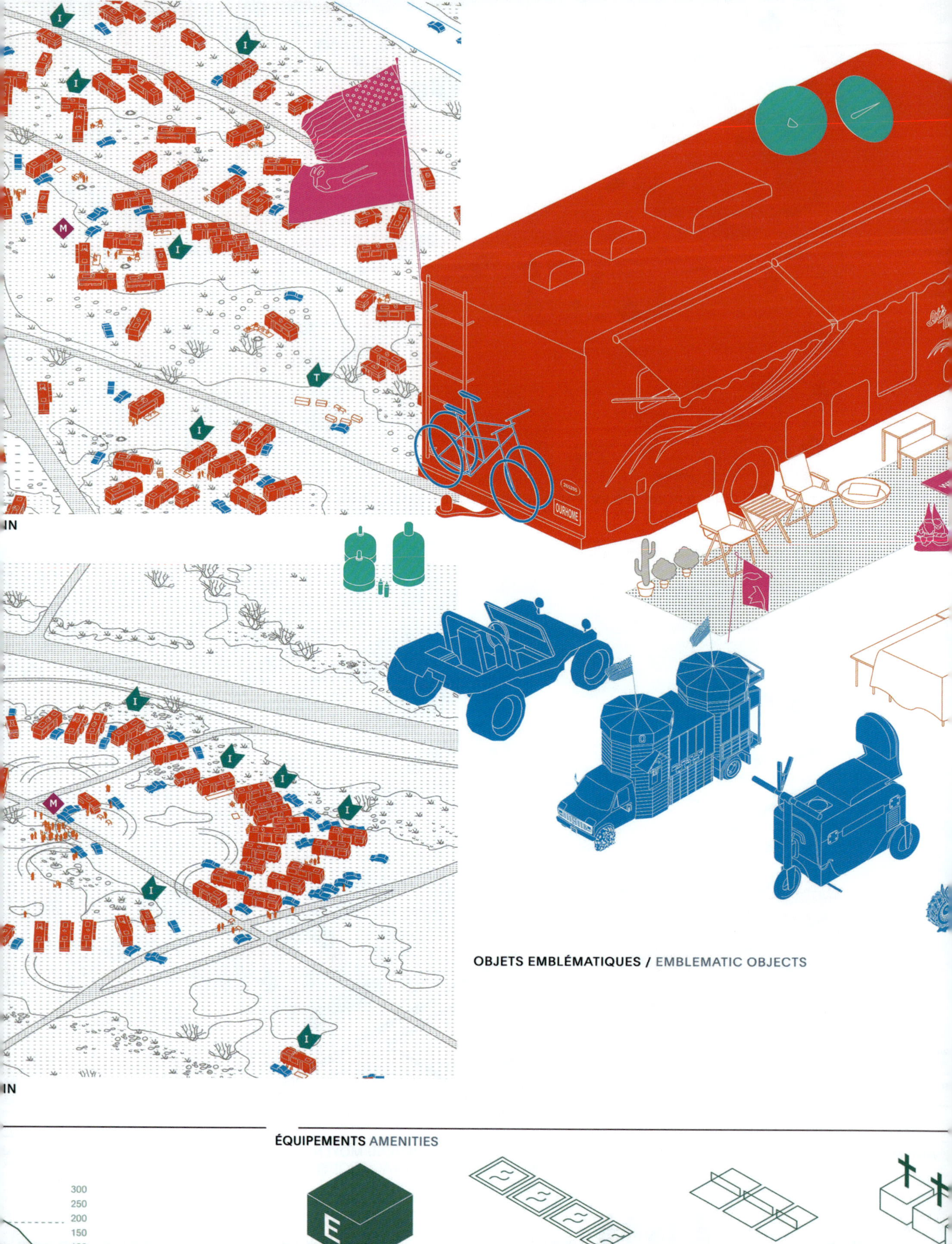

IN
OURHOME
IN
OBJETS EMBLÉMATIQUES / EMBLEMATIC OBJECTS
ÉQUIPEMENTS AMENITIES
300
250
200
150
100
50
0
Average temperature (°C)
Ideal temperature
E
268 000 ct

TYPOLOGIE "HOMEMAKING" / PAYSAGE DOMESTIQUE
TYPICAL OUTDOOR "HOMEMAKING" / LANDSCAPE DOMESTICATION

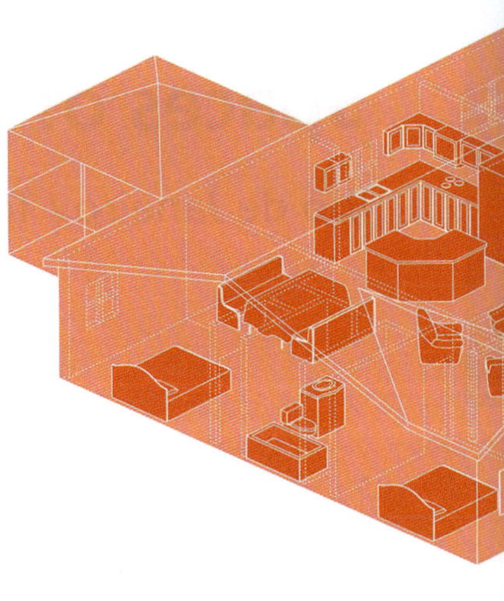

LA MAISON SÉDENTAIRE ET LA MAISON MOBIL
THE SEDENTARY HOME VS THE "MOVING HOM

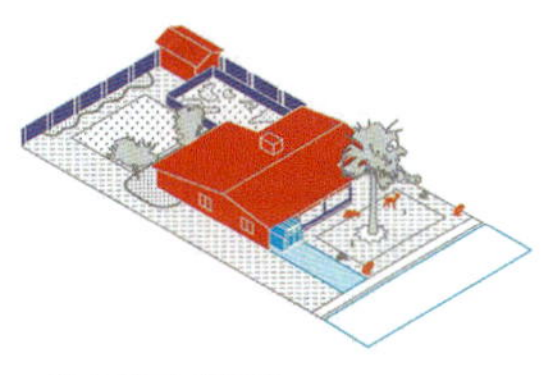

Youngtown, Arizona

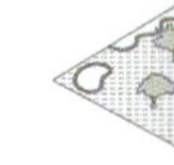

Sun Ci

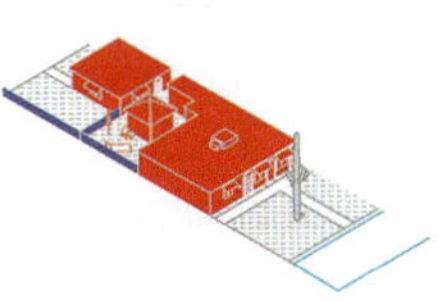

Youngtown, Arizona

Sun Ci

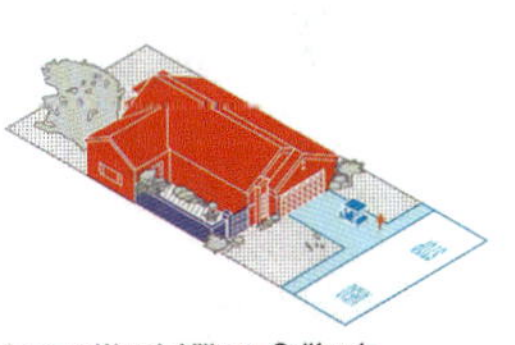

Laguna Woods Village, California

The Vil

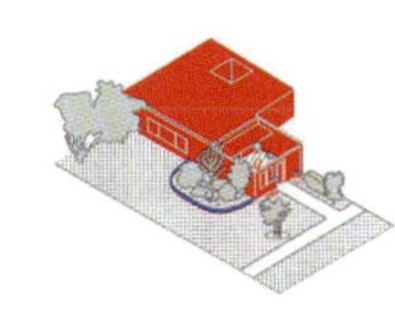

Laguna Woods Village, California

The Vil

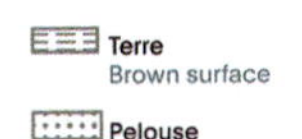

Terre
Brown surface

Jardin
Protected green

Eau
Water

Pelouse
Green surface

Sol artificiel
Artificial surface

Résidence
Residence

COMPARAISON DES TYPOLOGIES D'HABITATI

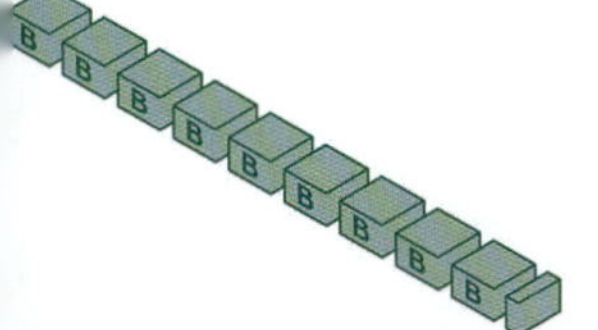

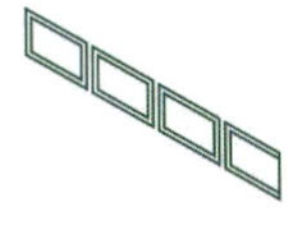

CAMPING-CARS MOTORIZED RVS

CARAVANES

Conventional

Van Camper

Mini

Folding

Spaces of Commoning

35

Rio de Janeiro / Tokyo

304

From Rio to Tokyo, anatomy of common spaces

In response to the inability of public authorities to create and maintain public programmes and spaces, citizens' communities are set up to take charge of the production and management of common spaces, which are places of conflict as well as interaction.
The study entitled *Spaces of Commoning* analyses these spaces in two apparently highly contrasting urban contexts: a favela in Rio and a working class suburb of Tokyo. It analyses our practices, the way we organise them in space, and the rules we play by. Could they be similar in two places so far from one another? What is the role played by cultural identity and local traditions? Can they produce a harmonious and enduring sense of "commonality", or are they merely reproducing models of segregation?

—

ETH Zurich / **PUC** Rio de Janeiro / **IAS + Y-GSA / TU** Berlin

The research project *Spaces of Commoning* investigates space as an asset for collective interaction. Considering the fact that public spaces and spatial commons are increasingly threatened by privatisation and corporate control, practices of 'commoning'-the collective management of shared resources- are changing its nature.

What are the programmatic and architectural components of today's collective spaces? Who establishes, manages and maintains these spaces? Who are the providers and who are the active users? Which groups take part and who is excluded? What is the institutional framework that guarantees the production of spatial commons and who takes care of their everyday performance? How much do these spaces rely on self-organisation and to what extent are they supported by governmental structures and formal regulations? What are the practices that sustain spatial commons and their actor constellations? *Spaces of Commoning* presents twelve exemplary cases from a research project exploring relations between urban space and collective organisation. It seeks to identify the various constellations that enable the formation of collectives and the creation of shared spaces. While the research project is ongoing and conceived as an open archive for collecting case studies from diverse regional contexts, the present selection focuses on a direct comparison between examples from Rio de Janeiro and Tokyo. In order to unfold the various aspects that contribute to a critical understanding of collective spaces, based on different cultural backgrounds and scales, the cases are shown through various forms of visual representation detecting the variety of components that have to be assembled in architecture and urban design for the production of collective places.

The diverse manifestations of *Spaces of Commoning* illustrate the need for redefining collective space according to its specific cultural, social and economic conditions. As soon as we start to trace the various connections between spatial commons and their actors, we also realise that space as common resource is often highly contested—run by privatised entities and bound to existing relations of power, subverted by the market and dismantled by neo-liberal regimes, *Spaces of Commoning* cannot, by default, be considered socially sound, inclusive and sustainable.

Instead of idealising commoning practice as the only remaining alternative to the proliferation of privatised interests, a critical understanding of the controversial nature of spatial commons serves as a reality check.It facilitates a proactive approach for contemporary architecture practice by researching the preconditions for the design and production of spatial commons. The constellations of human and non-human actors required to cope with the social transformations of today's urban reality equally involve top-down governmental practice and bottom-up movements of a self-organised civic society. Aiming at the development of tools and strategies for the improvement of collective spaces, the research project embraces commoning practice in its manifold cultures and contradictions, and it reveals negotiations and conflicts between formal institutions and informal appropriations, between solidarity networks promoting social values and exclusive associations following commercial interests.

Whether we look at public spaces, streetscapes, community centres, neighbourhood amenities, or cultural and religious places, *Spaces of Commoning* remain the most fundamental resources and the basis for the realisation of democratic societies and the collective project of the city.

Mobility Hub
Centre de mobilité
Place, Endroit :
Entrance Favela Vidigal,
Zona Sul
Rio de Janeiro
#003
Carnival Stadium
Sambódromo,
Cidade Nova
Celebration

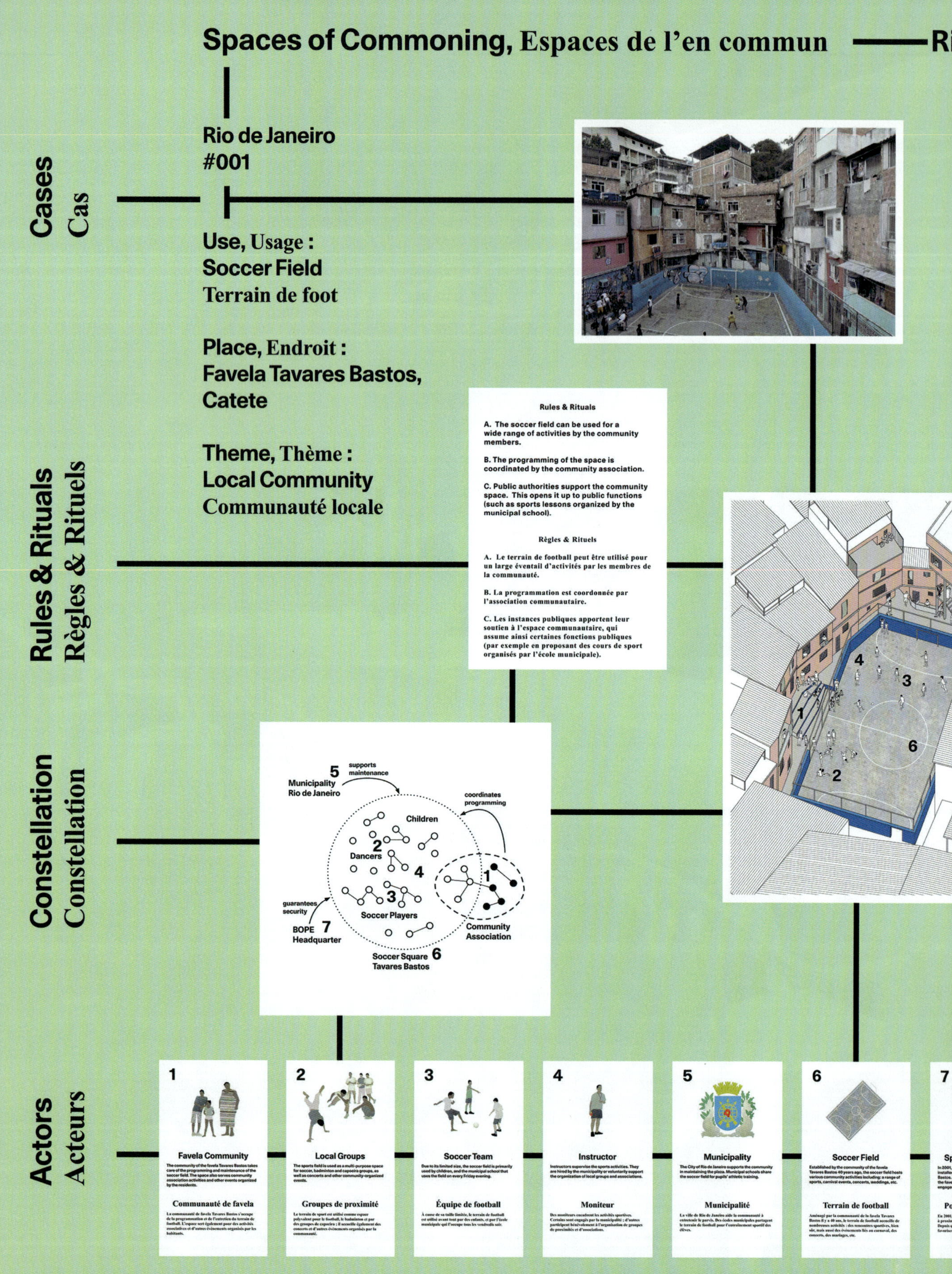

Spaces of Commoning, Espaces de l'en commun
Ri
Cases
Cas
Rio de Janeiro
#001
Use, Usage :
Soccer Field
Terrain de foot
Place, Endroit :
Favela Tavares Bastos, Catete
Theme, Thème :
Local Community
Communauté locale
Rules & Rituals
Règles & Rituels
Rules & Rituals
A. The soccer field can be used for a wide range of activities by the community members.
B. The programming of the space is coordinated by the community association.
C. Public authorities support the community space. This opens it up to public functions (such as sports lessons organized by the municipal school).
Règles & Rituels
A. Le terrain de football peut être utilisé pour un large éventail d'activités par les membres de la communauté.
B. La programmation est coordonnée par l'association communautaire.
C. Les instances publiques apportent leur soutien à l'espace communautaire, qui assume ainsi certaines fonctions publiques (par exemple en proposant des cours de sport organisés par l'école municipale).
Constellation
Constellation
5 Municipality Rio de Janeiro
supports maintenance
coordinates programming
Children
2 Dancers
4
3 Soccer Players
1 Community Association
guarantees security
7 BOPE Headquarter
Soccer Square Tavares Bastos 6
4
3
1
6
2
Actors
Acteurs
1
Favela Community
The community of the favela Tavares Bastos takes care of the programming and maintenance of the soccer field. The space also serves community association activities and other events organized by the residents.
Communauté de favela
La communauté de favela Tavares Bastos s'occupe de la programmation et de l'entretien du terrain de football. L'espace sert également pour des activités associatives et d'autres événements organisés par les habitants.
2
Local Groups
The sports field is used as a multi-purpose space for soccer, badminton and capoeira groups, as well as concerts and other community-organized events.
Groupes de proximité
Le terrain de sport est utilisé comme espace polyvalent pour le football, le badminton et par des groupes de capoeira ; il accueille également des concerts et d'autres événements organisés par la communauté.
3
Soccer Team
Due to its limited size, the soccer field is primarily used by children, and the municipal school that uses the field on every Friday evening.
Équipe de football
À cause de sa taille limitée, le terrain de football est utilisé avant tout par des enfants, et par l'école municipale qui l'occupe tous les vendredis soir.
4
Instructor
Instructors supervise the sports activities. They are hired by the municipality or voluntarily support the organization of local groups and associations.
Moniteur
Des moniteurs encadrent les activités sportives. Certains sont engagés par la municipalité ; d'autres participent bénévolement à l'organisation de groupes de proximités et d'associations.
5
Municipality
The City of Rio de Janeiro supports the community in maintaining the plaza. Municipal schools share the soccer field for pupils' athletic training.
Municipalité
La ville de Rio de Janeiro aide la communauté à entretenir le parvis. Des écoles municipales partagent le terrain de football pour l'entraînement sportif des élèves.
6
Soccer Field
Established by the community of the favela Tavares Bastos 40 years ago, the soccer field hosts various community activities including: a range of sports, carnival events, concerts, weddings, etc.
Terrain de football
Aménagé par la communauté de la favela Tavares Bastos il y a 40 ans, le terrain de football accueille de nombreuses activités : des rencontres sportives, bien sûr, mais aussi des événements liés au carnaval, des concerts, des mariages, etc.
7

Rio de Janeiro #002

Use, Usage :
Mobility Hub
Centre de mobilité

Place, Endroit :
Entrance Favela Vidigal, Zona Sul
Entrée de la favela Vidigal

Theme, Thème :
Commuting
Transit

Rules & Rituals

A. Together the municipality of Rio and the local community association set the prices for local transportation.

B. Residents pay 2 R$ per trip to access the top of the favela hill.

C. The local community association is in charge of improving the quality of the service and taking care of the plaza equipment.

Règles & Rituels

A. La municipalité de Rio et l'association communautaire locale fixent ensemble les prix pour le transport de proximité.

B. Les résidents paient 2 R$ par trajet pour accéder au sommet de la colline de la favela.

C. L'association est chargée d'améliorer la qualité du service et d'entretenir les équipements du parvis.

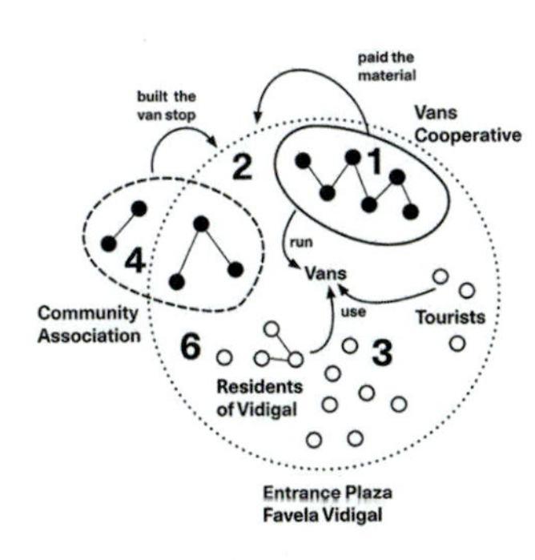

1

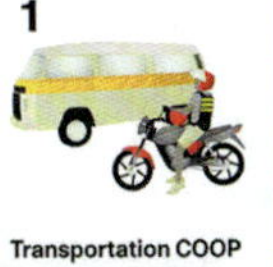

Transportation COOP

The van cooperative consists of a dozen drivers who collectively coordinate and set the price for transportation in coordination with the Municipality. For special events, tourists and visitors pay more than local residents. Motorbikes are also available for local transportation and are organized informally.

Transports coopératifs

La coopérative des minibus comprend une douzaine de chauffeurs qui coordonnent les trajets et établissent les prix en accord avec la Municipalité. Pour les événements spéciaux, les touristes et les visiteurs paient plus cher que les résidents. Des motos sont également disponibles pour le transport de proximité : ce moyen de transport est organisé de façon non officielle.

2

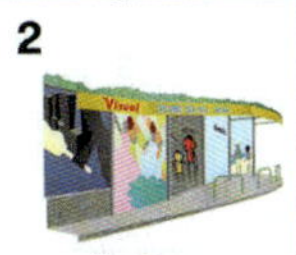

Van Stop

The van stop along the street was established by the community and is comprised of several components: a medicinal green roof, wall graffiti depicting the history of Vidigal, a bench, advertising and a TV.

Arrêt de minibus

Installé par la communauté, l'arrêt comporte plusieurs éléments : un toit végétal, des graffitis qui représentent l'histoire de Vidigal, une banquette, de la publicité, et un écran de télé.

3

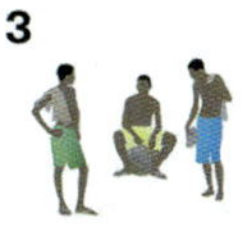

Community

Today, the favela of Vidigal is home to around 12 000 inhabitants. The community is located in a central area, close to one of the wealthiest neighbourhoods in Rio de Janeiro. Due to the topography and the proximity to the sea, the favela offers spectacular views that are contributing to the gentrification of the community.

Communauté

Aujourd'hui, la population de la favela de Vidigal est d'environ 12 000 personnes. La communauté est située en zone centrale, à proximité d'un des quartiers les plus aisés de Rio de Janeiro. La favela bénéficie de vues spectaculaires grâce à sa topographie et à sa situation proche de la mer, ce qui contribue à l'embourgeoisement de la communauté.

4

Community Association

Every year, the residents of Vidigal are asked to elect a president for their community association. The association has different tasks: establishing a dialogue with the municipality, mediating conflicting interests within the community and promoting local culture.

Association communautaire

Chaque année, on invite les résidents de Vidigal à élire le président de leur association communautaire. Celle-ci a différentes missions plurielles : établir un dialogue avec la municipalité, servir de médiateur au sein de la communauté en cas de conflit et promouvoir la culture locale.

5

Municipality

In 2010, the municipality created the local system for public transport (STPL) with the goal of regulating illegal vans in the city. Together with the help of community association, the public authorities define the transit lines and fix prices. A tender delegates the right of use to an official van cooperative.

Municipalité

En 2010, la municipalité a créé le système local de transport public (STPL) dans le but de limiter l'utilisation des camionnettes de transport illégales dans la ville. Avec l'aide de l'association communautaire, le conseil municipal définit les lignes de transport et fixent les tarifs. Les droits d'exploitation des lignes sont accordés à des coopératives officielles qui répondent à des appels d'offres.

6

Local Commerce

The favela Vidigal entrance plaza acts as a mobility hub and attracts diverse local commerce : shops along the street front, a kiosk in the middle of the plaza and informal street vendors.

Commerce de proximité

Le parvis à l'entrée de la favela Vidigal sert de pôle de mobilité et attire beaucoup de commerces de proximité : des magasins tout au long de la rue, un kiosque au centre du parvis et des marchands ambulants.

7

UPP Police

The so-called 'pacification unit' was established in 2009 as a special unit of the police. It guarantees the security in the favela and prevents the community from being taken over by the drug mafia and other criminal fractions.

Police/BOPE

L'« unité d'apaisement » fut établie en 2009 comme unité spéciale de la police. Elle garantit la sécurité dans la favela et empêche la mafia de la drogue et d'autres groupes criminels de développer une emprise sur la communauté.

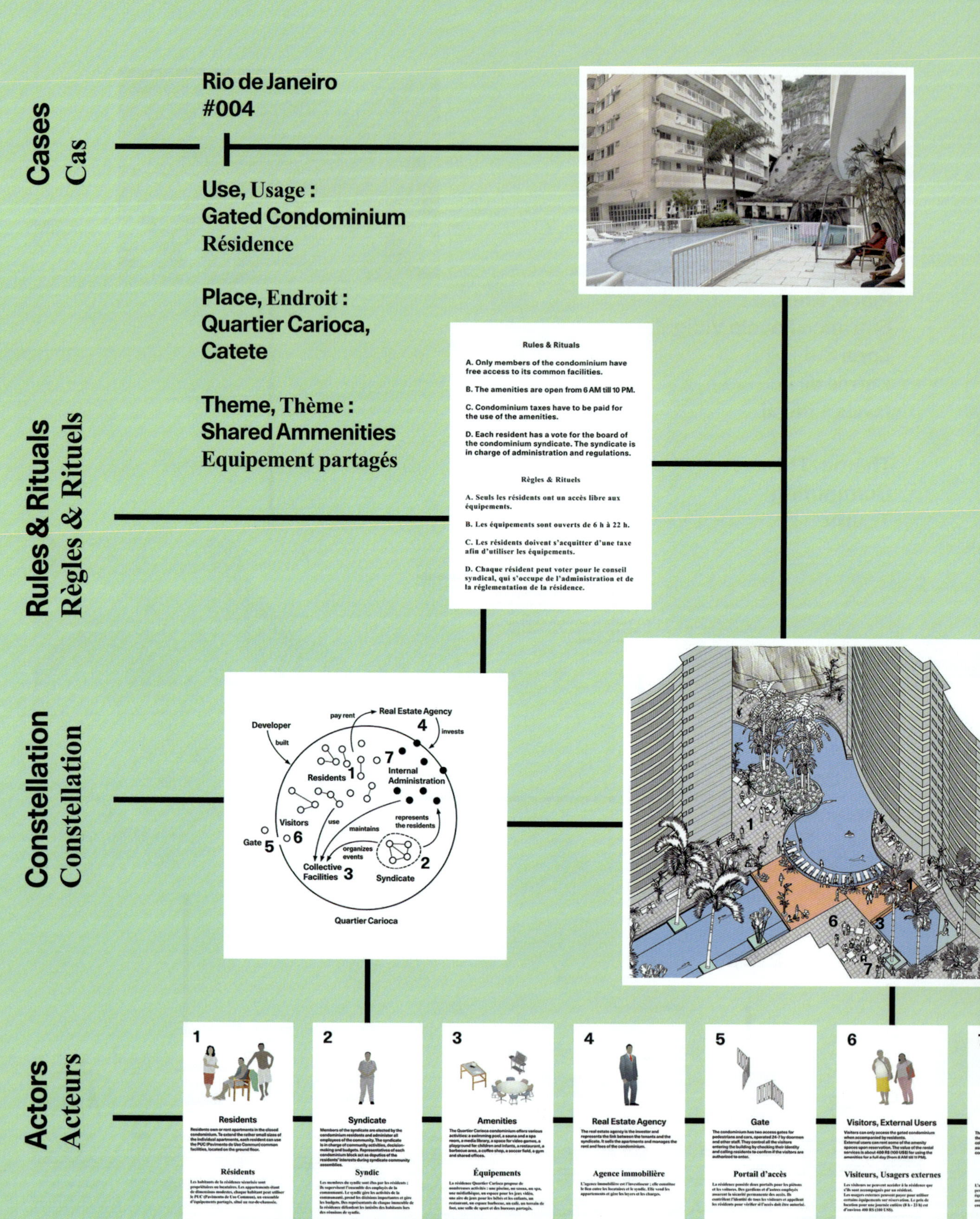
Cases
Cas
Rio de Janeiro
#004
Use, Usage :
Gated Condominium
Résidence
Place, Endroit :
Quartier Carioca,
Catete
Theme, Thème :
Shared Ammenities
Equipement partagés
Rules & Rituals
Règles & Rituels
Rules & Rituals
A. Only members of the condominium have free access to its common facilities.
B. The amenities are open from 6 AM till 10 PM.
C. Condominium taxes have to be paid for the use of the amenities.
D. Each resident has a vote for the board of the condominium syndicate. The syndicate is in charge of administration and regulations.
Règles & Rituels
A. Seuls les résidents ont un accès libre aux équipements.
B. Les équipements sont ouverts de 6 h à 22 h.
C. Les résidents doivent s'acquitter d'une taxe afin d'utiliser les équipements.
D. Chaque résident peut voter pour le conseil syndical, qui s'occupe de l'administration et de la réglementation de la résidence.
Constellation
Constellation
Developer
built
pay rent
Real Estate Agency
4
invests
Residents 1
7
Internal Administration
use
maintains
represents the residents
Visitors
Gate 5
6
organizes events
Collective Facilities 3
2
Syndicate
Quartier Carioca
1
6
3
7
Actors
Acteurs
1
Residents
Residents own or rent apartments in the closed condominium. To extend the rather small sizes of the individual apartments, each resident can use the PUC (Pavimento de Uso Commun) common facilities, located on the ground floor.
Résidents
Les habitants de la résidence sécurisée sont propriétaires ou locataires. Les appartements étant de dimensions modestes, chaque habitant peut utiliser le PUC (Pavimento de Uso Commun), un ensemble d'équipements partagés, situé au rez-de-chaussée.
2
Syndicate
Members of the syndicate are elected by the condominium residents and administer all employees of the community. The syndicate is in charge of community activities, decision-making and budgets. Representatives of each condominium block act as deputies of the residents' interests during syndicate community assemblies.
Syndic
Les membres du syndic sont élus par les résidents : ils supervisent l'ensemble des employés de la communauté. Le syndic gère les activités de la communauté, prend les décisions importantes et gère les budgets. Des représentants de chaque immeuble de la résidence défendent les intérêts des habitants lors des réunions de syndic.
3
Amenities
The Quartier Carioca condominium offers various activities: a swimming pool, a sauna and a spa room, a media library, a space for video games, a playground for children and infants, a restaurant, a barbecue area, a coffee shop, a soccer field, a gym and shared offices.
Équipements
La résidence Quartier Carioca propose de nombreuses activités : une piscine, un sauna, un spa, une médiathèque, un espace pour les jeux vidéo, une aire de jeux pour les bébés et les enfants, un restaurant, un espace barbecue, un café, un terrain de foot, une salle de sport et des bureaux partagés.
4
Real Estate Agency
The real estate agency is the investor and represents the link between the tenants and the syndicate. It sells the apartments and manages the rent and fees of the condominium.
Agence immobilière
L'agence immobilière est l'investisseur ; elle constitue le lien entre les locataires et le syndic. Elle vend les appartements et gère les loyers et les charges.
5
Gate
The condominium has two access gates for pedestrians and cars, operated 24-7 by doormen and other staff. They control all the visitors entering the building by checking their identity and calling residents to confirm if the visitors are authorized to enter.
Portail d'accès
La résidence possède deux portails pour les piétons et les voitures. Des gardiens et d'autres employés assurent la sécurité permanente des accès. Ils contrôlent l'identité de tous les visiteurs et appellent les résidents pour vérifier si l'accès doit être autorisé.
6
Visitors, External Users
Visitors can only access the gated condominium when accompanied by residents.
External users can rent some of the amenity spaces upon reservation. The value of the rental services is about 400 R$ (100 US$) for using the amenities for a full day (from 8 AM till 11 PM).
Visiteurs, Usagers externes
Les visiteurs ne peuvent accéder à la résidence que s'ils sont accompagnés par un résident.
Les usagers externes peuvent payer pour utiliser certains équipements sur réservation. Le prix de location pour une journée entière (8 h - 23 h) est d'environ 400 R$ (100 US$).
7

Rio de Janeiro
#005

Use, Usage :
Car-free Highway
Autoroute piétonne

Place, Endroit :
Aterro do Flamengo, Flamengo

Theme, Thème :
Recreation
Recréation

Rules & Rituals

A. The highway is closed to traffic on Sundays and public holidays from 7 AM till 6 PM.

B. Special events require authorization from the municipal authorities.

C. The municipality of Rio de Janeiro provides maintenance and security.

Règles & Rituels

A. L'autoroute est fermée à la circulation le dimanche et les jours fériés entre 7 h et 18 h.

B. Les manifestations spéciales doivent obtenir une autorisation du conseil municipal.

C. La municipalité de Rio de Janeiro assure l'entretien et la sécurité.

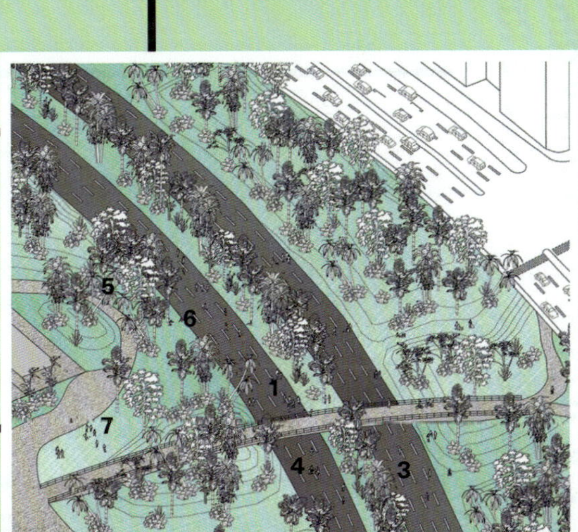

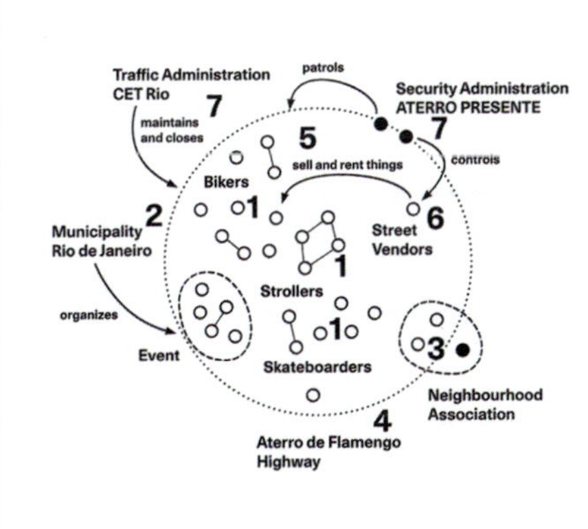

1

Park Users

The walk along the highway offers spectacular views of Rio's remarkable landscape and skyline. The smooth asphalt surface is attractive for people from all social backgrounds and in particular for bikers, skateboarders and runners who can appreciate the lane being free of vehicular traffic.

Un espace de loisirs

La promenade offre des vues spectaculaires sur les alentours de Rio de Janeiro. La surface goudronnée attire des gens de tous les milieux, notamment des cyclistes, des amateurs de skating et des coureurs, pour lesquels l'absence de circulation sur la voie constitue un atout majeur.

2

Municipality

Municipal organizations manage and maintain the space: CETRIO opens and closes the road and controls the car traffic, ATERRO PRESENTE guarantees security with special police reinforcement, and COMLURB manages sanitation and garbage collection.

Municipalité

Les organisations municipales gèrent et entretiennent l'espace : CETRIO ouvre et ferme la route et contrôle la circulation, ATERRO PRESENTE garantit la sécurité grâce à la présence renforcée de la police spéciale, et COMLURB gère les installations sanitaires et la collecte des déchets.

3

Civic Society

Several neighbourhood associations organize cultural activities in the park: Caminho do Rio, A(R)TERRO collective and LOTTA institute. Various people actively involved in local civic society occasionally arrange larger events : for example demonstrations, the Rio marathon, bike races, and carnival events.

Société civile

Plusieurs associations de quartier organisent des activités culturelles dans le parc, notamment Caminho do Rio, A(R)TERRO collective, et l'institut LOTTA. Des acteurs de la société civile organisent ponctuellement des événements plus importants : manifestations, marathon de Rio, courses cyclistes, événements liés au carnaval, etc.

4

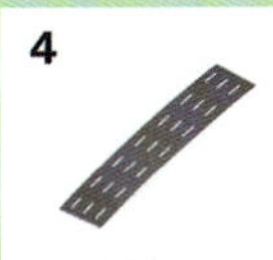

Highway

Since 2009, the municipality of Rio de Janeiro has blocked vehicular traffic on Sundays and public holidays, permitting leisure use only. This reestablishes urban space for pedestrians and encourages recreational cycling.

Autoroute

Depuis 2009, la ville de Rio de Janeiro interdit la circulation des véhicules le dimanche et les jours fériés ; seul les activités de loisir y sont autorisées. Cela rend l'espace urbain aux piétons et contribue au développement du cyclisme.

5

Vegetation

The highway is embedded in a park on a landfill that was conceived by the landscape designer Roberto Burle Marx. It features more than 200 different tree species from all over Brazil and is considered one of the most significant works of modernist landscape architecture.

Végétation

L'autoroute est intégrée dans un parc aménagé sur un vaste remblai, conçu par le paysagiste Roberto Burle Marx. Planté de 200 variétés d'arbres provenant du Brésil tout entier, on le considère comme l'un des exemples les plus marquants du paysagisme moderniste.

6

Street Vendors

Various activities emerged from the introduction of the closed highway: mobile academies, bike rentals, bars and street vendors selling food.

Services commerciaux mobiles

De nombreuses activités ont émergé depuis l'inauguration de l'autoroute fermée : location de vélos, bars, marchands ambulants vendant de la nourriture, etc.

7

Municipality

The municipality of Rio de Janeiro is the initiator of the car-free highway. The municipal government aims to improve the urban quality by promoting the use of public spaces on weekends, in turn guaranteeing the security of Flamengo Park.

Municipalité

La municipalité de Rio de Janeiro est à l'initiative de l'autoroute piétonne. Elle souhaite améliorer la qualité de la vie urbaine en encourageant l'utilisation des espaces publics le week-end. En contrepartie, la sécurité du parc Flamengo est assurée.

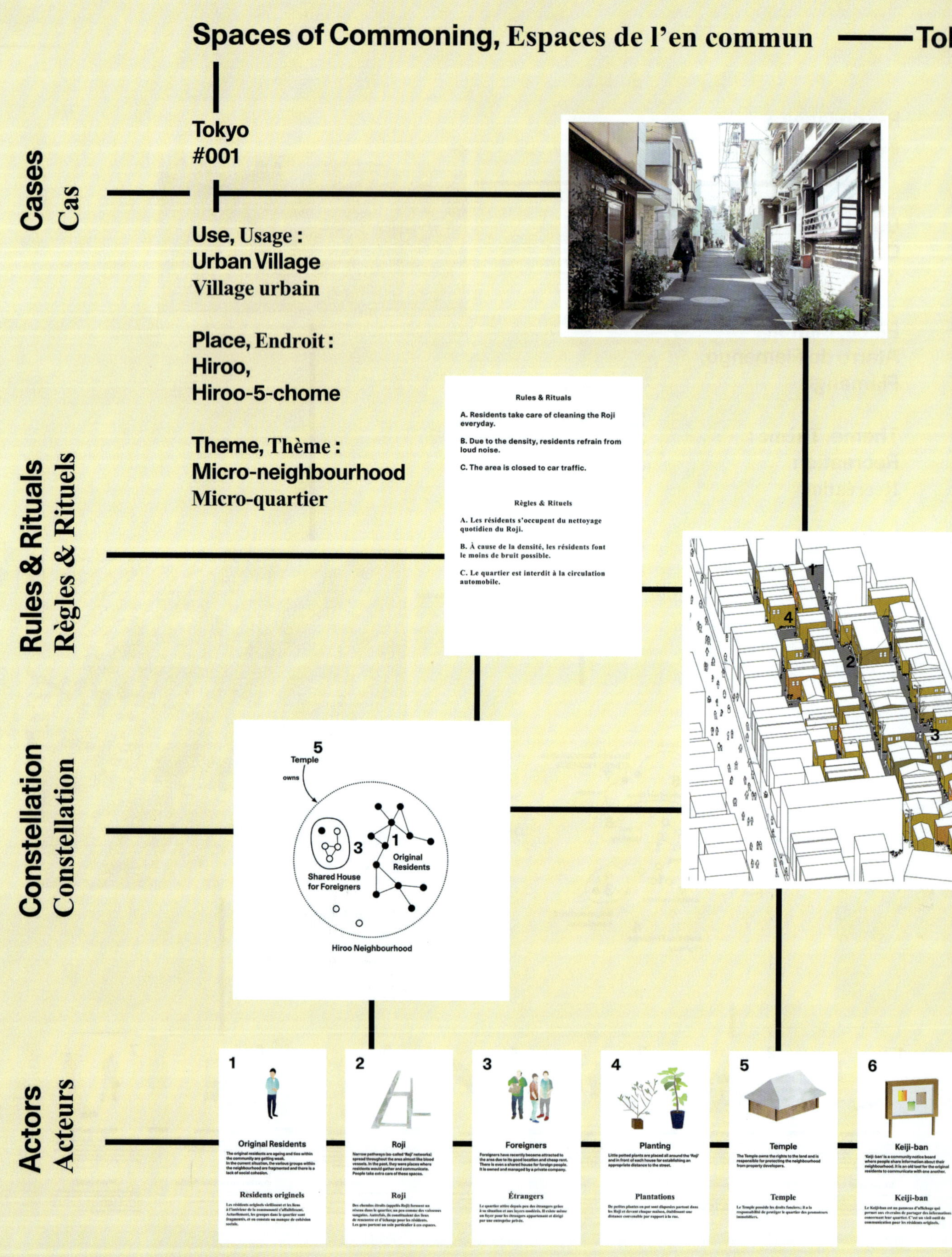

Spaces of Commoning, Espaces de l'en commun
Tok
Cases
Cas
Rules & Rituals
Règles & Rituels
Constellation
Constellation
Actors
Acteurs
Tokyo
#001
Use, Usage :
Urban Village
Village urbain
Place, Endroit :
Hiroo,
Hiroo-5-chome
Theme, Thème :
Micro-neighbourhood
Micro-quartier
Rules & Rituals
A. Residents take care of cleaning the Roji everyday.
B. Due to the density, residents refrain from loud noise.
C. The area is closed to car traffic.
Règles & Rituels
A. Les résidents s'occupent du nettoyage quotidien du Roji.
B. À cause de la densité, les résidents font le moins de bruit possible.
C. Le quartier est interdit à la circulation automobile.
1
4
2
3
5
Temple
owns
3
Shared House for Foreigners
1
Original Residents
Hiroo Neighbourhood
1
Original Residents
The original residents are ageing and ties within the community are getting weak.
In the current situation, the various groups within the neighbourhood are fragmented and there is a lack of social cohesion.
Residents originels
Les résidents originels vieillissent et les liens à l'intérieur de la communauté s'affaiblissent. Actuellement, les groupes dans le quartier sont fragmentés, et on constate un manque de cohésion sociale.
2
Roji
Narrow pathways (so-called 'Roji' networks) spread throughout the area almost like blood vessels. In the past, they were places where residents would gather and communicate. People take extra care of these spaces.
Roji
Des chemins étroits (appelés Roji) forment un réseau dans le quartier, un peu comme des vaisseaux sanguins. Autrefois, ils constituaient des lieux de rencontre et d'échange pour les résidents. Les gens portent un soin particulier à ces espaces.
3
Foreigners
Foreigners have recently become attracted to the area due to its good location and cheap rent. There is even a shared house for foreign people. It is owned and managed by a private company.
Étrangers
Le quartier attire depuis peu des étrangers grâce à sa situation et aux loyers modérés. Il existe même un foyer pour les étrangers appartenant et dirigé par une entreprise privée.
4
Planting
Little potted plants are placed all around the 'Roji' and in front of each house for establishing an appropriate distance to the street.
Plantations
De petites plantes en pot sont disposées partout dans les Roji et devant chaque maison, établissant une distance convenable par rapport à la rue.
5
Temple
The Temple owns the rights to the land and is responsible for protecting the neighbourhood from property developers.
Temple
Le Temple possède les droits fonciers ; il a la responsabilité de protéger le quartier des promoteurs immobiliers.
6
Keiji-ban
'Keiji-ban' is a community notice board where people share information about their neighbourhood. It is an old tool for the original residents to communicate with one another.
Keiji-ban
Le Keiji-ban est un panneau d'affichage qui permet aux riverains de partager des informations concernant leur quartier. C'est un vieil outil de communication pour les résidents originels.

Tokyo
#002

Use, Usage :
Jogging Track
Parcours de jogging

Place, Endroit :
Imperial Palace Outer Circuit, Chiyoda Ward

Theme, Thème :
Recreation
Recréation

Rules & Rituals

A. Runners can only jog in a counterclockwise direction.

B. For safety reasons, runners are not allowed to use their phone while jogging.

C. Runners must give priority to pedestrians.

D. Use of the running stations requires membership.

Règles & Rituels

A. On doit courir dans le sens inverse des aiguilles d'une montre.

B. Pour des raisons de sécurité, il est interdit d'utiliser son téléphone portable en courant.

C. Les coureurs doivent donner la priorité aux piétons.

D. Il faut être membre pour utiliser les stations de course.

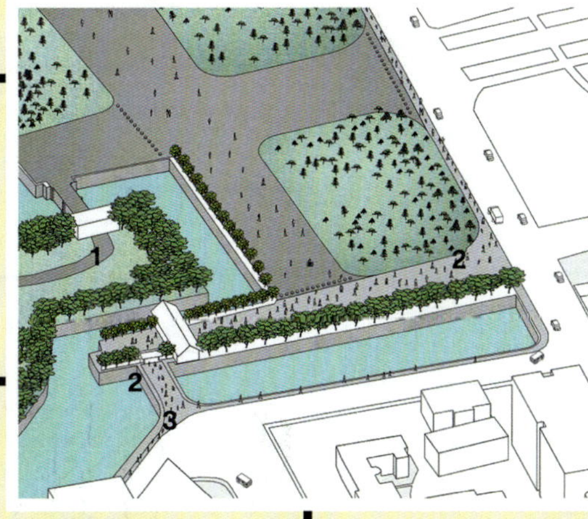

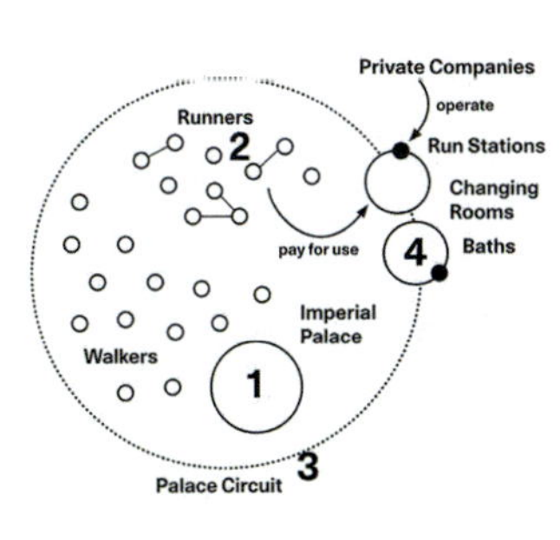

1

Imperial Palace

The Imperial Palace is the residence of the Emperor of Japan and is located in the center of Tokyo. It is surrounded by a moat and covered with greenery.

Palais imperial

Le Palais impérial, résidence de l'Empereur du Japon, est situé au centre de Tokyo. Il est entouré par des douves, au centre dans un écrin de verdure.

2

Runners

People working in the surrounding area use the outer circumference of the Imperial Palace as a running track for their daily exercise, from 5:30 PM till 9:00 PM in particular.

Coureurs

Des personnes qui travaillent dans les alentours utilisent le chemin qui entoure le Palais impérial pour courir, surtout entre 17h30 et 21h.

3

Jogging Path

The outer circumference of the Imperial Palace is approximately 5 km, making it easy for the runners to keep track of the distance they cover. Several places, including 'Sakurada-mon gate', are used as starting points.

Piste de footing

L'enceinte du Palais impérial fait environ 5 km de circonférence, ce qui facilite la mesure de la distance parcourue pour les coureurs. Plusieurs endroits, dont la porte Sakurada-mon, servent de points de départ.

4

Running Stations

With so many people jogging around the Imperial Palace, private companies have developed 'running stations' where people pay to use changing rooms and showers. The facilities are available to members only.

Stations de course

Le nombre de coureurs est tellement important que des entreprises privées ont créé des « stations de course » où les gens paient pour utiliser des vestiaires et des douches. Ces équipements sont réservés aux membres.

5

Jogging Apps

People use running apps in order to record their time spent jogging. Furthermore, they share their data through social networks, enabling joggers to compete with each other. These virtual communities motivate more and more people to jog around the palace.

Applis de Course

Les gens utilisent ces applis pour enregistrer leurs temps de parcours. Ils partagent ces données via les réseaux sociaux, ce qui permet aux coureurs d'entrer en compétition les uns avec les autres. Ces communautés virtuelles motivent de plus en plus de gens à courir autour du Palais impérial.

6

Website

Through the Website www.palacerunning.com information about running stations, events, rules and behavioral protocol is provided to the runners.

Site Web

Le site www.palacerunning.com fournit aux coureurs des renseignements sur les stations de course, sur le programme des événements, sur les règles à respecter et les comportements à adopter en courant autour du Palais impérial.

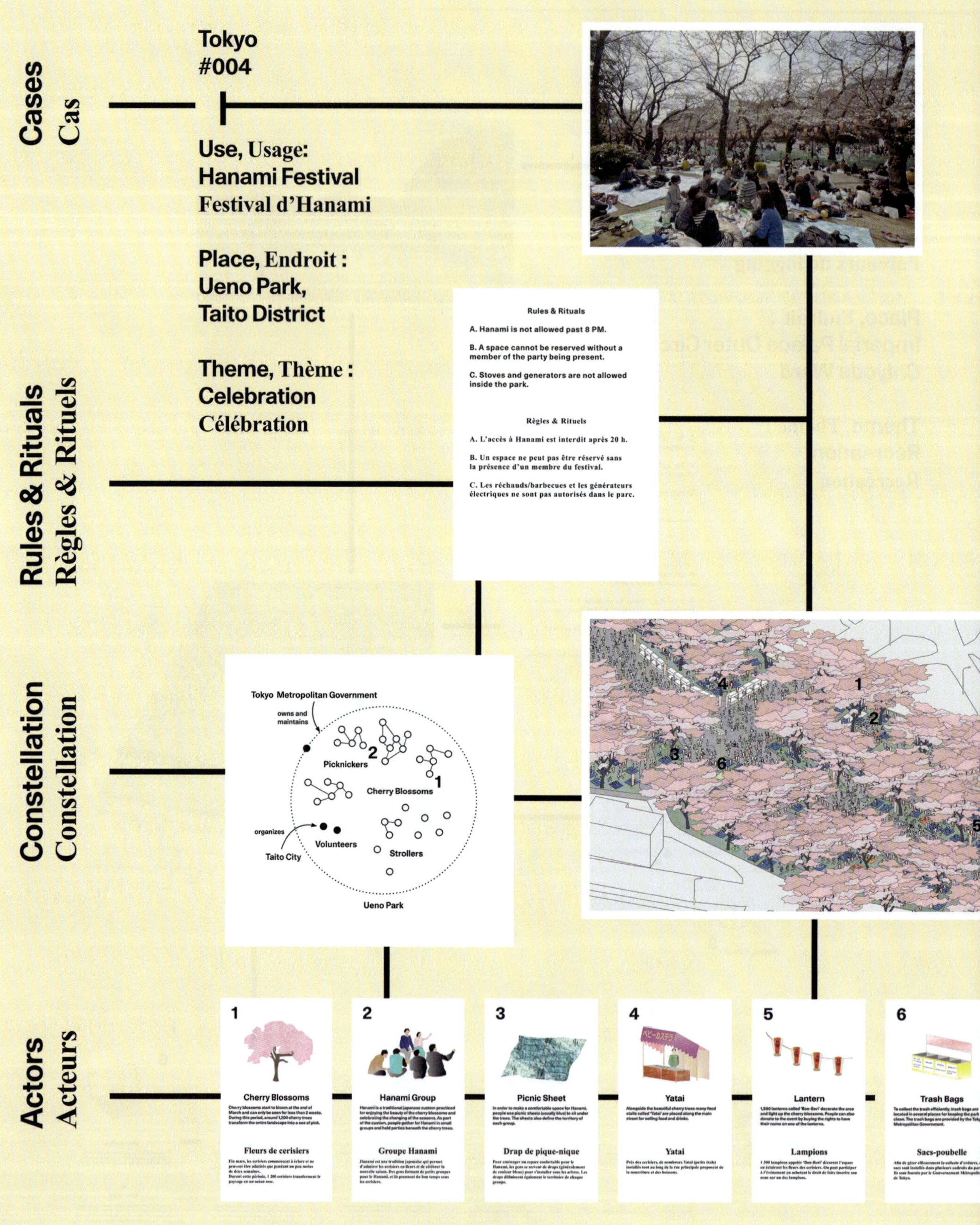
Cases
Cas
Tokyo
#004
Use, Usage:
Hanami Festival
Festival d'Hanami
Place, Endroit :
Ueno Park,
Taito District
Theme, Thème :
Celebration
Célébration
Rules & Rituals
Règles & Rituels
Rules & Rituals
A. Hanami is not allowed past 8 PM.
B. A space cannot be reserved without a member of the party being present.
C. Stoves and generators are not allowed inside the park.
Règles & Rituels
A. L'accès à Hanami est interdit après 20 h.
B. Un espace ne peut pas être réservé sans la présence d'un membre du festival.
C. Les réchauds/barbecues et les générateurs électriques ne sont pas autorisés dans le parc.
Constellation
Constellation
Tokyo Metropolitan Government
owns and maintains
2
Picknickers
1
Cherry Blossoms
organizes
Volunteers
Taito City
Strollers
Ueno Park
4
1
2
3
6
5
Actors
Acteurs
1
Cherry Blossoms
Cherry blossoms start to bloom at the end of March and can only be seen for less than 2 weeks. During this period, around 1,200 cherry trees transform the entire landscape into a sea of pink.
Fleurs de cerisiers
Fin mars, les cerisiers commencent à éclore et ne peuvent être admirés que pendant un peu moins de deux semaines.
Durant cette période, 1 200 cerisiers transforment le paysage en un océan rose.
2
Hanami Group
Hanami is a traditional japanese custom practiced for enjoying the beauty of the cherry blossoms and celebrating the changing of the seasons. As part of the custom, people gather for Hanami in small groups and hold parties beneath the cherry trees.
Groupe Hanami
Hanami est une tradition japonaise qui permet d'admirer les cerisiers en fleurs et de célébrer la nouvelle saison. Des gens forment de petits groupes pour le Hanami, et ils prennent du bon temps sous les cerisiers.
3
Picnic Sheet
In order to make a comfortable space for Hanami, people use picnic sheets (usually blue) to sit under the trees. The sheets also define the territory of each group.
Drap de pique-nique
Pour aménager un espace confortable pour le Hanami, les gens se servent de draps (généralement de couleur bleue) pour s'installer sous les arbres. Les draps définissent également le territoire de chaque groupe.
4
ベビーカステラ
Yatai
Alongside the beautiful cherry trees many food stalls called 'Yatai' are placed along the main street for selling food and drinks.
Yatai
Près des cerisiers, de nombreux Yatai (petits étals) installés tout au long de la rue principale proposent de la nourriture et des boissons.
5
Lantern
1,300 lanterns called 'Bon-Bori' decorate the area and light up the cherry blossoms. People can also donate to the event by buying the rights to have their name on one of the lanterns.
Lampions
1 300 lampions appelés 'Bon-Bori' décorent l'espace en éclairant les fleurs des cerisiers. On peut participer à l'événement en achetant le droit de faire inscrire son nom sur un des lampions.
6
Trash Bags
To collect the trash efficiently, trash bags are located in several places for keeping the park clean. The trash bags are provided by the Tokyo Metropolitan Government.
Sacs-poubelle
Afin de gérer efficacement la collecte d'ordures, de
sacs sont installés dans plusieurs endroits du parc.
Ils sont fournis par le Gouvernement Métropolitai
de Tokyo.

Tokyo
#005

Use, Usage :
Drinking Stand
Buvette

Place, Endroit :
Yurakucho Station,
Yurakucho District

Theme, Thème :
Commuting
Transit

Rules & Rituals

A. The space is used by people who buy drinks from the vending machines.

B. People clean up after themselves before leaving the space.

C. Smoking is permitted in designated areas.

Règles & Rituels

A. L'espace est utilisé par des gens qui achètent des boissons aux distributeurs.

B. Les gens doivent laisser l'espace propre en partant.

C. On peut fumer dans les espaces prévus à cet effet.

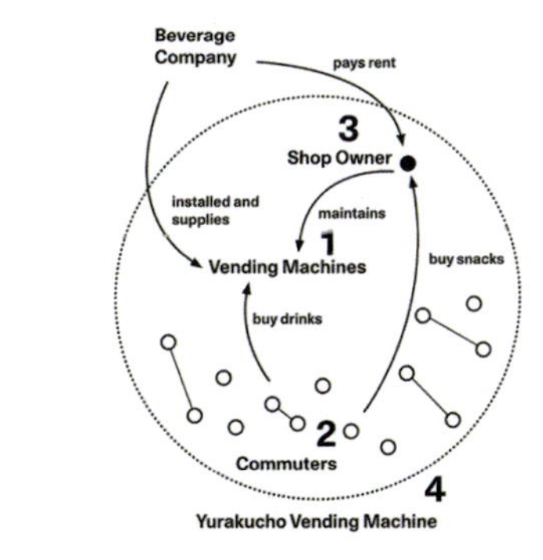

1

Vending Machines

Vending machines are placed inside the niche and provide non-alcoholic as well as alcoholic drinks. They also give a decent level of illumination to the space, shining onto the street.

Distributeurs

Des distributeurs de boissons alcoolisées et non alcoolisées sont installés dans la niche. Ils contribuent également à éclairer l'espace et la rue environnante.

2

Office Workers

Yurakucho is one of the busiest business districts in the center of Tokyo. Office workers use this place as a rest stop on their way home or before going out to a nearby restaurant or bar.

Employés de Bureau

Yurakucho est un des quartiers d'affaires les plus animés du centre de Tokyo. Les employés de bureau s'arrêtent à cet endroit en rentrant chez eux ou avant de se rendre à un restaurant ou un bar dans les environs.

3

Shopkeeper

The shopkeeper manages the drinking stand and sells snacks throughout the day. He can choose when he wants to be there. Since the place is somewhat organized by the vending machines themselves, he doesn't need to be present 24/7.

Commercant

Le commerçant gère la buvette et vend des en-cas toute la journée. Il peut choisir ses heures de présence : grâce aux distributeurs, il n'a pas besoin d'être là en permanence.

4

Elevated Rail Track

The drinking stand is located under an elevated rail track. It provides a space to smoke and acts as a refuge for the local office workers.

Voie aérienne

La buvette se trouve sous une voie aérienne de chemin de fer. C'est un endroit où on peut fumer, et il sert de refuge pour les employés de bureau.

5

Smoking Area

Since the numbers of smoking areas are limited, many smokers use this place as a rest stop to relax with a coffee or a beer.

Espace fumeurs

Puisqu'il existe un nombre limité d'espaces fumeurs, beaucoup de fumeurs s'arrêtent ici pour un moment de détente avec un café ou une bière.

6

Stainless Steel Table

Little stainless steel tables are placed in front of the niche and are used by people to hold their bags and drinks. The entire space is carefully designed by the placement of these stainless steel tables and their relation to the vending machines.

Table en inox

De petites tables en inox sont installées devant la buvette ; on peut y poser son sac et sa boisson. La configuration de l'espace dépend de la disposition savante des tables par rapport aux distributeurs automatiques.

South West Resilience

Johannesburg / Uzeste / Detroit

Inhabitant expertise

Bordeaux architect Christophe Hutin starts with the observation that inhabitants are the experts of their daily lives, and that they often drive new ways of inhabiting the world. In critical urban situations in Detroit, Johannesburg and Bordeaux, he meets people who have positioned themselves as leaders and who are changing the status quo within their communities.

In this video installation, he presents testimonials alongside documentary photographs and simple but ambitious projects that strongly involve the local population. Top-down points of view disappear, and instead the visitor is placed in a direct relationship with people who are changing their day-to-day lives on a daily basis. According to Gilles Deleuze, "the minority is everyone", and what the architect shows us here is a process of bottom-up democratic inclusion.

www.christophehutin.com/CH/Christophe_Hutin.html

—

photographies and videos © Christophe Hutin
comic strip: Nicolas Hubrecht

Christophe Hutin Bordeaux

How do we inhabit the world?

If we consider that the world's inhabitants are the experts of their own daily lives, they are able to answer that question. This installation calls on their expertise via testimonials and documentary photographs, and projects they are involved in with students as part of educational programmes focusing on architecture. Where politics fails, they have become organisational "leaders" within their communities and their environment. Their work and on-going initiatives also have a documentary value.

The idea is not to look at the world in a self-centred way but to bring the world in, gathering the information and knowledge it holds. Continuing on from his book *Le Parlement des invisibles,* the movement set in motion by Pierre Rosanvallon aims to give "silent" individuals the opportunity to express themselves by removing not only the filters between the public and the subject, but also instances of exterior, top-down expertise.

The visitor comes into direct contact with unique dwelling situations, reflecting Gilles Deleuze's words: "The minority is everyone". The situations shown here escape urban planning—we might call them examples of social and spatial invisibility.

The exhibition focuses on three cities—Johannesburg, Detroit and Uzeste—showing inhabitants in their everyday environment and artists interrogating the world around them.

Si le gouvernement pouvait nous aider.

IBRE AVEC la
héâtre Amusicien

La Garonne est un océan qui coule à Kliptown

Nicolas Hubrecht

This semi-autobiographical narrative is based on my experience over a period of ten years or so in two places, the district of Bègles in the south of Bordeaux (France) and the district of Kliptown in Soweto to the southwest of Johannesburg (South Africa).

On the French side the story describes my early investigations between 2005 and 2006 as an architecture student in a social housing estate, the Yves Farges estate which was part of a major urban redevelopment scheme (the Borloo demolition and reconstruction law), and thus in a process of significant transformation. On the South African side, the story focuses on my on-the-spot experience as a teacher in the "Learning from 2014" workshop run by Daniel Estevez and Christophe Hutin (École Nationale Supérieure d'Architecture in Toulouse) in the Kliptown area where we were running a community project with students to reopen a local cinema, the Sans Souci.

Although these two districts are different in many respects (culturally, socially, in urban terms) and are about 8,000 kilometres apart, they are both areas that suffer, or have suffered, from economic and social problems and can thus teach us a great deal.

Beyond their stigmatised architectural forms (high-rise estates in Bègles, a township of shacks and slums in Kliptown), I wanted to show "slices of life" and was naturally drawn to their inhabitants and the way they live their daily lives. My role, as a student or an architect, was to be present, to listen, to observe and to learn about these local residents who are, first and foremost, actively involved in their own lives.

Plates 6 to 10 are inspired by and show daily life in the Yves Farges estate in Bègles, in particular the labourer and priest Pierre Dubois (1938-2008) who lived for many years on the 14th floor of Block E. Actively involved in the estate (nobody knew it like he did) until it was demolished—the final years of the estate as he knew it—he fought to highlight not only the value of the residential buildings themselves but also their identity and the people who lived there. The book is dedicated to him. He sparked my curiosity as a young architecture student.

The South African section of the story illustrated by the first five and last five plates attempts to transcribe the daily lives of volunteer community workers in Kliptown including Prince Massingham, Sophy Wentzel and Ginger Mallhamvu whose project involved reopening a local cinema, which is in ruins although it was, in the past, a local institution and remains a powerful symbol.

These insights into day-to-day approaches, transcribed via the narrative protocol of a graphic novel, teach us an essential lesson about how to design embodied architecture.

Nicolas Hubrecht

C'est une vue magnifique que vous avez là Pierro.
Oui tout mon univers est là sous mes yeux.
La verrerie d'Aquitaine, la salle Saint-Maurice, la Garonne, le pont François Mitterrand, la rive droite, puis Bouliac, son église, Cadaujac, c'est infini.
Oui, on pourrait rester des heures à regarder...
Mais les gens ne se doutent pas que nous avons une telle vue ici.
Oui, en effet. Quel dommage, ce paysage, il en dit des choses pourtant.
Ce paysage c'est mon univers. J'en ai partagé toutes les facettes, les tristesses, les bonheurs depuis que je suis arrivé à Bègles il y a 40 ans.
Depuis quand vivez vous dans la cité?
Ça fait 12 ans que j'habite ici, avant j'étais à l'Eglise Saint-François.

Tu vois le problème de Kliptown c'est que tout est négligé... Regarde nos WC et nos égouts..

Nous n'avons même pas l'essentiel... alors maintenir notre patrimoine dans ces conditions c'est encore plus dur. Mais nous ne baissons pas les bras pour autant.

Ah tiens, voila un bel exemple de notre persévérance du quotidien, le jardin de Ginger!

Ginger est un personnage incroyable.. Avant c'était un bandit, il volait pour survivre. Il a fait pas mal de prison alors qu'il était assez jeune.

Puis il est revenu ici. S'occuper des jardins du quartier et des voisins l'aida à se réintégrer à la communauté.

Differently human

Difference only serves the complementarity of knowledge—a sap to be savoured
It's time to be differently human and to offer the world our love

If your family tree is a rainbow eucalyptus too
If you too know the magic of combining materials that only art can teach you
If you too have heard of the legend of the flood and the great ancient ark
Then you know that Humanity is just one people seen from way up there
A single people with several languages several cultures and several skin colours

If you too dream that peace is being prepared down there and upstream in the love poems
If you're able to learn to speak all of the world's dialects in a true act of bravery
Because difference only serves the complementarity of knowledge—a sap to be savoured
Then you know that Humanity is just one people seen from way up there
A single people with several languages several cultures and several skin colours

If you too in the silence of the city ask the stars to locate you
Somewhere between the fibre of your soul and the colour of the fabric it came from
Taking the fingerprints of History by looking for people who look like you
Then remember that Humanity is just one people seen from way up there
A single people with several languages several cultures and several skin colours

Souleymane Diamanka

Friday 23 September 2016

créolisations
Conversation + music & dance organised by **Christophe Hutin**, architect, relating to his South West Resilience project with:
Andrew Diamond, historian
Erik Howard, photographer
Sacramento Knoxx, musician
Hamid Ben Mahi, choreographer

Nuit créolisation

In reference to Édouard Glissant's *Tout-monde*, artists associated with each situation can produce a blended artwork reflecting the theme of the exhibition. The aim is to put the spirit of the show into practice via a cultural programme involving the people who appear in the videos: inhabitants of Johannesburg, Detroit and Uzeste. The event will take place on 23 September 2016: it will suggest how it is possible to inhabit the world, here and now, by experimenting with creolised cultural creations.

Conversion of 530 flats

37

Bordeaux

Taking care of a high-rise and the people who live there

For Anne Lacaton, Jean-Philippe Vassal, Frédéric Druot and Christophe Hutin, high-rises are "exceptional territories" whose transformation brings an economical, efficient and qualitative response to housing needs. This stance, which is radically different from current urban renovation policy, which focuses more on demolition and reconstruction, is reflected in the Grand Parc district in Bordeaux where, along with the social housing body Aquitanis, they are developing a process whose value was demonstrated by their last two projects.
Thanks to conservatories added to the façades, the flats gain in surface area, comfort and light, and offer residents improved quality of life. As Philippe Ruault's photos show, the minimal and repetitive architecture takes a back seat with respect to the many different uses it makes possible. The simplicity that characterises the project is, paradoxically, highly unusual.

www.lacatonvassal.com

—

photos: © Philippe Ruault

Lacaton & Vassal, Frédéric Druot Paris
Christophe Hutin architect Bordeaux
Philippe Ruault photographer Nantes
with aquitanis

Gounod, Haendel and Ingres residential buildings

GHI: génération d'habitat innovant
3 blocks/ 530 flats/ Grand-Parc district, Bordeaux
Build began **in 2012**: 20-30 month schedule
Budget: **28 million euros**
Architects: **Lacaton & Vassal** (Équerre d'argent 2011)
Frédéric Druot and Christophe Hutin, associate architects
Client: **aquitanis** (Bernard Blanc directeur général)

G.H.I. (Génération d'Habitat Innovant: generating innovative housing) is a project that increases dwelling space by starting with the occupant. Highly standardised cell-like flats are extended with conservatories, extra rooms whose use is not predefined. Grafted onto existing façades over 15 storeys, these exterior structures give each flat 25 to 45 square metres of extra space, providing the opportunity, as in a house, to live outside while remaining at home. Further interventions are planned: enlarging the bathrooms, creating exterior lifts and bike and pushchair parking areas, and landscaping.

Attitude

lt's a matter of never demolishing, subtracting or replacing things, but of always adding, transforming and utilising them.
"To have elements judged in advance as being very negative be seen as very positive, be it due to reversal or excess, means to bring about a development contrary to that of the disenchantment a place has been subject to." (Jean Nouvel)
This is a job of work whose goal is precision, delicacy, amiability and attentiveness: being attentive to people, uses, buildings, trees, asphalt or grass surfaces, to what already exists.

lt's a matter of causing the least inconvenience or no inconvenience at all.
lt's a matter of being generous, giving more, facilitating usage and simplifying life.

It's a matter of rethinking those arbitrary acts which seek to satisfy the inhabitants of the dwellings and to focus people's concerns on superficial or superfluous issues: the insulation of facades on the outside, the treatment of hallways, "residentialisation", the so-called "urban project", which is usually limited to dotting the built space with paving, granite kerbs, fencing, roundabouts, boundary markers, rows of plants, lighting, obsolete or useless urban principles of composition, etc., a set of obsessions that leaves the required thinking about the qualitative evolution of the dwellings to one side and denies changes in lifestyle and the demands of progress.

It's a matter of recreating the impact of postwar reconstruction, which had initiated the move from insalubrious to salubrious housing, and of instigating the pleasure of living in it.
This means embarking on a positive revolution whose aims are the exact opposite of demolition and reconstruction.

lt is frightening to observe that the only development housing has witnessed in the last forty years has been produced on the basis of norms and regulations.
Just as it is incredible to observe that, right now, demolished apartments are 15% larger than the ones that are being built now, when what ought to be recognised is a demand for different and bigger dwellings.

From Frédéric Druot, Anne Lacaton and Jean-Philippe Vassal, *Plus*, Gustavo Gilli, 2007

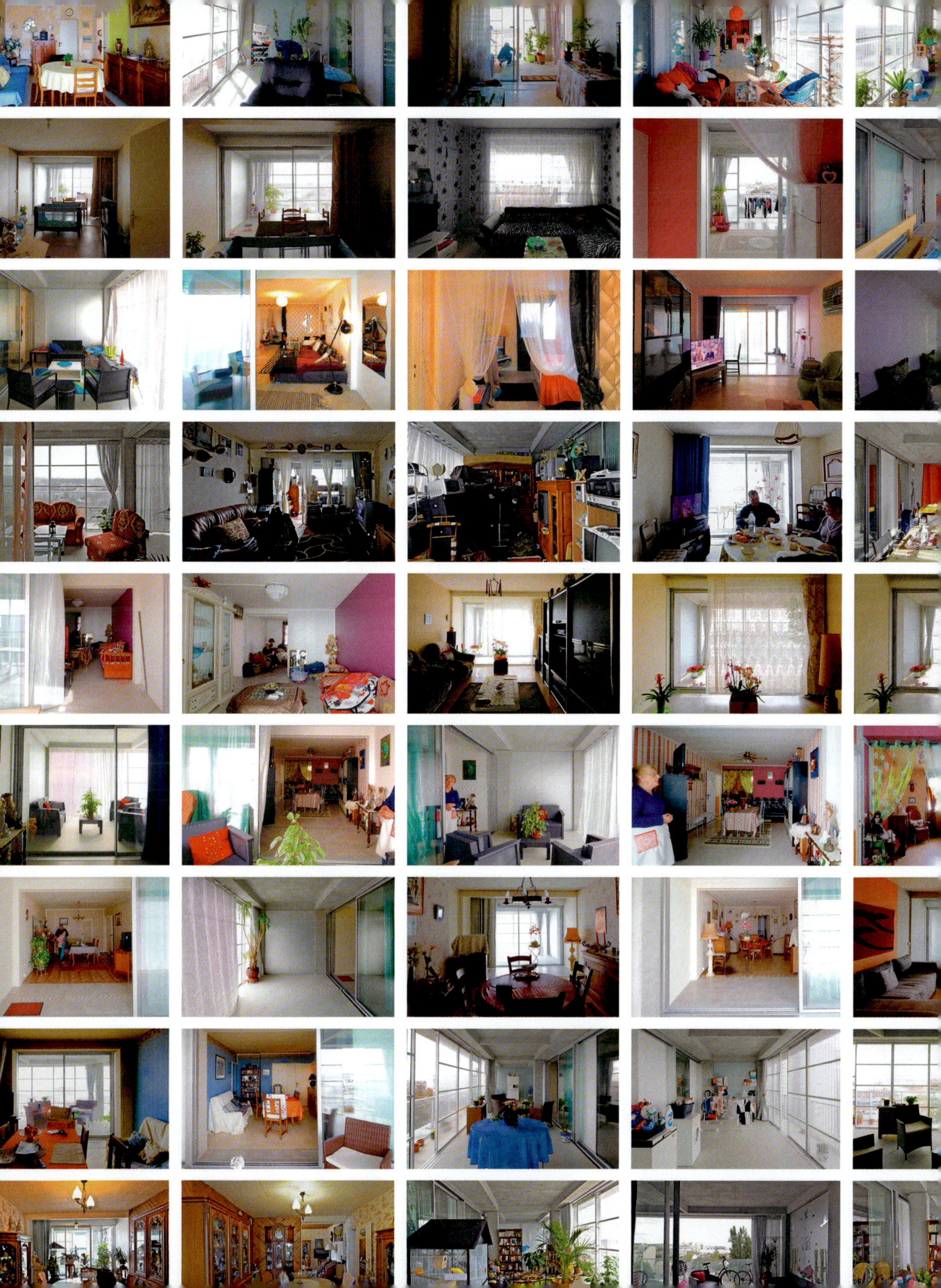

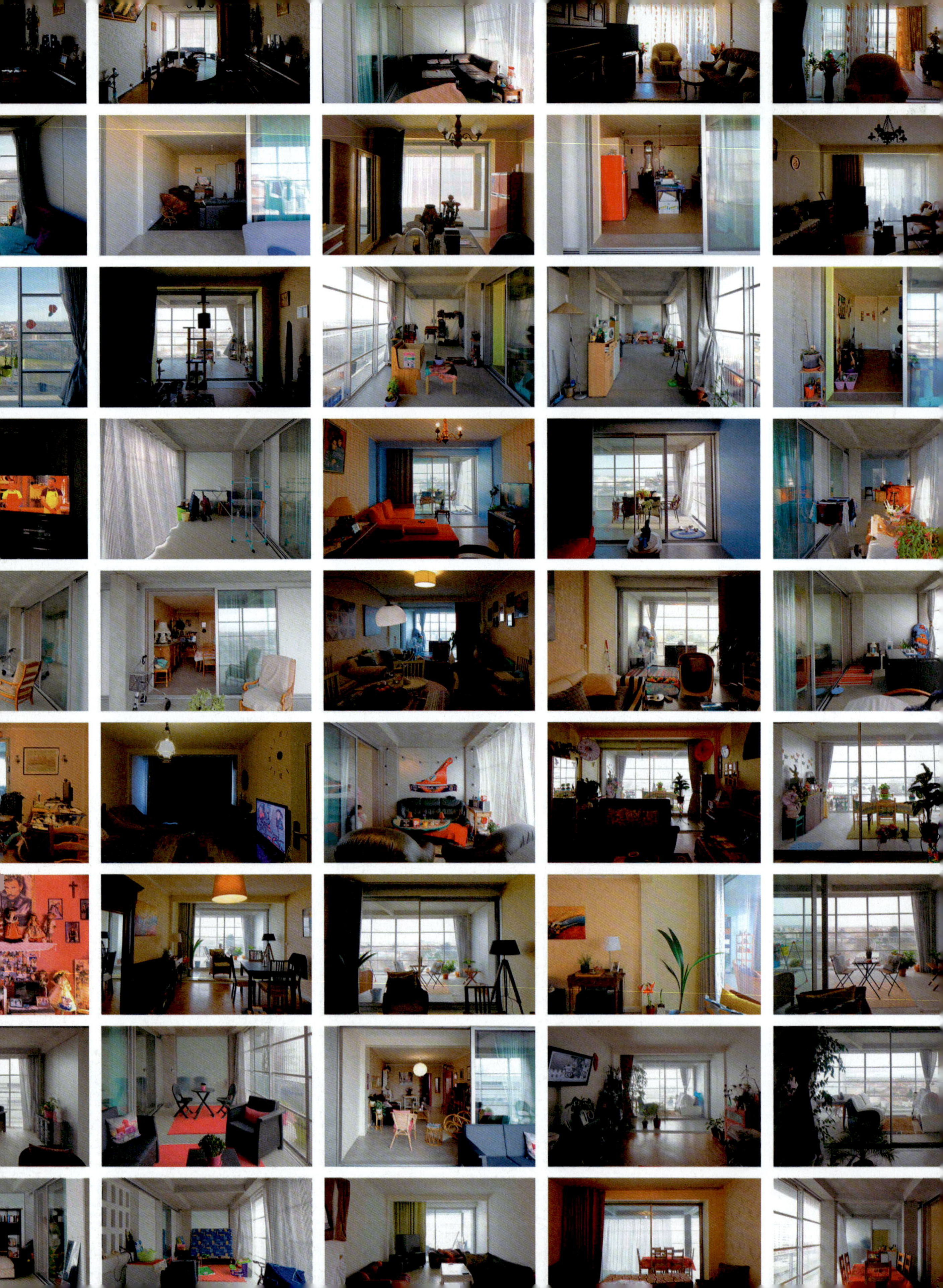

Urban-Data Complex

38

Gaza

Investigating the theatre of war

The Forensic Architecture firm works in areas of conflict such as the Palestinian Territories and Syria. Partnered with international organisations, it acts as a kind of forensic scientist of space, analysing the ruins left behind by armed conflict and precisely reconstituting events: the position of a sniper, the time of the attack, the type of ammunition used, and so on.

Like a forensic police unit for architecture, or like archaeologists of recent history, Forensic makes the urban context into a subject for judicial investigation. It cross-references information, collects testimonials, makes videos, and carries out inspections. Space holds an enigma where proof of a crime or a lie might be concealed: that of military propaganda, for example, whose arguments Forensic manages to disprove one by one.

www.forensic-architecture.org

Forensic Architecture London
Eyal Weizman

This project shines a light on the reality of Syrian detention centres. The forced "disappearance" of people who are thought to pose a political threat to the government is common practice under the current regime. People are held in atrocious conditions where torture is used as a means of social control. Although these acts take place in interrogation rooms, the doors are often left open so that the screams can be heard throughout the prison. This means that torture goes beyond physical pain: it is broadcast as sound through the corridors of the building. The conditions of imprisonment and the architecture of the prison are thus also used as instruments of torture.

This installation will consist of 4-6 screens arranged in a circle, showing interviews with former inmates describing their experiences. The audio descriptions will be broadcast simultaneously, and will thus intermingle. On a pedestal in the centre of the ring of screens, there will be 3D-printed model of the prison distorted by the memory of the survivors. The collective artefact of these shared experiences is a space that is warped by true-life accounts of torture and imprisonment.

Najjar Hospital
Hamdam wedding hall
Yussuf al-Najjar crossroad
supermarket
Uruba street / orooba St
Abu Shawarb building
watertower
Al Buyuki Area
Al Buyuki A
Sala al-Din Street
Al Buyuki Ar
Sala al-Din Street

tanks in AM shelling area
Tabit Zare'
Saaid Sayal Camp
Sala al-Din Street
Salah Eddin Street
Zoloda road

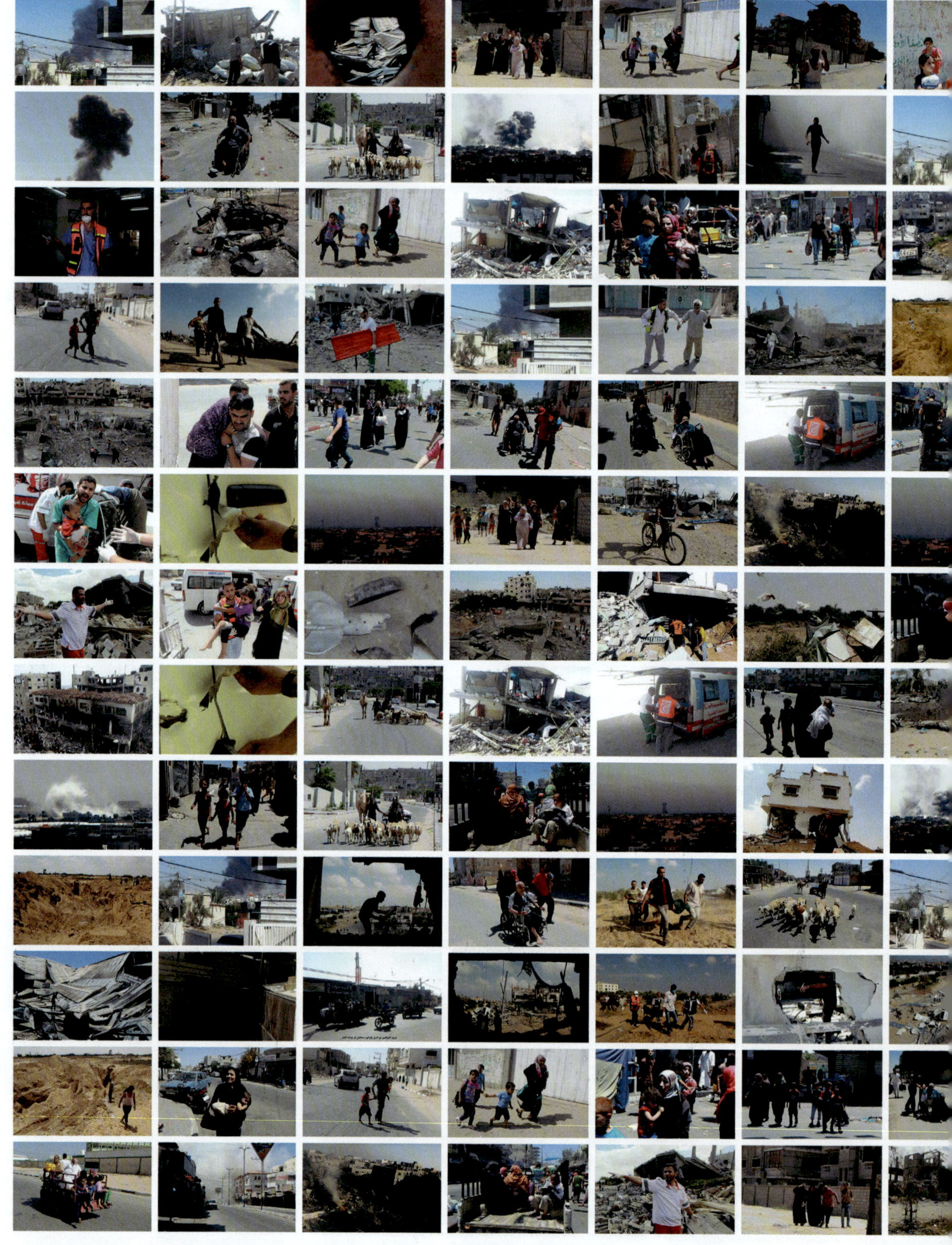

> previous pages
The master drawing of the Rafah investigation includes viewpoints and plume measurements from every photograph and video sourced, craters from airdropped bombs and artillery observed on the satellite images, tank paths and armoured vehicles on the move, identifiable buildings and reference points, possible tunnel routes as well as testimony mappings. The base image is a Pléiades satellite photograph of eastern Rafah, taken on 1st August 2014,11:39 am local time.

> left
When bombs started raining on the city, people took their cameras out to record events around them, often risking their lives in the process. They have photographed from the streets, from higher windows and rooftops, sometimes before running or instead of escaping, despite knowing that the Israeli military's open fire instruction is to shoot-to-kill anyone directing a camera at soldiers. The production of visual evidence that must be studied carefully. Reading these images is not a passive act, but one that requires construction.

> next pages
The Architectural-Image-Assemblage Architectural models provided an optical device and a means to compose the relation between all images and videos in space and time.

Vertical Gym

39

Caracas

Gyms in kit form in the middle of the slums

The slums on the slopes of Caracas, the capital of Venezuela, are among the most densely populated places in the world. In the light of this ultra-density and the need to provide elementary amenities, the local government and the Urban Think Tank team are creating sports and cultural complexes that literally stack up buildings on former football pitches, which are the only parts of these working-class districts that have not been built on. These Vertical Gyms, where the running track overlooks the basketball court or indoor football pitch, act as communal spaces in areas where violence is rife. They complement the urban cable car system that has already been constructed by the city authorities.
From a structural point of view, the facilities are assembled in kit form, which makes it easier to bring the necessary materials into often inaccessible areas. This system of public facilities and public transport contributes to the process of inclusion for working-class areas of Caracas.

www.u-tt.com

—

photos: © Iwan Baan; © Daniel Schwartz for UTT

Urban Think Tank Zurich

Urban think tank

Our work does not merely contemplate the city. We change it through direct intervention on its three scales: metropolitan, urban, and architectural. The projects have accordingly ranged from the design of a transportation hub (City Lifter), to the provision of housing in the Anglican Church, to a social/cultural centre (Vertical Gym). Rather than producing a symbolic or autonomous architecture, our practice has adopted concrete strategies for physical appropriation and production. Moreover, our work has aimed at reversing the top-down hierarchy of governance in the public sphere in favor of bottom-up, locally driven action. This reversal sets up new opportunities both for sustainable development in the informal city and for using on-the-ground experience to inform future theory. Ideal situations do not concern us. Our work is about avoiding catastrophes.

Ceiba

AMOR
Barinas

VIM, housing project

40

Bordeaux

A model for building our habitat together

Referencing Jean Prouvé's Métropole building, the structure of the 14 participative flats in the Benauge district of Bordeaux is simple, elementary and economical. Featuring a post-and-beam design with concrete floors, it is designed as a framework within which the future residents will be free to define the limits of their homes.
An essential tool for the participative experiment, a 1:20 scale wooden model of the building serves as an interface between the architects, the client and the residents. This collaborative system allows everyone to become their own interior designer by playing with furniture and partitions that can be inserted into the structural model.

www.atelierprovisoire.com

—

photos: © Gaëlle Deleflie
© Agnès Clotis + IO Studio Photographie

Atelier Provisoire Bordeaux
with aquitanis

Essential habitat: a flexible approach

In the era of BIM (Building Information Modelling) and smart buildings, where technology is king in terms of energy saving, the VIM project adopts an alternative approach. The project is based on low tech, structural economic solutions and an appropriate use of space. Inspired by Jean Prouvé, what is known as the "essential habitat" is based on values of simplicity, elementarity, logic and honesty, making aesthetic features arise from ethical principles. This notion, which has become a fundamental element of the Aquitanis sustainable development approach, gradually takes shape in this unique building. It is not predefined; instead it is the result of an "active conversation" between the architects at the Atelier Provisoire and the Aquitanis teams.

together
séparément
together
séparément
erforming Social Landscapes
Galerie / Gallery / Galeria
OGARDO ARAGÓN
ésoamérique : l'effet ouragan

The VIM housing development consists of a physical environment that is provided but whose spaces are not functionally predefined, making it possible for residents to extend the dwelling areas themselves according to their needs. The heated floors are open: the walls are installed with the future occupant based on a preliminary survey carried out by the architects and using a catalogue of lightweight components: dividing walls, doors, and room-dividing furniture units.

Location: Bordeaux
Programme: 14 flexible homes
Client: aquitanis OPH (Bernard Blanc directeur général)
Architects: Atelier Provisoire
Engineers: Cétab
Design: 2014-2015
Build: 2016-2017
Floor area: 1,525 sq.m.
Budget: €2,015,000 +tax

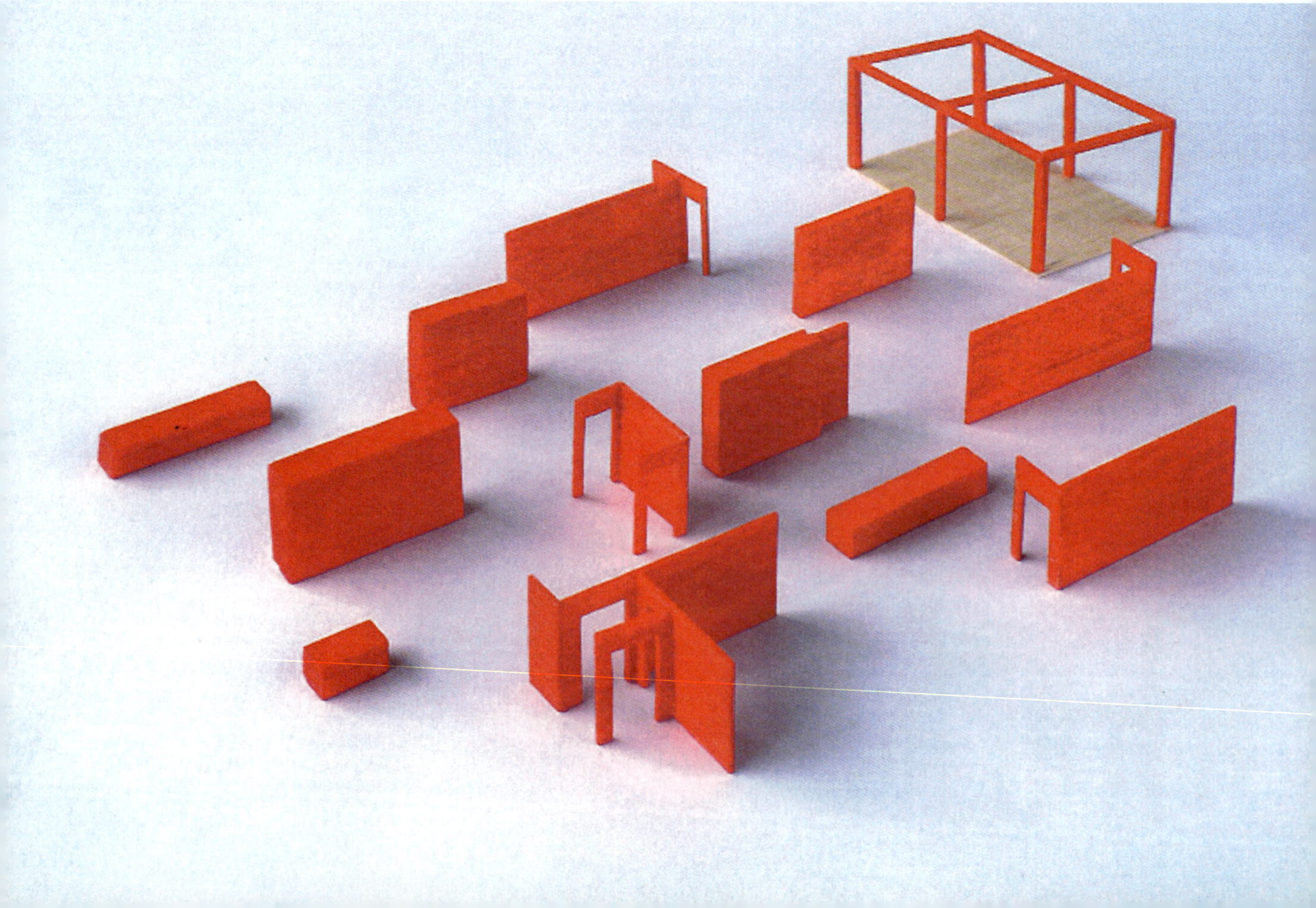

A visit to Kraftwerk

41

Zurich

Cohabitation between the private and the collective

The history of residential cooperatives in Switzerland goes back to the late nineteenth century. This type of housing, which allows groups of residents to live more affordably by pooling services, now accounts for 8% of property in the country and up to 20% in large towns.
In the Kraftwerk building in Zurich, the types of flats are deliberately varied in terms of layout so as to cater for very different lifestyles: flat-sharing in twelve-room apartments, families in more traditional flats, and so on. All social classes are represented. The scale of the buildings makes it possible to share services such as a grocery and a cafeteria, and collective projects abound although residents are free to choose whether they take part or not. "Living apart together" relies on a simple principle here: residents don't own their flats individually but collectively own the building.

www.martinetienne.com

Zurich

_ large city, population **1.3 million_ reference** in Europe for social housing_ cooperatives, 60,000 units, are the **leading provider** of housing _ **social innovation** driven by community pressure _ cooperatives are independent from the authorities, **democratic** and non-profit _ **density**, the cooperatives drive urban **regeneration** in outlying areas _ plots **made available** to the cooperatives by public authorities, under certain conditions _ design competitions organised by the municipality for the cooperatives, a vector for **quality architecture _ tenants are also co-owners** through the cooperative_ **affordable**, rents are 30% lower than market prices_ **a bold initiative,** 25% of the housing belongs to the cooperatives, the city aims to achieve 33% over the coming years.

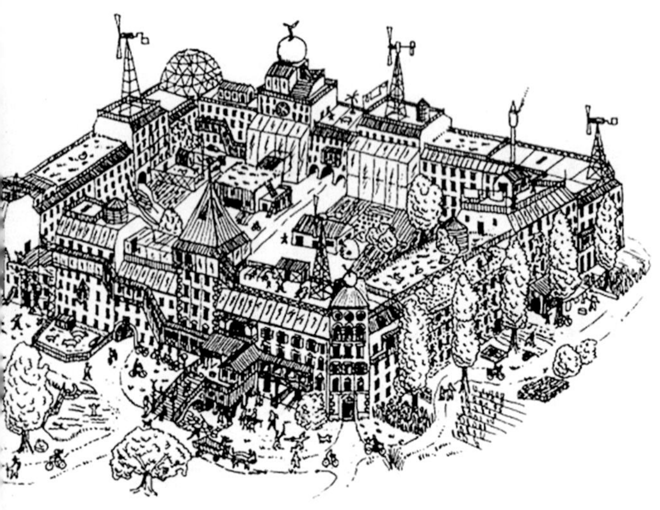

An "Urban Bolo" able to accommodate 500 people: illustration from the book by P.M. Bolo'Bolo, 1983

We plan …

… to create somewhere for hundreds of people to live,

… to create somewhere for hundreds of people to live,

… to show enough tolerance and generosity to respond to all kinds of different expectations,

… to manage contradictions creatively,

… to make affordable buildings in the framework of an ecologically and architecturally responsible project.

… to live without cars, but to avoid discriminating against people who think they need them,

… to embrace a multi-facetted, intense urban lifestyle, while taking into account the needs of the most vulnerable groups,

… to develop forms of collective mutual aid in these times of increased unemployment and social uncertainty,

… to preserve our unique characteristics while remaining open to the realities of the district and the city.

That's why we want to carry out our Kraftwerk 1 project on a recently vacated industrial site in Zurich.

Would you like to join us?

Kraftwerk1
DEUX LUXE WEST
coiffeur-salon

Drawings from *Voyage à Kraftwerk*,
Criticat n°11, spring 2013

Après moins de 15 minutes de trajet depuis la gare centrale de Zürich, le tramway me dépose sur la Hardturmstrasse, pile en face d'un immeuble à l'enduit rouge-corail sur lequel est écrit en gros "Kraftwerk 1". C'est bon, je ne me suis pas trompé d'adresse.
Derrière ce premier bâtiment composé de commerces à rez-de-chaussée et de plateaux de bureaux en étages se trouvent trois autres immeubles de logements, dont deux de dimensions et d'aspect similaires au premier. Au centre de l'ensemble, comme protégé par ses trois petits gardiens rouges, s'étire un immeuble beaucoup plus grand et revêtu de brique brune. C'est le coeur du dispositif et c'est dans celui-ci que se concentrera ma visite.

Après avoir traversé de long en large la parcelle, être rentré dans tous les halls, avoir gravi chaque escalier, ne sachant où exactement j'ai rendez-vous (je constate avec surprise que je peux rentrer partout, aucune porte n'est fermée) je finis par retrouver P.M. Son accueil est chaleureux, il prend le temps de me faire visiter les lieux de fond en comble, m'expliquant en détail le fonctionnement de cette "petite société" et me livrant bon nombre d'anecdotes sur l'histoire de Kraftwerk 1. Plus tard dans la journée, je retrouverai Andréas Hofer qui me parlera avec le même enthousiasme de ce projet auquel tous deux ont donné vie.

P.M. est un des membres fondateurs de Kraftwerk 1. Il est écrivain, enseignant à la retraite et toujours très actif au sein de la coopérative.

Andréas Hofer est lui aussi à l'origine du projet. Il est architecte (son agence est installée dans Kraftwerk 1) et s'investit énormément dans le développement de nouveaux projets Kraftwerk.

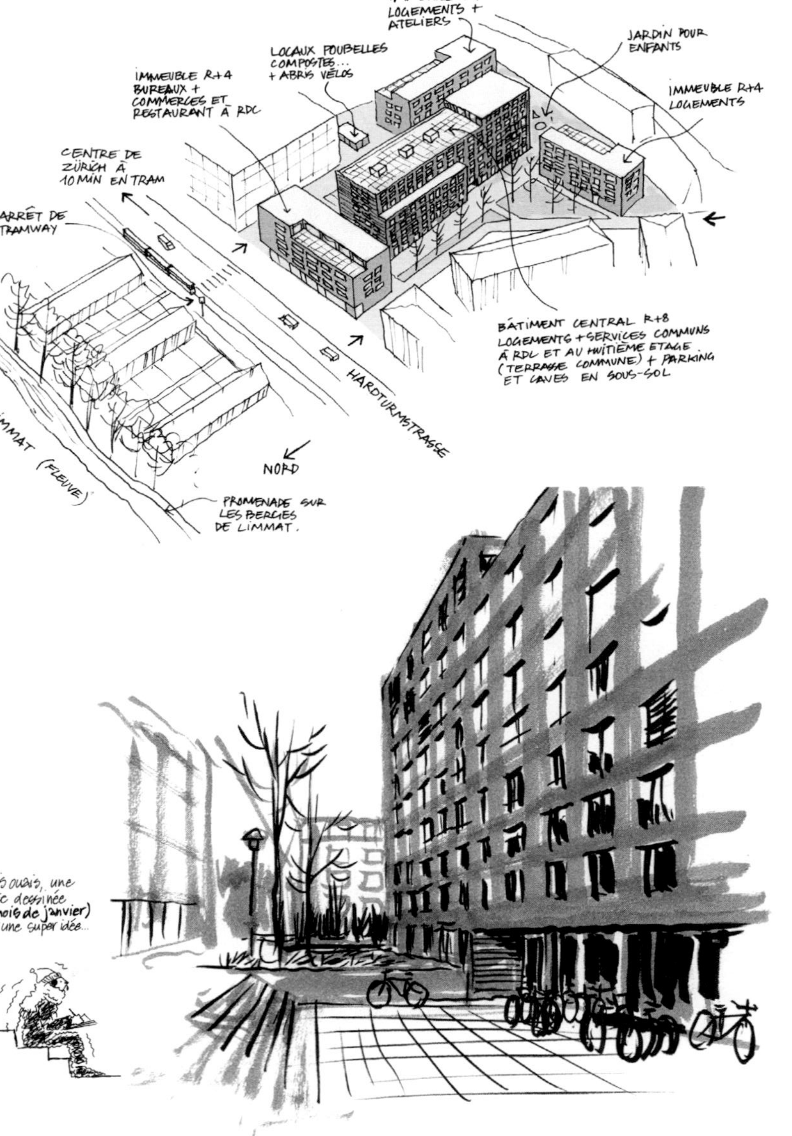

étagère pour l'échange de livres entre habitants.

laverie

poireaux bio achetés à l'épicerie

encore des livres

épicerie

"café pantoufles"

panneau d'info et de petites annonces échanges de services, évènements, etc

poussettes, vélos d'enfants et autres jouets stockés dans les sas d'entrée.

Dehors il pleut, alors les enfants jouent dans le hall

Le hall du bâtiment central s'étire en longueur pour desservir quatre cages d'escalier, des locaux d'activité, une crèche, un petit appartement (que chaque résident peut louer pour héberger des invités) et au centre : une laverie, une épicerie, une cafétéria.

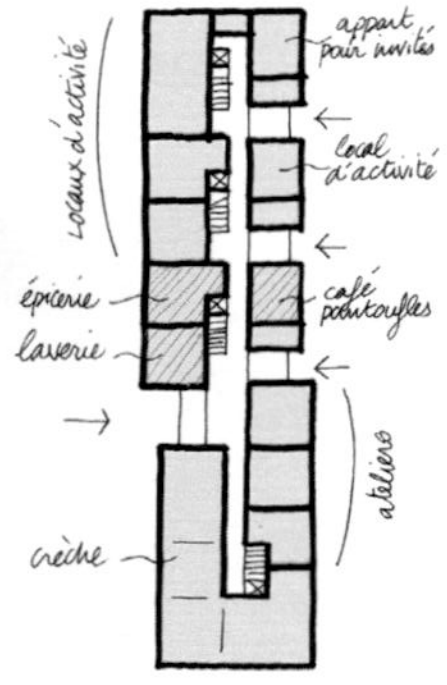

appart pour invités

local d'activité

café pantoufles

ateliers

locaux d'activité

épicerie

laverie

crèche

* les locaux d'activités, l'épicerie et la crèche ne sont pas réservés exclusivement aux habitants de Kraftwerk

Aucun des appartements de Kraftwerk n'est équipé de machine à laver. Tout le monde vient faire sa lessive dans ce "salon de lavage" ouvert sur le hall et largement vitré sur le jardin

La cafétéria, dite "café-pantoufles" est en libre service. On peut y descendre (en pantoufles donc...) à toute heure pour y boire un café, prendre l'apéro, lire les journaux du jour, s'affaler dans les canapés pour regarder le match à la télé.

INCROYABLE!!!
Y'a un cadenas sur le frigo! C'est la seule porte fermée à clé de tout l'immeuble. Les bières, ça doit être sacré chez Kraftwerk.

!!!

L'épicerie, gérée par un des habitants, est ouverte tous les soirs. On y trouve, entre autres, des fruits et légumes cultivés à quelques kilomètres de Zürich, sur des terrains appartenant à Kraftwerk. Une coopérative laitière livre chaque jour des produits frais. Evidemment, ici tout est bio.

Alors que je suis en train de dessiner dans le hall, un chat, visiblement seul habitant intrigué par ma présence, vient s'asseoir à mes côtés. J'apprendrai plus tard que son propriétaire a déménagé il y a quelques mois, mais le chat a préféré rester.
Il passe d'appartement en appartement, les habitants le nourrissent tour à tour, c'est désormais le chat de la coopérative.

Un baby-foot trône devant les boîtes aux lettres, les couloirs d'étage sont remplis de porte-manteaux, chaussures, petits meubles de rangement, jouets d'enfants... Tous les espaces communs sont investis et agréablement partagés.

Andréas m'invite à boire un café chez "lui". Il partage un duplex de près de 300m² avec 11 autres occupants ! Les profils sont divers : suisses, étrangers, célibataires, couple avec enfant, jeune étudiant, actifs plus âgés... Mais tous ont en commun ce désir d'habiter à plusieurs (et à Kraftwerk). Dans leur immense salon soigneusement meublé, règne un calme loin du désordre que j'aurais pu supposer.

Mais alors, comment vous faites pour les courses ?... Vous dînez toujours à 12 ?... Et quand vous voulez inviter des "amis" ?...

Sur un ton lassé, Andréas me répond : "Tout ça, ce sont des problèmes théoriques." Je crois qu'il a trouvé la parade parfaite à ces questions qu'on a dû lui poser 260000 fois. Déconcerté, je change de sujet.

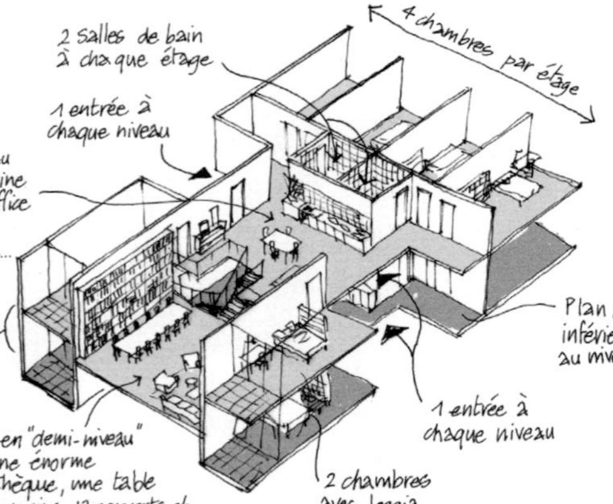

4 chambres par étage

2 salles de bain à chaque étage

1 entrée à chaque niveau

1 cuisine principale au niveau bas et 1 cuisine secondaire qui fait office de deuxième salon, entrée, coin bureau, etc... au niveau supérieur.

2 chambres avec loggia

Salon en "demi-niveau" avec une énorme bibliothèque, une table pour au moins 12 couverts et plein de canapés.

2 chambres avec loggia

1 entrée à chaque niveau

Plan du niveau inférieur identique au niveau supérieur.

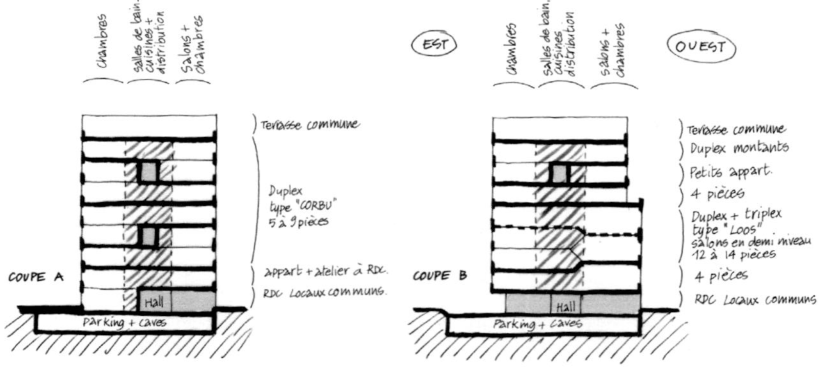

COUPE A

chambres | salles de bain + cuisines + distribution | salons + chambres

Terrasse commune

Duplex type "CORBU" 5 à 9 pièces

appart + atelier à RDC.

RDC Locaux communs.

Hall

Parking + caves

EST

OUEST

COUPE B

chambres | salles de bain, cuisines distribution | salons + chambres

Terrasse commune

Duplex montants

Petits appart.

4 pièces

Duplex + triplex type "Loos" salons en demi niveau 12 à 14 pièces

4 pièces

RDC Locaux communs

Hall

Parking + caves

A B

NIV. 3

Duplex type "CORBU"

grands duplex et triplex type "Loos"

Les 4 cages d'escalier et la régularité de la trame constructive ont permis une grande variété typologique de logements, du 2 au 14 pièces, assurant ainsi une diversité des modes d'habitat : personnes seules, familles, cohabitations plus ou moins grandes, jusqu'à 15, dans les triplex que je n'ai malheureusement pas pu voir.

Je visite aussi un appartement de 4 pièces, l'agencement y est plus conventionnel, mais les volumes restent spacieux.

Le salon comme les chambres sont éclairés par d'immenses baies vitrées.

CH. CH. CH.

Tous les mercredis soirs, une quarantaine d'habitants se retrouvent pour dîner dans la grande salle commune du dernier étage. P.M. m'invite à me joindre à eux, l'ambiance est conviviale. Il m'explique que les cuisiniers changent chaque semaine, tour à tour les membres de ce petit club cuisinent pour les autres. Mes voisins de table me parlent de plusieurs autres événements de ce type organisés tout au long de l'année, mais me précisent que la participation de chacun n'est absolument pas une obligation. C'est là, à mon sens, que réside l'intelligence de cette coopérative, elle met en place des dispositifs capables d'accueillir des pratiques collectives sans pour autant exclure des modes de vie plus autonomes.

Le lendemain matin, je reviens dessiner sur la terrasse en toiture. C'est l'hiver, évidemment je n'y croise personne. Mais les nombreuses plantes en pot et chaises de jardin laissent supposer qu'à la venue des beaux jours les résidents doivent apprécier ce belvédère donnant d'un côté sur d'anciens terrains industriels petit à petit reconquis par la ville et de l'autre sur des quartiers résidentiels construits à flanc de coteaux en surplomb de la Limmat.

Avant de reprendre mon train pour Paris, je refais un tour au pied des quatre immeubles et contemple à nouveau ces volumes simples et leurs façades neutres, où la même fenêtre est répétée indéfiniment quelle que soit la pièce à éclairer. Le plus surprenant et admirable est sans doute le contraste entre cette architecture imposante par sa matérialité et sa capacité à s'effacer pour ne pas entraver la diversité des usages qu'elle abrite.

M.E.

Warka Water

42

Ethiopia

A drinking water collector to supply the village

In rural communities in Ethiopia, getting enough water is a daily struggle. The Warka Water experimental project offers a simple water collection system designed to be managed collectively by its users. Energy self-sufficient, cheap, and easy to assemble and move, it takes the form of a 9-metre tower. Inside the vertical bamboo structure, a fine-meshed net traps rainwater and atmospheric moisture, which then run down into a collector.
The construction does not only offer a fundamental resource; it can also become a social space in the heart of the village, like a contemporary palaver tree. Since 2012, twelve different prototypes have been installed across the country.

www.architectureandvision.com

—

photos: © Architecture & Vision

Our Story

During a trip to Ethiopia in February 2012, while visiting isolated rural communities on a high plateau in the northeast of the country, I witnessed a dramatic reality: the lack of drinking water. The villagers live in a beautiful natural environment, but often without running water, electricity, toilets or showers. To survive here, women and children walk every day for miles towards shallow, unprotected ponds, where the water - often contaminated by human and animal waste - is teeming with disease-carrying parasites. They scoop the water up in dry carved gourds and carry it back in old plastic containers, which are extremely heavy.

Recent studies show that only 34% of Ethiopia's population has access to an improved water supply. This implies that some 60 million people lack access to safe water.

To address this dire situation, I made it my mission to find an alternative solution and help these people. This was the genesis of the design of Warka Water: an environmentally, socially and financially sustainable solution for providing clean water.

It started as a voluntary initiative in 2012. Since then, my architecture office 'Architecture and Vision', with a group of collaborators, have designed and built several prototypes on different scales to test various aspects of the project.

In May 2015 we reached an important milestone with the construction of our first pilot prototype on site in Dorze, an isolated rural community in Southern Ethiopia.

Arturo Vittori

Warka Water > beyond the walls

13 May – 6 June 2016 > Bordeaux City Hall

15 June – 25 September > Botanical Gardens, Bordeaux

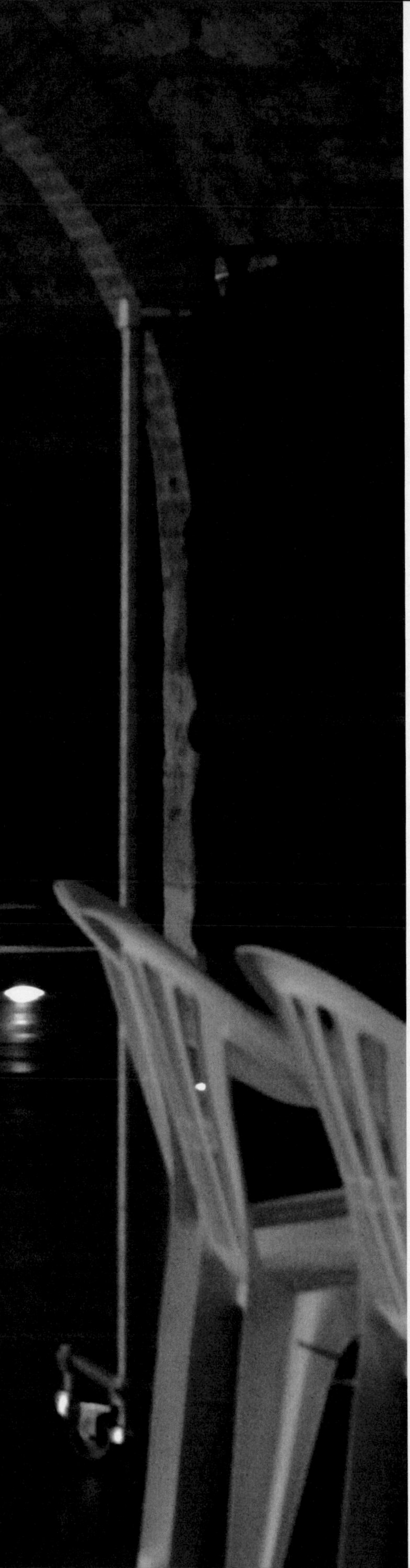

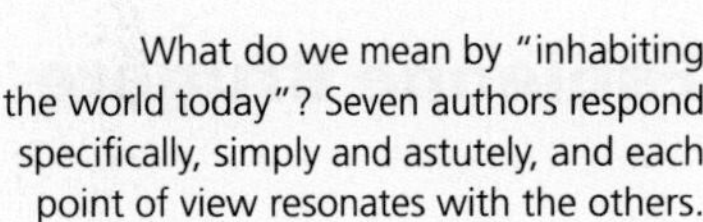

What do we mean by "inhabiting the world today"? Seven authors respond specifically, simply and astutely, and each point of view resonates with the others.

talks

Fabienne Brugère philosopher

394 **What does inhabiting the world mean?**

Inhabiting the world means building a relationship with nature and other people at the same time.

It means building a relationship with nature in the sense that we live in a finite universe, with resources that are also finite, in the context of a constantly growing population.

Thinking about our relationship with nature means bearing in mind the possibility of sharing land and resources, and it means really taking the global population into account.
This in turn involves the possibility of inventing an alternative form of globalisation based on sharing.

But inhabiting the world also means building a relationship with others. This clearly involves taking their cultural and political differences into account.

Today this is a crucial question, especially in the European context, where there is a tendency for inward-lookingness.

Does inhabiting the world mean inhabiting an environment? And does inhabiting an environment mean taking care of it?

Inhabiting the world today means living in an environment in the sense that humans always need an environment to live in. In a way, we never live in a city centre, a suburb, or a rural area without being able to make it our own. It seems to me that inhabiting an environment primarily involves appropriating one's surroundings, which means being able to deploy one's own subjectivity there, being able to use a territory. It's a kind of *droit de cité,* literally the "right to use the city": the right to appropriate the environment we live in. If we don't do this, anything can happen, and we can expect the worst. We've seen a few examples recently.

But inhabiting an environment also has a somewhat different meaning, which involves the notion of care. For the people who live there, "taking care" means caring about their lives and caring about their collective histories, which are not often the same. "Taking care" also means caring about their development, about how their lives unfold. Taking care of others means being able to organise, in a particular area, collective, communal life that fosters various forms of sharing and is associated with living environments that are not just places where things are consumed.

How can we rethink the role of democracy in the city, based on the power of residents to discuss or decide things? How should we approach the relationship of horizontality and verticality referred to in the ethics of care: a form of sensitive democracy?

It's often said that democracy as "power of the people" emerged in Greece from the possibility of direct democracy in a public square, and more precisely from the opportunity for people to engage in debate, to discuss a number of subjects that were important to the community.

This reference to direct democracy has become a necessity for a lot of people: examples are occupations of squares and other places where a number of people get together to engage in debate and to practice direct democracy. The underlying idea is that there's not enough horizontality in our society, and that we need to be able to deploy that horizontality in a number of places.

This is fundamental in France as we try to define a democratic way of inhabiting our surroundings. It's important because we're in a very centralised country where there's always a top-down process that goes from State to citizen. But what we probably need to develop in France today are bottom-up processes that start with citizens, collectives and NPOs and finish up at State level. It's also a way of thinking about the French state in terms of how good it is at listening to people. We should say to those that govern us: "Listen to people, develop your ability to listen, acknowledge your mistakes, introduce proposals that are also inventions." It's a real political challenge.

Guillaume le Blanc philosopher

What does inhabiting the world mean?

You can't live somewhere without an address, or without a letterbox. I think the letterbox creates the place, the house where we live, the flat. And starting from this local element, we can think about what's global. You always need local things for global things to exist.

Without this little point on Earth, without this "somewhere", the individual cannot have his share. And this share, which comes to us via the place we live, creates the possibility of "seeing the world" in the strictest sense.

A philosophy of the world is always rooted somewhere. There's nothing worse that thinking about the world without reference points, without some kind of rootedness. At some point, they are roots that move, they are rhizomes, they are lines of perspective. But without those lines, it's impossible to plough our furrow in life.

The fragility of the act of dwelling comes from the fundamentally precarious relationship between what is local—the possibility of living somewhere—and what is global. You need a roof so that the concept of "home" can radiate beyond your physical home.

Does inhabiting the world mean living in the environment? Does living in an environment mean taking care of it?

There's a kind of crazy futuristic fantasy that combines with today's individualism, according to which it's possible to live anywhere, as a matter of pure arrogance, with no concern for the environment. There's even a kind of Promethean dream of building beyond the limits of the world.

I think we have to get back to a form of modesty where the concept of dwelling is concerned. In actual fact, we know full well that living somewhere means finding a kind of ecological nest, and experiments all over the world bear this out: it's about building in the world that surrounds us, in a world we suddenly have to take care of.

In this sense, I think the best way of taking care of the world is to take care of one's nest, of one's dwelling. It's the point from which we radiate.

It's true that the contemporary violence of war, terrorism, dictatorships and poverty always involves the destruction of dwellings and of the world around us. And this twofold destruction is what makes today's world so fragile.

How should we approach the relationship of horizontality and verticality referred to in the ethics of care: a form of sensitive democracy?

We now have to assert both *le droit de cité* (the right to be somewhere, to exist) and *le droit à la cité* (the right to take part in a broader community: the *cité* or *polis*). The idea is that each individual, each inhabitant, is a participant who cannot be evacuated from this "world around us" that is the city. So we have to extend the scope of *droit à la cité* by making sure that people who are invisible, who are on the periphery—on the periphery of power, on the periphery of the architectural centrality of the city—can take part and do their part, either by voting in local elections or via other forms of political activity.

We have to imagine the political horizontality of tomorrow's cities. I think this is one of today's great utopias. The democratic horizontality of tomorrow's cities is necessarily connected to the radical idea that, in a true democracy, there is no centre. There must no longer be a centre. There must only by a creative periphery, forms of free activity linked to all the peripheries of the world that come together in the *polis*.

I dream of a *polis* built on the free, joyful exploration of all creative peripheries. That's what we should aim for.

Michel Lussault geographer

When we say we "live" somewhere, we usually talk about living in a particular place, at a precise address, or in a city: so what does "living in the world" mean?

First of all we should remember that we mustn't confuse the words *résider* and *habiter*. These words are often confused. People often think they are synonyms, but that's just not true.
Résider is synonymous with *loger* or *demeurer* [to live/stay], which imply, respectively, that we have a *logis* or a *demeure:* a home. Some of us have several, because in today's world it is not uncommon to be, as the geographer Mathis Stock says, "polytopic"—living in more than one home. This is nothing out of the ordinary.
So *résider* is an extremely important human activity. Whether we are sedentary or nomadic, at some point we have to "reside" somewhere.
This action of "residing somewhere" is very important because it gives our daily lives one of its anchor points. It's what anchors us to a particular place, giving us a firm base and somewhere to stay. But such an anchorage—like a ship's mooring—is also a place we can move away from, towards new anchorages and other places.
Résider—living in a place we call home—is thus an important concept. constellation.s tackles this question by focusing on a number of cases that show how human beings live in a place, occupy it, make it meaningful, and try to shape it, develop it and make it their own, in more or less easy conditions.

But *habiter* is more than that: it is a much broader concept. It points to the origin of the notion of the word "habitat": a notion that was created in the 19th century in the fields of ethology and botany. These "natural sciences" defined habitat as the living environment of a species. By extension, human habitat is the living environment of a particular species: humans.

My residence, my home, is only one of the places that I "inhabit". My habitat, my living environment, is much larger than my place of residence. If we think about it, our habitat, our living environment, creates a state of tension between three things.

The first dimension of habitat is anchorage: this refers not only to places where we live, but also to places where we work, play, learn, or just wander around for the sake of it, and places where there are sports facilities.

The second dimension is movement: there are places where I can be, but also be in motion. What better examples of movement than the mobility of cars or public transport or bikes, or even my experience of walking by the river in Bordeaux? When I move, I have a relationship with space that is different from when I "reside" in it or when I'm in my place of anchorage.

The third dimension of habitat is connexion. Because I connect, I'm in contact with others and other spaces via that connexion. I connect when I go into a station to get on a train that will take me somewhere else, or an airport that will allow me to discover unknown places. But I also connect when, using my smartphone, my connected object or my computer, I contact other individuals who have other realities, while I'm walking along, or when I'm driving somewhere—sometimes over long distances.

For each individual, "inhabiting" means bringing life to a habitat, which is a subtle combination of anchorages, movements and connexions. constellation.s tries to show what constitutes that habitat. In this perspective, the fact that we "inhabit" the world is quite understandable.

We inhabit the world in two ways. We inhabit it collectively, as the human species, as a set of societies. Ultimately, the world is what accommodates our respective habitats and the collective habitat—that of the entire species. This is how we should consider Planet Earth. But each of us also inhabits the world individually, because we tend to "inhabit" on a larger and larger scale—in particular because society is becoming more urban, mobile, and connected.

Look at contemporary migrants—including illegal immigrants. These migrants create tension in the places where they stay: movement and connexions on a scale that goes well beyond that of the "home" or the "anchorage". This is why we take the idea that Man inhabits the world seriously.

What impact does urbanisation have on our ways of inhabiting?

Global urbanisation changes the situation insofar as it's not simply something that transforms living environments. It's also an urbanisation of ways of being, of "types of life". It changes the way we conceive our existence.

First of all this urbanisation transforms anchorages from within. It does not destroy them; on the contrary, it makes them more complex. Because of what urban societies are becoming, a number of individuals—not only wealthy people, indeed often very poor people—find themselves part of more and more complex anchorage systems. If we go back to migrants, we see that their geographical anchorage system is extremely complex. Indeed it leads to thinking about memory-based anchoring processes referring to the native land they, or they ancestors, left behind.

Another consequence of urbanisation is to make mobility and connexions more complex. Research and observation show that urbanisation simplifies nothing and makes the habitat of each human—and thus of the human species—more complicated, subtle and ambiguous. It also complicates the relationship we have with our own habitat and that of others. It complicates cohabitation between each of us and the people we come into contact with.

What is the role of local initiatives?

Local initiatives are essential. We're at a historic point where many individuals and groups, operating locally and in the field, are taking their future into their own hands and using local action to decide to change the way their social group lives.
This blossoming of local initiatives is very striking, especially as it's people who we tend to think of as subordinates and who possess little economic capital—poor people or people who are somewhat on the fringes of existing networks—who are most actively reclaiming the individual and collective ability to influence our habitat and the way dwelling and cohabitation are envisioned.

One question still arises, however: how can we hope to change the global habitat using local initiatives at a time when, as we know, we face considerable challenges as a species?

These challenges are of three kinds.
I'd describe the first challenge as environmental or ecological: we are entering the Anthropocene. Global change shows us that we now face a new situation where the inhabitability of the planet is called into question by the very efforts of human activity. We have never experienced this before in the history of global human development.
The second challenge is that of social justice.
And the third major challenge is political. How can we find forms of government that will ensure an environmental and social balance able to provide a human habitat that is both environmentally sustainable and socially fair?

These two types of challenges must be tackled both globally and locally. We can't hope to tackle them using top-down rulings alone. Public authorities have to take action and draw up a roadmap. COP 21 and other such events are steps in the right direction, but it's networked local initiatives that will really allow us to bring about change.

How can we produce a model based on successful local experimentation that can be transposed to other contexts? How can we ensure, thanks to this reproducibility, that we can solve similar problems elsewhere? This is a fundamental political question. We don't have the answer, to be honest. Ours is not an age of certainty. We don't know quite how to do it, but a lot of us think we have to take the question seriously: the question of the empowerment of local stakeholders and the idea that local experiments can become examples and, even better, transposable models. It's a kind of gamble: the gamble referred to in constellation.s. It's a collective political gamble.

Dominique Boullier sociologist

When we say we "live" somewhere, we most often talk about a place, a precise address, a city...

First and foremost living in the world means thinking about how we can produce an outer skin on a global scale—how we can feel "inside".

What we call globalisation causes shifts to occur and gives rise to a number of different situations. In "top-down" globalisation, to use Jacques Donzelot's term, these situations are those where we stay in Hiltons or Radissons. And in "bottom-up" globalisation, we stay in ramshackle shelters in jungles. But in neither case are we actually "living" anywhere.

"We don't live anywhere" means we cannot durably occupy and transform the technical system that is our habitat, and that is also what will transform us. It is this reciprocity that is made difficult. We no longer take care of ourselves, nor of the environment. And in our brand of globalisation, something is shattered.

And yet, in the current period, we find ourselves facing the need to think from the point of view of the interior—from the point of view of a habitat. The consequences of industrial progress and the indefinite extension of damage caused to "nature" call into question a modern vision of the world, where the Earth is finally just a place we can visit, occupy and exploit. This view can no longer hold, because the consequences of all this behaviour are coming back to haunt us. And now, these consequences make us realise to what extent we have occupied the Earth without thinking about how to really live in it—and about the very fact that we do live in it . The Earth itself responds to us and forces us to consider ourselves as being within it. If we want to tackle environmental or ecological issues, we have to think about them as "inhabitants of the Earth".

This is a historic opportunity—linked, it is true, to the imminent nature of the disaster—that forces us to think anew about the way we relate to "nature", no longer seen as something exterior. As Philippe Descola has shown, "nature" is a concept that made it possible to consider phenomenon in which we are completely immersed as exterior. We now have to think about how we are linked to them: how we're connected by all the links and attachments we have with what we call "nature" and "the environment".
The political question currently being posed is the question of how our way of looking at the world has to change: how to leave behind the modern world of occupation—which is, in a way, very close to colonisation—to move towards a vision of "inhabiting" according to which we are "at the heart of everything", but not as masters of the world On the contrary, we are *inside:* caught up in the network of these attachments.

How can we square mobility with this notion of "living inside"?

Mobility creates what is probably the key problem in today's world: climate change caused by atmospheric pollution, in turn caused by mobility, especially vehicular mobility. So we need to think about the link between living in the world and this mobility.

But this mobility has shaped the layout of our cities, to the point where it has created problems in the way residential space is distributed, because the results of mobility are so intrusive and generate so many costs… It's something that is becoming unmanageable, and yet it remains the predominant model for urban development.

So why do we have to change our point of view on this issue? Until now, we thought we could just replace cars with public transport. But we didn't really understand what "attachment to cars" was all about. It mainly involves the fact that we "live in" a vehicle. This is what makes the attachment so strong, and what makes it so difficult to sever the connection. It's not just about considering the technical functionality of cars. Advertising has understood this: they never sell you just a way of getting from A to B or an engine performance; sure, they sell you a dream or a fantasy, but they also sell you an *interior* and the idea that you'll feel at home in it, that the car will suit you down to the ground, that you will be able to transform it and that it will transform you. This coupling process, which is the key process of the act of "inhabiting", this reciprocal transformation of technology and the human being, is something that creates very powerful connections and that makes separation very difficult, even for reasons that seem completely justified. The bubble created by the envelope is what I call *an habitacle* [= vehicle interior, passenger compartment]. Along with the notions of *habitat* and *habit* [= clothing], with which it shares the same root, an *habitacle* makes up the third technical envelope. This "third envelope" has a value that goes beyond the function of the vehicle. From this point on, comparing it with public transport and new ways of living becomes very difficult.

Questions of mobility have to be reconsidered in the light of the way we "inhabit" our journeys, how we create envelopes that must interpenetrate—as Peter Sloterdijk says when he talks about "foam"—envelopes that are, in a way, co-dependently fragile, but which, at the same time, have to act like bubbles. There's still a lot of progress to be made in the way we invent the transport of the future, which will have to tackle both climatic issues and anthropological questions relating to the *habitacle*—the interior.

Can we "live in digital"?

Until now, in the technical development we have experienced, including digital, we've mainly stacked up layer upon layer of networks. It's what's called electrosmog. And we might say that digital is a layer or a technical envelope whose long-term consequences we are unaware of. But we've also stacked up applications, systems, and technical objects, without really thinking that we have to find an organisational principle other than simplicity.

With smartphones in particular, which are very close to us,very close to our skin, which we carry around all the time, this stacking process ends up creating something called the *personal data ecosystem*, which doesn't just connect us to the device, but to a whole set of social worlds we can enter according to the situation. This phenomenon is all the more significant because two thirds of humans now have such as device.

This represents an anthropological transformation: a population gets a device that allows it to connect remotely to extremely varied worlds and to switch between them very fast. But this process causes problems, especially from the point of view of privacy. People become aware that the system is full of holes and that personal data can't be controlled. They also face problems of ease of use and access to devices.

This is why I suggest thinking about digital and all these layers we build up as "envelopes" and as a "habitat". I coined the word *habitèle*, which refers to the Web and not distance. This is what's important: it's what we weave out of all the networks that connect us. If we don't change our way of looking at how we relate to that environment, we could say that we "stay" in digital just as we might "stay" in a particular habitat, in the sense that we are subjected to a technical system that is in many ways very unreliable, whereas we'd really like to make it our own. The demand for personalisation is colossal. It goes hand in hand with a demand for data control and control over the worlds we're connected to. This is the world we live in. In the morning, as soon as they get up, people switch on their mobiles (if they're switched off), and they're connected to the world all day long.

This is a new way of living in the world. It's a new way of living with all these connexions, which are permanent and extremely frequent. We have to think in a new way about the development of applications, the options we offer clients and consumers, and the political choices relating to technical architecture. We have to think about all this in terms of habitat, considered as an *habitèle*.

Anne-Sophie Novel economist and journalist

What does "inhabiting the world" mean?

The first personal awareness I've always had is that I'm lucky to have been born in a rich country, in a healthy family, and to have always had a roof (or several) over my head. Not everyone is so lucky.

The second awareness, that I came to later—but I think it's developing in more and more people's minds nowadays—is an awareness of interdependence.

I can't live in my world if I am not aware of the conditions in which others live. This means that, when I eat something, when I buy clothes or furniture, or when I do something that has an impact in the world, I can't get away from the idea that it might affect someone else.

I think that living in the world today means developing these forms of awareness to move more towards solidarity and being aware that not everyone has the same roof over their head or the same kind of habitat.

Natural disasters and climate change: what impact do they have on our habitat?

Climate change doesn't have the same impact on everyone. Some people will be hotter, some will be colder. Some will experience drought, others floods and frequent storms. We're moving towards more and more natural disasters.

There's also significant impact on biodiversity, on the migrations of certain species, on animals and plants. And we're only at the beginning of our observations. We now know with certainty that something is happening, that temperatures will rise by more than 2 degrees over the next few years. So we're also moving towards many uncertainties. We'd be well advised to anticipate the effects of what's happening.

Consuming, pooling, sharing: how does our economic behaviour adapt?

In response to climate change and the awareness we're now developing with regard to dwindling resources, growing waste and all kinds of pollution, new economic models are emerging.

There are, for instance, so-called "circular" economic models, in the sense that the idea is to recover and reuse resources, to think of them in terms of a life cycle that is not linear (where you take something, transform it, then throw it away). Waste can now become a raw material that can be used again and again, *ad infinitum*.

We can also develop a so-called "economy of functionality", which involves paying to use things instead of owning them. Everything that now relates to the sharing economy is based on this notion of use where, when I need something, I can change the way I consume.

There are also economic models where we refer more to "symbiosis". We can develop, in a given area, a set of new models that grow locally and enrich the area—whereas today we allow these assets to escape.

Observing these new models is fascinating: it shows that opportunities to take action are now within our grasp.

Pierre Rosanvallon historian

When we say we live somewhere, we usually talk about a place, a precise address, a town or city: what does "living in the world" mean?

The French word *habiter* has two meanings. In the legal sense it refers to what you put on your ID papers: the place where you live. But the strong meaning of the word *habiter* is much broader. *Habiter*—to inhabit—means to make a place your own. We "inhabit" our body and we "inhabit" a place, in other words *habiter* refers to the process by which we become, in a sense, the co-owner of a particular space. This means that "living somewhere", in this particular meaning of *"habiter"*, doesn't mean just living there because we have to. Living somewhere is something we do actively, so as to feel something in common with a given space.

Of course, when we live in a flat or a house, it's a space that's determined by the rules of ownership and the facts of family life. But living in a city means feeling something in common with the other people who live there. Consequently, there's no distinction between the definition of "living in one's city" and "living in the world".

It relates to the way we construct our existence in terms of how we relate to others. Either we stay indoors with the shutters closed, or we open the windows. And today we can say that the more information we get about what goes on in the world, the more easily we become "inhabitants of the world".

This means that it's the way we look at people and things that gives substance and depth to the act of "living somewhere".

Is there a tension in democracy between the local, the national and the global? Does living in the world today mean living in an environment? Isn't there a risk of making nature into a mere instrument of the "act of inhabiting" rather than an authentic living environment?

It's not simply democracy, it's not simply an intellectual truth: there's a sense of citizenship that needs to be experienced and shared, in a sensitive, civic-minded way. That's why public squares, for example, have always been seen as arenas for civic action—like the forum and the agora. They're places where we feel that we're physically together as one.

Now, at the end of April 2016, there's a field of experimentation in Paris (it's not really a social movement) taking place around the "Nuit Debout". These are people who are building something, in the same place, physically. We might say that all such specific initiatives—initiatives out there in the field—have this value of giving what we might call a physical dimension to citizenship.

But we mustn't forget that citizenship isn't just a physical thing. It has a "redistributive" dimension. This is, in fact, what characterises belonging to a nation-state. Political citizenship leads us to share the nation-state and takes us into an arena where shared redistribution can take place. This is the real difference, it seems to me, between the national area and the European area.

The European area has a shared history. There are past evils we want to keep at bay. There are forms of legal organisation that we want to build. There are customs barriers we want to remove. But while there are things we have in common, we mustn't forget that the EC budget only accounts for 1 % of the GDP of the member countries. In a nation-state like France, we share about 50 % of GDP.

Citizenship is thus not defined merely in sentimental, intellectual or historical terms. It is defined with respect to the material conditions under which we share things.

And it's also what makes the distinction between national and global citizenship. European citizenship can be seen as a way of experimenting with globalisation on a small scale. But the idea is of a similar order: it's about sharing a legal arena, hopes for peace, and the organisation of trade. But it's much less about redistribution.

And finally there's distinction to be made between the national level and the local level. One of the characteristics of local tax is that it is redistributive. When you pay your property tax in France, it's calculated according to the size of your home or the piece of land you own, not according to how much you earn. The *commune*, the local administrative area, is more an area for the management of common assets and collective utilities, with social redistribution and correction of inequalities often playing a less important role. Having said this, each level has its own pedagogical value and takes particular forms.

You've worked a lot on political representation and you've recently focused on an amplification of executive power: does this mean that the government of towns and cities should be understood only in the perspective of a reinforcement of executive power, or are there political initiatives that lie outside the regulated procedures of government?

It's not only a question of possibility. It's a question of necessity, because we live in different spaces. And as we live in these different spaces, we are either visitors, or we are users. We use collective services, we take part in public events, we have a personal or family life in a given space, and we're citizens and tax payers.

So it's these different personal life scenarios that put things into a hierarchy. It's not theoretical thought that does this. But in different cases, what's involved is a different representation of oneself and others.

In one framework, the most local case, our representation of self and others is related to friendliness, which is related to meeting people, which happens when we share a bus, an underground carriage, a busy square, or a tram platform. But there are other experiences we have that occur through information and images rather than through direct encounters with people. It's what we see on TV—on the problems with refugees coming from Syria, Afghanistan and other places on makeshift boats—that in a sense expands our sensitivity and our understanding of what connects us to other people.

Paradoxically, this points to a growth in sentimental or sensitive citizenship that's not always accompanied by a corresponding increase in material or financial solidarity. That's the contradiction we also have to resolve today. The media increase the scope of our sensitivity, but they don't increase our sense of solidarity.

We mustn't idealise this. We have to take it for what it is: a level, a form of experience. For a lot of people, especially very young people, it's also an early form of understanding of citizenship, at a time when the voting booth can seem very far away, especially in a period when politics seems devalued. Here, there's a form of closeness that makes things meaningful.

Miguel Benasayag philosopher and psychoanalyst

When we say we "live" somewhere, we most often talk about a place, an address, a city: what does "living in the world" mean?

We might think that living in the world today is, for example, being in front of a computer screen and getting news of what's happening in the world. Actually, it's not that at all. Living in the world means finding the world. Finding it not in front of a screen, like something abstract, but in a very concrete way, in our neighbourhood, in our city, in local things. We have to find what's at stake in the world and how that manifests itself in each place. In other words, the world is not the sum of all the places in the world. The world is what actually exists in each place. If we talk about neoliberalism, we shouldn't think about liberalism per se, but about how it exists in our particular world. We talk about ecological disasters as they exist in our local environment. Each big question is targeted to the unique place each of us lives in.

Your approach emphasises the understanding of areas of fragility in existence, but far from serving sad ends, this is to increase opportunities for joy. In what sense is there a joyful way of living in the world?

Fragility is often seen as a weakness, mistakenly in my view. It's as if we wanted to be tough, not fragile. But fragility is the very condition of living things. It's the condition for living culture, for living beings. Fragility means we can be affected by things. And if we can't be affected by the world, we can't act in the world. Fragility means we're neither strong nor weak. We're connected in a fragile way of being in the world. Joy exists under condition of this fragility. This means that we cannot be joyfully passionate, in a joyful life, if we don't come to terms with our fragility. If we seek to be strong and tough, we deprive ourselves of joy. So joy exists on condition that we come to terms with the fragility of life.

You closely examine the micro-inventions of ordinary lives. How do they help us to build an irreducible home?

What you call "micro-inventions" refers to initiatives where people, not individually but linked together, can create ways of living that differ from the norm, which involves eco-destruction: the destruction of living cultural diversity. These inventions, which I prefer to call resistances or creations, make it possible to carry out a large number of concrete experiments that highlight the potential to imagine alternative ways of living.

None of these local inventions or creations is restricted or irreducible or irreversible. On the contrary, they come and go. But this creative explosion may, I hope, become the ground from which a new social and historic mindset and alternative ways of living can emerge.

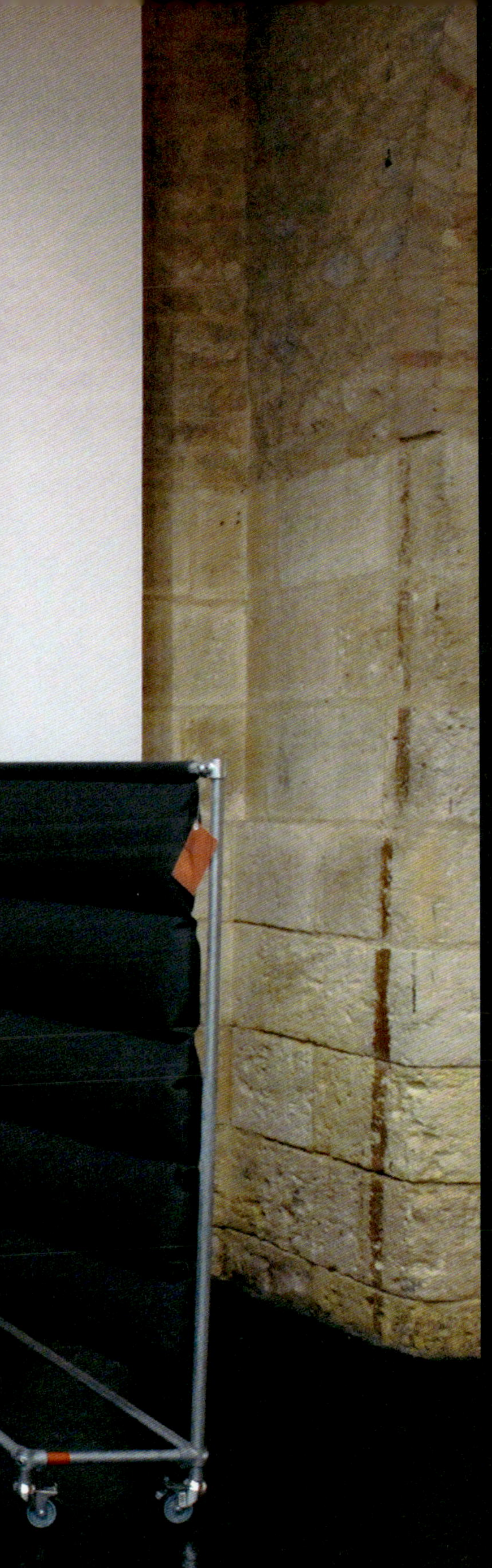

videos

Lawrence Abu Hamdam United Kingdom

The All-Hearing

Cairo, 2013, 13′, English subtitles

KARAOKE

Bruno Boudjelal France/Africa

Harragas

2011, 5′

Jan Rothuizen, Martijn van Tol and Dirk-Jan Visser / Submarine Channel
Netherlands

Refugee Republic

Cairo, 2013, 13′, English subtitles

Marc Johnson France

YùYù

China, 2015, 15’

Gideon Mendel South Africa

The Water Chapters

2007-2015, 15′

25

Bruce Bégout

New Underground

Furtive artists

1. It was quite by chance, like a dog wriggling into a gap and finding itself in a kitchen, that I met the *New Underground* art collective. I was on a scientific mission on one of the islands of Franz-Joseph Land, an archipelago in the far north of Russia. I was supposed to count the gannets that live in this hostile, uninhabited place-the northernmost island group in the world. I was heading up a small team of Swiss and Russian scientists assembled for the purpose. We were to stay for the two summer months, taking samples in the field and living totally self-sufficiently in an improvised camp. The beauty of the place, with its basalt cliffs and volcanic cones, would make the remoteness and solitude more bearable. However an arduous task awaited us.

2. On an expedition to a rocky islet called Koelitz, one of my Swiss assistants fell into a crevasse. It was a deep, narrow hole, from which we could hear his cries for help. We abseiled down to get him. Iouri was lying in a dark, smelly pool of water. He had fallen eight metres and might easily have been killed. Fortunately he only had a broken leg and a few scratches on his faces. While two people looked after him and got him into a cradle to be winched out, I took the opportunity to inspect the large dark chamber.

3. It was part of a large network of caves with walls covered in mauve lichen. Daylight falling on the rock crevices formed grotesque shapes. But there was something even more strange than these tricks of the light: a deep, muted silence, a silence I have never experienced anywhere else. It was the silence of desolate, unknown lands; the silence of the tombs of knowledge.

4. I was almost lost, a long way from the hole the Swiss assistant had fallen into, when I was attracted by a pallid glow. It wasn't an effect of the daylight, even filtered by the earth and ice. It had an artificial quality, like a halogen lamp. I wriggled between two walls of jagged rock and, at the end of a bottleneck, I came face to face with a kind of art installation. A red neon light was leaning against a big rock, forming a 45 degree angle with the ground. The glass tube twisted and turned, forming a few words. Cocking my head sideways, I read what it said: *Energy is eternal delight*.

5. How had the neon light got there? And who put it there? I confess that I was stupefied by this discovery. The islands were not inhabited and received few visitors. They were very difficult to get to, not only because of the climate, but also because of all the endless red tape. And I couldn't imagine a hard-working Russian or Finnish fisherman setting up an artwork that no one would ever see in a remote, inaccessible cave. It was perfectly clear that the neon light was not there by chance, but had been placed deliberately in the cave, far out of sight. What's more, it was ingeniously powered by a solar battery that recharged automatically thanks to the sun's meagre rays entering, with calculated precision, through a tiny hole.

6. No one knew anything about the installation. My Russian guides, like the Arkhangelsk authorities I asked when I got back to the mainland, had never heard of an artistic expedition to the archipelago. The work was unsigned, and a long search on the Web taught me next to nothing. The photos I'd taken did not make it possible to identify a known artist. A lot of artists work with neon tubes as an expressive material, but no one could help me identify the creator of *Energy is eternal delight*.

7. For months on end I followed up the smallest clue that might begin to explain the presence of that artwork concealed in a remote corner of the globe. I adopted the same dogged methodical approach as when I carried out my work as a naturalist. But my search, which sometimes seemed like an investigation by a private detective looking for a missing person, was fruitless. The silence of ignorance was as powerful as what I had experienced underground on the rocky island. Meanwhile, a resident of Kem had received authorisation from the Russian authorities to organise trips to see the red neon light.

8. I'd almost given up trying to solve the mystery of the Master of the underground cave when one weekend I got an odd phone call. I didn't expect such a call: a recorded, toneless female voice gave me a date and a place to meet. At the end of the message, which played in a loop every thirty seconds, the voice, scrambled to make it impossible to identify, reminded me of the neon light in Franz-Joseph Land.

9. A fortnight later I got off the bus from Sucre to Potosi, in southern Bolivia, at a deserted crossroads with a dirt track leading off to the left. The voice message told me to follow this rocky track that only donkeys and SUVs could use. After an hour and a half under the beating sun of the Altiplano at an altitude of over 4,000 metres, my energy flagging, short of breath, I spotted a ruined church nestling in a hollow. I knew then that this old building, of which all that remained was its white bell tower, was my destination.

10. I waited over an hour among the ruins, pushing stones with the tip of my shoe and gazing vaguely at the surroundings. I seriously began to think I was the victim of a practical joke, and I almost returned the way I had come. For several months I'd moved heaven and earth to find the mysterious creator of the red light. Perhaps I'd stumbled on something I shouldn't have seen. Maybe I'd disturbed someone as I searched for the truth. I was cursing myself, and my childish thirst for knowledge, when a pickup truck appeared and drove down the slope in a cloud of brown dust.

11. I spent the next few hours bound and hooded in the back of the truck. Men wearing Mexican wrestlers' masks had leapt out of the vehicle. I wasn't hard to catch. After a long drive, my back in agony from all the bumps and potholes, we stopped. It seemed that we'd arrived. I heard orders being barked in Spanish, and several people crowded round the vehicle. I was bundled off the truck and (if the echoing footsteps were anything to go by) taken into a large room. Only after another long wait did someone take off my hood.

12. Facing me, sitting calmly on chairs set in a semicircle, were a dozen men and women. They were not masked, and did not look like members of a terrorist group. Their clothes, their attitude, and their faces seemed to indicate that they formed a secret but peaceful assembly. After a length of time it was hard to estimate, a young Asian woman wearing a long white tunic stood up and came towards me. She said, loud enough for everyone to hear: *"I am the Master of the red neon light"*.

13. I lived with them for several weeks. I learned about their way of life and the principles that governed their community. In the beginning, they were on their guard. They maintained a certain reserve, and did not wish to give me clear, precise information about their way of life. They had been surprised by my discovery and had resolved to spy on me. In a way, someone, some day, had to stumble upon the red neon light, but they wondered why I'd been so eager to find out its origin and meaning. My curiosity kindled their own. Then little by little, perhaps realising that my intentions were good, they explained in detail the meaning of what they were doing and the secrets of their mysterious behaviour.

14. The little community I found myself in was just one of the many groups forming the *New Underground*: that was the name of this invisible brotherhood scattered across the world. It was a secret society of contemporary artists who turned their backs on celebrity and decided never to show their works. The created, sculpted, cast, painted, wrote, danced, set up video and sound installations, filmed and screened, composed and recorded, but they refused to exhibit the fruits of their creative labour in known, accessible places. They had neither names nor images. They were, they told me, "anonymous and anoptic".

15. Only the artworks mattered to them, not the fact that they might be seen. Like stones and stars, they were to exist perfect autonomy, completely free from the aesthetic relationship with a viewer that would pollute them with endless points of view and comments. And so, with a skill at concealing things that would make the intelligence services green with envy, they managed to put them discreetly in the remotest corners of the world, where no one would suspect they existed.

16. I was the first to discover them. Over a period of over thirty years they had been camouflaging their works in various corners of the world, and no one had been lucky enough to find them. Only that unfortunate fall revealed part of their existence, and my love for geology did the rest. For them, I was an object of curiosity. They weren't angry with me, although they would have probably preferred it if I hadn't ventured into that narrow passage. The fact is, they didn't really know what to do with me. I was the only witness to what must remain unwitnessed.

17. I dodn't know their real names. They used ironic pseudonyms borrowed from art history: George Michelangelo, Anthony Beuys, Franklin Matisse, Helen Cage, and so on. They came from a range of different countries and formed a community of about a hundred members scattered across the globe in autonomous groups. Thanks to strict rules and quasi-religious devotion, they'd managed to remain incognito among people who sought to become known. Fame was of no interest to them; still less money. They were not envious of celebrities, exhibitions, and critics. Only art-a meteor in a sky without humans-mattered to them, and the safe, lasting presence of the artworks in the blind spots of existence was enough for them. They never thought about the dreaded moment of discovery. They were convinced their creations would remain secret for centuries, and that they would survive everything.

18. I was able to come and go as I pleased in the village they'd restored in the mountains. I was fascinated by this society that had vowed to vanish. My questions didn't bother them. They replied with a frankness that was all the greater for being, for the most part, parcimonious. I learned that other works-thousands of them-had been cleverly concealed in the most improbable places, inside ancient trees, in the DNA of a mollusc, under the huge expanse of a glacier, in the chimney of a nuclear reactor, and on a communications satellite: anywhere people would never dream of looking. But the exact locations were never revealed to me; I was only given vague hints. Actually, I'm not even sure they know themselves where all their artworks are.

19. At the end of my stay, they gave me permission to write this: the only trace of my encounter. The only condition was that I should respect the absolute rule of their society. It wasn't very hard to guess what that was: I had to bury the manuscript in such a remote place that it would be completely protected from prying eyes. For days and days, I wondered what this ideal location could be. I became obsessed: I imagined places that are impossible to reach, and places that don't even exist. I saw myself climbing mountains and traipsing across the tundra. Then, remembering a short story by Edgar Allen Poe, I found it. It was both obvious and discreet. I had now become one of them: a furtive, invisible artist of the *New Underground*.

#02
Les liens matériels et immatériels foisonnent et tissent de nouvelles cultures spatiales qui remodèlent nos espaces de vie. À la manière d'écumes, ils sont pluriels, multiformes et changeants.
Tangible and intangible connections are everywhere, creating new cultures of space that are reshaping the places we live in. They are as diverse, multiform and shifting as sea foam.

Complex and shifting, the urban world is not easy to depict. Images allow us to get closer, and to express, sometimes via emotion, a reality that is sometimes hard to grasp. But they also create a distance—a space in which to think. These images are also symptoms of what is happening in the world, destabilising our certainties but also providing opportunities for us to control our shared future.

photos

Juan Aballe

Country Fiction (Spain, 2014)

Somewhere in the Iberian Peninsula, Juan Aballe photographs people who have left the city for an idealized countryside of dreams, living their "fragile utopia" in caravans or renovated houses.
www.juanaballe.com

Calle
de la Fuente

442 Gösku Baysal

Far away from state, close to the clouds

(Berlin, Germany, 2013)

May 2013. Turkey was in turmoil after police violently suppressed a demonstration on Taksim Square. Goksu Baysal recorded these days of revolt, photographing crowds up close in the streets denouncing attacks on freedom, press censorship, and government corruption.
www.goksubaysal.com

446 Valentino Bellini

The Bit Rot Project (Italy, 2013)

"Bit Rot" is a colloquial term used in computing to refer to the gradual decomposition of digital data. Valentino Bellini uses it in his way to follow the globalized journey of the voluminous e-waste (electric and electronic) that is constantly growing, until its final elimination.
www.valentinobellini.com

—

Massimo Berruti

Gaza, Miracle Water (Italy, 2015)

In Gaza, successive Israeli military offensives have destroyed infrastructures and deprived inhabitants of vital resources.
In the ruins of the city, Massimo Berruti photographs the people of Gaza in their search for water, which has become a precious commodity.
www.massimoberruti.net

—

454 Toufic Beyhum

Za'artari Champs-Élysées (United Kingdom, 2014)

In the Za'artari camp in Jordan, over 130,000 Syrian refugees survive while awaiting a hypothetical return to their homeland. On the main avenue of the camp, nicknamed the Champs Élysées, shops have been set up and life continues.
www.toufictbeyhum.com

معرض مرام

Anne-Laure Boyer

55 mètres / Déménagements (France, 2008-2010)

Anne-Laure Boyer immortalises from the same angle, the 18 floors of the Grand Pavois in Cenon under demolition. In the next photo, she has recreated "the apartment" with furniture and objects collected from residents relocated in the district of Floirac.
www.annelaureboyer.com

Stéphane Couturier

Alger (France, 2013)

In the heights of Algiers, the Climat de France housing estate, built between 1954 and 1957 by Fernand Pouillon, brought hopes of modernism. 50 years later, 50,000 residents live in this monumental building that is now run down and full of drug dealers.
www.stephanecouturier.fr

—

468 Nicolo Degiorgis

Hidden Islam (Italy, 2014)

Italy has a Muslim population of 1.5 million, but only a handful of official mosques. Within the stronghold of the Northern League, which is openly hostile to immigration, Nicolò Degiorgis opens the doors of garages, warehouses and gymnasiums where, in the absence of places of worship, makeshift mosques are set up.

www.nicolodegiorgis.com

—

FALLI
TIME OUT
TIME OUT
FALLI
PERIODO
BONUS
LOCALI
OSPITI
Cassa Rurale
di Trento
BANCA DI CREDITO COOPERATIVO
RISTO3

s.r.l.
condizionamento
329.4151953

Cédric Delsaux

Nous resterons sur Terre (France, 2009)

In this series of 137 photos taken throughout the world, Cédric Delsaux explores the symbolic places of post-modernity: oilfields, steelworks, waste dumps—desolate landscapes both created and then ruined by Man.
www.cedricdelsaux.com

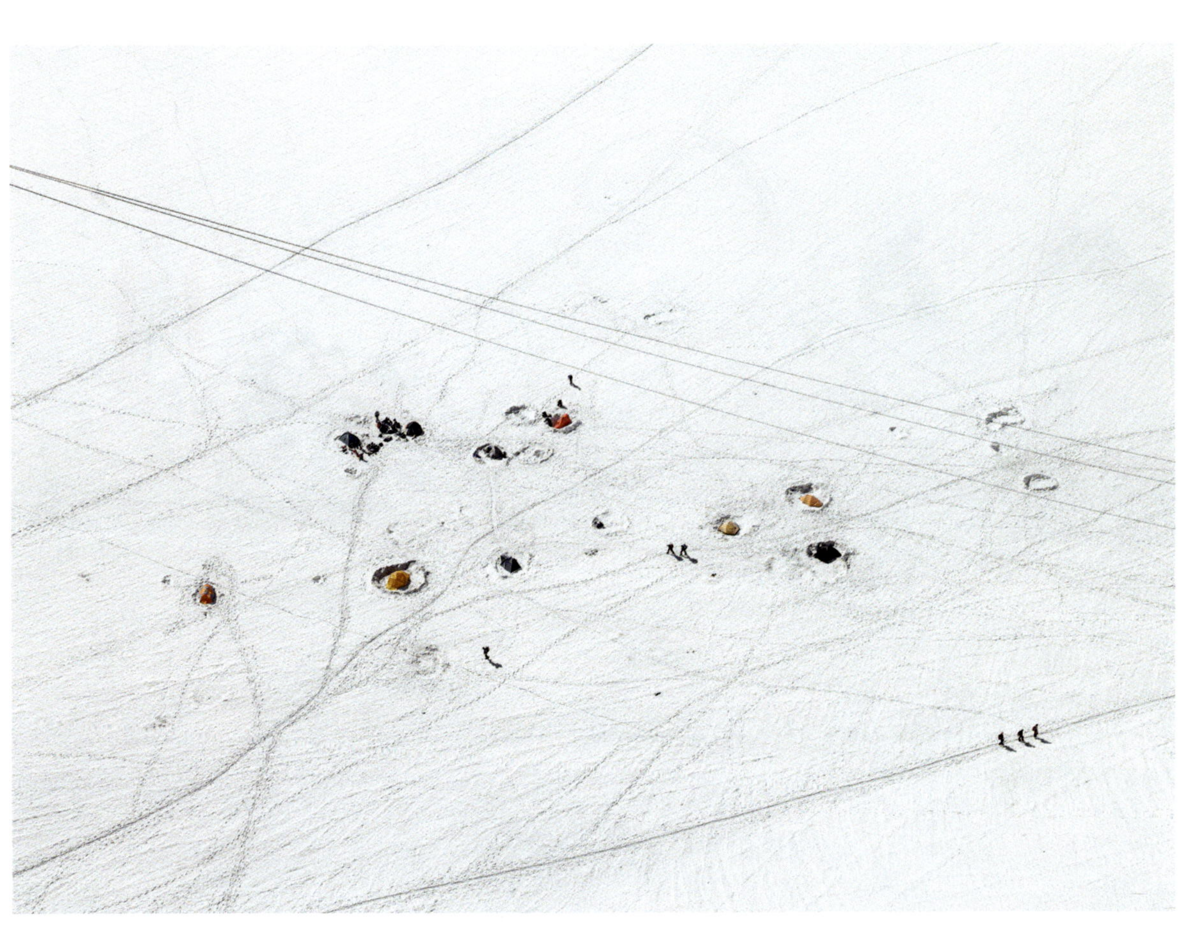

478 Isabelle Eshraghi

Le football féminin au Qatar / Arabie Saoudite : Les femmes en marche (France/Iran, 2010-2014)

The work of Isabelle Eshraghi looks at the role of women in Muslim society. In Saudi Arabia, she photographs businesswomen, doctors and artists whose independence opens the way to changes in mentality. In Qatar, she shows the enthusiasm of teenage girls who experience freedom by playing football in areas protected from the eyes of men.
www.isabelleeshraghi.com

—

ALIA
4
TAR
7

482 Tim Franco

Metamorpolis (France/China, 2009-2014)

In Chongqing, central China, the last remaining farmers cultivate the land at the foot of the skyscrapers, waiting to be devoured by the city. Since 2009, Tim Franco has been documenting the incredible sprawling development of this city with a population of 30 million, one of the most populous in the world.
www.timfranco.com

486 Jorge Fuembuena

Wood Stories (Europe 2011-2013)

From Spain to Notre-Dame-des-Landes, Jorge Fuembuena met with independent communities fighting for "rewilding" and using virgin lands to develop a way of life in direct contact with nature.
www.jorgefuembuena.com

—

490 Zhang Kechun

The Yellow River (China, 2010-2012)

Travelling along the legendary Yellow River that crosses China from West to East, Zhang Kechun offers a languid and unsettling view of the river, capturing the overwhelming grandeur of its landscapes, which mirror the excesses of China's own development.
www.zhangkechun.com

494

Dieuwertje Komen

An Altering Climate (Netherlands, 2010-2014)

In the Netherlands, where a quarter of the land is below sea level, climate change is a particularly urgent issue. Dieuwertje Komen photographs these shifting landscapes that will ultimately disappear, submerged in the more or less distant future by the rising waters.
www.dieuwertjekomen.nl

Gideon Mendel

Drowning World (South Africa, 2010-2014)

Throughout these "submerged portraits" of flood victims in Haiti, Pakistan, Australia, Thailand, Nigeria and the United Kingdom, Gideon Mendel shows the extent of climate change and the shared vulnerability that unites victims beyond frontiers and cultures.
www.gideonmendel.com

—

502 NASA

Earthrise (1968)

This "Earthrise" behind the Moon, photographed by the astronaut William Anders during the Apollo 8 mission changed the way we see our Blue Planet forever. Revealed for the first time in this now iconic picture, it appears in all its fragile beauty.
www.nasa.gov/multimedia/imagegallery

—

Jürgen Nefzger

Fluffy Clouds (France, 2010)

Peaceful scenes of daily life with a sense of looming menace: the chimneys of the nuclear power plant are never far away. In this series, Jurgen Nefzger photographs contemporary European landscapes that are emblematic of the changes taking place within a consumer society in crisis.
www.juergennefzger.com

—

Martin Parr

Playas (United Kingdom, 2007)

For almost thirty years Martin Parr has been photographing beaches throughout the world. In Valparaiso as in Punta del Este in Uruguay or at Mar del Plata in Argentina, his outrageous photos reveal, with humor and irony, the absurdity of our societies of leisure and consumerism.
www.martinparr.com

—

514 Huang Qingjun

Online Shopping Family Stuff (China, 2003-2013)

All across China, even in the most remote regions, Huang Qingjun photographs families at home, displaying all the purchases they made online as if they were organizing a garage sale.
www.huangqingjun.com

518 Philippe Ruault

Untitled (France, 1993-2006)

From the Latapie House in Floirac (a family home) to the renovation of the Palais de Tokyo in Paris (a major centre housing contemporary art), the approach of architects Lacaton & Vassal is clear: to create generous, affordable spaces that shun standard criteria while providing an array of climatic atmospheres, broadening the capacities of use.

IMMIGRATION
PAYS DESTINATION
POOR
RICH

Allan Sekula

Fish Story (United States, 1993)

From 1989 to 1995, Allan Sekula (who died in 2013) crossed the oceans on container ships, photographing the great international industrial ports and the men who work there, taking a critical look at the globalized economic system of maritime trade.

—

"Panorama. Mid-Atlantic." from Fish Story, 1989-1995.
Courtesy of the Allan Sekula Studio

Pieter Ten Hoopen

Tokyo 7 / Tsunami (Netherlands, 2011)

For seven days, Pieter Ten Hoopen followed seven young Tokyoites to discover a city and a country deeply affected by the tsunami of 2011. He photographs the daily life of a new generation, open to the world and broken away from traditional society.
www.pietertenhoopen.com

—

第三大和丸

532 Ambroise Tezenas

Le tourisme de la désolation (France, 2014)

From Rwanda to Tchernobyl, from Sichuan to Cambodia, places where contemporary disasters or genocides have taken place are becoming popular tourist destinations. Ambroise Tezenas has joined some of these macabre package tours and photographed our ambivalent relationship with death and History.
www.ambroisetezenas.com

—

2008-5-12

534 Guy Tillim

Jo'burg (South Africa, 2004)

Jo'burg, the nickname of the birthplace of Guy Tillim. More than twenty years after the end of apartheid and the radical urban transformations that took place, he photographed the squalid districts that are home to the forgotten in the capital of the richest province in South Africa.
www.agencevu.com/photographers/photographer.php?id=137

—

Ulster

odacom

538 Patrick Zachmann

Mare Mater (France, 2009)

Himself the son of a mother who crossed the Mediterranean from Algeria to France, Patrick Zachmann now tells the story of young people who cross the sea to Europe to meet mothers whose children have gone, echoing his own family history.
www.magnumphotos.com

—

constellation.s
films
After Tomorrow
Toufic Beyhum, Carl Gough
2015 - 53 min
Alpi
Armin Linke
basé sur un projet de recherche de
Piero Zanini, Renato Rinaldi et Armin Linke
2011 - 62 min
Bidonville :
architectures
de la ville future
Jean-Nicolas Orhon
2013 - 82 min
Changement
de propriétaire
Aurélien Lévêque, Luba Vink
2015 - 66 min
Habitations
Légèrement
Modifiées
Guillaume Meigneux
2013 - 76 min
Hamou-Beya,
pêcheurs de sable
Andrey S. Diarra
2012 - 72 min
Les messagers
Hélène Crouzillat,
Lætitia Tura
2014 - 70 min
Sud Eau
Nord Déplacer
Antoine Boutet
2014 - 109 min
Unfinished Italy
Benoît Felici
2010 - 33 min

films

Toufic Beyhum, Carl Gough

England, Lebanon, South Africa

After Tomorrow

2015, 53 min, documentary, colour

www.tbeyhumphotos.com

For 200 years, members of the Bdoul, a Bedouin tribe, have bred livestock and farmed the land near the caves of Petra. In 1985, to attract more visitors to this very popular site, the Jordanian government moved them into sedentary dwellings on the outer edges of the area. For two months, Toufic Beyoum filmed the way their traditions have adapted to the phenomenon of tourism, which is central to globalisation.

The "Nan Shui Bei Diao"—literally *South Water North Transfer*—is the largest water transfer project in the world, taking place between southern and northern China. Following the development of this colossal project, this film maps out a land of engineers where cement covers the plains, rivers overflow, deserts become forests… and little by little voices are heard calling for justice and freedom of speech. While matter decomposes and people become increasingly alarmed, an unnatural science fiction landscape emerges.

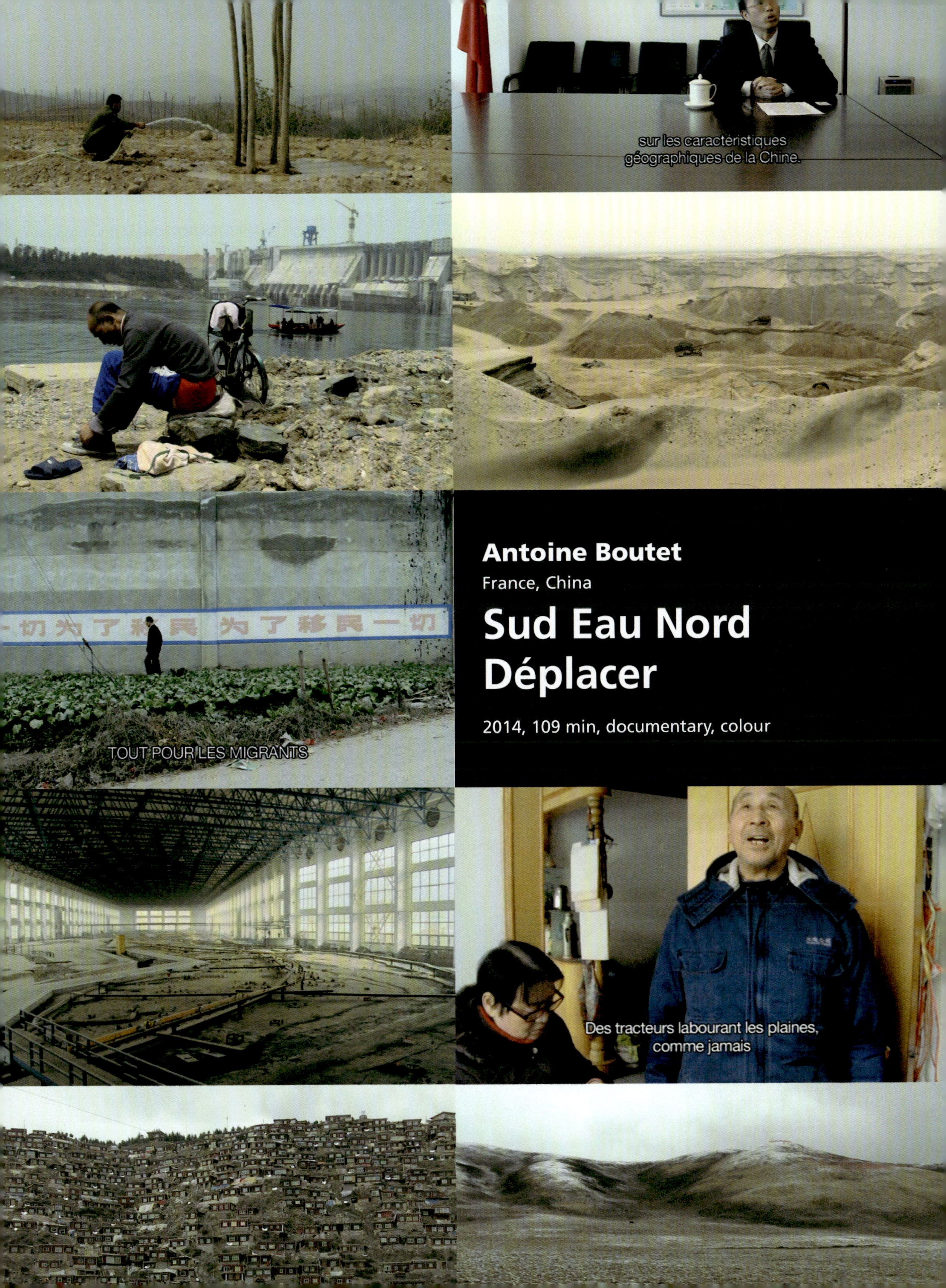

Antoine Boutet

France, China

Sud Eau Nord Déplacer

2014, 109 min, documentary, colour

Hélène Crouzillat, Lætitia Tura

France

Les messagers

2014, 70 min, documentary, colour

www.laetitiatura.fr

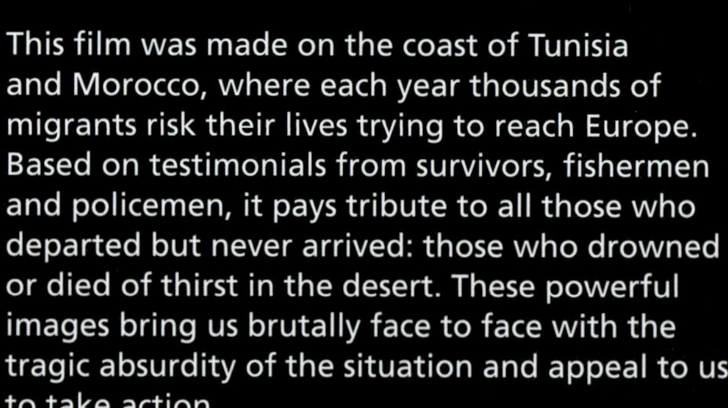

This film was made on the coast of Tunisia and Morocco, where each year thousands of migrants risk their lives trying to reach Europe. Based on testimonials from survivors, fishermen and policemen, it pays tribute to all those who departed but never arrived: those who drowned or died of thirst in the desert. These powerful images bring us brutally face to face with the tragic absurdity of the situation and appeal to us to take action.

On décide qu'ici on attend la mort.
D'ailleurs en ce moment,
la mer remonte des morts.
SEPULTURE
DE
L'an mil neuf cent et le 17 fevrier
je soussigné, de cette Paroisse ai célébré les
obsèques religieuses de
né le
fil de et de
épou de , décédé sur
cette Paroisse
muni d sacrement d et d
En foi de quoi,
SEPULTURE
DE
L'an mil neuf cent et le 17 fevrier
je soussigné, de cette Paroisse ai célébré les
obsèques religieuses de
né le
fil de et de
épou de , décédé sur

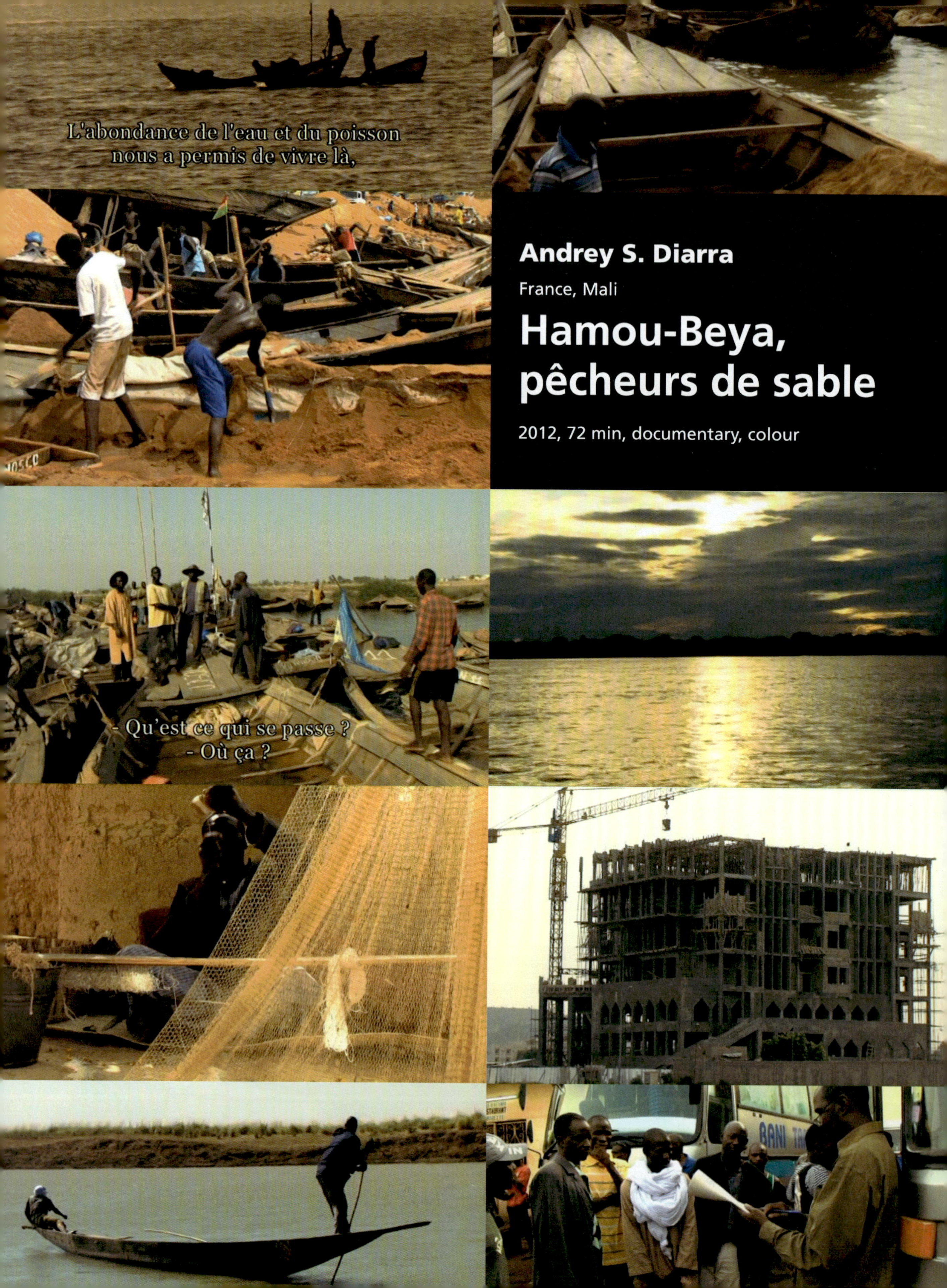

Andrey S. Diarra

France, Mali

Hamou-Beya, pêcheurs de sable

2012, 72 min, documentary, colour

From the area around Mopti, famed for their skills as fishermen, the Bozos now extract the river sand to meet the growing need for concrete in Bamako. This film follows the fortunes of Gala Sabé and depicts an uprooted generation unable to return to its traditional lifestyle and uncertain about its future.

Benoit Felici

Italy

Unfinished Italy

2010, 33 min, documentary, colour
www.benoitfelici.com

des hôpitaux sans patients
et des garages sans sorties -

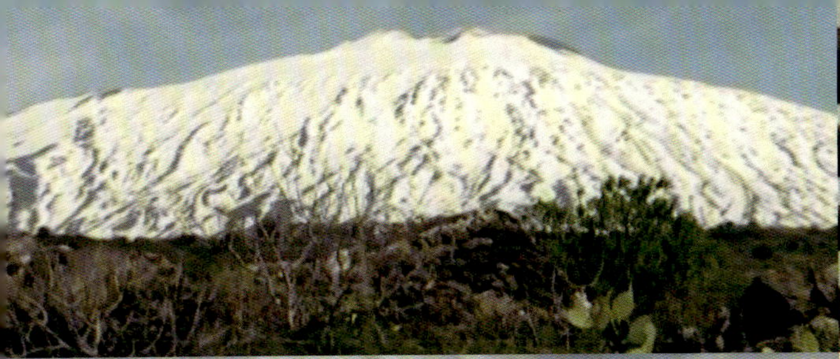

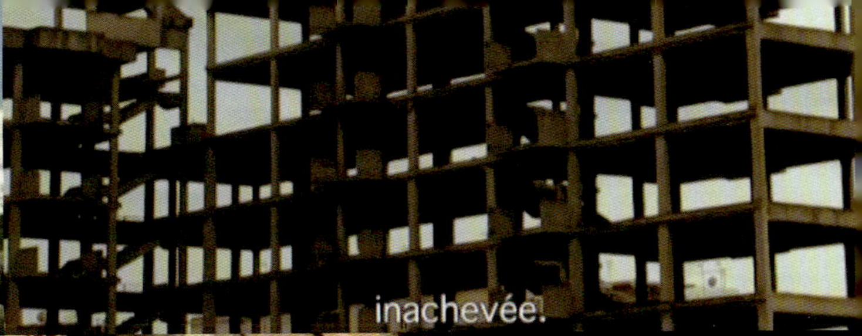
inachevée.

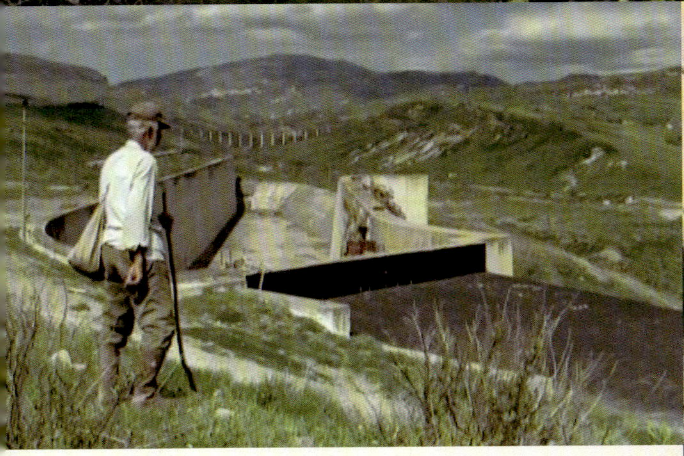

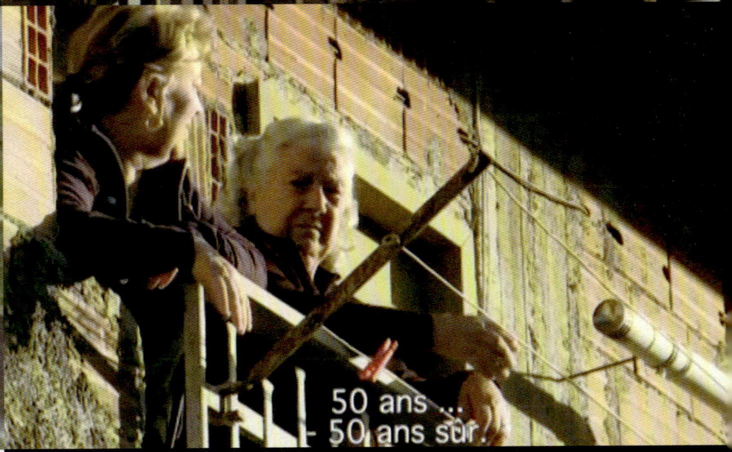
50 ans ...
- 50 ans sûr.

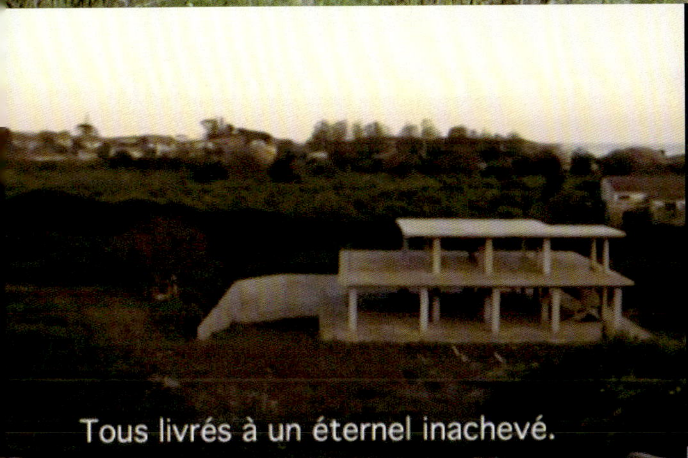
Tous livrés à un éternel inachevé.

On the road in Sicily, Benoit Felici films buildings left unfinished over the past forty years, where Nature has gradually taken over. Some are abandoned and stand oddly in the landscape; others have been renovated. Little by little, the filmmaker reflects the poetry of these modern ruins and shows the local people who have learned to lived alongside them.

PD A247
Moi je n'aime pas les choses
inachevées.

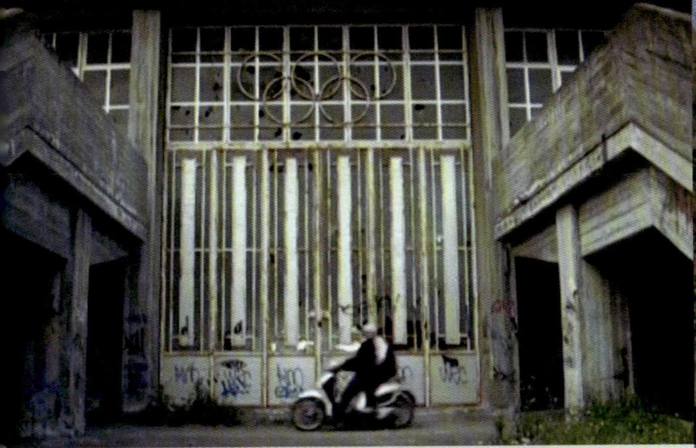

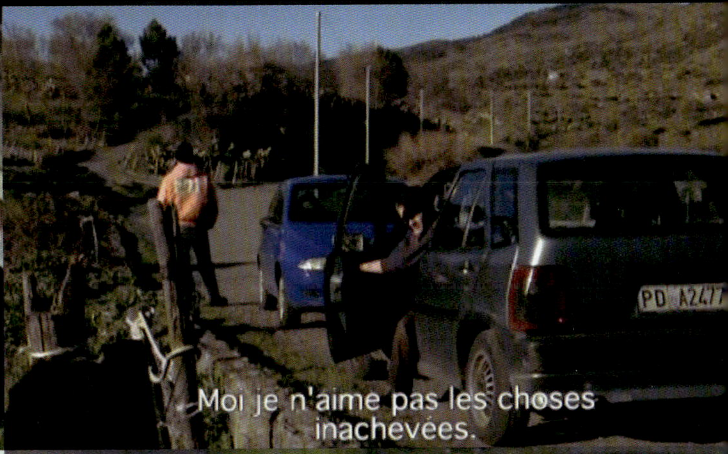

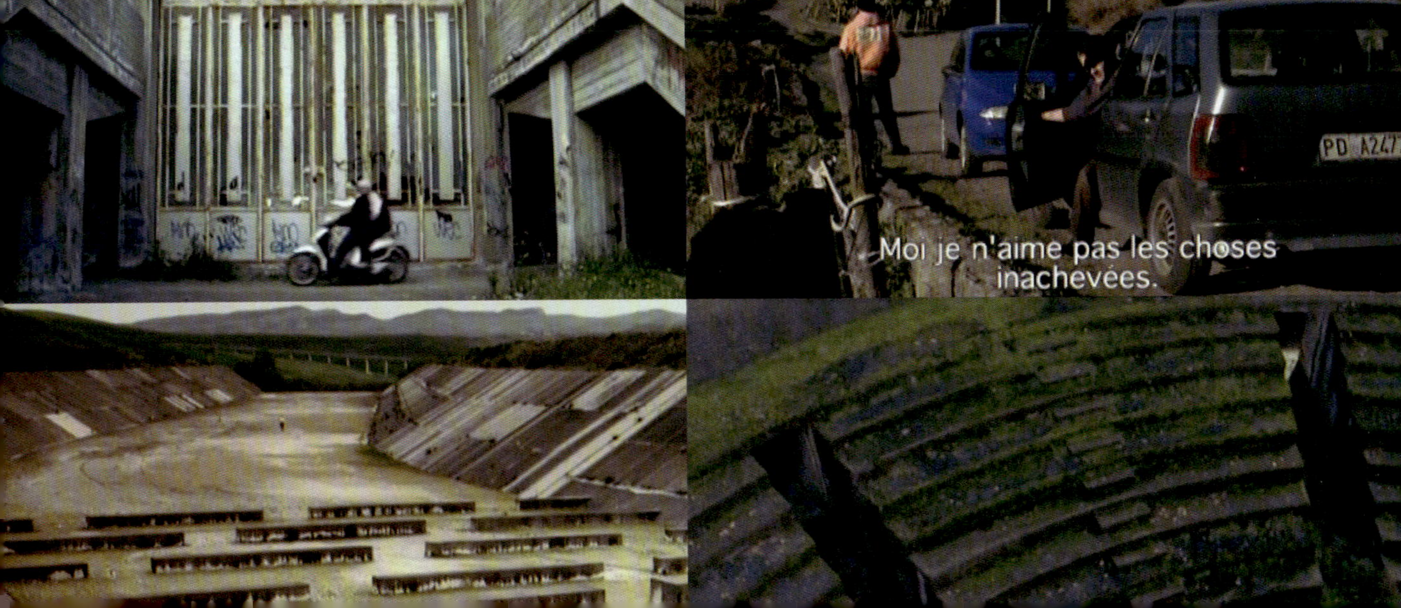

Aurélien Lévêque, Luba Vink

France

Changement de propriétaire

2015, 66 min, documentary, colour
www.changementdeproprietaire.com/Le-film

Terre de Liens is a community movement that sees land as a communal asset. For two years Luba Vink and Aurélien Lévêque followed these activists as they attempt to move industrial farming towards ecological and traditional methods. Their documentary *Changement de propriétaire* focuses on the economic models that the association has invented and perfected since it began.

Armin Linke, based on a reseach project by Piero Zanini, Renato Rinaldi and Armin Linke

Germany

Alpi

2011, 62 min, documentary, colour
www.arminlinke.com

Alpi explores contemporary perceptions associated with the landscape of the Alps. In this film, Armin Linke juxtaposes situations and places that reveal the numerous economic, social and political networks active in the region. He shows what lies behind images of the pristine natural landscape, and reveals the artifice and illusion of the modern world with a hint of irony.

Guillaume Meigneux

France

Habitations Légèrement Modifiées

2013, 76 min, documentary, colour

During the transformation of the Bois-le-Prêtre Tower in Paris by architects Lacaton & Vassal, Guillaume Meigneux recorded the desires, anxieties, hopes, enthusiasms and reluctance of local inhabitants on the subject of this renovation scheme intended to improve their daily lives. The film's colourful testimonials and images of a range of interiors contradict the prejudice that associates high-rise estates with anonymity and uniformity: the building emerges as a true living environment that forms a setting for relationships with others and with the city at large.

Jean-Nicolas Orhon

Canada

Bidonville : architectures de la ville future

2013, 82 min, documentary, colour

www.jnorhon.com

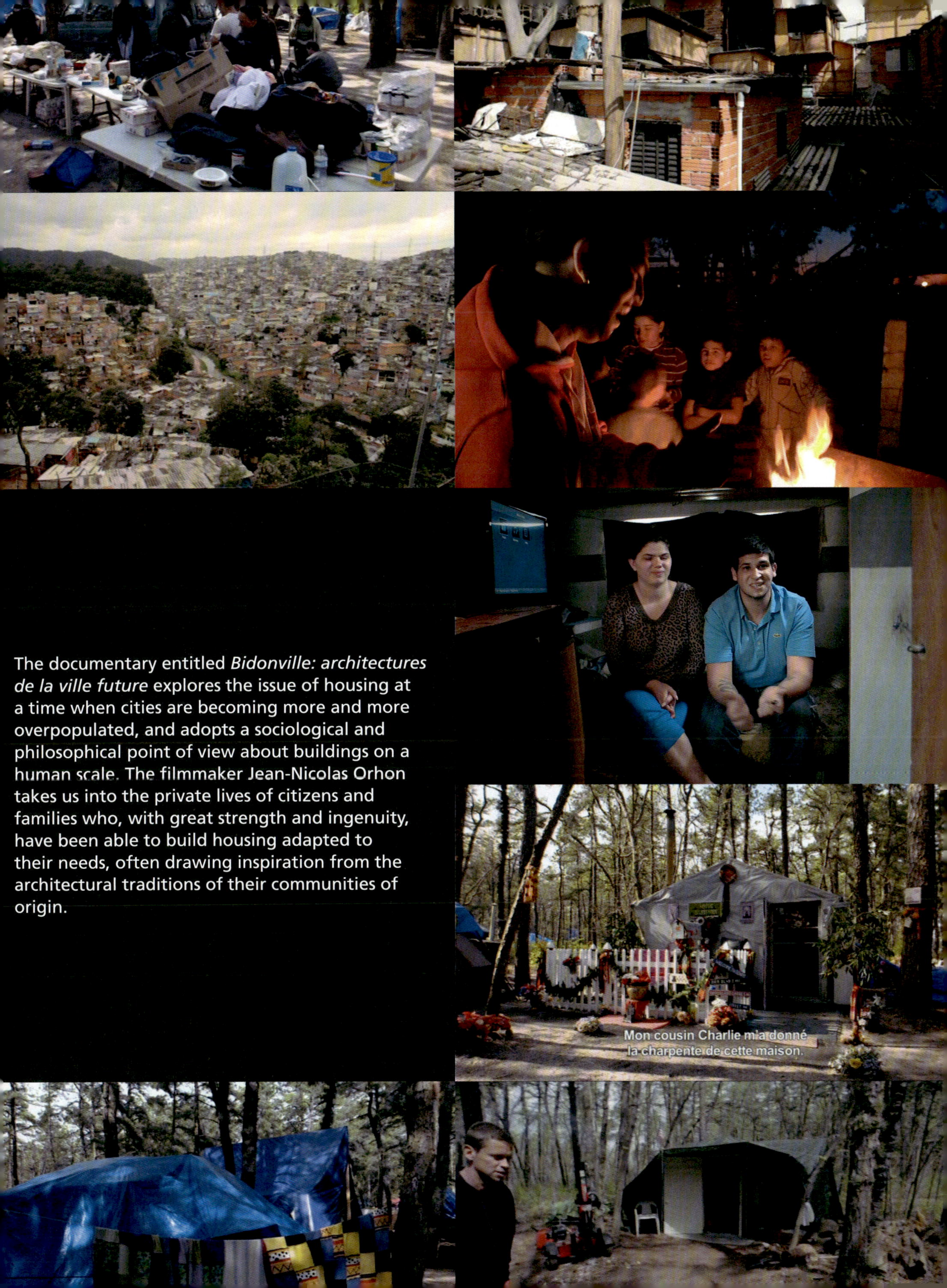

The documentary entitled *Bidonville: architectures de la ville future* explores the issue of housing at a time when cities are becoming more and more overpopulated, and adopts a sociological and philosophical point of view about buildings on a human scale. The filmmaker Jean-Nicolas Orhon takes us into the private lives of citizens and families who, with great strength and ingenuity, have been able to build housing adapted to their needs, often drawing inspiration from the architectural traditions of their communities of origin.

The ways we inhabit the world are shifting and complex, and they require an intellectual approach that is agile, open-minded and flexible. Twenty contributors—anthropologists, architects, economists, geographers, philosophers, political scientists, sociologists—discuss their points of view regarding the issues and mechanisms that determine the way we live in the world.

20 texts

towards an ethic of local care

constellation.s aimed to highlight a new direction for architecture and planning: a path they have seldom taken. It reflects a trend that has captured the attention of global societies for at least a generation, along with an increasingly strong awareness of urban globalisation and its consequences, a gradual awareness of the dawning of the Anthropocene[1], and a sense of the vulnerability of human settlements and the destructive potential of global change. One of its major characteristics, among those we have discussed, is doubtless a renewed interest, on the part of individuals, in the places where they anchor their existence and go about their daily lives. Without going into detail here, we can nevertheless emphasise the fact that many activists, NGOs, international institutions, thinkers, specialists in environmental sciences and workers in the field are focusing on the local scale as it lends itself to the implementation of strategies for coping with and adapting to global change. Alongside the necessary mobilisation of global societies and the implementation of new *ad hoc* global geopolitical strategies, the premise is that we must start from places where daily life actually takes place to experiment with and validate more modest approaches, and to be more actively concerned with the environmental cycles that will keep the ecumene[2] inhabitable. The local sphere is becoming a place where individuals can more effectively gain awareness of their unavoidable and indispensable involvement in what some are presenting as an epic struggle to redefine civilisation and a new way of conceiving the cohabitation of humans and non-humans. It is here that we might actually become aware of the modalities and effects of wasting resources—an awareness required to trigger people's willingness to act. The local sphere, in its countless guises, may well be the new frontier in the struggle against global change[3]!

Taking "care" seriously

This observation should lead us to define more precisely a corpus of principles that might drive a local strategy of adaptation to the consequences of the nascent Anthropocene. The social sciences and the philosophy of the environment have asserted themselves over the past few years as new academic (inter) disciplines that attempt to embrace this new intellectual necessity[4]. In the framework of scientific debate, I will try to define an ethic and a politics of care for the vulnerable local and global ecumene. I will also explore the philosophical aspects of the notion of care, which I feel is eminently transposable to a comprehensive approach to societal space. I refer especially to Joan Tronto's phrase in *Moral Boundaries: "A Political Argument for an Ethic of Care[5]"*.

The term *care* is tricky to translate into French as it refers both to attention to others and the practices and activities undertaken for the benefit of the people we care about. This duality must not be thought of as an inconsistency; Joan Tronto proposes a broad definition of care as "a generic activity that includes everything we do to maintain, perpetuate, and repair our world by linking different elements (our body, ourselves, our environment) into a complex network in support of life[6]." This insistence on the generic nature of care indicates that, for Tronto, care is not reserved for a category of recipients—the weak, the poor, women, "subalterns"—even if they clearly form an "audience" for whom it is most immediately necessary. Care is, in fact, a basic principle of human life. We also note that the philosopher does not reduce it to relationships with others, but extends it to those we establish with everything around us—one might say all the human and non-human realities that surround us, the very realities that architecture and planning aim to include in a "composition" that makes it possible to "keep together", albeit temporarily, "compositions[7]" of humans, non-humans, materials, ideas, and the bodily affects of voice, sound and light. The value of this approach as we move towards the notion of "spatial care" is immediately obvious, thanks to its insistence upon the "complex network" of all the components of individual and social life. This definition aims at nothing less than *"rethinking the entire decorum of contemporary political society"*, which Joan Tronto states to be the intellectual aim of her work: *"What would it mean, in contemporary society, to take the values inherent in care seriously, to consider them part of our definition of a good society? Thoughtfulness, responsibility, educational attention, compassion, and attention to the needs of others are […] traditionally precluded from being given any public consideration[8]."* It is now my turn to take this approach seriously and to attempt to grasp the scope, for a geographer, of the concept of universal care, which defines the modalities of relationships between social realities (individuals, objects, non-humans) that are not only ethically fair but also efficient (it is important, as Joan Tronto says, to think about how the requirements for dignified existence can be met). By making care into a central and essential activity of fragile human life, we shape the kind of relationship that has to be established with any creature, any natural element, any thing that needs to be cared for because it is as intrinsically vulnerable as we are. As a result of this generalised caring and the horizontal relationships it establishes, *"all social and spatial links are redefined, and a collective force imposes itself"* based on the individual and his/her attention to others and other realities. It's tempting to extend this analysis to the local ecumene, insofar as it is the construct of what supports us, surrounds us and exists within us, via the values and imaginary characteristics we attribute to it, the knowledge and norms we attach to it, the actions we undertake in relation to it, and the artefacts we place within it. We necessarily share this ecumene, which both contains us and forms the basis for our actions with others (including non-humans, whose right to exist within it is now attracting more and more attention).

Consequently, I propose to approach spatial care by embracing Joan Tronto's definition with a slight modification (in italics):

"a generic activity that includes everything we do to maintain, perpetuate and repair our habitat and the principles of our local and global cohabitation, *so that we can live as well as possible in our ecumene*.

With this in mind, I consider spatial care to have a twofold dimension that refers to two types of relationship that must be established between inhabitants and their ecumene:

1. Care for the vulnerable system of a habitat (on any scale): this means making it possible to identify and collectively objectify weaknesses in the ecumene for cohabitants (humans and non-humans)—without excluding, of course, questions of asymmetry in social relationships. The aim is to build the notion of vulnerability into social and political contracts and to make it into a communal and public fact that forms part and parcel of shared spatial cultures. At the IPCC (Intergovernmental Panel on Climate Change), at the COP, and in the countless organisations focusing on global change, it seems to me that there are scientists who are helping to clarify these processes and consolidating the concept of the Anthropocene—a good example of collective and democratic objectivisation. We are seeing the gradual development of a new geographic approach (I agree that the process is neither simple nor rapid) that is changing the ways we analyse weaknesses in the terrestrial ecumene in general and in its local manifestations, prompting individuals to become the protagonists of this analysis by designing and carrying out the necessary initiatives. This work also helps us to define the weaknesses that are acceptable, those we can reconcile ourselves to, those we can, in a sense, make our own, protecting ourselves from them and even entering a relationship of "familiarity" (e.g. exposure to storms on the Breton coast, to tsunamis in Japan, or elsewhere to predators that attack livestock, etc.), and those we need to turn away from and whose effects we should not have to suffer (the excessive warming of the atmosphere, brutal reductions in biodiversity, the predatory exploitation of resources, and radical challenges to local ecosystems).

For any habitat, it would be useful to consider that part of the social contract governing communal life is based on a shared and constantly evolving definition of what makes it vulnerable and sensitive to damage, without excluding social questions from this approach. After all, social injustice, poor housing, lack of access to public facilities for many people, and the ostracism some groups suffer—among others—are all things that can threaten the very idea of cohabitation. This brings us to an idea that is at the heart of a book by Frédéric Worms[9], who also sees vulnerability as fundamental to life, considered from the standpoint of "viability" in the sense of "ability to live". He underlines the possibility of constructing an ethic and a politics of care based on constant attention to others. Only such attention makes it possible to highlight the vulnerability we all share and which applies to ourselves and to others. I propose to extend this process to all the elements that are assembled and interlinked by cohabitation within our habitat. "Spatial care" is thus based on a shared concern for the vulnerability of the local sphere, where the latter is most visible, tangible and open to debate, via "care" that operates as a kind of collectively elaborated symptomatology.

2. Care for the stabilising characteristics of a habitat and its ability to tackle and overcome inevitable crises (Japan is inevitably exposed to tsunamis and implements an *ad hoc* spatial culture), without preventing change and adaptation to new situations. This care is a collective effort that must never cease, at the risk of failing to ensure that the living environment is able (albeit minimally) to resist crises of vulnerability—major disasters, for instance.

The spatial dilemmas of cohabitation

The tandem of attention and care required to make the ecumene inhabitable for all allows us to lay down, in exploratory fashion, a few major principles that will help flesh out the notion of "spatial care".

a) At the root of this notion is the act of taking into consideration the *actual activity of cohabitation* among humans and between humans and non-humans. This activity, which is, as we have pointed out, constant, establishes and stabilises spatial commons (habitats) that make us all undergo the experience of "spatial communism", an expression that should be considered in an elementary sense here: i.e. the need to share spaces with others, which we never quite escape from. Within this framework, it is very interesting to start with local spatial installations where we can best observe the ordinary facts of cohabitation and rediscover the primordial nature of certain gestures of "viability" and "concreteness" in social environments[10]. The ecumene we need to focus on is not a natural given, but a composite construct given concrete form by the long-term co-action of human and non-human entities interacting more or less intentionally. Spatial care does not sweep us up into the ethereal realm of abstraction; it brings us back to the observation and consideration of spatial reality itself, in which we find our anchor points, our places of sojourn, the springboards for our departures, and the roads that make our mobility possible.

b) I see spatial care as *a practical theory based on the principle of the involvement and empowerment of stakeholders,* in particular the weakest individuals and subalterns. This is close to Joan Tronto's approach (and Carol Gilligan's); for her, politics is not primarily a matter of sovereignty or authority, just as social relationships cannot be reduced to top-down relationships. She sees politics in terms of the diversity of the social sphere, of ordinary lives, and of that which constitutes their (vital, social or environmental) vulnerability: in other words, in terms of horizontal networks. The politics of care does not involve a process of power; instead it is rooted in the initiatives of "non-decision-makers", demands that their initiatives be made visible, and promotes an insistence on "spatial justice" that allows everyone to inhabit the world in the best way possible. Research in the social sciences increasingly analyses cases where "weak" local societies outstrip entrenched "geo-powers[11]" by insisting on the recognition of their expertise as inhabitants and their ability to define a future for their shared living spaces. Spatial care thus proposes a redistribution of the flow of power: I see it as subverting the established order, but based on a pragmatic approach to "attention to" and "care for" the ecumene: the common asset that we establish and share. This fits perfectly with what many of the cases exhibited in constellation.s have shown us.

c) Trying to define the act of "caring" also makes it possible to give *new importance to the question of dependency,* which is central to Joan Tronto's theory and that of many other thinkers concerned with the notion of fragility. These approaches to dependency remind us that the word can actually have two meanings. On the one hand it denotes the power of one individual (or phenomenon) over another, who finds himself weakened and subordinate. Being dependent means being under the authority or domination of someone/something else, for whatever reason. Productivism and the prevailing moral and political ideology, which encourages autonomy and promotes the power of the individual, often point to the negativity of dependency as the result of a weakness that hinders self-fulfilment—which is why strategies for dealing with fragile individuals (which show clear intellectual similarities to territorial risk prevention strategies) exist. But we tend to ignore another meaning, highlighted by the caring relationship, which points to the possible existence of solidarity between two or more elements (people or things). This is *the positive nature of interdependency,* whose mutuality we recognise, and which arises from the bond that necessarily develops between people who share the same vulnerability.
If we transpose this to spatial care, we can consider that the human habitat is particularly qualified to support the insistence on positive interdependence between all the human and non-human components of the ecumene, which does not express weakness but possesses social strength, provided we leverage the potential that this network of links represents. We should point out that interdependence does not necessarily mean symmetrical relationships. The great (and troubling) idea in the theory of care is to claim that asymmetry is not an obstacle, and that on the contrary it opens up many possibilities. Because it both arises from and creates differences, it allows us to highlight the strength that arises from the dependency of every human with respect to other humans. If we then move on to

spatial care, space and local spatiality provide a vehicle for the analysis of constructive interdependency, a form of mediation that makes it visible, and a way of dealing with it politically.

With this in mind, we might completely reframe the question of the hospitality we are willing to extend to migrants, refugees and asylum-seekers by postulating the effective interdependence of each member of the host society and each refugee. At this point, how is it possible, for example, when we look at the response of public authorities to the so-called "migrant crisis" that Europe has been mismanaging since 2014, to ignore the fact that the way the migrants' living environment—the slum, the makeshift camp, the squat—is organised and the attempts at radically separating that space from that of the "natives" are obvious symptoms of the current inability of many European societies to engage in true spatial care (which is also a way of saying that I am not unaware of the doubtless somewhat ironic nature of my proposal). On the other hand, the engagement of people working towards an ethical response to the questions raised by this shortfall in hospitality involves completely redefining the relationships between living environments by trying to see borders as places of constant exchange and not as fences[12] and striving to make care visible in the landscape.

Spatial care also makes it possible to highlight the importance of *human/non-human interdependence,* which is at the heart of all habitats and all dwellings—a fact that has long been underestimated. This makes it possible to radically change our approach to the way people relate to one another within a system of links that are admittedly asymmetrical, but where nobody and nothing can be automatically seen as an unwanted guest.

It makes us identify and care for the most exposed vulnerable elements of the ecumene: non-humans (and even non-living entities) can then be seen as more vulnerable than humans, and we have to define the local conditions for the care and attention we give them.

d) The logical consequence of the above is that spatial care should lead us to raise a series of elementary questions for each situation of cohabitation that necessarily involves collective regulation: what must be maintained, protected, established, and cared for? What must we share? What can we/must we develop? What can we agree to abandon and to see disappear? What records should we make of this? How can we reconcile the recognition of acceptable fragility with the economic production required to ensure habitability for all? On the latter subject, the issue leads us to think about a non-speculative version of the economy (and indeed to return to the etymology of the word "economy": that which makes it possible to maintain one's dwelling—here considered as the ecumene) and non-superfluous habitats. We must define the conditions for a mode of habitation that frees itself from the focus on power and performance that characterises standard architectural, urban design-related, planning and engineering approaches. It means asking ourselves how we can organise spatial environments and ensure they function as effectively as possible while consuming the least possible resources to meet the needs of the greatest number—including the real social need for entertainment, culture, spending, and even excess.
Although the above questions are general in scope, the answers to them are specific to each situation and each configuration of the habitat that we consider to be appropriate. In this sense, the world in its globality unquestionably constitutes an "appropriate situation" (we have to ask ourselves if it does), just like any other place for which all the problems relating to care arise, however blinkered we decide to be. We should point out that such situations can only be defined when concrete action is taken, and that the existence of a reliable and solid democracy is the primary condition for true spatial care—and we are nowhere near achieving this, even in many democratic countries.

In any case, we are seeing the emergence of concrete "moral dilemmas[13]", which are actually spatial and ecumene-related dilemmas in the sense that they arise from spatial issues that pose a problem, point to vulnerability in the habitat, and oblige people to make individual and collective choices determined by observations, differences in points of view, and the interdependence—whatever they might think of it—of the different stakeholders. These dilemmas are all specific: they can only be solved by looking at the reality of cohabitation and the general questions it raises. The practice of spatial care might make it possible to model, simulate, and play out spatial dilemmas before they veer into actual conflict. It could, above all, ensure that such dilemmas remain open-ended, by refusing to use abstract ideas or values to shut the door on issues and by taking full account of the context (which expresses a specific arrangement of the ecumene) and of the modalities of cohabitation specific to each living environment.

e) Paying attention to the habitat and the inhabitable environment leads us to recognise and highlight *the labile nature of human installations and the uncertain and indeterminate nature of human initiatives*. This is a departure both from the prevailing ideologies shared by local and city authorities that generally promote the notion of the irreversibility and permanence of buildings (notwithstanding external threats from which they must be protected), and from the certainty of rational intervention. It also represents a departure from native identity-driven initiatives that essentialise local environments and their culture and claim that they are immutable and untouchable. But if we recognise that the vulnerability of each living environment is innate, insofar as it is one of the necessary conditions for its existence, and if we observe spaces while taking into account the interspatiality of individuals, then that changes everything.
We are becoming aware that all spatial situations are, in a way, makeshift, labile,

and fleeting; aware of how they depend on a particular moment in time and on the place where the people involved set up and arrange their realities according to their spatial needs, before moving on and settling somewhere else, thus forming new spatial situations[14]. The new approach to fragility that this attentiveness presupposes allows us to identify the importance of uncertainty with respect to cohabitation: we never know exactly what we're doing, nor what lies behind what we do, and yet we have to do something. This prompts us to approach the ecumene with care, delicacy, conciliation and restraint, applying a kind of active prudence based on common sense: that of the cohabitants themselves (a kind of *phronesis*), which determines what action needs to be taken based on observations of what constitutes the foundations of our habitat and what defines the inhabitable. Spatial care challenges and rejects the arrogance of certainty and probability (that of engineering, of management, and of insurance forecasting), focusing instead on the uncertain future of spatial life: its ambiguity, its open-endedness, the equivocal nature of its unfinished scenarios, its stories that are not only unfinished but impossible to tell in their entirety.

The notions of "attention" and "care" outlined above are inconceivable without allowing for the active participation of all the stakeholders in spatial situations, first and foremost the inhabitants, whose status as "dwelling experts" must be acknowledged and highlighted. Their expertise is based on ordinary everyday practices, but we would be wrong to see it as less significant than specialist know-how based on objectivisation and scientific reasoning. We might even say that the pragmatic expertise arising from first-hand knowledge, thanks to the effects of unquestionable truth and the power of individual experience, is always right. Every time this is forgotten, we end up with initiatives that are questionable—and will now

be increasingly called into question.
But we can't stop at this observation alone, at the risk of drifting towards a kind of "participation" that would be a mere forum for the expression of individual opinions—especially as, if we accept the idea that all inhabitants have to be involved, we can't just select what we see as the good, relevant ideas and reject the bad ideas that need to be held in check. We have to take everything on board and accept that asking people for their opinion can, rationally speaking, sometimes have disturbing results. Ruwen Ogien emphasised this in his book on education: *"Even if it's regrettable, rational thought can ultimately make values such as selfishness, fierce competiveness, reward for merit, and even money attractive*[15]*."* With respect to global change, we'll inevitably come across climate-change deniers spouting rationally constructed arguments, and we can't just make them leave the room. What we *can* do is put their words into perspective by placing them within a broader polyphony of "inhabitants' opinions". We thus discover that *spatial care is an educational process* whereby people are taught to care for the ecumene. Based on the shared local experience upon which such an approach can be built, the idea is to spark a transaction between very different individuals that can be seen as an intercultural learning curve where the group learns from each individual and each individual learns from the group (and where humans also learn from the non-human). The aim is to move towards a new ecology of ecumene-related knowledge, restoring the status, in particular, of everything that relates to the vernacular (the observation of so called "native peoples" has shown how important it is to take this into account).
To achieve this, we need to define ad hoc "specifications" that are explicit and accepted by all the participants. In such a framework, specialist technical and scientific skills are not placed over and above everything else; instead they form part of a polyphonic thought process and are seen as powerful educational instruments that make it possible to articulate different registers of knowledge within a single shared learning discourse, using media that make it possible to illustrate projects and develop narratives to describe them effectively. These skills are essential, and must allow the spatial reality of each inhabitant to find its place—and its meaning—in what we do to ensure that our world remains inhabitable.

1. At the 35th World Geology Congress in Cape Town, from 27 August to 4 September 2016, an official decision was made to consider the Anthropocene as a new "epoch" (part of the Quaternary "period" of the Cenozoic "era", to use the exact terms), and to consider that it began after 1945.

2. The ecumene is the living space inhabited by humans.

3. Michel Lussault, *Hyper-lieux. Les nouvelles géographies de la mondialisation,* Paris, Le Seuil, 2017.

4. Catherine Larrère and Raphaël Larrère, *Penser et agir avec la nature. Une enquête philosophique*, Paris, La Découverte, 2015 ; Bruno Latour, *Face à Gaïa*, Paris, La Découverte, 2015.

5. Joan Tronto, *Moral Boundaries. A political argument for an ethic of care*, London-New York, Routledge, 1993).

6. Idem, ibid, p. 143.

7. Bruno Latour, "An Attempt at a Compositionist Manifesto", *New Literary History,* vol. 41, n°3, 2010.

8. Idem, ibidem, p. 32.

9. Frédéric Worms, *Le moment du soin. À quoi tenons-nous ?*, Paris, PUF, coll. "Éthique et philosophie morale", 2010.

10. We recall the etymology of the word "concrete": *cum-crescere*, to grow together – a similar idea to cohabitation.

11. I have coined this concept with reference to Michel Foucault's "biopower". I define it as the power of bodies that intend to spatialise human (and increasingly non-human) activity in a normative way, in other words to conceptualise and construct standardised and prescriptive material spaces for existence.

12. Michel Agier, *Les Migrants et nous. Comprendre Babel*, Paris, CNRS Éditions, 2016.

13. Ruwen Ogien, *L'Influence de l'odeur des croissants chauds sur la bonté humaine*, Paris, Grasset, 2011.

14. Michel Lussault, "L'expérience de l'habitation", in *Habiter : mots et regards croisés, Annales de géographie*, n° 704 (4/2015), Paris, Armand Colin, 2015.

15. Ruwen Ogien, *La guerre aux pauvres commence à l'école*, Grasset, 2013, p. 93.

using the concept of *hors-lieu* to understand precarious areas

Michel Agier anthropologist

What is publicly revealed via the so-called migrant crisis (which is actually the crisis of nation-states with respect to mobility) is how hard it is to conceptualise mobility.
This is a difficulty that is well known in anthropology—in fact since its beginnings, since anthropology was founded as a form of ethnology that required unity between places, cultures and identities—and that is how it is still known. Transparency between the three terms probably never existed, but in any case ethnology, and in a way anthropology, gave it credence in their monographs and their monographic approach. Anthropology mapped out its territory in the social sciences and in philosophical thought based on this equation. But it's quite obvious that the equation no longer exists—if it ever did—since the advent of what we call human globalisation, the globalisation of merchandise, and the globalisation of cultures. Places, identities and cultures are now considered separately.
There is no longer unity of place because one can live in several places. We know that hardly anyone lives in the village or town where they were born, and yet we continue to hear people say that in a normal world, migrants should live in, and must thus return to, the place where they came from. Imagine if everyone here was told to go back to the place where they were born: we'd be in real trouble.
There's no unity of culture because it is no longer possible to associate cultures with places. Cultures move very fast; cultural items move very fast, putting themselves back together in new environments and new social and symbolic systems. We see widespread phenomena such as hybridisations, which make it hard to associate a particular cultural item with a particular place.
Last but not least, the relationship between identity and place and between identity and culture does not work either, because we are at a point where we can affirm one identity in the morning, defend another in the afternoon and demonstrate in support of a third in the evening, be it identity based on gender, nationality, skin colour or profession… There are thus a great many identities in which the relationship with place and culture is constantly being deconstructed by the practices we adopt as individuals or groups.
This crisis highlights the importance of mobility in the world and forces us to invent alternative methodologies and theories that place mobility at the centre of things. It's akin to what anthropology does: creating a kind of general reversal where, instead of being disturbed by mobility, we place it at the centre of our thinking about humanity in general and humans in society in particular.
The notion of *hors-lieu* strikes me as being one of the responses to this need. Without really claiming to elaborate a concept, I have tried to coin a term that makes it possible to describe a number of things temporarily. The *hors-lieu* is not in competition with the anthropological definition of place; it complements that definition. By putting forward the idea of the *non-lieu*, I think Marc Augé wanted to shake up our certainties relating to locality and point out that there are things that no longer work in the world as it is now—the contemporary world of the anthropologist. We can no

longer associate people with places. Places are becoming multiple and mobile. We lose ourselves in them, and it is this meaning that the term *non-lieu* refers to, with a pun on the absence of guilt: our general innocence with respect to what seems abnormal[1].

The *hors-lieu* is situated within this perspective: understanding the spaces in which lives are lived today. The *hors-lieu* is a little descriptive concept that I'm keeping just as it is, without wanting to make any more of it. It's very close to the idea of "heterotopia" developed by Michel Foucault, or Zygmunt Baumann's ideas on extraterritoriality. *Hors-lieu* is a notion that refers to something that is almost, but not quite, outside. It refers to a boundary, something we can see as being outside but which, since we can see it, is not so far away; not really outside. It's not absolute outsideness, and it's not radical otherness: it's on the edge. It's a little bit outside: it's relative exteriority.

I observe that a number of places are developing in a state of precariousness. And what is precarious, by definition, does not last, but we have to understand that those places also change. Let's say that the term *hors-lieu* can help us to understand the status of certain places that are generally associated with extraterritoriality and a certain existence of their own: an internal dynamic, so to speak. This is true of camps and encampments, but they need to be described and deconstructed because there are a great many configurations that can correspond to that reality.

To mark out that reality, and to go further than the descriptive concept of the *hors-lieu* and exemplify it, it struck me that one might use the concept of the *forme-camp*. This concept makes it possible to distinguish situations characterised by extraterritoriality, exception and exclusion—that is to say the geographical, legal and social elements that put people on the outside: an outside that doesn't exist, an invented outside, an outside that is a fiction

---

1. Translator's note: *non-lieu* literally means 'non-place' but its usual meaning is the dismissal of a court case: in legal terminology, a nonsuit.

invented for, or because of, a position that defines itself as central and which is founded on a negation of individuals akin to the negation of stateless people, supernumeraries, and so on.
Once again, it must always be said that we think "at a given point in time", because I try not to essentialise the word "space" and the word "person". Precarious situations are a more and more widespread and topical phenomenon, which is why we have to describe situations "at a given point in time". So today we can say that there are seventeen million people living in one form of camp or another. We can be more or less certain of that. But what will these forms of camps become? Camps or encampments that have been opened in various parts of Europe, around Syria, in the Middle East, as well as those that have existed for decades in Pakistan or Africa, are all changing. There are even camps that can, at some point, stop being camps. This is true of the outskirts of Khartoum, where camps have officially become suburban areas. They have at last been freed from their definition as camps. So we can say: today, as we speak, there are seventeen million people in the world who are in camps of one form or another, but tomorrow that will have changed. Of course, geopolitical and economic change means that all of this is in constant flux, but I think we need these concepts. The term *hors-lieu* is a little concept that makes it possible to describe a given moment in these precarious spaces and the precarious people that live in them.
If it's important to study the development of camps and encampments in Europe in their contemporary emerging forms, it is because they implicitly tell us about hospitality and the process of its disappearance, and it is also because of their ambivalence, or rather because of the ambiguity that forms throughout their long-term existence.

Hospitality as a relationship

Faced with the political challenges linked to the arrival of migrants in Europe, what the anthropologist can do is to entirely rethink the notion of hospitality by returning to what the anthropologist and historian Florence Dupont calls "Derrida's mistake", which consists in believing in the existence of unconditional hospitality, in other words a virtue or an ethical position that puts hospitality before everything else. Florence Dupont does not contest the principle, but the possibility of thinking further once this idea has been formulated. According to her, the translation of Xenos is not "foreigner". Xenos is the partner of Xenia, the host, and is thus a partner in the relationship of hospitality; this in turn implies that there is no absolute foreigner, as there is always a relationship. Florence Dupont critiques Derrida's arguments in texts he wrote in around 1995-1997. The 1995 assembly of the International Parliament of Writers produced a Cities of Refuge Charter, which was given concrete form in the same year in the Network of Cities of Refuge; this continued the following year at the Cities of Refuge Conference. These projects and institutions did not last long and failed to keep their promises, but they are echoed today in expressions of commitment such as the "network of hospitable cities" in which the Mayor of Grande-Synthe takes part, or the Cities of Refuge Manifesto signed by several mayors of major European cities, including Anne Hidalgo, mayor of Paris. At the 1995 Parliament of Writers, Derrida gave a speech, repeated at other seminars and in other discussions and texts, which was at once fascinating and unsettling. Derrida held that hospitality is unconditional: I host whomever I want to, and the foreigner is an absolute concept that only exists outside of all context. This makes real, pragmatic adhesion difficult. In concrete terms, the question is: "if I don't host everyone who comes, I am not within the ethics of hospitality: the right ethics". The problem of philosophy is that it talks about ethics without dealing with real life. What anthropology can do is resituate words within the context of their utterance. We can then ask the question again: "Whom shall I welcome into my home?" and the anthropologist answers: "I welcome into my home relatives, children, cousins, an uncle, maybe an aunt—unless I don't get on with them". There's "practical kinship" and there's "representational kinship," as Bourdieu said. For kinship to happen, we need people we get along with, and with whom a real relationship exists. But this goes beyond the private meaning of hospitality that René Schérer analysed so well: where does familiarity survive? Familiarity can still be seen in the spheres of trust we deploy in our immediate surroundings: in community work, in politics, in religion: in places where we can recognise people via the networks they belong to, via the trust we place in them, via the faith we share with them, and so on. In this chain and in these networks, there's a tipping point between what relates to private hospitality and what is always provided in a relationship, and something else that moves away from that without necessarily breaking away from it. The words "host" and "guest" share the same roots. Hospitality is the implementation of a prerequisite. It is only delegated when one can no longer state under what conditions, and within what kind of relationship, it will take place. But the condition is always there.

Historically, the origins of public hospitality date back to hospices in mediaeval towns and the work of Saint Vincent de Paul and the Sisters of Charity. Some writers consider that this period and these institutions are the historic roots of humanitarian activity. The role of the hospitality provider was delegated to the Church and gradually to public institutions. From that moment on, the fundamentally anthropological relationship based on gift and counter-gift, which established hospitality as a form of exchange, was left behind.
Moving a long way forward in history, we arrive in the 19th and 20th centuries where

public hospitality became an affair of State and disappeared at the same time, replaced by the right to asylum and refugees' rights. The Nation-State embraced the notion of asylum, then diluted it in policies designed to control borders, territories and movements. The word "asylum" is still used in two ways: one can provide asylum, and one can lock someone up in an asylum. In this terminology and these policies, all traces of hospitality have been lost, which explains the point of view developed by some people today according to which the idea of public hospitality is a deceptive metaphor used to talk about public policy. I do not share this point of view even though I understand the criticism levelled at the State. Paradoxically it idealises private hospitality, whereas anthropology resituates the practice in its social and historic context and makes it possible to rethink the admittedly complex continuity between private and public hospitality so that it can ultimately point to an alternative—and first of all a new narrative of hospitality.

Let's look at how the meaning of hospitality is being redefined today, based on what has happened in Calais. In April 2015, the Mayor of Calais asked for the migrants to be moved away from the town and placed in a State-organised camp. She intended the migrants, supported by associations, to be kept at a distance of seven kilometres in a specific area, surrounded and controlled by police patrolling the three roads surrounding it (the fourth being the motorway providing access to the port, separated from the camp by a very high fence topped with barbed wire). In other words, the migrants were told: "this is the only place where you're tolerated"—note especially the use of the word "tolerated". For months, expressions of solidarity came from various European countries, especially people signing up on line to spend a week or two in Calais to provide help. The place changed incredibly fast. The same thing happened as in refugee camps in Africa, the Middle East or elsewhere, but in these other contexts it took several years for such changes to take place . The amount of resources and level of commitment are far higher in Calais than in Africa, and things changed very fast. In late December, something that everyone ended up calling a "slum" emerged: something that apparently looked like a slum and no longer quite like a camp. Churches, mosques, schools, restaurants, a theatre, and a legal aid centre were built. In January, a Europe-wide movement got under way in France with the *appel des huit-cents*: a petition against the situation in Calais signed by eight hundred intellectuals and artists. Calais had become *the place to be*. Calais had become a political place, a place where people were starting to live in relative comfort—insofar as one can live comfortably in a slum. Some people even forgot to chase lorries at night in an attempt to get to the UK because, in the end, a lot of things were going on in the camp. Some people started to think they might stay and apply for asylum in France, not to stay in France but to stay in Calais, because living there wasn't so bad. With the help of all the solidarity surrounding them, people made a relatively hospitable place for themselves. One might call this "urban hospitality", arising from the sociability of the city's inhabitants. Within the same timeframe, the Mayor of Grande Synthe, a town about fifty kilometres away, also demanded a decent housing solution, in collaboration with Médecins Sans Frontières. He announced the opening of a "humanitarian camp".

A few days ago, the Paris City Council announced its support for the Babels research program at the Agence Nationale de la Recherche (ANR) on cities of refuge, borders and migrants. This signals a change of position, or at least an attempt at one, on the part of the City of Paris, not only with respect to the State but also with respect to other European capitals and cities such as Barcelona and Venice. The Paris Mayor signed an appeal for cities of refuge that was not widely disseminated in France—much more so in Spain and Italy. It announced that the Mayor intended to create, as in Grande

Synthe, a humanitarian refuge for migrants in Paris—and it's significant that it was to be in Paris and not outside the city. The Mayor of Paris wanted to follow in the footsteps of the Mayor of Grande Synthe, whose initiative was widely covered in the media, announcing that she would set up a "humanitarian camp". It would be interesting to reflect upon the use of this term, what it is supposed to mean, and if local mayors know what a camp within the humanitarian framework really is.
These are just words, of course, but in the current context words matter. For example, when the Mayor of Grande Synthe says: "I am the mayor of a town and in my town no one must starve or freeze to death", he returns to a principle of local hospitality, something between private hospitality and public hospitality that has been taken over, transformed and diluted by the State.
In the current situation, given the role of major cities in the world, the town or city can play a very important role in this relationship with solidarity and hospitality, even when this relationship turns out to be in conflict with the State.

The future of camp residents as citizens

When in March the government decided to demolish the southern section of the Calais camp, which was the most "slum-like" section where most changes had taken place, a dozen occupants sewed their lips together and went on hunger strike for a fortnight. They asked to meet a UN representative to say what they had to say. Unfortunately for them, they were only introduced to the HCR representative in France, which isn't much when you want to meet a UN representative! He told them more or less the same thing as the Minister of the Interior Bernard Cazeneuve, although he did listen to them for a little longer.
Several times, in various refugee camps in various countries, I've noticed that the people in camps are highly politicised. They're constantly engaging in politics: they demonstrate in front of "humanitarian

compounds", the areas where the offices and housing for the UN and humanitarian agencies are grouped together. When government or HCR vehicles go by, they stop the NGO vehicles and take them hostage, surrounding them for twenty-four or forty-eight hours until their demands are met—demands that are very often practical but which can sometimes be more complex.
For example, they get pastors in Sierra Leone to address camp leaders, because churches form in the camps and the pastors become the leaders of the discontented people who live in them. They bring lists of complaints to weekly camp government meetings. They organise a lot of political demonstrations, but each time it's hard to know who they need to talk to. It's like the Calais migrants asking to talk to "a UN representative".

In these cases, we are literally faced with what Etienne Balibar calls *le devenir citoyen* (the process of becoming a citizen), which I discuss in my book entitled *Borderlands*. Stateless citizens practice citizenship. What we don't see, what we see very little in media reports, not because they're dishonest but because I think journalists don't know what to say, are demonstrations and placards demanding that human rights be respected, demanding the right to mobility, demanding that borders be opened. Policy on migrants is also policy on borders: it raises the issue of crossing a frontier between one country and another and between one form of citizenship and another.

It's politics, and it's everywhere: it's in Idomeni, it's on Lesbos with the protests and the fire at the Moria camp, it's in Calais… it's in all those places. Camps are political places. Politics is played out in very precise areas: in the streets of Calais, in the port of Calais. When they decide to occupy the ferry, we arrest them saying that they're delinquents or wretched fools who believed they could get to England. That's not true, they're just people engaging in politics, occupying a strategic place on the border. Even if the media have really got their act together over the past year following the example of a handful of journalists at Le Monde, Libération and Médiapart, they still find it hard to treat this question as a political subject. But everyone finds it hard to see this as one of the new places where we can find the politics we're desperately looking for in town squares and wherever else. I think it's important to understand that the border is one of the new arenas for politics.

what does "living in precarity" mean?

Guillaume le Blanc philosopher

Today, the tragedy of life, of millions of lives, is the risk of being obliterated becase many people have nowhere to go on Earth. "Having a place", in the strongest sense, refers to the ability to occupy a space and to see that ability recognised. It is probably no accident that many current movements such as Occupy or Nuit Debout aim to reoccupy certain areas. It is also what is suggested in the title of *L'Occupation des sols* by Jean Echenoz: there can be no life without some form of land occupation. Knowing what land we can occupy makes life possible.

For Hannah Arendt, the pariah is the person who no longer has a place, who is obliterated in advance, who has no rights at all. Conversely, an integrated life, a life for which inclusion is not a problem, is a life that is sure of being "inside", sure to provide a job, a home, laws, ID papers, and health cover. "Inhabiting" is all that at once: it's a life that is guaranteed. We can't "inhabit" if we have a roof over our heads but no health cover. Inhabiting isn't just having somewhere to live: it is a principle of accreditation for existence in the world. Some lives have social properties given to them by the possibility of having a place. They are lives that are relatively sure of being inside. Then there are lives that are totally outside, unfortunately. The excluded person is the one who is outside, in the strictest sense of the word. In French homeless people are said to live "à la rue" (literally, "at the street"). One might wonder about the use of the word "à" (instead of "dans"), which expresses an openness to a regime of space, but which does not allow individuality to develop: a kind of radical exposure.

Precarity is often confused with exclusion, from a theoretical point of view. Precarity is both inside and outside—it touches on the notion of *hors-lieu* developed by Michel Agier. A person living in precarity has a set of qualities, of social properties, which allow him to inhabit; but he does not have all the social properties that allow him to inhabit durably. The person living in precarity lives in his space in a non-durable fashion. He is at once inside and outside. In this inside/outside scenario, the question is how to think about precarity as an in-between state between the inside of inclusion, which is obviously something of a pipedream, and the outside of exclusion. The precarious person wants to be included and, at the same time, he is afraid of becoming an excluded person—afraid of having a sort of "negative career".

This is why we have to think carefully about the fragility of the act of "inhabiting". To inhabit is to actively occupy a space without which existence itself becomes precarious. There's a risk of becoming a ghost, of seeing one's life disappear when this principle of habitat steps outside of its own existence. It's as if one's own centre of gravity were outside of oneself. We know full well that a building has a centre of gravity. But if we imagine that the centre of gravity of a building is outside, it collapses. There's a risk of collapse in the strictest sense for an individual when his habitat is in crisis. And his habitat is in crisis when one of the four properties of "inhabiting" is in crisis: a roof, papers (laws), health cover, and education. This is what happens to a lot of people.

When we analyse these precarious lives, these existences where the act of inhabiting is in crisis, it is important not to erase, with a theoretical and practical gesture of added violence, the fundamentally creative ability these precarious existences have to inhabit. The risk, basically, is to add to the objective precarity of a life the kind of violence that involves refusing to look at the inventiveness of the precarious person's way of inhabiting. Think of places such as unmapped slums. The effort of mapping a slum, the effort of giving voiceless people a voice, is part of a desire to recognise the richness of how precarious people inhabit. From this point of view, a "life in poverty" must not be seen as a "poor life".

Towards a policy of inhabiting

These thoughts lead us to consider the political dimension of habitation. Occupy and Nuit Debout are, of course, ways of experimenting with a place. But we must not forget what these movements convey, namely a challenge to the unequal distribution of wealth through which some people become place-grabbers. Let us remember the beginning of the second part of Rousseau's *Discourse on the Origin and Basis of Inequality Among Men*: *"The first person who, having enclosed a plot of land, took it into his head to say this is mine and found people simple enough to believe him, was the true founder of civil society. From how many crimes, wars, and murders, from how many horrors and misfortunes might not any one have saved mankind, by pulling up the stakes, or filling up the ditch, and crying to his fellows: Beware of listening to this impostor."* The act of taking over a space or a piece of land involves an unequal distribution of capital. The question of cohabitation is thus both ethical and political.

How much do different modes of existence matter to us? How do we fight against the spread of ghettos or, at best, separated places in cities? These questions invite us to think about neighbourliness, in the philosophical sense of the word. Today, space is taken over by neighbours. When we get ready to live somewhere, we function according to the famous social law: *"Birds of a feather flock together"*. People live according to a presupposed idea, which is to mimic their neighbour. But inhabiting consists, on the contrary, of settling in a place that precedes its own inhabiting. It is to recognise that the practice of one's existence, one's space and one's habitat is part of a history of habitat, and that it involves others. Inhabiting is being placed among others, it's being situated among others, it's being situated in the contingency of a set of existences that I cannot create myself, which was there before I existed, before I came here.

When we move house, we physically feel that we arrive somewhere that precedes us, not only a place in terms of a habitat, but also as a set of existences. We are preceded by existences who all have their own history, their own opaqueness, their own social, cultural, religious and political density. This means we are not in control. We are not the owners who will fence in the land. Today this philosopy of neighbours risks being replaced by a social law for neighbours that harms the antecedence of the place and increases self-centred attitudes.

This is the challenge we face as we think about the habitat, about the notion of inhabiting and the verb "to inhabit": what do we do to maintain a certain quality of habitat? What do we do to take care of a place? Think about that scene in *The Great Dictator* where poor Charlie Chaplin, who has lost his memory, goes back to his home, which has been transformed into a Jewish ghetto by the horrible dictator. Unaware of what has happened, he modestly starts to remove the cobwebs in his barber's shop: the occupation of a space begins with such modest acts of care. The life of Charlie Chaplin the barber also involves taking care of the people in the same area by shaving them and cutting their hair. It's a twofold idea: we take care of a place by taking care of the lives of the people who live there, and that demands a political strategy: a reflection on social justice.

the city and spatial justice

Edward W. Soja geographer

Paper prepared for presentation at the conference *Spatial Justice*, Nanterre, Paris, March 12-14, 2008.

The specific term "spatial justice" has not been commonly used until very recently, and even today there are tendencies among geographers and planners to avoid the explicit use of the adjective "spatial" in describing the search for justice and democracy in contemporary societies. Either the spatiality of justice is ignored or it is absorbed (and often drained of its specificity) within such related concepts as territorial justice, environmental justice, the urbanisation of injustice, the reduction of regional inequalities, or even more broadly in the generic search for a just city and a just society.

All of these variations on the central theme are important and relevant, but often tend to draw attention away from the specific qualities and meaning of an explicitly spatialized concept of justice and, more importantly, the many new opportunities it is providing not just for theory-building and empirical analysis but for spatially informed social and political action.

My aim in this brief presentation is to explain why it is crucial in theory and in practice to emphasise explicitly the spatiality of justice and injustice, not just in the city but on all geographical scales, from the local to the global. I will state my case in a series of premises and propositions, starting with an explanation of why the specific term "spatial justice" has emerged from literally nowhere in just the past five years and why it is likely to continue to be widely used in the future.

Why spatial ? Why now ?

1. Whatever your interests may be, they can be significantly advanced by adopting a critical spatial perspective. This is the premise that lies behind practically everything I have written over the past forty years and is the first sentence in *Seeking Spatial Justice*, the book I am currently writing.

2. Thinking about justice in spatial terms not only enriches our theoretical understanding, it can uncover significant new insights that extend our practical knowledge into more effective actions to achieve greater justice and democracy. Conversely, if we don't make the spatial explicit and assertive, such opportunities are less likely to arise.

3. After a century and a half of being subsumed under prevalent social historicism, thinking spatially has, over the past decade, spread across almost all disciplines. Never before has a critical spatial perspective been so widespread in its recognition and application—from archaeology and poetry to religious studies, literary criticism, legal studies, and accounting.

4. The development of "spatial thinking" is the primary reason for the attention that is now being paid to the concept of spatial justice and to the broader spatialisation of our basic ideas of democracy and human rights, as in the revival of Lefebvre's notion of the right to the city, of particular relevance here in Nanterre.

Whereas the concept would not have been easily comprehensible even five years ago, today it attracts a much broader audience than the traditionally spatial disciplines of geography, architecture, and urban and regional planning.

5. Thinking about space has changed significantly in recent years, from emphasising flat cartographic notions of space as a container or stage for human activity or merely the physical dimensions of fixed form, to an active force shaping human life. A new emphasis on specifically urban spatial causality has emerged, allowing us to explore the generative effects of cities not just on everyday behaviour but on such processes as technological innovation, artistic creativity, economic development and social change as well as environmental damage, social polarisation, widening income gaps, international politics, and, more specifically, the production of justice and injustice.

6. Critical spatial thinking today hinges on three principles:
a) The ontological spatiality of being (we are all spatial as well as social and temporal beings)
b) The social production of spatiality (space is socially produced and can therefore be socially changed)
c) The socio-spatial dialectic (the spatial shapes the social as much as the social shapes the spatial).

7. Taking the socio-spatial dialectic seriously means that we recognise that the geographical realities in which we live can have negative as well as positive consequences on practically everything we do. Foucault characterised this by showing how the intersection of space, knowledge, and power can be both oppressive and enabling. Building on Foucault, Edward Said states the following:
"Just as none of us is outside or beyond geography, none of us is completely free from the struggle over geography. That struggle is complex and interesting because it is not

only about soldiers and cannons but also about ideas, about forms, about images and imaginings."

8. These ideas expose the spatial causality of justice and injustice as well as the justice and injustice that are embedded in spatiality, in the multi-scalar geographical realities in which we live, from the space of the body and the household, through cities and regions and nation-states, right up to the global scale.

9. Until these ideas are widely understood and accepted, it is essential to make the spatiality of justice as explicit and actively causal as possible. To redefine it as something else is to miss the point and the new opportunities it opens up.

On the concept of spatial justice/injustice

1. In the broadest sense, spatial (in)justice refers to an intentional and focused emphasis on the spatial or geographical aspects of justice and injustice. As a starting point, this involves the fair and equitable distribution in space of socially valued resources and the opportunities to use them.

2. Spatial justice as such is not a substitute or alternative to social, economic, or other forms of justice but rather a way of looking at justice from a critical spatial perspective. From this viewpoint, there is always a relevant spatial dimension to justice while at the same time all geographical realities have expressions of justice and injustice built into them.

3. Spatial (in)justice can be seen as both outcome and process, as geographical realities or distributional patterns that are in themselves just/unjust and as the processes that produce these outcomes. It is relatively easy to discover examples of spatial injustice descriptively, but it is much more difficult to identify and understand the underlying processes producing unjust geographical realities.

4. Locational discrimination, created through the biases imposed on certain populations because of their geographical location, is fundamental in the production of spatial injustice and the creation of lasting spatial structures of privilege and advantage. The three most familiar forces shaping locational and spatial discrimination are class, race, and gender, but their effects should not be reduced only to segregation.

5. The political organisation of space is a particularly powerful source of spatial injustice, with examples ranging from the gerrymandering of electoral districts, the redlining of urban investments, and the effects of exclusionary zoning to territorial apartheid, institutionalised residential segregation, the imprint of colonial and/or military geographies of social control, and the creation of other core-periphery spatial structures of privilege at both local and global levels.

6. The normal workings of an urban system operation are primary source of inequality and injustice in that the accumulation of locational decisions in a capitalist economy tends to lead to the redistribution of real income in favour of the rich over the poor. This redistributive injustice is aggravated further by racism, patriarchy, heterosexual bias, and many other forms of spatial and locational discrimination. Note again that these processes can operate without rigid forms of spatial segregation.

7. Geographically uneven development and underdevelopment provide another framework for interpreting the processes that produce injustices, but as with other processes, it is only when this unevenness solidifies into more lasting structures of privilege and advantage that intervention becomes necessary.

8. Perfectly even development, complete socio-spatial equality, pure distributional justice, as well as universal human rights are never achievable. Every geographical reality

in which we live has some degree of injustice embedded in it, making the selection of sites of intervention a crucial decision.

Why justice? Why now?

1. Seeking to increase justice or to decrease injustice is a fundamental objective in all societies, a foundational principle for sustaining human dignity and fairness. The legal and philosophical debates that often revolve around Rawls' theory of justice are relevant here, but they say very little about the spatiality of justice and injustice.

2. The concept of justice and the way it relates to concomitant notions of democracy, equality, citizenship, and civil rights has taken on new meaning in the contemporary context for many different reasons, including the intensification of economic inequalities and social polarisation associated with neoliberal globalisation and the new economy as well as the transdisciplinary dissemination of a critical spatial perspective.

3. The specific term "justice" has developed a particularly strong hold on the public and political imagination in comparison to such alternatives as "freedom," with its now strongly conservative overtones, "equality," given the impact of a more cultural politics of difference, and the search for universal human rights, detached from specific time and place.

4. Justice in the contemporary world tends to be seen as more concrete and grounded than its alternatives, more oriented to present day conditions, and imbued with a symbolic force that works effectively across cleavages of class, race, and gender to foster a collective political consciousness and a sense of solidarity based on widely shared experience.

5. The search for justice has become a powerful rallying cry and a mobilising force for new social movements and coalition-building spanning the political spectrum, extending

the concept of justice beyond the social and the economic to new forms of struggle and activism. In addition to "spatial" justice, other modifiers include territorial, racial, environmental, worker, youth, global, local, community, peace, monetary, border, and corporeal.

6. Combining the terms "spatial" and "justice" opens up a range of new possibilities for social and political action, as well as for social theorisation and empirical analysis, that would not be as clear if the two terms were not used together.

A geohistorical look at the concept of spatial justice would take us back to the Greek *polis* and the Aristotelian idea that being urban is the essence of being political; it would take us through the rise of liberal democracy and the Age of Revolution, and eventually focus attention on the urban crises of the 1960s, with their most symptomatic and symbolic moments taking place here in Nanterre. Paris in the 1960s and especially the still understudied co-presence of Henri Lefebvre and Michel Foucault, became the most productive forum for the creation of a radically new conceptualisation of space and spatiality, and for a specifically urban and spatial concept of justice, encapsulated most insightfully in Lefebvre's call for taking back control over the right to the city and the right to difference.

The trajectory of these developments of a critical spatial perspective was both extended and diverted by David Harvey's *Social Justice* and the City, published in 1973. Never once using the specific term "spatial justice" in this book, nor indeed in anything else he has written since, Harvey chose to use the term "territorial justice", borrowing from the Welsh planner Bleddyn Davies, to describe his version of the spatiality of justice. In his "liberal formulations", Harvey advanced the spatial conceptualisation of justice, and his view would shape all English-language debates on justice and democracy from that time on. Despite his recognition of Lefebvre's contributions as a Marxist philosopher of space, Harvey's Marxism moved him away from spatial causality and from a focus on justice itself, and he would rarely mention the term "territorial justice" again, although the notion of the urbanisation of injustice would be carried forward and Harvey, very recently, would write again on the right to the city.

The first use of the specific term "spatial justice" that I can find is in the unpublished doctoral dissertation of the political geographer John O'Laughlin, entitled *Spatial Justice and the Black American Voter: The Territorial Dimension of Urban Politics*, completed in 1973. The earliest published work I have found using the term in English is a short article by G.H. Pirie, "On Spatial Justice" in 1983, although almost there in 1981 was a book by the French geographer Alain Reynaud, *Société, espace et justice: inégalites régionales et justice socio-spatiale*. From the 1980s to the turn of the century, the use and development of the term "spatial justice" became almost exclusively associated with the work of geographers and planners in Los Angeles… and this brings me to my conclusion.

Conclusion

Los Angeles has been a primary centre not just in the theorisation of spatial justice but more significantly in the movement of the concept from largely academic debate into the world of politics and practice. I believe it can be claimed, although it is almost impossible to prove conclusively, that a critical spatial perspective and an understanding of the production of unjust geographical realities and spatial structures of privilege have entered more successfully into the strategies and activism of labour and community groups in LA than in any other US metropolitan region. Spatial strategies have played a key role in making Los Angeles the leading edge of the American labor movement and one of the most vibrant centres for innovative community based organisations. New ideas about community-based regionalism, locational discrimination, electoral redistricting, and environmental justice have propelled such organisations as SAJE (Strategic Action for a Just Economy), the Los Angeles Alliance for a New Economy, Justice for Janitors, and the Labor/Community Strategy Center (one of the leading organisation that have written written on Henri Lefebvre) into the forefront of contemporary struggles over spatial justice and the city.

Perhaps the most dramatic example of the impact of specifically spatial approaches in the search for justice is the Bus Riders Union, an organisation of the transit-dependent immigrant working poor that successfully challenged the locational biases of the Metropolitan Transit Authority and their plans to create a multi-billion dollar fixed rail system that would primarily serve relatively wealthy suburban areas at the expense of the more urgent needs of the inner city working poor, who depend on a more flexible bus network given their multiple and multi-locational job households. A court order was issued in 1996 demanding that the MTA give first budget priority to the purchase of new buses, reduction of bus stop crime, and improvements in bus routing and waiting times. Similar civil rights cases based on racial discrimination had been brought to court in other cities and failed. In LA, the notion of spatial and locational discrimination and the creation of unjust mass transit solutions were added to the racial discrimination arguments and helped to win the case. There are many complications to the story, but the end result was a shift of billions of dollars of public investment from a rail plan that would benefit the rich more than the poor, as is usually the case in the capitalist city, to an almost unprecedented plan that would benefit the poor more than the rich. The bus network today is among the best in the country, and is being used as a model of efficiency in other cities.

More recently, and of special relevance here, Los Angeles and in particular the Urban Planning Department at UCLA has become the focus of a national movement centred on the notion of "rights to the city". Informed by Lefebvre and others espousing a critical spatial perspective, the local movement has been joined on a global scale by the World Social Forum, which in 2005 presented a World Charter of the Rights to the City.

I hope I have been of some help in explaining why, after thirty or so years of relative neglect, Lefebvre's passionate ideas about *le droit à la ville* have been so actively revived.

the courage to exist: thoughts on the political implications of dwelling

Cynthia Fleury philosopher and psychoanalyst

In what way do we inhabit cities today? The notion of "ways of inhabiting" owes much to the great lecture given by Martin Heidegger in 1951, whose contemporary relevance I shall return to later. I shall also be examining the political implications of the notion of dwelling based on the connection between courage and irreplaceability, analysing individuation in the Rule of Law and the types of engagement individuals can make in order to inhabit the polity.

Dwelling: a condition for humanism extended to all our habitats

In a way, Heidegger's lecture title *Building, Dwelling, Thinking* shows the "nodality" of the word "dwelling". Dwelling is not simply a function among others. Vladimir Jankélévitch wrote that courage is a cardinal value, and one might say the same here: "dwelling" is a cardinal principle, in the sense that the individual cannot work well if he has no fixed abode, cannot move around comfortably without stable periods of rest, and has a hard time emotionally and in terms of human relationships if he is likened to a vagrant. There's a "node" here—a sense that "dwelling" forms part of a matrix. Dwelling in a space—truly inhabiting it—makes it possible to do other things: to go calmly to work, to feel that one is not in exile, to move around without anxiety. We're all the more "mobile" when mobility is wished-for and not suffered, and when we know that we have an accessible "home". Without this node, human life is wounded, cut to the quick, and in danger.

Being human requires setting up a vital spatial and temporal environment: a space and time we make our own. The first vital space for Mankind is time: when Man can no longer inhabit time, he perishes. And God knows that it's a constant fight to inhabit time, because time passes so fast, because we live in worlds of total acceleration, because there's no time left, because time is constantly being confiscated by instrumental rationality. Getting time back and having time to ourselves—time whose purpose we ourselves define—allows us to inhabit time, and thus to inhabit space: the two are tightly connected. Having a place, of course, helps us to have time. Modern living tends to push us out of our own space and time.

From a psychoanalytical standpoint, the human being is sick when he is no longer able to inhabit time, to be mobile within time. In analysis, this manifests itself when the patient is not longer able to remember—to move in the past—without bursting into tears or saying: "I don't know… I don't remember". It also manifests itself in a series of acts of concealment or repression that are so powerful that the person can no longer move in the future either: projection no longer occurs. From the point at which a human being no longer moves in the past or the future, he's in danger. His subjectivity and agency are under threat, caught up in a process of vulnerability. As a result, vulnerable people can no longer project. Their future is stolen from them—even in their imagination. So "dwelling" means inhabiting both time and space.

Heidegger describes the essential dialectic between inhabiting the land, inhabiting the world, inhabiting one's own life, and having the ability to "be in the world". The philosopher reminds us that "dwelling" has to preserve the "fourfold" (*das Geviert*), the four major functions that make it possible to unpack the definition of dwelling. Dwelling is not merely having an address: we inhabit the world physically, but also metaphysically. Being on Earth also means being under the heavens: having a relationship with the vertical, the sacred—not in the religious sense, but in the sense of a connection with the transcendent. Dwelling means creating the conditions under which we can gain access to that which transcends us. Architecture tries to respond to the question: how can we give that which transcends us a place on Earth? This is not restricted to the architecture of holy places (cathedrals, temples, mosques): any place can relate to the transcendent. There's the vertical, and then there's the horizontal: the connection with the human community. How can we identify as mortals, embracing our finiteness, and at the same time transcend that finiteness?

This "fourfold" of dwelling allows Man to transform his humanity and to bring forth his humanism. We must remember that humanity and humanism are not the same, insofar as humanism is a creation of Man linked to his environment: it is constructed by creating a transcendent, respectful, dignified link to others. Our connection with nature contributes greatly to this humanism. Heidegger was one of the first to observe the disfigurement of nature and reason caused by technology: by taking control of nature, we compromise our humanism. As soon as natural resources are placed in danger, the question of humanism becomes much more tenacious: Man may flourish, but not humanism. The conditions under which this humanism can be preserved involve a form of "dwelling" that respects the natural and human environment.

Before moving on to the notion of irreplaceability, we might recall Gaston Bachelard's view on the function of the words *maison* (house), *grenier* (loft), *refuge* (refuge) and *foyer* (home) as metaphors of intimacy and of the frontier with the outside world. For Bachelard, the *maison* is the necessary interface between cosmos and self, the self of Man. It is an aura of the self. We all need a "dream-house", the dream of a house in our minds that guides our way of inhabiting the world. Either we have a childhood home, or we have a dream of a childhood home, or we dream of a house we'd like to build one day, and this shapes the way we inhabit the world. When we don't own a house, says Bachelard, we still have this dream-house whose mental picture allows us to inhabit the world.

From this point of view, the subprime crisis in 2008 is a travesty, a total perversion of economics conceived as a science of the *oikos*—the home or the house. Today's economics, especially thanks to asset securitisation, contradicts the primary meaning of the economy—having a roof over one's head. Our economies create people without *oikos*, without roofs: they no longer allow us to inhabit the world. Conversely, and fortunately, territorial insularities emerge in which thinking about "commons" is fundamental. The Aalborg Charter (1994) on resilient cities brings together architects, local officials, citizens, academics, entrepreneurs and members of NPOs with a view to regenerating our spaces—especially our public spaces. The French word *réhabilitation* (renovation, regeneration, refurbishment) is not neutral. A major challenge of "dwelling" involves regenerating what already exists, not building over and over again and destroying protective natural ecosystems. The idea is to work with what is already there, to regenerate what was once abandoned, like the High Line in New York. Every year we build the equivalent of 1 % of the existing built surface area. The biggest challenge facing people and cities is thus the transformation of our existing habitats for "improved dwelling" in the future.

Besides the human habitat, nature and ecosystem resources also have to be preserved. The social and natural contracts are inextricably linked. *"Indifferent to the climate,"* writes Michel Serres, *"except when they're on holiday—you've recognised us, the men, the citizens, the tourists—when in their clumsy, Arcadian way they rediscover the world, they naively pollute what they do not know, which seldom hurts them and never concerns them. Dirty species, monkeys and motorists quickly drop their rubbish because they do not live in the space they are passing through, and so allow themselves to foul it."* We pass through, but we no longer know how to inhabit. We foul what we don't know how to inhabit: we abandon it; we lay it waste; we destroy it.

Behind the question of interlinked social and natural habitats, there's the question of inhabiting the world, of the desire to inhabit the world we must all have, so that we want to create a world worthy of being inhabited. James Lovelock presented Man in terms of this function that creates an ability to inhabit the world. When he considers that the atmosphere is a dynamic extension of the biosphere and that human activities can destroy it, Lovelock points to the Anthropocene and the epistemological break with the past it entails. We might compare the atmosphere to a bird's feathers—the extension of a living system designed to preserve an environment. We are put in mind of Peter Sloterdijk, who defines Man as an "atmosphere designer"—whether that atmosphere be toxic to, or protective of, the environment. If the atmosphere represents the feathers of the bird/man, then it is impossible to live without it. It becomes a natural extension of ourselves, and allows us to maintain ourselves as Subjects. This is a definition that might echo that of Aldo Leopold, who defined the political community extensively as that which connects the living and the dead. We must extend this definition to the soil, to rivers, to nature, to the Earth, and even to the atmosphere.

The Apollo 11 space mission in 1969 was essential to the development of our awareness of Earth's fragility. Michael Collins, who was on the mission with Niel Armstrong and Buzz Aldrin, reported that what he discovered once they landed on the Moon was neither outer space nor the Moon, but the Earth. Awareness of our "dwelling-place" arises most often when we are "somewhere else": either in exile or in a situation where we feel a sense of profound delocalisation.

Irreplaceability as the expression of a concern for oneself linked to a concern for the world

How can we connect these thoughts on dwelling and "irreplaceability" to the protective implement that is courage—the courage to exist? What do we "build" together, in Heidegger's sense of the world "building"? What are the material and intangible aspects of our shared building endeavours?

Beauty carries a city along. A city without beauty is but a parody of a city. Beauty refers, of course, to the material characteristics of architecture. But intangible aspects structure the city in equal measure. The intangibility of a city is the hope we feel when we come into contact with it and when we move through it; it's the way the city gives us a taste for the world. The solidarity that connects us means that inhabiting the world involves finding the most dialectical combination between tangible and intangible aspects. The notion of "irreplaceability" attempts to address this.

When the Rule of Law, under the influence of rampant neoliberalism, constantly makes us feel, as Subjects and as individuals, that we are replaceable and interchangeable and that we are not entitled to inhabit the world;

when concern for our habitat is such a low priority for the neoliberal state superstructure, then our uniqueness is destroyed. This alone is a disastrous act that should be condemned. What is less perceptible is the Möbius strip between individuation and the Rule of Law: by making individuals precarious in the extreme and by no longer allowing them to inhabit the world and the polity, the Rule of Law destroys itself, because only the bodies of Subjects constitute the body of the Rule of Law: there can be no Rule of Law without the constant revitalising input provided by individuals/ Subjects.

The political equivalent of the feeling of replaceability is the disappearance of responsibility for, and engagement with, the Rule of Law. It leads to the emergence of a feeling of resentment, which in turn leads to support for the most populist regimes. The historic lessons of replaceability are well known: Hannah Arendt brilliantly defined them in her theory of the banality of evil. Adolf Eichmann's imposture was to consider a replaceable subject, disempowered as a subject and dissociated from the Law, to be a mere "cog" in the machine. Today, the effects of replaceability survive in new, unwanted forms, producing deep-seated discouragement, depression, and burnout. People are exhausted, ground down because they feel like mere chattels. How do this discouragement and resentment translate into politics? History has shown us how: certainly not as the durability of the Rule of Law… Individuals who no longer feel like Subjects, who feel like mere products or merchandise, cease their involvement in public affairs—in other words, they abstain—or vote for explicitly xenophobic, fascistic or populist parties with inward-looking policies. Consequently, when the subject is harmed, he is no longer able to defend the Rule of Law—he no longer even cares, as concern for oneself (the protection of subjectivity) and concern for the Rule of Law are closely interconnected.

In a sense, "inhabiting" refers to one of the ways in which concern for the self and concern for the Rule of Law are linked. We have to build cities and areas that give us the feeling that we can invent, or take part in the invention of, a common narrative. What is a public space? It's not just a space anyone can walk across. A public space is not merely fonctionalised, in other words instrumentalised. It is an enabling space: it can be defined by the person who crosses it, at a particular point in time. The Nuit Debout movement is an example: suddenly, it redefined the Place de la République. What was designed as a place of circulation, with a precise function, was redefined by citizens, who inhabited it in a new way precisely because it is a public space. A city produces this enabling effect when citizens regularly demonstrate their ability to inhabit it in new ways. In cities that fail to give inhabitants the feeling that they can reinvent their lives, all they want to do is leave. In a hyper-functionalised city, access to the Metro might be limited to this precise function: "Nothing else can be done here". Or, on the contrary, it can become something else: "Look, I don't know what this place will become, but I want to put a piece of my story into it so that tomorrow it will have an enabling effect—so that it wlll be a place for invention". Inhabiting intrinsically involves invention, in the sense of inventing emergence.

Irreplaceability reflects this concern with constantly embracing the question of "being- in-the-world". In *Les Irremplaçables*, I attempted to analyse three major thresholds of self-knowledge, which in turn make it possible to identify three processes of individuation. First, individuation arises from *imaginatio vera*—true imagination. Here, our connection with reality (as distinct from social reality, which refers to the theatre that surrounds us) entails invention. Reality is the potential for emergence, for events to occur. It might be what will create tomorrow's social reality. Our truth as Subjects is not to subject ourselves to social reality; it is to make reality spring forth, and this happens via imagination, via the invention of reality. Our ways of inhabiting the world must always arise from this ability to invent reality. In our ways of inhabiting the world, we will make reality spring forth.

Second, individuation occurs thanks to *pretium doloris*, the price of pain. Man's primary activity is thinking-as-action. What constitutes *Homo sapiens* is precisely the fact that he does not dissociate action from thought. Thought entails risk, because it is what causes things to arise. But we live in worlds that have split the two activities: on the one hand we have people who think, on the other those who (supposedly) act. The split upon which today's world is built is pretty disastrous: it goes hand in hand with the disqualification of both those who think and those who act. We have to return to the profoundly coherent principle according to which Man thinks in order to act, and according to which Man acts when he thinks. We are back with Heidegger again: inhabiting is inseparable from thinking, and that's what building is.

The third individuation process arises from *vis comica*, comic force. When habitat is no longer possible, or when the habitat we live in is appalling, comic force is a way of creating a space-time continuum. We usually need a touch of humour to transcend absurdity, desolation or horror. Humour is a way of inhabiting the world because, when space and time fail us, it allows us to create something elsewhere. Concentration camp literature is hugely important in this regard. When there are only counterfeit ways of inhabiting the world, fortunately we still have humour: an ability to transcend everything, which carries us away so that we can find, elsewhere and in new ways, a place where we can exist in our own minds.

Many cases of dissidence or civil disobedience are closely associated with ways of inhabiting space: Occupy Wall Street, Occupy Gezi, Nuit Debout, Notre-Dame-des-Landes, and so on. In every case, citizens do not simply want to discuss theory; they want to develop, in space and time, new ways of inhabiting the world, however short-lived they may be. These movements choose a place, not a personality, to embody them. There must be a sense of embodiment, of making things real via the body, via the flesh, and perhaps also via the creation of ways of inhabiting. Suddenly, inhabiting becomes an eminently political issue.

creating, resisting, sharing

Fabienne Brugère philosopher

It is possible to gauge our thinking about inhabiting the world according to three verbs: "to create", "to resist", and "to share". These three verbs reflect fundamental and potential actions of human beings in all domains: not only in architecture, but also in art and life.

"Creating"

In Europe, creation and the possibility of creation are the very powerful tenets of what we are able to imagine. From the nineteenth century on, a certain figure of creation and a certain figure of the artist came to the fore, expressed via a differentiation between creating and manufacturing: on the one hand there was the possibility of creation with all that implies in terms of singularity and the engagement of individuality; on the other hand, manufacturing was conceived as the act of developing products and carrying out projects. "Creating" implies the possibility of expression, singularity, invention; it involves imagining something as a "work". Manufacturing refers more to an industrial world, to a product, and to anonymous development, especially via the image of cars made on production lines throughout the twentieth century.
In the field of architecture, the Grande Arche is a rather interesting example of this. In his book[1], Laurence Cossé very accurately recounts the adventure of the Grande Arche, from design to construction. It is precisely in the district of La Défense that an interesting scene was played out: one that allows us to reflect upon the verb "create". The tender for the building that would become the Grande Arche was won in the early 1980 by a Danish architect by the name of Johan Otto von Spreckelsen. He had developed a crazy project of great purity, the result of a drawing of a cube and a cloud. The project fired everyone's enthusiasm, in particular that of the French president at the time, François Mitterrand. Little by little, the project took shape. But the architect pulled out half way through, seemingly because he thought that his project was not being sufficiently well carried out by the person in charge, due to the constraints imposed by the French government. He had to work with a French architect, Paul Andreu, who was actually more of an engineer—he designed the two major Paris airports. What Laurence Cossé shows very effectively is that there was a sort of duel, a conflict, between, on one side, an architect who put himself forward as a creator, who arrived with the purity of his cube and his cloud and who was absolutely determined that the building should be a reflection of that; and on the other side, an entire system, a kind of machine linked to the French state, a number of architects, and high-ranking officials at the Caisse des Dépôts, who saw the project in quite a different light. The latter had in mind a product that would be as functional as possible, in a precise district. With hindsight, we can see that the arch was a failure in functional terms. There was thus a conflict between an architect who was a creator and who refused to accept

1. Laurence Cossé, *La Grande Arche*, Gallimard, 2016, 368 p.

a number of concessions, and an architect who was an engineer supported by an entire retinue of officials.

So the question of the singularity of creation and that of the possibility of appropriating a project are reactivated. The Danish architect probably though of himself as a genius, in the sense defined by Emmanuel Kant in the 18th and 19th centuries.

Creating inheres in the possibility of transgression, in a singular expression that is not immediately recognised and that generates dissent before that form of expression is finally acknowledged and digested. The Grande Arche, which remains a landmark at La Défense, can be seen as a desperate attempt to create. Creating is expressing something that is unique: it's being able to make something and hold it up not only as an outcome, but also as a way of life. We are entering a new era and we are probably at a point where the notion of creation is increasingly problematic, because we are hindered more and more often by rules, standards, systems, and the market. The notion of "creation" is, without any doubt, in danger.

"Resisting"

The second verb is "to resist". It has an immediate topical resonance: resistance via social and political movements has been organised in France over recent months. First of all, one might say that resistance presupposes that one can defend oneself and fight strength with strength. Resistance presupposes persistence, and being able to strive against that which harms or subjugates us.

According to Gilles Deleuze, to create is to resist. Creating means resisting via ideas that are potentially engaged in a particular mode of expression, be it architecture, painting or literature. Moving from creation to resistance means highlighting the expressive potential of a subject or individual. An individual who creates, like an individual who resists, is an individual who expresses himself. Resistance

raises the question of the individual and the subject within a collective. This is precisely what differentiates creation from resistance, that which separates the verb "to create" from the verb "to resist": in resistance we can move, or we must move, from "I" to "we". This makes the verb "to resist" into an essentially political word.
Gilles Deleuze identified "passive resistance" as the possibility of breaking away from traditional society and conformism. He bases his analysis of "passive resistance" on a short story by Herman Melville, *Bartleby*, when the character Bartleby says: *"I would prefer not to"* . With Bartleby, resistance entails answering "I would prefer not to" to all requests and suggestions, so that he gradually abandons all activities, including his job as a copywriter, which means he finally ends up in prison, where he dies. In this text, the possibility of resisting passively exists, but it ultimately leads to death. In his reading of *Bartleby*, Gilles Deleuze points out the perils of indifference and non-involvement. In a way, resistance echoes the image of Bartleby and highlights the importance of a political meaning for resistance and the construction of a "we" in action. If we remain alone in passive resistance, there is no way out.

"Sharing"

"To share" is clearly a verb that it is impossible to think about in the context of solitude. Sharing can't happen alone. We can imagine a form of solitude in the verb "to create", and we can imagine a form of radical resistance that might prevent us from joining others, but sharing can't be done alone. The verb "to share" expresses a concern for others and the essential character of a bond or relationship. It seems that sharing can only exist if a number of conditions are met. For sharing to occur, everyone has to be able to make use of a territory and find his or her place there. Sharing is impossible if individuals fail to appropriate space; this presupposes, of course, that sharing can only take place if everyone has the means to adhere to a territory, a space, and be able to make it their own. In our cities, there are areas that individuals cannot make their own, which makes sharing difficult. Second, to be able to share within an urban area, it is not only necessary to relate to the built city; we have to relate to the *polis*. We have to take part in the constitution of a common world and have the opportunity to actively involve ourselves in a project that might extend further than ourselves and in which we can combine our dreams with those of our neighbours, friends, and colleagues. In a way, it's a way of opening up to others via a common project.
Last but not least, it seems to me that for sharing to take place, there must be a certain level of decency in society. Wealth inequality erodes the opportunity for sharing because it erodes the very spirit of sharing and the value of examples as experiences of sharing. Sharing takes place on different scales. There's a spirit of sharing, and "global sharing" is a long way off, precisely because decency is impossible due to financial inequalities. Sharing on a national scale in France might be based on a reconsideration and re-examination of the notion of social status. The local scale, often highlighted in constellation.s, is now the most hopeful link in the chain. Opportunities for sharing begin at the level of individuals (in the wake of a number of failures on the part of those that govern us). As the exhibition shows, sharing on a local scale gives rise to many initiatives.

inhabiting digital

Dominique Boullier sociologist

The semantic worlds of habitat and digital technology seldom coincide. The digital lexicon refers more to connexions, flows and networks. And yet, in addition to this fluidity that prevails in digital terminology, we have words such as *hosting* (servers that host) and *home*, omnipresent in all mobile operating systems and applications—the *desktop* metaphor being preferred for computers. In this article we will not be discussing "smart cities" or "connected cities" that base their marketing on this ultimately superficial relationship between human habitat and digital tech. We will be more fundamentally exploring the anthropology of the "technical environment" that is digital.

The choice of the neologism *habitèle* to deal with this specific dimension of the act of dwelling harks back to the work of Jean Gagnepain, for whom *habit* [=clothing] and *habitat* constitute a specific human skill he refers to as "schematic", which involves equipping subjects with what he calls *peaux techniques* [technical skins]. Of course, social markers of all kinds are applied to these skins. The relationship between a body and a technically elaborated envelope can be characterised as "transductive", to borrow a term from Gilbert Simondon: it jointly defines the envelope and the body, and these elements set out independently would not enter into a relationship.

"Inhabiting" thus makes it possible to take seriously our animal and corporeal dimensions of "being in the world" and "governed beings" not only via enlightened decisions and rational choices, but also via "habits". For Peter Sloterdijk, the function of the habitat is to provide inhabitants with habits; but he immediately adds, quoting Flosser, that this is in order to usher in the non-habitual. *Habere* certainly refers to "habits", but it also refers to "having". When we talk about skin, this "having" refers to a "reciprocal possession": which defines society according to Gabriel Tarde. So, as Jean Gagnepain pointed out, to inhabit somewhere (*habiter*) is not to stay somewhere (*loger*). True enough, the "shelter" function is common to all animals, it's not the same as "inhabiting". "Dwelling"—actually living somewhere—as many researchers have noted (Jacques Lévy 2012, Michel Lussault, 2007), is a process, or even a skill, that presupposes reciprocal transformation. This is not the case for a few nights in a hotel, where we merely *stay*. However it is possible to live in a tent—apparent technological precariousness is not a distinctive criterion in this case.

How can we now export these dimensions of the act of dwelling into an environment made of waves, radio-electric emissions, wires, terminals and processing? In reality, it was when mobile phone use took off—in 1998 in France to be precise—that it became possible to think about digital in terms of human habitat. In 2007, 50 % of humanity was already connected to a mobile: in the same year, 50 % of humanity was living in an urban environment. The implications of this observation in terms of the pace of technological change are mind-blowing: it took several thousand years to arrive at this level of urban development, but it only took fifteen years to provide two thirds of humanity with a mobile or smartphone. This historically unheard-of change of scale in terms of the dissemination of a technology is the "key element" as Marshall McLuhan always used to say (and this does not refer to the content of the interactions, nor the specific applications). A new state of "connectedness" has thus been invented and adopted with matchless enthusiasm.

Until very recently, the *habitèle* was not restricted to the mobile phone. It included all the systems that had some measure of "portable identity": ID papers, access keys and cards, credit cards, and so on. Now all these dimensions are being built into the mobile terminal—the phone. This leads us to focus the *habitèle* on the mobile phone—while other things that we carry in our wallets and handbags (most of them clothing-like) remain non-embeddable: umbrella, makeup kit, medicines, keepsakes, and so on. This agglutinative process is happening before our very eyes: we're changing unwittingly, because we treat our relationship to the cellphone as a mere manifestation of consumerism.

Technical attachments

It is useful to associate digital with habitat because it helps us to grasp the anthropological implications—and thus the considerable political implications—of such a change. We have already experienced this inability to think about our "envelopes" with the motor car. The private car was "only" the technical transposition of the horse-drawn carriage—just one more vehicle—whereas it should have been thought of as an *habitacle* [a "passenger compartment": the car's interior], so enduring is our attachment to the car. This functional reductionism has obscured all thinking relating to change in the sphere of cars. It's true that we have developed a philosophy of mobility (John Urry, 2005), but we have ignored our powerful attachment to this technical marker of our identities, this new "envelope" that is the car interior. And these powerful intimate links have helped to push back as far as possible the acknowledgment of the consequences of a means of transport based on the combustion engine and fossil fuel, which have caused the biggest climate disaster in human history. The urban forms of the twentieth century are entirely dependent on this proliferation of motor-driven vehicles, with familiar disastrous consequences on urban sprawl. And yet our attachment to the car, as an *habitacle*, is such that, even when we look at the best argued forecasts, it remains difficult to abandon this deadly technical system. This power of attachment and bonding with our artificial skins should alert us to what is happening with cellphones, with what some see as "connection addiction". Here too, technical and climatic factors (the electrosmog generated by all the radio-electric emissions from aerials and terminals) are being underestimated, whereas there has been a phenomenal change of scale over the past twenty years. Similarly, the choice of technical architecture, and in particular the predominance of certain providers, systems and platforms, cannot be discussed politically as key issues in the "good life" we should be seeking to build. The enjoyment of our personal bond with the terminal as we attempt to produce an *habitèle* is such that we reject increasingly frequent arguments alerting us to the dangers of changing attention spans, platform dependency, and threats to our privacy.

By formulating this theoretical proposition of the *habitèle*, our concern is thus to facilitate a reappropriation of political choices with respect to the design of our technical systems and to avoid reproducing the same kind of blindness to reality that occurred with the motor car.

Dwelling in three dimensions

"Until then, dwelling essentially meant not being able to leave. What can the creature of habitat that is the human being become if he experiences the fact that habitat means the ability to be here and elsewhere?"

Sloterdijk introduces us to the question, already broached by others, of the "polytopic habitat" (M. Stock, 2007). The specific power of digital consists not of being successively here and elsewhere (as in timeshares), but simultaneously here and elsewhere, in the space of a second or even at exactly the same time (multitasking). Making this situation inhabitable means making it liveable, and it's uncertain whether system designers have fully understood the anthropological implications of this transformation.

"Inhabiting" ("dwelling") describes a process of co-allocation that transforms the "sojourn" into a "dwelling" and the "occupant" into an "inhabitant". The inhabitant doesn't arrive in a dwelling: he establishes himself as an inhabitant by transforming his place of sojourn into a dwelling, which then transforms him in return. Dwelling is a *devenir-habitant* [an act of becoming an inhabitant] as Gilles Deleuze would say, and thus a "becoming-with" as Donna Haraway puts it. This presupposes that we recognise the agency specific to the built environment that both "makes" something and "has something made" whilst also being affected in the coupling process. From a cosmo-political point of view, we might even refer to a "becoming-within" (D. Boullier, To Become Within, 2015) to indicate that it is impossible to apprehend this process from the outside—which constitutes a challenge to all architects and all moderns who *"deny ever having been inside"* (P. Sloterdijk, 2003). This approach harks back to the work of Bruno Latour (1992) on the anthropology of the moderns, as well as the work on the status of non-humans highlighted by Actor-Network Theory (M. Akrich, M. Callon, B. Latour, 1988) in research on scientific activity and technological innovation.

Dwelling has several dimensions, which we shall attempt to identify in digital systems. Dwelling generates a home (*oikos*) as a situating principle (G.-H. de Radkowski, 2002). It presupposes anchoring (M. Lussault, 2007), a position, a residence, and it results in "places". We see here what Henri Lefebvre (2001) saw as a key dimension of the city, namely centrality. At this point the risk would be to produce a form of egocentrism that would lend substance to identity and make it impossible to be both here and elsewhere. If we want to keep alive the process and the competence of dwelling, we have to maintain them as tensions and abstractions, as the ability to compose many different statuses and places that are independent from a site or from "roots", whilst at the same time reinventing them. Dwelling is doubtless closer to ecology than egology, as it presupposes thinking about oneself as part of a relationship before thinking of oneself in terms of substance.

A dynamic process, dwelling also generates access. Technical access control systems are part of the built environment: doors, thresholds, barriers, passageways, and thus choices: "flow management" preferences in relation to the exterior. Accessibility is the second key quality of the city according to Henri Lefebvre. The challenge of access can lead us to mark out areas which, once they are politically charged, can become territories or, on a smaller scale, what M. Lussault (2007) calls *domaines*. In Peter Sloterdijk's work, however, membranes mobilise the immune system, which is not an insulation but a filter and a channel: a set of permanent exchanges regulated in various ways at different points in time according to needs and energy capacity. These membranes allow care, attention, protection, and "sparing and preserving" (M. Heidegger). They are not watertight, nor are they even unique, because they are characterised by co-fragility: the fragility of what Sloterdijk refers to as *foams*, which are our contemporary ways of producing envelopes. If *"men are doomed to produce interiors"*, we now produce a multitude of interiors by increasing the number of more or less transient worlds we belong to, all of which affect one another.

Last but not least, dwelling generates a tension between centrality and accessibility, between anchorage and access: this in-between space produces a climate, an atmosphere, or, for P. Sloterdik, a *"tension in the inner chamber"*. Dwelling is a very different experience according to the way anchorage and access are fine-tuned. A state of relative openness or closure is not only a question of decision, as we are all affected by atmospheric exchanges; atmospheres that we detect and which determine whether we feel good or not in someone's home are affected by smells and air quality, and no one can claim to have control over them. Feng shui attempts to grasp what circulates in an interior and also what constitutes that interior.

Digital and the three dimensions of dwelling

Let us now try to transpose these three dimensions of the process of dwelling onto the digital world. The situating principle that constitutes anchorage can be immediately transposed to a node in a network. A difficulty quickly appears: a network node can be described empirically and geographically if we locate a set of servers in physical space (for instance, the essential role of Internet eXchange Points (IXPs), some of which are located at the arrival point of physical underwater cables (D. Boullier, 2014). But the "proximities" of digital topology are the result of algorithmic processing, and they are very different from physical proximities. M. Heidegger thought about this: *"This is a mathematical space which is a no-space, without space nor place."* This is echoed in Sloterdijk: *"The network is a concept based on points without extent that lines bring together on interfaces: a world for people who fish for anorexic data"* (2005, p. 226). This is the real problem in thinking about the dimension of anchorage in digital, despite the tendency of services to geo-localise everything to reassure the user by making his presence in physical space and his existence as an IP in a network topology coincide. The anchorage and the *oikos* that constitute dwelling are thus reconstituted fictionally via GPS coordinates—via the omnipresence of Google Maps… This is also what is attempted in social networks when our "friends" end up forming a community that revolves around us, but which nevertheless just represents an act of topological positioning, even if it is made up of links from activities on Facebook or other networks. In both cases, the information system seems to reorganise itself around an ego, but this is not at all the equivalent of "anchoring" and "home", whose centrality functioned via a connexion to something beyond the ego that gave it *a* place (ancestors, gods), but not an all-embracing or central place.

Doors and thresholds, the second dimension of dwelling, seem to be omnipresent in digital networks. Passwords are used in all kinds of interactions. Setups make it possible to select or be selected to gain "access". But ordinary experience shows that this access configuration and control are actually delegated, implicitly, to others, so opaque are these systems when they operate "by default", and so complex are they even when setup options are available. According to P. Sloterdijk, *"the twentieth century has made the habitat explicit"*, which comes via an unfolding (*ex-plicare*) of all its attributes, via restraint, via the end of decorative aspects, via an insistence on networks and the machine for living. Digital is part and parcel of this explicative undertaking, because processing presupposes explaining everything to make it processable. So if processing takes place everywhere in mobile devices, on social media, etc., it is becoming more and more opaque and automated. Terms of Use are hard to read, and thus never read; and algorithms that provide guidance or allow customisation have become totally opaque thanks to Machine Learning. To "dwell" here, you have to be able to use access rules and not be subject to spam, constant notifications from applications, or unwanted ads on your favourite websites.

From that point on, in this ersatz habitat made up of network topologies and opaque personalisation, we are not surprised by the strange atmosphere—the third dimension of dwelling—that prevails in these digital living spaces. For anyone who is used to using them, there are many opportunities for satisfaction if you accept all these intrusions and don't mind being on permanent alert and seeing the pathways of all your applications stacked up in your phone. But this atmosphere is not one of care, nor one of "sparing" that one expects from the habitat: it's closer to the welcome you get in a bar, where rumours, witticisms and scapegoats make it possible to put up with a type of bond which, by definition, cannot be appropriated. The race for recognition via reputation indices (likes, friends, etc.) is like "looking for a bit of company", as people used to say when talking about places all too hastily dismissed as "dens of iniquity". These places, which are neither public nor private, produce clans, moments of excitement, and sometimes addictive experiences—things that are hardly negligible in these times of generalised detachment. But this is not enough to allow "dwelling" to take place. This is where a major question, not only for anthropology but also for all policies aimed at managing our digital architectures: is it enough to talk about networks to generate the conditions for a liveable life? How can we recover the benefits of the envelope that make it possible to generate an ability to dwell in an apparently wide-open digital environment that is constantly being destabilised by innovation? And is "being connected" enough to "institute" things, in the meaning P. Legendre (1985) gives to the word *instituer*—can connection "institute" life?

The architects of the digital climate

To test the hypotheses arising from philosophical discussion and summary observations, we have, along with Maxime Crépel and Audrey Lohard and a network of seven foreign laboratories, carried out an in-depth study of mobile phone use (420 people surveyed in eight countries: France, the UK, the US, Brazil, Tunisia, Nigeria, India and South Korea).

To assess how and to what extent this digital envelope was being constructed, we supposed that home screen customisation might be a significant indicator. However only 50 % of users do this. However, attachment to one's phone number is clearly manifest everywhere, including in countries where so-called number portability is not always available.

Terms of Use are hardly ever known, and the ability of platforms, information agencies, applications and suppliers to use data without our knowing is widely recognised. However, reasoning of the type "I know, but anyway" (O. Mannoni) is generally applied: "I know my data is used, but anyway I know there's no risk and I get too many benefits from using this service or this system". This leads to the abdication of all control over one's digital environment. Those who have understood this risk have had to learn methods to become "self-counterfeiters", supplying false addresses and phone numbers, creating multiple email addresses and fake social media accounts, using different handles, and so on.

Far from generating a habitat, contemporary digital systems, in the format given to them by the major groups that dominate the market, force us to "stay" with them. Be they telecoms providers, Internet access providers, or platforms such as Google, Apple (iTunes), Facebook, Amazon, Microsoft (now with LinkedIn) and Twitter, we do not own our workspaces, our footprints, or our data. On digital networks, we're at best in a hotel (leaving our data there at will), or in a bar; in any case, we don't make the law regarding these spaces. Amazon retains the rights to digital books it has sold without actually passing on ownership. Facebook changes its conditions, its interfaces, its personal data use without the account holder being able to do much about it. According to the quality of the hotel, it can't be denied that the staff and services can be of a very high standard: Apple constantly promotes the concept of distinction and the "club effect" to show its customers that they're staying in a highly selective luxury hotel. Platforms even highlight the fact of having all the services to hand with no effort required thanks to network speed, and the fact that they have abandoned the traditional regime of ownership, so much so that the service providers themselves have become precarious guests—as is the case for Uber drivers. The hotel guests (users of platforms, apps and services) are even tempted to forget their "guest" status when the service is free, even when their online history and activities are sold for advertising purposes. Consequently, the room is paid for by brands, which then systematically and more or less discreetly attract your attention via advertising as you go about your most private business. An in-depth revision of legal categories will be necessary to make this transactional space inhabitable. So-called "personal" data cannot be substantively processed and stored in a safe because the very condition of their existence is to be transactional. The bank account itself is never MY bank account, but an account arising from a service transaction between a bank and an individual, which authorises the bank to know everything about account movements. This shows the enormity of the task at hand, which is just as time-consuming and complex to carry out as implementing specific rights such as property law. This law must, by definition, be international, which further complicates things, as data and waves circulate without borders—except in dictatorships that can restore those frontiers, as is the case in China.

The GAFA Grand Hotel

In the absence of this law, firms, with GAFA at the top, have taken charge of digital planning and regulation. They have now acquired all the trappings of sovereignty formerly reserved for sovereign states, including the power of life and death over accounts. They host us according to their own rules and terms, while offering us our favourite "bed canopies". Peter Sloterdijk tells us that the great seafaring explorers would travel with a bed canopy precisely reproducing the night sky in their country of origin with the position of the stars they had always known. The conquest of the globe was thus psychologically facilitated by this mobile anchorage in the home sky, which prevented them from being too affected by their discoveries and allowed them to continue projecting their native references onto the New World. And this is precisely what the customisation services now offered on all platforms do. The real traveller, as F. Jauréguiberry (2016) shows, sets off with his bed canopy— with his Facebook and Instagram accounts—and updates it in real time. But some people experience the loss of all opportunities to meet others or to find surprise and affection. On this level, GAFA's policies as hosts do differ, however, and merit closer examination.

Google and Facebook create a total "vault", to borrow Yves Citton's term, which soon turns into a kind of bewitchment[1]. In digital payment systems, based in particular on credit cards, "token vaults" have been created, in other words protection systems that generate a one-off code that the user obtains from *ad hoc* terminals, then keys in to make the transaction. Protection using a vault is not a habitat, that's for sure, and it makes it possible to protect both the client and the service provider. But when Facebook manages to keep all its members on its app—even when they were pointing towards external media sources—it lastingly captures users in its universe, which no longer has an exterior. Similarly, Google has become a response engine, not a search engine, because it no longer encourages us to click on links to look elsewhere, but instead offers *its own* response in position 0, i.e. before the sponsored links and after the links provided by PageRank processing. Because of this, and thanks to the relevance of its responses, most users don't bother looking elsewhere and stay on Google, be it for weather reports or to calculate their journey times. This quality in terms of results is only possible thanks to the systematic collection of data and digital footprints, which

1. Translator's note: A play on words: *envoûtement* (sorcery, bewitchment) contains the word *voûte* (vault).

at Google might even involve analysing emails, or posts and likes at Facebook. This is why it is becoming essential for both organisations to bring together the majority of the population on their platforms. Google and Facebook claim to be becoming *"substitute civil registers"*, and this is made easier by the fact that we tend to give our "real" identities—those recognised by the State—when signing up for these accounts. As soon as we use our Facebook or Google accounts to access new services (and this is often a requirement), we give these organisations control over access—a constituent part of our competence to "dwell" that manifests itself, for instance, as keys in our physical habitat.
Our survey also shows how predominant and widespread the egological construction model for digital networks is. We are clearly not talking about a system of "public space", in the urban or political sense. The connections identified in the survey show very little diversity in terms of activities or social worlds. This is also true of the mobile phone, although social networks tend to foster an extended family model that focuses on relatives and friends considered as family, even at the very heart of professional activities where certain selected links are part of the same quasi-familial regime. This parameter alone explains the intensity of the relationships. Hypotheses regarding the permanent possibility of switching between several social worlds, harking back to what Georg Simmel wrote about urban sociability, are thus proven wrong. The technical architecture of platforms produced by major digital groups thus primarily extend the familial dimension of the networks and produce affections that are more familial than societal, in the political sense of the word, and in any case make no reference to political opinion (D. Boullier and A. Lohard, 2012). Staying at the Google and Facebook hotel has a price: that of showcasing egos and the family worlds that surround them. This might at first sight seem to foster a "habitat" that is often assimilated with this traditional dimension of kinship, but choices are made on behalf of the occupants of Facebook and Google and they are not allowed to create their own atmospheres. For their part, Apple (via iTunes) and Amazon aim to capture our passions through systems that trace and manage our preferences and tastes. The "vault" they create resonates with neighbouring tastes, revealing communities of interest that do not know one another but which are part of the same clusters in the algorithms used on both platforms. They make intensive use of recommendations to keep us on the website, and also of our supposed community of interest. Unlike Google and Facebook, the aim here is not to offer an alternative anchorage or "home" centred on our identities, but to manage access to our preferences, to cultural worlds that create phonotopes for music, for example. These dimensions are just as important for creating an atmosphere of affiliation and loyalty.

Is a digital world without urban planners liveable?

But these shared atmospheres are not "instituted" in the sense that they have never given rise to debate or political explanation. They are "sub-political" (Ulrich Beck, 2001). In the world of consumerism, entertainment, and sociability, the usefulness of legislating or engaging in political debate on these issues is called into question. And yet if we place the challenges of digital in line with those of human habitat, we can no longer adopt such a lax approach: cities, districts and buildings are subject to more deliberation, checks, regulations and residents' participation than any app or digital service. The "architecture" and "planning" of our lives are thus designed with a total lack of transparency, justified by the fact that the services offered are free and high-quality (the "pampering" that Peter Sloterdijk identifies as one of the key components of contemporary life—the other dimension, he says, being stress). In this regard, digital networks have nudged humanity into new territory by accelerating the pace of the attention-grabbing. What has all this got to do with habitat? The atmosphere habitat creates has to make it possible to adjust the amount of tension in the inner chamber. But when that chamber is constantly subjected to notifications and alerts, the air conditioning stops working or lets all the outside influences in, effectively sabotaging the very possibility of an interior. We can't properly "dwell", for example, when platforms such as Twitter include a Retweet (RT) function in their architecture, which ramps up the mental contagion with automatic repetition. The non-habitual is forcibly introduced via a constant barrage of notifications that are as harmful to our attention spans as diesel particulate emissions are to our respiratory systems. But we have to recognise that, for now, this experience, as with cars, triggers such a strong sense of attachment that platform users desire the constant buzz and love being part of the state of tension.

What is at work here is "digital financial capitalism" that captures beliefs and desires (G. Tarde, 1890). The platform effect, which depends on the financial power it procures, is an all-enveloping force that knows how to make use of people's contributions, beliefs and desires. The envelope thus created is nothing like a habitat—it's more a form of bewitchment. It provides nothing for the inhabitant to grasp hold of, and it works by encroaching on the hostee. Significantly enough, network architecture has been entirely focused on speed to the detriment of security. Speed makes it possible to foster contagion and real-time responses; by definition it weakens the immune systems not only of individuals but also of the network itself. Security isn't just a matter for the police, it's also a question of caring and sparing: the necessary conditions for the emergence of an interior. This culture of speed at any cost is embedded in the very design of the networks. A state of algorithmic urgency governs all the decisions made by designers, and the proposed user experience is based on a constant state of high-frequency alert. But *inhabiting* presupposes *habits*, and designing a habitat presupposes the existence of rights. In both cases, the time allowed for habituation and decision-making is crucial, and it is one of the conditions for the production of a liveable world. From this point of view, the statement *"Connecting is not instituting"* can be applied to both designers and users, to both the architects of the digital world and would-be inhabitants prevented from dwelling by not being given enough time for habituation. The spaces thus produced are unanchored (they have no home), unfiltered (access is uncontrolled), and devoid of liveable climate control. Under such conditions, we can say that we don't inhabit digital; instead we shack up temporarily in standard shelters that are exposed to the four winds and subject to extreme tension.

Conclusion

Using the concept of the *habitèle*—extending our ability to dwell to digital environments—makes it possible to highlight the digital malaise that exists in civilisation, just as the concept of the *habitacle* makes it possible to highlight the disaster that is the motor car. The result is not a hatred of cars, nor of digital technology. We have produced these monsters, and it is our duty not to abandon them—and even to love them. Our attachment to cars, just like our general excitement with respect to digital connection, merit serious consideration—without suggesting that we must sweep them away with disdain and start over. The shortcoming of these "envelope technologies" lies simply in the fact that they were not seen as such at a sufficiently early stage, and that they have been treated from a purely functional perspective. A similar mistake was made in Europe in the post-war years with the industrial production of mass housing as a matter of urgency. We are still paying the price for that. It is also the case for the car, whose industrial production should have been tempered by an awareness of our attachment to the vehicle interior (the *habitacle*), which could have given the car a different status from that of a constrained and monopolistic everyday mode of transport. Similarly, for digital, it is still possible to create the conditions for a *habitat*, if we now become aware of what we have created, its power, and its fantastic ability to mobilise beliefs and desires. A political strategy of the *habitèle* is now required, and it needs to be the equivalent not of a housing programme, but of an urban planning scheme that places *urbanity* at its core, to make this new shared world liveable. To make it possible to "institute life" in this way, a number of mainly legal conditions must be established.

We must invent a system of rights for "connected individuals" that would make the multitude of connections inhabitable: no longer merely user-friendly design or personal data protection, but a set of newly formulated conditions for the digital habitat. The production of digital envelopes is a much more crucial task than the endless extension of networks and their capacities. It is even probably necessary to deliberately slow down the headlong dash entirely focused on network speed, in order to shift the focus back onto security, not only from a technical point of view but also from a legal standpoint. Standardised or blanket regulations cannot respond to such challenges. The diversity of situations, moments, and possible choices must be preserved in an area (digital) that has a clear advantage over the built environment: its plasticity. It's easier to rebuild an information system than a city, provided plasticity is not used as an argument in favour of negligence and acting-out, as is the case with Internet institutions and certain interpretations of "agile" development methods. There is no absolute rule, only issues and problems where all the stakeholders have to take the time to invent solutions outside of the state of urgency that the culture of finance has ended up extending to all types of activity. As we have seen, the design of our *habitèle* has to allow flexible anchoring, access and atmospheres, because they form the necessary conditions for dwelling.

Moreover, modern legal frameworks concerning ownership are longer viable given the accelerated circulation of goods, services, and interactions and their diverse values.

A return to commons, rooted in Mediaeval tradition, is one of the most promising avenues to explore (E. Orstrom, 2010). Marc Bloch (1939) highlighted the remarkable advantages of the participatory legal regime that prevailed, especially in rural areas, before the Renaissance and modern times. The same asset—in this case a piece of land—could be linked to several regimes of ownership at once: a system closer to the *dominium* of Roman law than to the right to supposed exclusive ownership. Inhabiting digital cannot be the same as establishing a right of ownership because digital life depends on transactions and interactions. The task is doubtless more complex, but it requires stepping beyond the legal models of the moderns. The setting on the air conditioning for digital could be switched to "collective intelligence" (Levy, 1997) instead of "competitive". All the would-be inhabitants of digital would benefit, as in so many other fields.

Last but not least, interface design really matters. It's no longer just a marketing ploy: the interface is the physical point of contact between a device and a would-be inhabitant. It must be designed with the aim of producing an interior: a "sparing" environment, not just a mass of functionalities as is currently the case. It's a mammoth task, and the potential for innovation is endless, but the concept of the *habitèle* can fuel genuine creativity, not just a few recipes for flash-in-the-pan designs. Peter Sloterdijk reminds us of *"The internal links between two types of architecture: developing standards and building houses"* (2005). As we have seen, the condition for the existence of the digital house, beyond the mere "occupation" of the radio-electric spectrum, is the invention of standards that make it liveable.

References

AKRICH M., CALLON M., LATOUR B., "À quoi tient le succès des innovations ?" L'art de l'intéressement. Gérer et comprendre, *Annales des Mines*, n° 11 (1988).

BECK Ulrich, *La Société du risque*, Paris: Aubier, 2001 (1st edition, 1988).

BLOCH Marc, Feudal Society, University of Chicago Press, 1964.

BOULLIER D. et LOHARD Audrey., *Opinion Mining et Sentiment Analysis : méthodes et outils*, Paris: Open Éditions Press, March 2012.

BOULLIER D., "Internet est maritime: les enjeux des câbles sous-marins", RIS, *Revue Internationale et Stratégique*, n° 95, autumn 2014, pp. 149-158.

BOULLIER D., "Les conventions pour une appropriation durable des TIC. Utiliser un ordinateur et conduire une voiture", Sociologie du Travail, n° 3, 2001, pp. 369-387.

BOULLIER D., *L'Urbanité numérique. Essai sur la troisième ville en 2100*, Paris : L'Harmattan, 1999.

DAMASIO Alain, *Le Dehors de toute chose*, La Volte, 2016.

GAGNEPAIN Jean, *Du vouloir dire*, vol. 1, Institut Jean-Gagnepain, Matecoulon-Montpeyroux, 1982-2016, digital edition.

HARAWAY Donna, *The Companion Species Manifesto: Dogs, People, and Significant Otherness*. Chicago, IL: Prickly Paradigm Press, 2003.

HEIDEGGER Martin, *What is a Thing?* Gateway Editions, Washington, 1968.

HEIDEGGER Martin, *Build Dwell Think* and *Poetically Man Dwells*, in Poetry, Language, Thought, tr. Albert Hofstadter, Harper Colophon Books, New York, 1971.

JAURREGUIBERRY Francis and LACHANCE Jocelyn, Le Voyageur hypermoderne. Partir dans un monde connecté, Toulouse, Éditions Érès, 2016.

LATOUR Bruno, *Nous n'avons jamais été modernes. Essai d'anthropologie symétrique*, Paris : La Découverte, 1992.

LEFEBVRE Henri, *Espace et politique*, tome 2. *Le Droit à la ville*, Paris, Anthropos, 2001.

LEGENDRE Pierre, *L'Inestimable Objet de la transmission. Étude sur le principe généalogique en Occident*, Paris: Fayard, 1985.

LEVY Jacques, *Habiter sans condition*, in Brigitte Frelat-Kahn et Olivier Lazzarotti, *Habiter. Vers un nouveau concept*, Paris, Armand Colin, 2012.

LEVY Pierre, *L'Intelligence collective. Pour une anthropologie du cyberespace*, Paris : La découverte, 1997.

LUSSAULT Michel, *L'Homme spatial. La Construction sociale de l'espace humain*, Paris, Le Seuil, 2007.

MANNONI Octave, *Clefs pour l'imaginaire ou l'Autre scène*, Paris: Le Seuil, 1969.

OSTROM Elinor, *La Gouvernance des biens communs : pour une nouvelle approche des ressources naturelles*, Commission Université-Palais, 300 p., 2010.

RADKOWSKI, Georges-Hubert de, *Anthropologie de l'habiter: vers le nomadisme*, Paris, PUF, 2002.

SEGAUD Marion, *Anthropologie de l'espace. Habiter, fonder, distribuer, transformer*, Paris : Armand Colin, 2010.

SLOTERDIJK Peter, *Bubbles: Spheres Volume I: Microspherology*, Los Angeles, Semiotext(e), 2011

SLOTERDIJK Peter, *Globes: Spheres Volume II: Macrospherology*, Los Angeles, Semiotext(e), 2014.

SLOTERDIJK Peter, *Foams: Spheres Volume III: Plural Spherology*, Los Angeles, Semiotext(e), 2016

SLOTERDIJK Peter, *Neither Sun nor Death*, Semiotext(e), 2011.

STOCK Mathis, *Théorie de l'habiter. Questionnements*, in Paquot T., Lussault M. et Younès C. (éd.), Habiter : le propre de l'humain, Paris, La découverte, 2007.

TARDE Gabriel, *Les Lois de l'imitation*, Paris, Les empêcheurs de penser en rond, 2001.

can we still disconnect?

Francis Jauréguiberry sociologist

Never has a technical innovation been so successful so fast and on such a scale... The mobile phone and its successor the smartphone have clearly struck a chord with respect to the expectations, needs, desires and fantasies of our contemporaries, to the extent that we can't imagine doing without them. Two processes constantly drive their use. First, feelings of integration and belonging. The social circle to which one belongs, which until not so long ago defined the individual quite well, disappears and is replaced by a set of more or less transient identity- and activity- related bubbles that scarcely intersect. This is a classic theme of modern sociology: the contemporary individual is a fragmented, versatile plurality, and mobile phones have doubtless arrived in the nick of time to help us cope with this lack of unity in terms of our identity and our occupations. They make it possible to move immediately from one "tribe" to the next; they make journeys more reassuring and profitable; they increase opportunities to meet people; and they've become indispensable for coordinating activities on the fly. By activating the right network at the right time, it's possible to share things remotely and to be recognised despite one's absence: integration increasingly depends on connection. At the same time, mobiles also tighten strong links that already exist, despite geographical distance or the passage of time. The integrative success of mobiles is to be found in the synthesis they make possible between openness and refocusing, between random jumps and continuity. They "reify" the lost unity of connections that no longer intersect in space or time. As mediating objects, they seem to condense what is scattered and thus help the individual to cope with his fragmented existence and his many instances of belonging, between here and elsewhere. They also give the impression that they do not cut themselves off from what, a century ago, Georg Simmel called the "multiple possibles" that the excitement of life in big cities allowed modern man to glimpse, although he did not really engage with them and later felt nostalgic for them. With smartphones, contacts, phone numbers, and e-mail addresses are stored away, awaiting possible reactivation. Our friends are on Facebook, our work contacts are on LinkedIn, traces of our past are on Instagram, and people we've forgotten can doubtless be found using search engines: nothing is lost, nothing is far away, everything is within our reach.

The second process that makes us log on is efficiency and performance. Here, the motivation is not emotional or relational reliance, but usefulness and profit. All the services offered on Internet are an obvious example of this, and it's hard to see how we could do without them now. Have we measured how many e-mails, on-line databases, booking websites, webcams, and dedicated geolocalised applications have helped make our lives easier and our daily experience more practical and efficient in terms of time spent versus results obtained? Smartphones provide access to these services and this data wherever we are, making them even better at helping us do what we do. If

we add how reassuring it is for people inclined to anxiety to be connected (“if I run into trouble, I’ll call a specialist or ask for help”), it’s hard to see what would make us log off: the advantages clearly seem to outweigh the possible disadvantages.
And yet, over recent years, muffled complaints have been making themselves heard with increasing force (“I’m completely snowed under”, “I’m inundated with emails”, “I can’t spend my entire life on the phone”, “I’m fed up with getting notifications”…) So much so that an unexpected desire seems to be emerging: the desire to log off—at least from time to time…

1 – Logging off as a form of escape

The most spectacular disconnections, and those that have given rise to the most widely broadcast testimonials, are also the most extreme. They all reflect an attempt to escape from a kind of connection overdose. They involve people running away from crises, people who have had enough or who find themselves too much in demand, people who suffer from a surfeit of information, from cognitive overload, from the harassment or surveillance that makes them feel lost or overwhelmed. In extreme cases of burnout, rejection of technology is an integral part of attitudes of defence that allow the individual to survive when he no longer has the energy to fight. These cases are fortunately rare; more than voluntary disconnection aimed at controlling communication flows, they tend to involve mechanical disconnection designed to avoid being carried away by something uncontrollable. Like a fuse blowing when there’s a power surge, disconnection is merely a reaction. Testimonials from people who have experienced burnout all show that disconnection is not voluntary but automatic, just like immediately stopping work.
Burnout is often presented as a kind of personal collapse under the weight of too much work or too much pressure from other people making demands. But clinical cases

show that they primarily involve a growing feeling of not being able to cope or not having a reason to face up to one's problems. "Not coping" means not having enough time, cognitive resources, cultural capital, and energy to deal with emails or text messages that are clearly too numerous to manage, or to reply to phone calls that are so frequent that they become a problem, or to satisfactorily maintain our on-line social networks without always having the impression that we're falling behind. "Not having a reason to do things" means that when you keep having to drop everything to attend to urgent and important things that turn out to be insignificant, and when you keep suffering from the paradoxical need to involve yourself in projects fully and for long periods in a world dominated by flexibility and adaptation, reasons to believe are eroded and reasons to hope disappear altogether. It's in this depressive state that burnouts occur. ICT itself doesn't cause burnout, but using it blindly and constantly and never stepping back from it does.

2 - Logging off voluntarily

Voluntary logoffs we have observed all fall short of such extreme responses. Indeed they aim to avoid entering the burnout red zone and suffering unbearable situations of information overload. They occur when the desire for disconnection goes beyond complaining or tiredness ("I'm snowed under", "I've had enough", "I'm inundated with emails"), and expresses itself in actions, behaviours and effective tactics. For example they involve turning your mobile off in certain circumstances or at certain times, disconnecting your email software and choosing to check it only occasionally, agreeing not to be constantly connected to social networks or refusing to be geo-locatable wherever you are. In any case, the decision takes place after a realisation, either by accumulation (the situation can't continue, something has to be done), or by a critical incident (an event that suddenly shifts your point of view).

Disconnection is never permanent but always occasional, partial, and situated in contexts where "too much" really is too much, where "again" becomes meaningless and where "more" becomes unbearable... The idea is not to abandon ICTs, but to try to control their use by introducing breaks, temporal cutoffs, and distancing strategies. One form of disconnection that is often mentioned involves putting your mobile in silent mode (and, as some insist, leaving it in your bag so that you don't see the screen light up when you get a call); another involves leaving your laptop at the office. Going out shopping, having a coffee or going running without your mobile are all ways of disconnecting, as is deciding not to check e-mails over the weekend. These are non-spectacular "mini-disconnections" that are not talked about in the media, but they actually represent almost all disconnections. Reading transcriptions of dozens of hours of interviews carried out with people who disconnect highlights the importance they attach to time. ICTs are fanstastic time management tools; they help us coordinate what we do more effectively, making our schedules more agile and precise. Being immediately informed of last-minute hitches, public transport schedules, altered appointments, etc., is a way of saving time and energy and often reducing stress. The smartphone becomes a smart diary: key in a time or a date and you get sent to the relevant email, avoiding time-consuming searches and memory lapses. If you're in a Cloud, the information is sent to all your devices. ICTs should thus save us time—and yet that's exactly what the disconnectors complain that they fail to do!
By constantly "pushing" unsolicited information towards the user, ICTs force him or her to process it. This pressure might come from your boss, your spouse, or your friends: the obligation is professional, status-linked or relational. ICTs don't create this dependency, but they make it more dense, to the extent that they sometimes make it too heavy to carry. Pressing emails and text messages from

a superior or colleague, frequent calls from a spouse or worried mother, or abundant notifications from social networks end up producing feelings of weariness, of being gradually ground down, that are expressed via exasperation, mood swings, or an impression of being overwhelmed. This is where the idea of the disconnected break comes into its own: a "time for yourself" where you can bring things back to your own pace and reconnect with the meaning of things such as length of time, waiting, deep thought, and focused attention.

3 - Professional disconnections

There are jobs where logging off is simply not an option during working hours. Jobs involving telemarketing (calling potential customers), giving information, making reservations, or providing rapid intervention services are examples of this. But ICTs have, in just a few years, become a vector for information overload, which has become an added burden in jobs that require a certain amount of concentration, demand continuity in the way they are carried out, and do not necessarily require uninterrupted connection. The obligation to report almost continuously on progress, multiple checks and inspections carried out while tasks are being carried out, and the general obsession with information in companies disturb and often destabilise employees, to the extent that an important new concept has emerged: the right to disconnect. Tentative experiments are being carried out in this regard, for instance at Volkswagen in Germany where sending professional emails is not allowed after 6 pm and at weekends, or very recently, in France, where a labour agreement for IT consultancy firms includes an "obligation to disconnect". It seems that after twenty or so years of being told to "communicate more" and pressure to be constantly connected, the time has come to think hard about what seems bearable in psychological terms and in terms of what is desirable from a social and organisational point of view. It's more this second point (the danger of counterperformance) than the first (psychological/social risks) that motivated the first management studies on the subject of disconnection. With cases of dysfunction starting to be a serious source of worry because of their cost, company directors began to think about disconnection in terms of managerial performance alone. Their concerns intersected with studies carried out in management sciences focusing on the idea of information overload. Information and knowledge overload is seen as having an impact on the rationale of organisational decisions and overall corporate strategy, and it is thus important to measure its negative aspects.

But for the time being, this is what all our surveys in work environments have shown: everyone does their best to improvise bearable ways of using ICTs allowing disconnection times… but not all employees and managers are equal in terms of their room for manoeuvre and their ability to implement such practices. Not to put too fine a point on it, we might say that one the one hand you have people who have the power to disconnect, and thus to impose on others their (relative, if they have voicemail) inaccessibility, and on the other hand the ones who don't have that power; on the one hand, those who have the power to impose permanent availability on others, and on the other hand those who are forced to bow to this; on the one hand those who have the power to disconnect, and on the other, those who have a duty to remain connected. The "new poor" of telecommunications are no longer those who have no access, but those who are now forced to respond immediately and who are thus unable to escape having demands constantly made on them. And the "nouveaux riches" of telecommunications are those who can filter information and thus maintain a certain distance from such demands.

Of course it's not ICTs that build up this kind of inequality from scratch. It derives from hierarchy, power relationships, status, and ultimately types of power that already exist in companies, organisations or networks. So the question is not whether to consider communication technologies as *sui generis* producers of new forms of exploitation, but whether the simultaneity in telecommunications they make possible tends to reinforce existing inequalities (in the form of relationships of control and dependency—or whether, on the contrary, it tends to weaken them (by making it possible to experiment with new forms of organisation paving the way to greater autonomy and responsibility for all).

4 - Private disconnections

It is on this point that the surveys carried out for the DEVOTIC project surprised us the most. We didn't think that by researching disconnection practices we would garner such serious and profound considerations. Disconnection refers to nothing less than the meaning of life, existential questions, and force of engagement. We didn't expect these themes to emerge, at least not with such force and regularity. Of course, they did not appear immediately in what people said to us. What the vast majority describe as leading to disconnection practices is the desire to (in the respondents' words) "take a breather", "take a step back", "clear your head", "get away from the turmoil", and even "stop feeling knocked out". What they seek is thus part of the same process of distanciation, of temporarily stepping away, of rest and quiet that we can observe in professional settings.

When not governed by defensive or evasive tactics intended to cope with too many unwanted demands, disconnection is always presented as the result of a choice: in this case it is always voluntary and proactive. Here, disconnection is often explained as a way of defending one's own time in a context of generalised synchronisation, of preserving one's own rhythms is a world that urges acceleration, of asserting the right to be left in peace in an environment of intrusive telecommunications, and of expressing the will to be focused on what we do in an environment that lends itself to channel-hopping and lack of focus. Waiting, isolation and silence, which used to be pushed back against because they were seen as synonyms of poverty, confinement or loneliness, reappear in this context no longer as something we submit to, but as something we choose.

These disconnections can be of very short duration and are mostly partial and targeted (choosing not to check email but leaving the phone switched on; putting the phone in silent mode but checking who has phoned from time to time; using geolocation to find an address, then switching it off). People seem to be developing increasingly innovative expertise as ICTs become more complex: we draw from our everyday experience to establish forms of disconnection adapted to the situations we encounter. All these strategies involve managing our attention and entail a set of almost technical rules (knowledge of what the smartphone and its applications are capable of), assessment skills (in strategic terms or in terms of social appropriateness) and the ability to act (to make choices). The aim is to articulate different types of engagement either sequentially (logging on and off) or in the form of modulations (switching off email, but not the phone; total disconnection except three incoming numbers; visual filters, etc.) It all becomes a question of choice and priority.

5 - Disconnection as a personal test

When disconnection is not experienced as a mere act of retreat in response to too many demands or as a way of taking a rest or a break, and when it is not mainly motivated by the desire to be "entirely focused on the task" or "entirely available" or "entirely absorbed by the spectacle we are watching", it is described as a way of "breaking away" or of "distancing" or "isolating" oneself, with the aim of "having some alone time" or "taking stock". It opens the way to a dialogue with oneself: a moment of reflexivity. This experience of interiority is never simple. It enters a tense relationship with processes of recognition and gain that motivate connection. With disconnections of this type, there are no emails, no calls and no social networks to attest to one's existence in the eyes of others, no tweets or Internet to inform people of how the world goes round! There's no more outside stimulation, no more notification, no more distraction or immediate occupation. There's nothing outside of the marks that are left on us, which then have to be organised to make them meaningful. The choice, our respondents told us, is always tricky and difficult to make. It involves giving up—if only for five minutes—everything that might reach them via these channels they decide to temporarily switch off.

What is hard to give up is exactly the same thing as what drives them to frantically check their inbox, their voicemail or their social networks. At this point, many people talk about "addictive" behaviour; and the vocabulary used by our respondents ("I'm hooked", "you become totally dependent", "I can't do without it"...) tends to confirm this. But in most cases "addiction" is a misnomer: it's more like curiosity and a huge desire for new events. It's a vague but constant desire to be surprised by the new and unexpected, by a call or a text message that will change the course of the day or evening by giving it more density or diversity, and ultimately by making one's life more interesting and intense. So it's not addiction that makes it hard to disconnect, but the fear of missing out: FOMO, as the Americans call it.

The result of such a disconnection can be very striking: when the state of almost permanent connection becomes the everyday norm (to the extent that not answering your phone requires justification), disconnection (if it lasts for more than a few hours) represents such a break that it almost automatically makes essential questions emerge. The contrast is such that boredom often no longer has a place: the brutal confrontation with the meaning of one's life occupies the entire space. Silence beckons us, distance questions us, and the past reappears. The search for coherence and self-continuity and the constant striving for intimate significance, to which modernity has condemned humans by making them aware of their autonomy in a changing world, stand out in sharp relief.

There is no reason to mechanically contrast connection and disconnection: it even seems that one cannot exist without the other. Or more precisely, controlled connection (or at least striving towards it) involves forms of disconnection; and by the same token disconnection is only meaningful because the rest of the time there is connection. When extremes come together, a non-controlled connection can lead either to the dissolution of the self in structure-destroying hyper-connection, or else to implosive disconnection (aka burnout). La Boétie described voluntary servitude as that part of our freedom that we delegate so that we can live in a world that is practicable by the greatest number. Here, voluntary disconnection refers to what we agree to relinquish in terms of safety, information or distractions to preserve our own private space: a form of anonymity and reflexive distance where individuals can think of themselves as subjects. If, as far as ICTs are concerned, the protagonist is the person who communicates on networks, the *subject* is the person who gives this communication meaning. But to achieve this, that person has to be able to disconnect from time to time. It is in this respect that the oscillation between connection and disconnection is a perfect indicator of hypermodernity and the uncertainty it constantly produces.

how can we exist in the digital world?

François Jullien philosopher and sinologist

Notions of privacy, influence and existence are three ways of approaching connexion and the digital world. We say that digital transformation calls privacy into question: what is left of privacy under these conditions? We say we're influenced by digital waves, or that they pass through us. How should we approach that influence? What is this thing that has resisted European thought and philosophy for so long? What is influence? By considering the notion of existence from the standpoint of its etymology, "standing outside," I shall be looking at digital in the light of the following paradox: "inhabiting while standing outside".

What is left of privacy in the digital age?

In French, the notion of *l'intime*—which means both privacy and intimacy—is not only complex; it is also paradoxical. *L'intime* does not just refer to what is private or the subjective dimension of what is private. It goes much deeper than that.
As language and the dictionary defines it, *l'intime* has two contradictory meanings. First of all it means "that which is deep inside"; this meaning is connected to expressions such as *sentiment intime* [profound feeling], *conscience intime* [deep-seated awareness], *sens intime* [deep meaning] and *intime conviction* [deep-seated belief]. *L'intime* refers to what lies deep within ourselves, what it most remote, what goes furthest back in time, beyond which we cannot go. At the same time, *l'intime* refers to a relationship with Others, as in phrases like: *je suis intime avec X* [I'm on intimate terms with X] or *"nous sommes intimes"* [We're on intimate terms.] *L'intime* is thus hidden deep within me, and at the same time it points to a relationship with others. There's a tension in the term. *L'intime* refers to both withdrawal and sharing.

To understand the interior of the self, we should first go back to the Latin terms *intus* "inside", *interior* "further inside" and *intimus* "the furthest inside". The latter term is a superlative that has no equivalent for the "outside". *L'intime* is not the interior, it is "further in than the interior", which is itself an opening to the outside—even an opening to infinity. *L'intime* is a kind of cavity inside us that opens us up to infinity, which explains why the term is so subjective.

L'intime escapes thought because it has neither principles nor causes. It is a category that explodes dualism, because it is at once sensual and sexual [*parties intimes*: private parts, genitals; *rapport intime*: sexual intercourse], and it is also highly spiritual. This category challenges the standard, stiff, dualistic dichotomy of the sensual and the spiritual, in the sense of the infinite: openness to the infinite within the finite.

The history of *l'intime* is not insignificant: its discovery goes hand in hand with our modernity. It is not a Greek word. When, on the walls of Troy, Hector and Andromache play their big scene as a married couple while Greeks and Trojans are busy killing each other below, we might think of it as an "intimate-private" moment. But in fact, both have their own positions and plead for their respective causes: Hector for glory, Andromache for survival. Astyanax, the child who is frightened to see the top of his father's helmet, makes an intimate/private gesture, but it doesn't fit with the idea of *l'intime*. Similarly, when Plato talks of the soul, he is not referring to *l'intime*, but to the transparency of minds. The Greeks were not familiar with the notion of intimacy/privacy; in was Augustine who opened up the idea in Rome. Indeed he used the word to refer to openness to Christianity: God found himself to be "more inward than my innermost self", *interior intimo meo*.

The notion is not taken up by Montaigne either, although he constantly talks about the self. But he expresses himself in an aphoristic, sententious way, and in his own words he "talks about himself". *L'intime* remains sententious when he talks about himself—his deepest self—or when he talks about his relationship with others, with his wife, and above all with La Boétie, of whom he wrote *"because it was him, because it was me"*. In Montaigne there is no reference to *l'intime* in the relationship sense ("we're intimate"). In *La Princesse de Clèves*, a great love story, there's still no notion of intimacy. There's never a sense of "us" between the Duc de Nemours and his conquest, the Princesse de Clèves, who knows that if she gives herself to him, she will lose herself, or rather she will lose love. Even in the scene where they write the letter together, there's no sense of intimacy. Similarly, in the final scene, they are alone; unseen by others, they can talk to each other at last... and yet they continue to plead their own cases.

L'intime becomes essential in Jean-Jacques Rousseau's *Confessions*, whose title he borrowed from Saint Augustine. Rousseau read the translation of Augustine so well that a new possibility arose: that of talking about the Self and relationships with Others. In history, intimacy is both the most singular and the most communicable notion. In Stendhal's novels, especially *Le Rouge et le Noir* and *Lucien Leuwen*, as in many 19th century novels, there are two parts: the provinces and Paris. The image of women conveyed in the two parts touches on intimacy. The provinces represent an opportunity for intimacy, whereas intimacy is impossible in Paris. In *Le Rouge et le Noir*, the Stendhalian character is a man who, having made an amorous conquest, discovers and achieves something previously unimaginable: intimacy. First, Julien wants to seduce Mme de Rênal, then the reverse of the conquest occurs, in other words a power game with the Other and the end of one's ambitions and plans involving the Other. This is when "intimacy" begins: when the power struggle and projection cease. With Mathilde de la Mole, there's a conquest, but no intimacy. Similarly, in *Lucien Leuwen*, intimacy is possible in Nancy and impossible in Paris at Mme Grandet's home. What characterises Stendhal's characters is their access to intimacy. Before intimacy, Julien Sorel is an ambitious man; Lucien Leuwen is a fop, content with his books, his wealth, and his father's wealth. By attaining intimacy, they discover new subjective possibilities and unexpected new resources.

L'intime describes the subject, unlike love. When we say "I love you", we make the Other into an object (*je t'aime, je te mutile*: I love you, I mutilate you, as the saying goes). When we say "I'm intimate with you", we are intimate, so we are in "subject" position. Moreover, love is declarative. Saying that we love someone has something theatrical about it, which intimacy destroys because it is not said: it is tacit and implicit. Intimacy is not an event, it's always a process. All in all, intimacy does not need to be communicated; when we're intimate with someone, silence equals words. When two intimate people get together, they don't say anything, they just convey intimacy. When you can stay with someone for two minutes without being embarrassed, there's intimacy between you. With intimacy, there's no need to talk. And this characteristic of intimacy is essential to understand what is at stake in the digital world.

So silence equals words—but in order to say what? What does intimacy communicate via the rapport it establishes? The idea of a "rapport" or implicit understanding between two people can be expressed in French by the word *connivence*, which is worth looking at a little more closely. *Connivere* in Latin means "to understand each other with one's eyes tightly closed"—in other words, to understand one another without needing to say so. The notion of *connivence* also refers to the idea of *connaissance* (knowledge), which is the great subject dealt with in Greek philosophy. The major turning point between Greek and other thought can be seen at the beginning of Plato's *Theaetetus*. Socrate is asked what wisdom is, and he answers: *"Wisdom is science"*. This illustrates the great tipping point in Greece that led from wisdom to science. Such a mode of thinking is not neutral. It creates a framework, an envelope… a bubble we think inside. We have decided that the mantle that clothes thought is knowledge. But what do we leave to one side, no longer seeing it? To what extent is our thought walled in? What has the philosophy of knowledge passed by? What status do we give to that which is forgotten, covered over, or buried? Consequently, the notions of *connivence* and intimacy (intimate words, intimate silence) convey knowledge. *Connivence* is knowledge's Other. And poetry is the language of *connivence*.

The notion of *connivence* has become especially relevant today, in particular via the question of digital and the inhabitable environment. All instances of "inhabiting" involve *connivence*, because inhabiting involves entering into a relationship of tacit mutual understanding. *Connivence* presupposes time: it involves a process. It is not something sudden, chosen, or decided. But it's not a matter of habit (*habitus*) either. *Connivence* is what implicitly and tacitly develops, creating a form of intelligence that can be described as *connaissance*—knowledge. *Nous naissons connivents*: we are born in a state of *connivence*. The child at its mother's breast, or on her lap, is *connivent*. Then gradually, from this initial *connivence*, we develop knowledge: *connivence* becomes *connaissance*. At school, we learn things, we organise our knowledge, we become familiar with things, and we construct knowledge that is communicable. But with our families, in private, and on holiday, it's all about *connivence*. We flip-flop between *connaissance* and *connivance*—knowledge and implicit understanding. Knowledge develops through exteriorisation, as we map things out and distinguish them in a communicable way. Conversely, *connivence* involves inner thought. One day, A Bordeaux wine grower said to me: *"In the end, the relationship we have with the vine is one of* connivence*. Knowing how to prune vine stocks is about* connivence*, it's what we call* 'le biais du gars'*."* "Le gars" means the craftsman (here, the winegrower), and "le biais" means his technique. What's the best way of pruning a vine? Craft is all about *connivence*. We are *sujets connaissants* and *sujets connivents*—subjects who know, and subjects who share implicit understanding—and we never stop flipping between relationships based on *connaissance* and relationships based on *connivence*.

So now let's explore the notions of *habiter*, *habit*, *habitation* and *habitacle* in the light of this notion of *connivence*.

Digital affects us as an *"influence"*

With digital, people are affected, indeed invaded, by notifications—just as they are affected by the waves passing through them and influencing them. But the notion of *influence* seems to resist European philosophy: in Europe, we don't know how to approach the notion of *influence* in philosophical terms. The term comes from *influential astrology*, which describes the supposed influence of the stars on human destiny. The word appeared in the Middle Ages; its origin lies in astrology, not ontology, which means that it's seen as highly suspicious, because it refers to the occult: the knowledge that European rationalism rejected and marginalised from the Renaissance on—just as it rejected everything that lay beyond the heroic construction of reason that took place in the 16th and 17th centuries, and beyond the Great Adventure of classical science.

The notion of influence undermines and shakes the foundations of what European thought holds most dear: the idea of ourselves as autonomous subjects, in other words subjects of initiatives with freedom as their primary attribute. Influence passes through us without our realising it. Influence is not frontal: that's what sets it apart. When I'm attacked head-on, I can fight back; but influence is ambient, fraught, invasive and penetrating. I can't face up to it, so I can't resist it. I don't know where it comes from, and I can never contain it as an adversary. It will not be confronted. It is diffuse, and will not be isolated. Influence is something we can't control. It is not part of the category of being. Influence is the unassignable *par excellence*: I don't know where it comes from, how it gets to me, how it passes through me; I cannot confront it. Influence is not present; it is pregnant: weighty with potential.

By the same token, digital is not present either, in the Latin sense of *para esse*, which means "what is before me", because I either see or don't see what is before me. Digital is "pregnant" and ambient and, like influence, it infiltrates, it insinuates itself, and it penetrates from all around without alerting us and without our noticing. Influence does not stand out, so it is not noticed, which is why European thought, while it acknowledges the phenomenon, has been so uncomfortable about approaching influence and has done so little to develop the concept. And yet Freud says that between a psychoanalyst and his patient there is a relationship of influence (*Beeinflüßung*). European and Greek thought did not tackle it because they are a philosophy of causality, of principle, and of beginnings.

Chinese thought, on the other hand, considers influence to be at the beginning of everything, and is rich in perspectives when it comes to thinking about digital, especially if we consider influence and the waves passing through us. The fact that waves pass through me in an ambient, pregnant and invasive way, challenging my position as an autonomous subject and my subjective initiative, gives rise to a question that is specific to European culture. Chinese thought is thought based on influence. It's a philosophy based on flows. Thanks to the *chi*—breath, breathing—the world is made up of flows and interactions that are constantly placed in a state of tension, like yin and yang.

The first concept of Chinese politics is transformative influence. A regime or a kingdom is looked at in terms of the quality of the influence that imbues it, impregnates it, and passes through it. At the time of the Chinese principalities, before the Empire was reconstructed, a principality was assessed according to its influence. The wind is the great theme of Chinese thought: we cannot see it, but it discreetly passes through everything. As Confucius says: *"When the wind blows, the grass bends"*. There are two possible translations: in the most dictatorial periods of Chinese history, it was translated as *"the grass lies down"*, but the translation not subject to the Chinese ideology of authoritarian power is *"the grass bends"*. This phrase lies at the source of Chinese political thought. The good prince is like the wind: a bending, ambient, pregnant, penetrating force that influences the people. China only imagined one political regime: that of the prince, the monarchy. Still today, the Communist Party is a kind of monarchy. The Chinese word for country is *guójiā* (国家) which means "that which belongs to the family".

The good prince influences his wife, who influences their children, and from beginning to end influence spreads out like a wave to the ends of the earth, under the sky.

Conversely, the notion of influence has been a structuring principle of critical thought in China. In China, there is no critique as we know it comparable to *J'accuse*. There's no critique of opposition, no democratic critique where I raise my hand and say "No". There's no Greek-style criticism, made up of rebuttals, *logos* versus *logos*, discourse versus discourse. In China, there's no agora, no public space where one can talk face to face. Influence dissolves face-to-face situations, and influence cannot be resisted. Just as the prince could not be criticised, and just as one could be beheaded for even thinking about criticising him, one would express oneself poetically, through images and in a diffuse way, and this evasive picturesque discourse would allow criticism of the prince to get through. Political criticism does not directly express an opinion; it is distilled in a more poetic way. Poetic imagery allows you to say just enough for the other person to understand, but not enough to lose your head. This kind of compromise and non-committal haziness is the cornerstone of Chinese politics.

So Chinese culture knows nothing of persuasion, and Greek culture knows nothing of influence. If I convince someone, he realises he's convinced, whereas if I influence him, he doesn't realise it. Influence is not direct; it is discreet and ambient. It will not be confronted head-on. It is diffuse, and will not be isolated.

The theme of the landscape helps us to define this specific trait of Chinese thought relating to influence, in the light of European thought focusing on the subject and its discourse. In the 16th century, first in Holland and Italy, then in France, a philosophy of the landscape emerged in painting. "Landscape" is a European term, present in all European languages (pays/paysage ; Land/Landschaft ; land/landscape).

What makes a landscape? According to the Petit Robert, a landscape is *"une partie de pays que la nature présente à un observateur"* [an area of land that nature presents to an observer]. I find this definition characteristic because it involves the typical western subject. When he looks at a landscape, the viewer isolates an area of land and places it in front of himself as an object. When the landscape entered painting, it introduced a relationship between subject and object, between perceiving subject and perceived object.

"Landscape" in Chinese is *fēngjēng* (风景), "mountain water". There is no perceiving subject, but an interaction, an interflow between high and low, between that which is motionless (the mountain) and that which moves (water), between that which has a shape (the mountain) and that which is shapeless (water), between what we cannot hear (the mountain) and what we can hear (water). The landscape is an interaction, a correlation, an instance of tension in which what we Europeans call "the subject" finds itself involved. The Chinese philosophy of the landscape considers that perception has an emotional dimension. China thinks in terms of complementary opposites, as demonstrated by yin and yang, sky and earth. In China, a landscape is qualified by the fact that there is a tension within it between complementary opposites, so that it passes through us and the split between inside and outside vanishes. The Chinese say: *"Landscape and emotion are no longer separated"*. We no longer know what relates to the landscape—the outside—and what relates to emotion—the inside. That which is perceptible becomes emotional at the same time, and that's what makes a landscape and qualifies it as a landscape. This is interesting when we come to the question of inhabitable space and related projects. Do the inhabitable world and the digital world not recall the Chinese idea of the landscape—something I find myself involved in, something that passes through me and influences me?

The question of "the unassignable" lies at the heart of thought relating to inhabitable space and the digital world. If we don't know where something comes from, that challenges the position of the autonomous subject. It basically unravels our philosophy of freedom: of the subject as free. Freedom poses a difficult question for China, and one that is still subject to caution. China has developed a system of thought without freedom—without detailing this property of the subject. It has considered

the subject more in terms of its availability, referring to a capacity for openness that puts everything within the subject's grasp. As Confucius says: *"Nothing I can do, nothing I cannot do."* I am open and available for everything. If something needs to be carried, I'll carry it. If it needs to be left behind, I'll leave it behind. In China, the biggest human fault is not error but partialness: dropping part of reality and not being open to everything. Chinese greatness lies in availability, not freedom.

How can we inhabit the digital world while remaining outside it?

These thoughts on influence and availability lead us to the question of inhabiting and digital. Digital is said to require new forms of adaptation, and we say that it is an important point in our evolution. Humans have never stopped evolving since life appeared on Earth, often by adapting via the survival of the fittest. Referring to "humans" and not "Man", which has his own definition, is not without significance. Using the word "human" means that we are in a process of humanisation whose beginning and end we are unaware of. "Human" suggests that we are aware of being in transition and that we are not defined by a horizon (in its etymological sense of "definition") made up of the senses—of human nature.

Digital marks the beginning of a new phase, creating a new envelope, a new skin, a new habitat we must adapt to. "The human" is no longer conceived as a phenomenon in transition; it is no longer seen as tightly defined and circumscribed by what Man is. There is something essential in the move from Hominoid to Hominid, from Hominid to Homo, from Homo to Homo habilis to Homo ergaster and finally to Homo sapiens. The work of paleontologists shows that there is no clean break between Man and what came before Man.

But is the concept of adaptation sufficient? Does digital lead to a new form of adaptation? In Latin, *ad aptus* means "making oneself able"; but is it not simplistic to see Man and his future as being the result of continuous adaptation? Yves Coppens, for example, is still working with the great logical concept of evolution and adaptation, whereas other paleontologists are highlighting something else. In fact, adaptation comprises the exit from adaptation, which some have dubbed "exaptation". In the digital age, the adaptation we are being forced to embrace (though some, like me, are digging their heels in) contains the question of a "way out". And perhaps we are already unknowingly in the process of developing the adaptive modalities that will prevent us from being stuck in this adaptation and provide us with a way out. Adaptation always secretes an "exaptation", a way out of adaptation. By defining this new world as a new layer, a new envelope, a new skin, we can already think about how to pierce the layer, break through the envelope, and slice open the skin. Isn't that what being human is really about? Isn't a human being someone who constantly opens the skin or the envelope, someone who has always punctured his ecological niche? Digital appears as a new ecological niche we have to puncture, just as we did with those that came before it.

We no longer believe in all those definitions of Man as a special being with a specific essence. There is no such thing as human exceptionality. But what has *manifested itself* as human, what has persevered and promoted itself as human, is a different matter: in this respect, Man has been able to make himself an exception and stand out from the rest. Is the human not the one who has repeatedly, randomly, dangerously, through trial and error, survived in the living world? Is he not the one who has found a way out—a side exit? Man is like an evolutionary sidestep, because he stands out and because he adapts. Humanity has found "a way out"— a way out of adaptation. That's what I think characterises human development.

The word "existence" describes this mode of development well. To exist—*existere* in Latin—means "to stand outside". But how can we exist as we inhabit, when to inhabit means "to be inside", when existing means "being outside the inside"? How can we promote the human dimension that involves providing a way out of adaptation via exaptation? How can we promote switching off, dislocating, pulling out of joint? In *Hamlet*, Shakespeare uses the expression *out of joint*, echoing the prefixes "un-", "dis-" and so on—what I call *dé-coïncidence*: dis-coincidence. Is the human being not one who dis-coincides? "Inhabiting" the digital world means "adapting" to it and "exapting" from it. It means residing within it and excepting oneself from it.

In the beginning, "to exist" was a theological verb that meant "to be outside the spirit of God". The premise was that we are in the spirit of God until He decides to make us exist in the world. We only exist because we are sent outside to inhabit the world. To exist thus primarily means to exit the spirit of God. If we remove the theological trappings of the verb, to exist means "to be outside" what constitutes the world, in other words totalisation and integration—according to my own definition of what constitutes a world. The world is an integrating whole, which is thus "inside". This means that to exist, in the Latin sense, means being outside the integrating whole that is the world. In the digital age, to exist means to be outside the integrating whole of the digital envelope. According to Martin Heidegger, *"only Man exists"*, in the sense that only Man is able to step outside his environment (*Umgebung*), to refuse to be contained within the integrating whole that is the world, to fail to adhere to the all-embracingness of the world. The digital envelope constitutes a world; digital adaptation exists; so a world is being formed through totalisation and integration. How can we exist by inhabiting this world? How can we inhabit freely?

Dégager [to free, to clear, to open up, to release] is an interesting term—not because of the way it relates to truth or morals, but because of the way it relates to behaviour and the notion of inhabiting. *Se dégager* means no longer being caught up inside something or sticking to it; it means recovering a sense of perspective: a "clear" view [in French: *une vue dégagée*]. We are put in mind of the famous slogan *"Dégage!"* ["Clear off!", "Get lost!"] used by protesters during the Arab Spring. *Dégager* means to clear an obstruction that bogs us down by making us stick to something. It is a verb that we have not explored philosophically in Europe, unlike the Chinese who have approached it as an ethical verb *par excellence*. The theme of untying or release is present in both Plato and the ancient Taoist thinker Zhuang Zhou. For both the Greeks and the Chinese, we must relinquish narrow vision and perception in order to release ourselves from what surrounds us.

We need to rethink the notion of freedom, not in the classical mode that no longer holds water (freedom given by God because we are in God's image). The era of Cartesian freedom, which begins the day I depart from divine power, and the age of Kantian freedom, which presupposes a necessary natural law I must abide by and which I can escape from because I belong to something else which is noumenal and metaphysical, seem to be over. We have to think about freedom in non-metaphysical terms. We have to think of freedom as a release, as an ability to open up the game, as a loosening of the vice of adaptation, as a path to exaptation. The future figure of the subject is that of the alert subject—as against the inert, soulless, dead subject. The alert subject is able to find exaptation in adaptation: a shifting away, a form of dissidence that makes it possible to exist by keeping outside our sense of belonging to the world, so that it no longer walls us in or covers us over or holds us down.

We live in a world where communication is so easy that it is likely to destroy the possibility of thought. Thought initiatives lead us to except ourselves, to exist, to find a way of staying out of the "in" that we inhabit, immanent and existent. What matters is not the way we have to adapt to digital, to the new world, to this new envelope, to this new skin, but how we're going to get out of it. How are we going to inhabit these changes without being its prisoners, stuck fast like birds on a wire? How can we make sure we don't just make it into an ecological niche, and if it's an ecological niche, how can we punch holes in it so that we can get out? How can we split this new digital envelope? How can we find outsideness on the inside? Does it have to be invented? How can we invent a way out where we go in? How can we "exist" in the digital world?

lightness

Anne Lacaton and Jean-Philippe Vassal architects

Living somewhere doesn't stop at your bedroom, your bathroom, your living room or your garden. It also means going to the library, to a museum, or going for a walk down the street, going to work (we often spend more time at work than at home, and there's no reason why offices shouldn't have balconies to allow people to take a breath of fresh air). Living somewhere is a permanent state, from bedroom to city to landscape. This is a fundamental notion. The space we construct must be defined in relation to this permanent state of dwelling. I also think it's about democracy. We continue to practise 19th century architecture and planning—it's a way of thinking that doesn't change: we really need to look at progress that has been made and experiments that open up new avenues in this domain.

J-P V

Africa raised a fundamental question for us: when it comes down to it, what does the practice of architecture mean?" I really wonder if I ever asked myself that when I was studying architecture. I don't think I did. In Africa, a poor person needs to build a shelter. He looks for some wood, and he soon realises that if he makes a tripod it stands up on its own, and that if he puts a coat on it he can use it to keep the sun off. In the beginning, you think that's a bit pathetic ("they're poor people") but after a while you realise that that person practises architecture every day: he goes from a situation where he can't stay where he is because there's too much sun, or where it's uncomfortable, to a situation where he's created an inhabitable space. You then start to understand that architecture is bout dealing with issues like that. Of course its more complicated than just making sunshades, but fundamentally it's the same thing. An perhaps what we brought back from Africa is a desire to always keep sight of this lightness of purpose, and to keep hold of the idea that there's no reason for processes to become cumbersome.

A L

That's where freedom lies, in every project: in the way we relate to a situation and in the way we manage what we do. It's true of projects like the Latapie House, but also the Cité Manifeste in Mulhouse, where there's a kind of garage structure with a professional greenhouse on top. This is where we find the most efficient and effective tools possible: the horticultural greenhouse with its ability to control the climate, and the prefabricated structure used in car parks that enables us to deal with the floor area and the 3D volume. The same goes for the house in Cap-Ferret, but the difference is that here it's an interaction between a forest and a steel-and-concrete structure that generates the situation. And the conversion of the Bois-le-Prêtre tower is the same: there's something that already exists, and we add things to it instead of knocking it down and starting from scratch. We have no lack of materials, and yet what we find interesting is to consider urban situations as materials: how we can discover and leverage opportunities within the complexity of the city.

A L and J-P V

a common world

Geneviève Azam economist

First of all, by way of introduction, I'm going to talk about the notions of the "common world" and the "world in common".

The "common world" is made up of all the human institutions that we inherit. It's also made up of objects, "durable works" in the words of the philosopher Hannah Arendt, for whom the common world is the world into which each of us is born and which each of us inherits. This common world is inconceivable without its habitat, the Earth, which we share we other species. The "world in common" refers to the way in which the inherited world is passed on, inhabited, recognised, and shared. It is also a world that has to be brought into existence, and that needs to be built in common.

Today the common world and the world in common are under threat from all sides: the idea of a common world, of the world in common and a world to be shared is being abandoned by part of the population that has broken away, by an oligarchy that seems to live outside the world, in an off-shore world to use a financial term. Added to that we have the partially irreversible harm done to our common habitat, the Earth.

At the same time, and the exhibition shows this, we see concrete initiatives emerging everywhere that show other ways of living in the world. Beyond the destruction, the threats and the ugliness in the world, they testify to a love for the world, an *Amor Mundi* as Hannah Arendt called it, without which the common world is under threat. Loving the world does not involve consenting to what exists, it's a way of putting reality to the test: it tests our sensitivity to what exists.

Loving the world means resolutely confronting the reality of the world to understand what is happening to us when the reality of the world tends to escape our grasp along with its sustainability. If there is no more stability in the world, if everything is moving, doomed to be destroyed or permanently challenged, then it is very hard to project ourselves into a common world for the future.

This difficulty in feeling the world can be seen in the profusion of non-worlds, what the anthropologist Marc Augé calls *non-lieux*, which are uninhabitable because they are entirely devoted to circulation, passing through, and consumption. The loss of the reality of the world is a major form of our alienation, especially as many filters prevent us from feeling it.

This reality manifests itself painfully in ecological imbalance. Life on Earth is threatened and utopias that imagined that we would be radically separated from Nature, which we could limitlessly dominate and control, are now obsolete. It's a very tough wake-up call: we're becoming aware that our habitat is fragile and that we must reconstruct commonality among ourselves by cooperating with nature and other species instead of trying to overpower them. We painfully discover that we have triggered phenomena over which we have no control. We made the mistake of believing that we were all-powerful, enlightened, in full control of our actions, and able to anticipate their consequences.

I'm thinking in particular about global warming, which is the unwanted consequence of our activities and social structures. But we can't negotiate with the Earth, with the atmosphere, or with the length of time carbon stays in the atmosphere. It's a brutal fact that we have to face and we have to take it into account as we build a world in common.

The tendency to destroy the world in common

What is the origin of the increasing fragility of the common world over the past thirty years, leading to "acosmism", that is to say worldlessness: not only the lack of a world in common, but of a world per se? To what extent has neoliberalism created this acosmism, this worldless world, and of course this world without a common world?

The neoliberal way of living in the world was formulated by Margaret Thatcher: "Society doesn't exist". Such a statement is the result of elaborate philosophical thought, in particular by Friedrich Hayek in the 1930s. To say that society does not exist is to assert the primacy of the individual, who is supposed not to have anything exterior to himself. Society boils down to a collection of individuals: it is an emergence, a shifting fabrication, a process built from contractual relationships between individuals. When all these private contracts are added together, you get society. And as the economist Milton Friedman pointed out, to make a society it is not necessary for individuals to know or like one another; you just need to find a coordination mechanism that spontaneously harmonises all the actions carried out by the different individuals. This mechanism is the market and the price system, which harmonise supply and demand.

Society has no prior foundation because it is in a constant state of re-emergence, it's a network, even an information network, that contains within it the automatic mechanisms of regulation. In societies that do not exist, and in an unanchored world, it is naturally hard to define a common world.

In economics, the point at which we moved from a world in which we could rely on stability to a world in which everything is adrift dates from the early 1970s. In this regard, President Nixon's decision in 1971 to abandon fixed exchange rates between different currencies and to let the currency market calculate exchange rates ushered in an era of general monetary instability. Floating exchange rates are a really good metaphor for the directionless world that emerged at that time.

And yet stability makes it possible to live in the world. Stability does not mean immobility, but an absence of stability sets everything adrift.

Some of these neoliberal movements were influenced by cybernetics, in other words by a vision of society as an interconnected network of information, with humans themselves becoming networks and storehouses of information based on genetic maps. Society was seen as a cybernetic machine in which everything is interconnected, shifting, flexible, liquid, with no possible exteriority. Modernity became liquid, in the words of the sociologist Zigmund Bauman. It is something that flows and slides; it is the illusion of the immateriality of existence; it is the apology of flows, of that which does not settle, of drifting.

Because everything always changes, we cannot oppose economic change, we just have to adapt, because change has become the essence of our condition. In a networked society, we don't have to interact (the primary condition for building commonality), we have to react to stimuli, to an abundance of information, in the most rational way possible. We can understand the success of behavioural sciences, techniques, and psychology, because they involve optimising reactions to a constant stream of information and managing risks. Just as we can understand the success of the archetype of the self-employed person, who manages his own life and his own business and becomes what is known in French as an *auto-entrepreneur*: a self-entrepreneur. But if we are the entrepreneurs of ourselves, it is because we consider that we don't have a world, that we are self-sufficient, asocial, ahistorical, apolitical, worldless creatures.

With society as a full-blown entity partly exterior to individuals disappearing in the neoliberal tradition, nature does not exist either: it is now even dead. This isn't about recognising ecological destruction; it is a way of saying that there can be no more nature without traces left by humanity, that nature is completely anthropologised: transformed by humans. Some people say that we should finish the job and go even further in this radical transformation of nature by humans, as far as re-manufacturing nature to tackle the dangers arising from the deterioration of ecosystems in the remotest corners of the Earth. If nature is entirely manufactured by humans, this also means that wherever we go all we meet is humans, that there is no longer anything outside of human experience, that there is no longer a boundary. Bio-economics, which aimed to study economic systems as subsystems of the biosphere, is reversed: liberal bio-economics, often called green economics, attempts on the contrary to treat the biosphere as a subsystem of economics, as natural capital that needs to be developed, like any form of capital.

For a very long time, in economics, nature was seen as an endless supply of resources we could draw from, like Jean-Baptiste Say, a 19th century economist, who talked about *le grand magasin de la nature* (the department store of nature). Nature was seen as a dead object whose purpose was to satisfy our desires and needs. The other sciences then taught us that nature is a living thing, not just a set of rich resources; it produces endless flows of what, in a purely utilitarian tradition, we call "ecosystemic services". It purifies air and water; it allows pollination; it captures carbon; it eliminates waste. But these ecosystemic services have been harmed (think about dying bee populations) and they must be protected and restored.

The response from the green economy is to preserve this interconnected network of ecosystems by submitting it to the logic of economics, according to which the problem of these services is that they are free, because anything that is free is doomed to be wasted according to that ideology. Establishing a market price is the condition for rational use of these services. Such an entrepreneurial view of nature brings nature into the cycle of capital. Consequently, nature, which used to be a form of exteriority and otherness, something that resisted us, something we didn't create or manufacture, something to lean on and a source of wonder, something that fired our imagination and sparked our creativity, now enters the platforms of productive capital. It becomes an infrastructure that will allow a new capitalistic leap forward. The absence of society, the absence of nature, the refusal of anything exterior to human experience and the neoliberal individual, removes all opportunities for a common world—and for a world per se.

The return of the commons

At the same time we are experiencing a return to the idea of "commons" and various practices and experiences that subscribe to that notion.
The notion of commons is ancient, since the Latin definition of *Res Communis*, common things, as compared to *Res Publica*, the public thing. In Europe, thinking about commons goes back to the 18th century in England

648

and gained momentum during the Industrial Revolution and the birth of capitalism. It was the response to the process of enclosure—where landowners enclosed common land, foreshadowing the emergence of private farmland and agrarian capitalism. This process led to the expulsion of the peasants who made their living from these areas of common land. The process spread to Europe, sparking strong resistance to the privatisation of land. For a long time these struggles were underestimated or devalued, reduced to the level of peasant revolts, especially by the productivist and industrialist Left. Until the early 19th century, common ownership, which presupposes a community that defines rules of use for common resources, was the response to the privatisation of land, forests and commons. The cooperative movement, which was one of the earliest labour organisations, was also organised on the basis of common ownership. It was workers' production and consumer associations that supported the 1848 revolution. At that time, commons were not defined in statist terms.
At the end of the 19th century and after 1945, in the dominant socialist or communist movements, the alternative to private property became State property. This is why discussions on the subject of commons disappeared; the very idea of commons was strongly devalued by statism, which held that the only sovereign community that could oppose private interest was the central State.

And yet for the past thirty years we have seen a return to the notion of commons in the public arena. This seems to be a reaction to a new and unusually far-reaching enclosure movement that began in the 1980s concerning the essential elements of life: water, the soil, energy, air, even life itself with ownership rights over living things. In addition to these so-called natural commons there are commons such as information, knowledge and culture, which are themselves subject to a privatisation process.

This return to the notion of commons follows theoretical pathways and gives rise to attempts to reclaim threatened commons and to invent new commons. The research movement followed an article by Garrett Hardin published in 1968 in the journal *Science*, entitled "The Tragedy of the Commons". To deal with the harm done to natural commons and the exhaustion of resources, Hardin stated that it is necessary to define precise public and private ownership rights, as free access to commons gives rise to predation and waste, according to a widely shared vision of the liberal individual as selfish and only concerned with his own interests.

In the United States in the years that followed, with the arrival of conservative and neoliberal coalitions that formed around Ronald Reagan, just one thing was remembered from Hardin's article: to avoid the tragedy of the commons, we have to set up private ownership rights. In this context, a researcher called Elinor Ostrom started a multi-disciplinary project on commons, based on fieldwork carried out all over the world, especially studying the management of alpine pastures and water. She showed, unlike Hardin and unlike the neoliberal approach, that commons are not freely accessible, and that a very long time ago the communities that manage them invented common rules of use that are not necessarily written down, but which are powerful rules that regulate the use of these resources. She arrives at the conclusion that in general, for all the cases she studied, the common management of commons is much more efficient than private or state management. Elinor Ostrom was awarded the Nobel Prize for Economics in 2009 (actually the Bank of Sweden Prize): she was the first woman to receive it on a subject that was not most economists' cup of tea, even if her methodology reflects mainstream thinking. Following that, many academic research projects began.
At the same time, social unrest all over the world took place as part of a process of

reclaiming the commons, in the context of struggles against the privatisation of water, energy and seeds, against land grabs, and against the appropriation of knowledge. The communities concerned might be large or small: towns, cities and regions also became involved. This reclamation process takes place via experiments in communal management.

While we regret the fact that these experiments to design an inhabitable world do not manage to connect to one another, coming together to discuss the idea of commons allowed links to be made between experiments, which instead of being fragmented were more widely disseminated.

The issue of commons once again raised the problem of ownership, which was no longer really being thought about. Very interesting forms of ownership emerged, in the form of property that is not appropriation. Instead, it involves granting right of use but requiring the user to maintain and give back the property, to ensure the long term existence of the resource for the community and for future generations.

With commons we highlight concrete alternatives, and not only the kind of abstract utopias that appeared in the 19th and 20th centuries, utopias that often drifted into systems because they were so far removed from the living realities of the world. These concrete experiments are sometimes regarded with disdain because they are too local and too concrete compared to the major abstract planetary challenges that lie before us. Such an attitude means neglecting what is within our immediate reach in the name of major necessary change. These millions of concrete utopias mean that anyone can set things in motion in places where there opportunities for life and experiment, and can thus feel the world, the concrete aspect of the world; anyone can feel that emotion, instead of the calculated economic reasoning that produces the non-world.

the economy: towards new forms of solidarity?

Anne-Sophie Novel economist and journalist

Any social change has to devise its economy, and although our societies seem confused in many ways, a number of emerging economic models seek to provide responses to the century's challenges. From degrowth to the blue economy, from the symbiotic economy or perma-economy to the positive economy, there are many terms to describe possible alternatives to laissez-faire and liberalism. What many of these models have in common is solidarity and cooperation, which run counter to the law of the jungle and the survival of the fittest dictated by the spirit of capitalism that has brought us this far...

To start with, let's look at the cooperative economy, the oldest of these models, which is often called the social and solidarity economy. The first consumer cooperatives appeared in the late 18th century to promote a more social economy. At that time, consumers got together to buy goods wholesale, giving each member the possibility of exercising rights and duties. In this social economy, groups of people aimed to meet collective expectations: cooperative networks as varied as Biocoop shops, power suppliers such as Enercoop, or banks like the Crédit Coopératif (whose processes echo those of production cooperatives) offer more than goods and services: they offer guarantees in terms of product quality, production methods, respect for humans and the environment, fair prices, and ultimately an alternative view of society. In this sense, their reasoning is not anti-capitalistic, but a-capitalistic: these initiatives do not stand in opposition to capital, but in its negation, and people replace capital in the ultimate goal of collective action. As Jean-François Draperi explains in *Rendre possible un autre monde*, "Adopting a social economy restores the connection between assets and capital. It brings together volunteers, each of whom has a voice, and only one voice, in decision-making independent from differences in financial investment. Money made is not considered as profit, but as a management surplus upon which the company constitutes reserves that cannot be shared out and are inalienable". This sector now has its own Ministry in France, has created 400,000 new jobs (more than the traditional private sector) in ten years and is currently moving forward on the question of its links with social entrepreneurship (under the impulse of Mouves, in particular) to determine whether broader acceptance of the statutes of the ESS and profit management could be extended.

Another model that is often talked about is the positive economy. Defined by Maximilien Rouer and Anne Gouyon in *Réparer la planète, la révolution de l'économie positive* (published in 2005 by JC Lattès Édition), the positive economy is defined in relationship to the negative economy (which harms the environment and is predominant today) and the neutral economy ("that of 1970s ecologists, which was less polluting but which in no way solved existing environmental problems," says M.Rouer in the interview). The positive economy is intended to repair the environment while making a profit. This economy applies "to all sectors, construction, agriculture, energy or consumer goods. It desectorises the environment, moving it from sectorial logic to mainstream logic, and changes our scientific, technological, economic and financial references points. It goes as far as to question the vulnerability of existing business models, products and services," points out Maximilien Rouer. Today the term is used by Jacques Attali, especially in the framework of the LH Forum held every September in Le Havre since 2012.

The third model is that of the circular economy. With the work undertaken by the Ellen Macarthur Foundation, the institute of the circular economy set up in October 2012 in Paris, the work of the Inspire Institute and the creation by Euromed Management of a research chair entitled "business as unusual" devoted to the subject, there have never been so many opportunities to move forward with this concept according to which one person's waste is another person's resource. Local policies are starting to adopt this model for the development perspectives it offers, for example the Aquitaine region since 2015 (see the RECITA website http://www.recita.org/ which maps out initiatives in Aquitaine).
In a similar but not identical vein, the economy of functionality is based on selling the use of a product and related services instead of selling the product itself. Unlike the usual service economy approach, it involves seeking environmental and/or social gains. In France, the Club Economie de la Fonctionnalité is keeping a close eye on the subject, and in 2013 the Inspire Institute was able to work with the Provence-Alpes-Côte-d'Azur region on a methodological handbook (the NOVUS method: Nouvelles Opportunités Valorisant l'Usage et le Service/New Opportunities Focusing on Use and Service) "aimed at preparing the region for a transition to an economy that consumes fewer natural resources while continuing to create value and new jobs". Among the pioneers of this approach, the best known in France is Michelin (which rents tyres to its professional clients) and the best known internationally is Interface (which offers its professional clients a carpet rental service).

The collaborative economy, which has been actively developing in France since 2012, focuses on access to property and encourages peer-to-peer interactions. After much initial enthusiasm, this economy has found itself embroiled in controversy (UBER / VTC in conflict with taxi operators, irregularities observed on the UBER platform, and so on), so much so that the term "collaborative" is increasingly criticised. The fact remains that web platforms that have arisen from this model have popularised age-old practices (bartering, gifts, exchange between private individuals, buying and selling second-hand goods, etc.) and offer the majority of users solutions in terms of purchasing power and social cohesion. Interestingly enough, the age of collaborative practices gives a new perspective to the deployment of the cooperatives processes described above. Combining the core values inherent in the social and solidarity economy with the flexibility and agility of collaborative processes clearly opens the way for a new economic and social paradigm.
In the same vein, some people prefer to talk about the contributive economy, such as the philosopher Bernard Stiegler who believes that our next working model will be anchored in knowledge and not in the consumerist model. For example, "in the field of energy, the contributive economy is very very important. There are several types of contributors. Individuals, first of all. I, for example, own a mill. I could put solar panels on 300 square metres of roof and sell 3 to 4 times what I use. But I don't do it because safety regulations dictate that I would have to invest a lot of money," he explained at Rue89 in February 2013. The key question is: how can we get away from consumerism? The current economic model has become toxic for both people and the environment and we have to turn towards an "age of contributive work, where the contributor is neither merely a producer, nor merely a consumer". And remember that the cooperative economy as it was originally designed is not contributive

because it does not fundamentally alter the industrial economy and develops side by side with the industrial model. The economy of contribution is a cooperative industrial model that is not "separate from the rest", while promoting freeware and everything that arises from decentralisation and decentralised networking (in the field of energy in particular).
Others prefer to talk about the horizontal economy, such as Daniel Kaplan, former director of the FING, who stated in an interview for the WithoutModel website in 2013 that "individuals who engage in these practices (eBay, car sharing, and so on) don't tell themselves that they're "collaborating"; they seek to do things more quickly, more cheaply, or in a more satisfactory way. And most of the economic value is captured by an intermediary". He believes that collaboration is reserved for people who exchange goods and services outside the commercial sphere. But much more than this, "the world of DIY, makers and Fablabs reveals another trend that may profoundly transform the industrial model. These emerging concepts at the very least foreshadow an important change in the domain of design and prototyping, and no doubt a transformation in terms of the life cycle of products and the way it is managed; and perhaps, in some fields, a new mode of production and assembly". Processes are becoming more fluid, as Joël de Rosnay has been saying for a long time, in particular in *Surfer la Vie*, or Jeremy Rifkin when he discusses the lateral economy in his reference work *The Third Industrial Revolution*.
In a long-term perspective, the economist Michèle Debonneuil believes that the pioneers of a "quaternary" economy are now emerging. "New technologies are full of potential and [the French classifieds website] Le Bon Coin is an embryonic illustration of everything that will be possible thanks to these new interactions on the Internet and on mobile phones. These technologies will make it possible to increase human mental abilities tenfold, just as mechanisation has allowed us to increase our physical abilities," she explains in an article by Laure Belot published in Le Monde in January 2013. The limit, in her view, is the risk of reverting to a barter economy "that would ignore the real contribution made by the market economy". Companies have to build these new processes into their methods, making themselves more open to new consumer needs and entering the age of co-creation. Michèle Dubonneuil also reminds us that digital technology should allow us to move from an economy based on "having more" to an economy whose aim is improved quality of life.

Meanwhile, in terms of cooperation and solidarity, the so-called "open source" economic model also offers some interesting perspectives. Highly developed in the field of software, this approach now also applies to hardware, so that we now have open-source cars, open-source tractors, and open-source boats that clean up after oil slicks. The people taking part are motivated by a desire to share, enrich and add to knowledge, and to make it easier to reproduce and move forward by leveraging creativity and transparency. The "makers" movement dear to Chris Anderson (and to Joël de Rosnay, who uses the term "doueur") also takes part in this open collective dynamic.
Last but not least, in an approach developed more recently by the agronomist Isabelle Delannoy, the symbiotic economy tends to integrate all the models described above. "The parallel and non-concerted emergence of these models shows that a real new wind is blowing, moving things forward independently and powerfully, bringing together more and more industrialists, countries, citizens and consumers in a movement that has gone beyond weak signals," she explains. What all these models have in common is that they pair economic profitability with restoring ecosystems and social resilience. Together they can open up a completely new road towards sustainable development, a form of development where Mankind doesn't do things "less badly" but instead does them well. In total, six principles

working in synergy govern this economy. It is an economy that is biomimetic (the so-called "blue economy"), leveraging the intelligence of ecosystems; it is collaborative; it is parcimonious; it is cleaner (less polluting); it tends to relocalise; and it tends to diversify. The symbiotic economy acts as a barometer to assess existing projects and helps us to build tools to improve and manage new projects. "It also makes it possible to offer new indicators to measure ecological, economic and social restoration processes," explains Isabelle Delannoy.

Symbiosis is probably the key to the new forms of solidarity that humans are seeking to implement. All that remains is to take inspiration from nature's precious gifts and reconnect with the living world. At that point, we'll be just a step away from talking about the "living economy"!

what digital technology does to the economy: the bright and dark sides of collaborative models

Yann Moulier-Boutang economist and essayist

When we talk about new economic models, the subject of so-called participative, collaborative or interactive platforms is omnipresent. This omnipresence is affected by, follows on from, and anticipates technological changes such as digital.

If we compare what economic organisation used to be like with the situation today, what is striking is obviously the global complexity of the socio-productive model: the overlaps between market and non-market aspects, and administrative prices regulated by the State and the public, in different forms, including what appear to be new digital commons. What is also striking is the highly collective nature of these new forms of organisation. Relationships prevail over substance, and the resulting mode of organisation is the network. We have bridges and points, and these points have no identity per se. Instead they consist of a mass of relationships that are constantly being redefined. This poses a series of problems and implies extreme ductility, porosity, and agility. It makes it impossible to think in terms of a rock of certainty (the company) from which we can jump to other rocks in a sea of uncertainty.

In fact, what we see in this new setting is the productive core of society, in other words the way society produces the conditions for its own existence, not only to give people things to eat, if possible in a way that doesn't poison them and is thus sustainable, but also to establish relationships, to get an education, and to continue to learn, work, be active, be inactive, be an employee or a freelancer, all through one's life. All these relationships are forged and supported by digital, which plays a similar role to the one played by steam engines or electricity in industrial capitalism.

Moreover thanks to digital it is possible to trace interactions that take place in this complex society: I'm talking about metadata. We can talk about "interactions of the multitude" insofar as the multitude means that it's a phenomenon in progress. It doesn't mean peoples or nations: it's much more flexible than that.

These interactions turn out to be an incredible arena for potential value creation: both the net creation of a new value of use, and more significantly (and this is where the ambiguity kicks in) the creation of values of exchange on a vast scale. This is what I call "the continent of externalities": everything that escapes the eye of the economists. To be perfectly clear: "the eye of the economists" was turned towards the market economy. Everything that was external to the market economy, in other words everything the market was unable to take charge of, was dealt with as part of the public economy or placed under the catch-all term "externality" which, by definition, is what's "outside". So the economist referred us kindly to the sociologist, the political scientist, the religious historian, etc.

Then, in this extremely short-sighted world, the panorama started to get wider under the economist's magnifying glass. We realised that what we were generating in terms of negative externalities, things that weren't being paid for but that would need to be paid for in the end (pollution, damage to the planet, phenomena described as relating to the Anthropocene) were starting to knock at our door.

What's more, we realised that a whole lot of new things were appearing. These new things had already been covered by the social and solidarity economy, both in workers' movements and in all kinds of NPOs. We soon realised that collaborative platforms were intellectual hotbeds and places of great technical inventiveness, and that we couldn't reduce the economy—the *oikos* in which we live, the "big house of the world", to the sum of goods sold, measured by an indicator (which was soon criticised): the GDP (gross domestic product).

These platforms are an arena for different forms of interaction between a multitude of different protagonists, paid or unpaid, whether they're in relationships of solidarity in the conscious (ideological, political, organisational) sense of the word, or whether they get involved unconsciously—and this is the main thing that digital brings to the table. When you're interacting with your Google search engine or your social network, there are loads of things going on that you have no control over but which appear in metadata and in Big Data generated by constant use. This gives rise to projects that form what is known as the data driven economy, which is essentially an attempt to control this vast universe which comprises both positive and negative externalities.

Transformation phenomena are obviously followed closely by social forces that have to tackle formidable problems such as ecological transition and energy transition. There's a sense of urgency, because we're beginning to realise that the amount of damage being done is quite alarming. Social forces look high and low, groping for solutions and innovating. constellation.s is a fine example of collective intelligence. There are new forms of subjectivity. In English they talk about "empowerment". There are opportunities to do things quite quickly, and in any case we can provide guidance that is in fact a critique of cumbersome planism or forms of government. That's the plus side.

But there's a dark side, too. When we look at bees, the trade in bee products (honey and wax—which nobody uses any more) is only worth a billion dollars a year. When we look at the effective contribution of bees to the *oikos* via pollination, which makes trees into trees and which means we can produce the food we eat, their importance is of a completely different order. In 2010 I estimated that they're worth something like 700-800 billion dollars annually for the market side of the economy. The latest assessment from the IPCC, which does not include wild pollinators and wild bees, is that they are worth 550-650 billion dollars a year. The difference is colossal.

With digital technology, you can capture 10% of the externalities of the life of a bee, of everything it produces during its life, and you can easily surpass GDP. That's why GAFA (Google Amazon Facebook Apple) dominate all the others from an economic point of view. They manage to capture, divert and suck up part of the pollen and this pollinating activity. It's the same thing for humans. Essentially, we give GAFA gifts (we should add Twitter and Uber to the list). There's an extraordinary potential for value that wasted no time manifesting itself and which can adopt forms that are all the easier for digital workers to use. The number of hours we spend every day on our mobile phones or computers is starting to compete with time spent watching television and official working hours. So if you capture 10% of the value generated by those activities, you're the kings of the world. This is what I call cognitive capitalism, a new kind of capitalism that is making the old systems obsolete. It's the "Uberisation" of all areas of life in society.

To summarise, new economic models and so-called collaborative platforms form something that is absolutely ambivalent and ambiguous, with a bright side and a dark side. We have to analyse and unpick all this, and see what we're going to call collaborative, participative and interactive; what we're going to call conscious and unconscious; what we're going to see as new forms of refined exploitation; and what we're going to see as expressions of freedom and autonomy.

at the source of current debate: the fundamental ambivalence of our economic models

Timothée Duverger historian

Along with the question of new economic models comes the already old question of regulation. Karl Polanyi talks of a dual movement in society, in particular since the nineteenth century. On the one hand we see a movement of market self-regulation or of liberalisation; on the other hand, we see a counter-movement, in other words a movement of self-protection undertaken by society whose aim is to create regulations that make it possible to avoid a number of evils arising from societal liberalisation. It's a power game that has been taking place since the nineteenth century and which has manifested itself in particular via the emergence of democratic regulations and initiatives in terms of social economics. For example the earliest mutual-aid organisations in France, which often concealed unions, emerged in a very special context: a Jacobin state that was repressive with regard to all these initiatives, especially via the Le Chapelier act that prohibited intermediate bodies and collective assemblies. Despite all this, initiatives emerged, in the name of a very "illiberal" democracy, to quote the term used by Pierre Rosenvallon. This counter-movement entered phases of institutionalisation—this was the case for the mutual-aid organisations. According to Philippe Frémeaux, Social Security arose from this legacy: the State organised the post-war social protection system as a natural extension of all the social initiatives that emerged in society.

This dual movement also concerns the social and solidarity economy, which is not devoid of ambiguity. The case of the mutual-aid organisations mentioned above sheds light on this other aspect of the question. Under the Empire of Napoleon III, there were approved societies and societies that were not approved. Those that were, in particular societies governed by local authorities, the mayor or the priest, were granted a degree of latitude. In this case we see both a philanthropic dynamic and social control expressed via a desire to manage the population in order to avoid revolution. These initiatives may thus be seen as ambiguous. Even within the SSE, the dual movement can be highly ambivalent. This social economy thus became gradually institutionalised from the end of the nineteenth century onwards until just after the post-war boom years (around 1975), and included cooperatives, mutual benefit societies and *associations* (non-profit organisations). Foundations were added to the list more recently.

To give a more statutory dimension to the social economy, we ask ourselves the following question: "How should we go about it?" The answer is defined by rules. One rule involves the democratic process by which one person equals one vote. A second involves restricting profit from such organisations, either by ensuring that they make no profit at all (in the case of NPOs) or by ensuring that they generate low levels of profit, in the sense that the redistribution of profits is limited (in the case of cooperatives).

From the 1970s-1980s, in addition to this statutory social economy rooted in the

19th century arose an economy of solidarity in response to new challenges faced by society. In response to mass unemployment and growing precarity, an entire sector devoted to jobs and social development sprang up. The second major challenge was the question of ecology, with the reduction of natural resources, global warming, and the erosion of biodiversity. This generated a number of green initiatives, especially as regards recycling and renewable energy sources. When these two aspects—the historic social economy and the emerging solidarity economy—came together, the result was what we call the "social and solidarity economy".

Today, we face a third challenge: digital technology. A true transition is under way. As Jacques Ellul points out, technology is not neutral but ambivalent. The question is to know what to do with it, and to know what forces are at work. The question of the collaborative economy also brings forces and regulation into play. For example, a platform cooperativism movement is emerging, and raises the issue of value sharing. Should we not set up a contributive dividend, since in effect we are pollinating value "like bees", as Yann Moulier-Boutang points out? Could there not be power-sharing? Could we not imagine regulations that would make it possible to include all the stakeholders in the governance process, via user committees for example? But if we observe major trends, there is reason to be concerned about the future of the collaborative economy. Pascal Terrasse's recently published report shows that the cooperative model is far from being the one most often adopted by leaders. On the contrary, we find ourselves faced with highly lucrative systems aiming at maximum profit.

Despite its ambiguities, the social and solidarity economy has a fundamental role to play in terms of incubating all the possible solutions. Let's take the case of "Uberisation" and the self-employment model. The SSE invented the model of business and employment cooperatives. How can we invent a form of entrepreneurship with collective regulations, with social protection and a protective framework for the entrepreneur? Business and employment cooperatives are, from this point of view, absolutely crucial. In response to increased precarity, how can we make employment less precarious by responding to the needs of companies, in a framework that provides flexibility for the company and security for the employee's career? I think, for example, that we should develop employer groups in rural areas to make those areas attractive to businesses and encourage local populations to stay. Today, intense segmentation is taking place between high-performance, high-employment metropolitan areas and rural areas where populations are relegated. The Gironde region is a case in point.

The word "commons" is more and more frequently used in the field of the collaborative economy. Commons are an invention of the cooperatives, and today's cooperatives preserve a residue of commons. At the source of the cooperatives, we find the great millenarist utopias inspired by religion. For example, in the 19th century, Étienne Cabet thought he could set up a new society (an "ideal city" he called Icarie) on virgin land in America. This utopian model drifted, via dissidence, towards the cooperatives, which became gradually institutionalised. The residue of "commons" can be found in questions of democratic governance and non-profit-making status. Today, by leveraging this "residue", how can we restore a sense of public interest and make it more possible for a utopia to emerge? In France, the SCIC model (Sociétés Coopératives d'Intérêt Collectif), which is undergoing a degree of expansion, raises the question not only of the interest of the members of the cooperative, but also that of the interest of communities and how the businesses can operate in local areas. Very concrete examples are emerging in a wide range of different domains.

Ultimately, we see clearly that these models and these new regulatory frameworks exist. The problem is that they are scattered far and wide. We have to bring things together, make the models converge, and find catalysts. How can the SSE be an accelerator for all these initiatives and transform capitalism a little more? How can it help us drive the required transitions? A democratic block needs to be built between civil society and the State, to help us to push these transitions forward.

alternative models exist in the very heart of our societies

Philippe Frémeaux economist and editorial writer

What are the new models currently emerging? Is there an alternative model? In my work on the social and solidarity economy (SSE)[1], I attach a lot of importance to thinking about how we describe our society. To do this we often refer to capitalism and the power of neoliberalism.

In France today, almost 50% of the wealth is redistributed and social protection accounts for 32% of GDP. Historically, the recent development of SSE is closely linked to the growth of the social State. Though it is true that the latter has made use of initiatives arising from civil society, it has then financed them and fostered their development as different forms of health and social care. In this perspective, the relationship of public authorities with the SSE, essentially where the latter takes the form of non-profit organisations, can involve instrumentalisation when state bodies use NPOs as mere subcontractors for policies defined elsewhere. But NPOs, when they preserve their strategic autonomy, can help to co-construct social policy, bringing to the table their in-field knowledge and their potential for social innovation.

Our democratic society thus socialises a large amount of wealth to place it at the service of the greatest number, via education, health and the funding of non-commercial services largely provided by NPOs. This means our society cannot be reduced to the term "capitalism" alone: it is, in fact, infinitely more complex than that.

And yet we live in a liberal society in the "good" sense, and this is especially reflected in the fact that we have the freedom to engage in enterprise. This freedom is not only economic; it is also political. It is the ability of anyone, if he or she has the means, to create an enterprise, to escape from the mainstream workforce, and to gain autonomy with regard to the State. Totalitarian states have always prohibited entrepreneurial freedom. Under the Ancien Régime in France, this was characterised, for example, by the fact that Jews were refused access to a whole range of professions; it was a way of denying their citizenship. By the same token, in the totalitarian USSR, it was impossible to do plumbing jobs for the neighbours and be paid for it.

In a democratic society, entrepreneurial freedom has to be framed by rules. When an enterprise develops, it must engage in social dialogue with its employees, and the latter must be able to organise themselves freely. But entrepreneurial freedom plays an important role in our society, just like the SSE insofar as it reflects the free organisation of citizens who aim to satisfy a need or provide a service by grouping together forming cooperatives, NPOs, or mutual benefit societies, using the power of numbers to oppose the power of capital. The SSE is fully legitimate

---

1. Philippe Frémeaux, *La Nouvelle Alternative ? Enquête sur l'économie sociale et solidaire*, Paris, Les Petits Matins, 2011, 157 p.

because it arises from spontaneous social initiatives that emerge within it to respond to social needs. It criticises, through its actions, the logic of capital by revealing that we can engage in enterprise with other aims in mind than becoming the richest person in the village. We can want to do things in the general interest, and within a collective framework.

The SSE currently accounts for 10% of jobs, but it is not a uniform entity. The really innovative and transformative part of society only represents a very small subset within this 10%. In our complex society, which is not just about capitalism, the SSE is not an outside element that has the potential to surpass the system. It is an element inherent in the model, performing an entire range of social functions which, if they were not provided, would lead to the collapse of society. Enterprises in the capitalistic commercial sector are incapable of responding to a wide range of social needs that the SSE takes care of.

Furthermore, orthodox economic theory describes a world where there are only Robinson Crusoes who, when they get out of the forest, find themselves in a clearing and establish contracts in their mutual and respective interest. An enterprise is not a collection of contracts that can be constantly called into question; it is first and foremost a human organisation in which it is necessary to spark cooperation, and to foster skills and collective expertise. All this takes time—a dimension that orthodox theory does not understand. Orthodox theory does not understand cooperation and long-term approaches because it thinks of the world as a set of isolated individuals who establish instant contracts. It can thus not understand the notions of time and cooperation, which are at the heart of how our economy actually works. In a nutshell, "capitalism" is a highly inadequate word to describe our society, and the new models that need to be constructed already exist within it.

Conversely, the model that is now developing can just as well be embraced by cooperative forms that bear hope for democracy and community living as by the most brutal forms of capitalism. There are extraordinary models such as Wikipedia, which represents a social and solidarity economy in the strongest sense of the word in terms of collaborative cooperation, and the Uber model, which has qualities but also a number of faults, especially in terms of social protection and real revenue for people employed by the platform.

Another observation is that indicators which, until now, measured change and progress in our society have now become obsolete. The GDP, which measures growth, no longer works. First of all, over the last twenty years, wellbeing has become unhitched from growth: more growth does not necessary mean more wellbeing. Material growth in production is thus no longer something satisfying. Moreover, GDP does not take into account negative factors external to production—factors relating to the destruction of capital and which determine the future of the planet. When we have to start paying for air, when we have to pay to enter a filtered area because urban pollution is so bad, and when the destruction of the very foundation of life becomes something that increases GDP, that's a very perverse process indeed. In parallel, we have the opportunity to communicate free of charge via Skype with our children, who unfortunately consume kerosene when they go on trips to the US or Brazil. Conversely, when we use BlaBlaCar, there's a car that's already been built that's going from A to B anyway: it just does so with three passengers instead of just the driver. This is a process that produces no value, but it produces more wellbeing, more economic satisfaction, without increasing the GDP. Forms of production that destroy value for the planet are counted in GDP, and certain forms of value creation are not. We must thus move on to more effective indicators. GDP is a conventional instrument that corresponds to a certain period in the history of capitalism. For decades it worked well as an instrument for regulating the sharing of value between workers and bosses, but it is extremely conventional. The question of progress indicators relating to society is primarily a democratic one. What really matters? What really has value? What has value for us? All this has to be at the heart of democratic deliberation.

The question we face today is how to build a more inclusive society while preserving what modernity has given us. Our society is both one of evil capitalism and one of autonomy and emancipation. From a certain point of view, capitalism has also made possible women's liberation and the end of the reign of the father, the priest, the party and all those wonderful things from the 1950s. Nobody misses that productivist, macho and, in some ways, totalitarian society. We must preserve the positive aspects of modernity while placing economic activity within the limits of the planet and expanding the scope of democracy. How can we make this constraint into an opportunity to make the economy serve wellbeing? It's all about interlinking global and local challenges. Then we should link politics and societal dynamics, because the former can do nothing without the latter and the latter are limited if they do not live in a world of rules that foster their development established at regional, national, European and even international level.

Then there's the challenge of the emergence of a society that produces more connections and less goods, a society that uses fewer resources and starts fighting against built-in obsolescence. Future technologies will doubtless not solve all the problems—that would be a very dangerous illusion; the idea is to rethink how we can reuse existing technologies.

We have to get away from an "or" culture (local OR global, state OR society, planning OR the market) and move towards an "and" culture that is obviously more open. We have to accept compromise between all these different levels[2].

---

2. To find out more: *Réinventer le progrès - Entretiens avec Philippe Frémeaux*, Laurent Berger and Pascal Canfin, Les Petits Matins, November 2016, 168 p.

societal innovation in urban policy: three inspirations and two revelations

Gilles Pinson teacher and researcher

What is innovation? Literature on the subject identifies three dimensions, three sources of motivation, and three models for social and societal innovation (including architectural and technological innovation) that I think are worth looking at again.

The first approach is inspired by neoliberalism. Oddly enough, we've been talking about societal and social innovation since the 1980s and 1990s, at the same time as neoliberal policies aimed at dismantling the Welfare State have been developing. David Cameron is the embodiment of this. He talks a lot about social innovation. Simultaneously, he supports the *Big Society* project, according to which removing the Welfare State, because it is expensive and produces scroungers, allows civil society to produce its own ways of innovating and shouldering social risk.

The second approach, which is close to the neoliberal version, is the Schumpeterian version. Joseph Schumpeter saw the entrepreneur as a modern day hero. He drew a contrast between the entrepreneur and the independently wealthy individual, the civil servant, and the person who does a routine job. This point of view can also be seen in the call for societal innovation, which considers that it's up to us all to be the entrepreneurs of our own lives and to think for ourselves about the way we fit into the world.

The third approach, whose inspiration is democratic and emancipatory, is much more interesting in my view. In many bodies of work, especially those focusing on the social and solidarity economy, societal innovation is presented as a set of actions that make it possible to transform social relationships of class, gender, race and production. This version of societal innovation makes it possible to emancipate individuals, inhabitants and professionals and encourages us to remove sectoral barriers and frontiers. The idea is to identify, in organisations, forms of collective action that generate a capacity for autonomy and freedom among individuals. In parallel, it's about stepping beyond forms that generate independent wealth, inequality, and the belittling of certain social groups. Innovation is clearly of interest when it frees us from a number of social constraints.

If we look at architecture and the city, we can observe that recent urban policies belong more to a process of regression than to one of innovation. Moreover, we note that innovation is promoted as an object of marketing. Two examples illustrate this regression and this way of marketing innovation. The first involves urban policy and its connection with urban renovation. When I talk about urban policy, I'm thinking less about the kind defended by Roland Castro than about Hubert Dubedout's version of urban social development. Despite all the bad things people say about it today, it was a policy whose aim was to create emancipation and make inhabitants better able to do things. From this point of view, urban renovation is a fundamental regression where urban policy sees itself eroded and diminished by the return of town mayors, the corporation of mayors and civil engineers, and repressed technocratic Jacobinism. The protagonists who worked on urban policy and who strove to implement local community councils and associations such as ACLEFEU and Pas Sans Nous are bitterly disappointed in the way urban policy has been destroyed by urban renovation.

Another example concerns the way innovation is touted for marketing purposes. When I went on a field trip on cooperative housing in Freiburg im Breisgau and Tübingen, I met the deputy mayor, who supported cooperative housing projects. He told me a surprising story. When they hosted some council officials from Bordeaux, they showed them around some pleasant neighbourhoods created thanks to cooperative housing processes. When they saw the architecture, The Bordeaux officials were delighted. But when they started talking about the system and the support processes for residents' collectives, the people from Bordeaux completely lost interest. Societal innovation, because of its processes and its liberating and emancipating qualities, is very visible in terms of marketing and PR. But in practice it's still lurking in corners.

towards
an ecology
of disorder

Djamel Klouche architect and urban planner

In recent times we have been experiencing some very difficult moments: most of the huge amount of information, ideas and questions that reach us through public networks is unfortunately toxic and brings us little joy. It is in this context that the exhibition entitled constellation.s reveals itself as not only necessary, but also highly relevant.

I would like to quickly introduce my contribution with a picture from the fresco by Ambrogio Lorenzetti, *The Effects of Good and Bad Government*[1]. I would like to see it as a powerful sign: inhabiting the world is, above all, a question of "good government". In this regard I would like to quote from a book by the historian Patrick Boucheron published in 2013 entitled *Conjurer la peur - Essai sur la force politique des images*, and read you an excerpt that I like very much and which, I feel, simply expresses this notion of inhabiting a city, of inhabiting a territory, and of inhabiting the world.

The passage is in a section of the book that has a very evocative title: "Ce que voit la paix : récits d'espaces et corps parlants" [What peace sees: narratives of spaces and talking bodies].

"Big spaces at last. The eye slips effortlessly along the slope stretching out before it, extending the vision of a city in peace. Nothing stops it, not even the clear line of the pink walls that slice the city wall into two equal parts. Here the sharp angles of the buildings, whose somewhat abrupt jostling compresses urban density, and which nonetheless agree to part so that the crowd of citizens can assemble; over there are rolling hills gently sloping towards the valley that cuts across the plain below, dotted with vines, pruned trees, carefully aligned hedges and lanes. On either side of the zigzag wall, people mill around and talk, unifying a space that is entirely occupied, in the streets and on the paths, although in a diverse way. This means that a single landscape stretches out, bearing witness to the intensity of the attentive care taken over "highlighting" it—as painters do, but also as urban designers and agronomists do[2]."

What this text talks about, and what I'd like to share with you today, is the continuity between the city and the countryside, the non-distinction, the non-dichotomy between inside and outside. Already in 1338, the effects of government were to fail to make the distinction between inside and out, in other words the countryside was as well treated as the city standing within its walls. If we apply this to the present day, to what we understand by the words "centre" and

---

1. *The Effects of Good and Bad Government*, an allegorical fresco painted by Ambrogio Lorenzetti between 1338 and 1340, Sala della Pace of the Palazzo Pubblico in Sienna, Italy. The fresco stretches over three walls: in the centre, on the north wall, is the representation of "good government"; on either side are the effects of "bad government", on a long western wall (war, fear, constrained bodies) and those of "good government" on the opposite wall (peace, freedom, conversation).

2. P. Boucheron, Conjurer la peur - *Essai sur la force politique des images - Sienne 1338*. Paris, Seuil (Points) p. 177, 2013.

"outskirts", we might consider that European society is probably too centred. Living in the world must lead us to look at the world from its margins, from its peripheries, from outside of it. Patrick Boucheron's text reminds us quite clearly and simply how the question of good governance or "good government" is raised in our civilisation. The fresco retains, I feel, much contemporary relevance: it shows us the need to think about the periphery as much as the centre; and it shows us how its delicate theme suggests, or brings to the surface, the notion of "inhabiting the world".

As architects, we have an incredible, sublime and fascinating profession, because our role is to construct spaces and atmospheres that make it possible for different populations to live together. We are asked to build something that has to allow different groups to live together, whereas in general those groups have absolutely not chosen to live together, to live in this space, to work in it or to live in this city and share its amenities with others. When we build a home or when we design part of a district or a section of a city, we have to provide an answer to an interesting, even fascinating, theoretical question, and to do this we call upon a whole series of thoughts, skills, philosophical writings, geographers and sociologists so that we can provide the best, newest, and most appropriate response.

As we seek to provide the most relevant response, we find ourselves facing a host of questions. They force us to be permeable an abundance of new expectations, new desires, new instances of resistance, new forms of sharing and mutualisation, reactions and regressions. We are faced with an entire range of toxic sets of information. We have to negotiate with good and bad ideas. When we set out fifteen years ago, we worked a lot on high-rise housing estates. As architects and urban designers, this was our primary aim, and it was very difficult to tackle certain ideas of enclosure—what was called "residentialisation" at the time—or the notion of the *tabula rasa*—by demolishing something, you make the problem disappear.

Our profession is fascinating, but it has to negotiate with a whole series of contingencies that do not necessarily converge and which, all too often, are even divergent. Raising the question of how to inhabit the world means asking how to navigate within this huge paradox.

Three notions with which we are—as architects and urban designers—obliged to negotiate seem to assert themselves in a positive way: they are climate, acceleration, and the notion of common space.

First, the climate has become a horizon that cannot be stepped over and with which we are obliged to work, negotiate, innovate, and initiate change. The notion of climate is a complex one. A strong trend tells us that we have to move towards a kind of degrowth, that economic development must be slowed down because it creates climatic problems.

Second, the notion of acceleration is emerging in English-speaking countries. Leading economists and scientists agree that liberalism is highly destructive, but that to win the battle against it, we have to accelerate and overtake it. The notion of acceleration also refers to the technological revolution that is in progress: digital and robotics.

The third notion that emerges is at the heart of constellation.s. It concerns commons, and more precisely to what extent we are able to rebuild commonality without slipping into communitarianism, without drifting into something we are merely subject to. That which is common must be chosen, naturally and neutrally, and it is this commonality I am searching for. As an urban designer, I constantly seek it via projects, but not necessarily on the scale of the micro-space, more on the scale of the metropolitan area. The narrative of commonality seems not to be a narrative of small scale, otherwise we fall into something that is closed in on itself. If we open commonality to the scale of a local region, a metropolitan area, or a city, there is potential for fulfilment in various different forms.

These three horizons with which we have to negotiate are not necessarily convergent, but I think they create highly paradoxical situations whose consequence can be a form of apparent disorder.

I believe that the notion of inhabiting, and new ways of inhabiting per se or inhabiting the world, involves bringing out the reality Cynthia Fleury talked to us about: the potential for transformation, for a future that has to constantly seek a form of embodiment in space. Making reality spring forth means transgressing the narrative that is given or sold to us every day, and it is via projects that we can get closer to inventing it.

Inhabiting the world probably involves militating for an ecology of disorder

As architects and urban designers, we are asked to organise space, to organise the world. But I want to disorganise space. I am fighting for an ecology of disorder. Inhabiting the world means militating for an ecology of disorder. An ecology of disorder that would take into account the challenges of climate, of the controversy of acceleration, and of the advent of commonality—a troika that is, of course, not exclusive but inclusive.

Perhaps inhabiting the world entails making every effort to redesign or rebuild new virtuous forms of proximity between things that we have gradually stretched and dislocated in the modern period.

When in recent projects and research we refer to Brussels or Rotterdam as productive cities, it's simply to make the observation that for centuries the place of production has been in the city, but that ultimately our emancipating civilisation has taken production out of the city and that we now have to find the instruments that will enable us to place production in close proximity to our habitat. Inhabiting the world also means producing things next to our habitat and finding new forms of mutualisation, new forms of sharing, and new forms of proximity.

In conclusion, I feel that constellation.s and its lectures have opened up a debate. But there should be a permanent exhibition and permanent debate if we want to construct a theoretical and practical counter-approach to projects fuelled by toxic ideas.

concerning Calais, and many other places…

Sébastien Thiéry political scientist

The following "decree", written a few weeks after constellation.s ended, expresses what underlies PEROU's participation in that crucial exhibition.

PEROU. Decree n° 2017-01 enacted on 1st January 2017. Steps to be taken to resist the policies of destruction and criminalisation of hospitality to refugees in France.

Given the existence of the French Republic, with fraternity as one of its founding values.

Given the current turmoil, the perspective of exceptional migratory movements, and the likely future increase in the number of "jungles" springing up all around.

Given that the "Jungle of Calais" was inhabited by over 20,000 refugees, not vagrants but heroes who have escaped the unimaginable, armed with infinite hope.

Given the colossal dreams of these stalwart walkers who actually lived, not merely survived in this place, and whose will our vetting systems, prison procedures and uninhabitable containers did their utmost to break so that they would become mere human rubbish to be managed, head-counted, parked somewhere, then told to move on.

Given that Mohammed, Ahmid, Zimako, Youssef and so many others turned out not to be poor vagrants or penniless vulnerable migrants, but inveterate builders who-despite the mud and the terrifying clamour, despite everything that insidiously treated them like stupid children-took just a few short months to build three churches, five mosques, three schools, a theatre, two libraries, a hammam, three infirmaries, five hairdressing salons, forty-eight restaurants, forty-four groceries, seven bakeries, and four nightclubs: unquestionable evidence of humanity that was reduced to the level of mere anecdote in official accounts of the "migrant crisis".

Given that, some distance from the historic centre of Calais, people lived, cooked, danced, made love, engaged in politics, spoke over twenty languages, sang about their hopes and their pain, laughed and cried, read and wrote, thus starkly contradicting the damning stories told by certain indignant, exasperated onlookers.

Given that between the motorway and the seafront each of the dwellings built, put up or pitched bore the imprint of a caring hand, an attentive gesture, and perhaps some words of faith, of hope for a better future: words that were too difficult for the bystanders to understand, their eyes only seeing chaos and open sewers and their mouths regurgitating nothing but the words "shame" and "misery".

Given that for one year, in both the city and the slum, hundreds of British people, Belgians, Dutch people, Germans, Italians, Greeks and French people built far more than was reasonable, distributed food and clothing, organised concerts and plays, set up radio stations and newspapers, provided legal advice and medical care, and at night slept in the dozens of beds at the Calais Youth Hostel, a temple of active solidarity, perhaps the only place of its kind in the world and the true centre of Europe if ever there was one.

Given that, before these officially dark months, local associations had never received so many donations and offers of voluntary work; but that during these admittedly extraordinary months the fables of collective exasperation, of widespread xenophobia, and of violence in Calais continued to be reproduced and exaggerated in the media, tarnishing the city's reputation just as effectively as the miles of barbed wire had disfigured it.

Given that Calais was, *de facto*, a global city, a pioneer of 19th century urban planning, whose attitude of denial, via brutal public policies, bears witness to a criminal blindness to the worlds of the future and an irresponsible contempt for the contemporary forms of hospitality that thousands of anonymous people took the risk of providing.

Given that, when this potential city had been demolished and its builders sent away, the town council, the regional council and the French government together planned to open a forty-hectare amusement park in Calais called "Heroic Land", an entirely artificial development devoted to video game heroes, an unimaginable "ghost town" costing 275 million euros and a monument to the vulgarity of today's public policy.

Given that what made the "Jungle" will not be made to disappear by brutal laws enacted on the edges of our cities as if gangs of criminals were hiding out there, nor by various attractions designed to numb people's minds and make them avert their gaze, nor by the abstract solutions proposed by "housing for all" whose containers, centres, and official camps costing millions of euros show the sickening dead end that has been reached.

Given that the negligence of public bodies and the stupidity of the solutions they propose are such that in future the Jungle of Calais will be reproduced a hundredfold, in France and Europe, and that, to help us at last invent public policies worth their salt, the only precious resource we have is the result of what the residents of Calais and the refugees tirelessly cultivated for months: namely a sense of togetherness.

It is hereby decreed:

1. That the destruction of the Jungle of Calais shall go down in contemporary French history as an act of war committed not only against buildings, but also against men, women, children, dreams, songs, and stories; not only against a slum, but also against what, in 2016, amounted to a fully-fledged town on the edge of Calais.

2. That to prevent such acts of devastation from happening again we must resist the denial of reality; we must contradict the sinister fables propagated by professional complainers and exasperated doomsayers; we must extol the beauty of the work of these fringe builders; we must make their hospitality famous; and we must open our eyes to the age-old spirit that drives them and the promises they make for the future.

3. That taking action in response to such situations, which will occur again and again in future, involves fostering the creativity of refugees and their hosts; it involves building palaces in their wake to provide people with shelter, human rights, and happiness; it involves using what we learn from them to build temples of reclaimed fraternity; and it involves risking alternative political approaches to hospitality, to the common good, and to our Republic.

This "decree" echoes a number of lessons learned from the "new ways of inhabiting the world" showcased at arc en rêve. In Calais, as elsewhere, it is clearly not only necessary but possible to build rather than demolish, and it is crucial to welcome, with renewed enthusiasm, the building work carried out by these men and women seeking refuge. The text is thus an extension of what we defended in Bordeaux, namely three ways of understanding and implementing the notion of resistance.

First, the "decree" urges resistance not only to the violence that currently prevails, but also to the irresponsible approaches mascarading as public policy that are adopted when slums, "jungles" and sprawling camps appear. PEROU engages with these dangerous situations, convinced of our own responsibility—in other words, literally, our power and duty formulate a "response" to them. So we ventured to build things illegally with the people living there, and to celebrate acts, gestures, spaces and forms of hospitality which, in the world that is still being imposed on us, are still against the law. Before we even take the risk of building with the tools of the architect's trade, we have to reclaim the notion of our ability and duty to take action, and thus reconstruct a legitimate political position for ourselves as agents of change. It's important to resist the torpor that takes over us whenever the question of the so-called "migrants" comes up—a question so poorly formulated that it automatically refers to someone else's responsibility, to the way the world is (dis)organised, and to a disaster whose sheer scale would, by definition, doom all our efforts to fruitless failure. In a political context where irresponsibility has become an argument, we have to take the risk of being responsible and see "taking action" as the most elementary way of exercising our political sovereignty.

Second, the "decree" urges resistance to the obsession with worst-case scenarios and the daily liturgy of TV and printed news describing *ad nauseam* the mud, the distress, the arrival of the demolition crews, and the desert that ensued. At PEROU, we've decided to focus on what is being invented, asserted, constructed and created in a spirit of dissidence. In the so-called Jungle of Calais, in spite of the cold and the violence, a form of urbanity has been invented, and will be invented once more. In the situations we work in, we strive to describe and re-describe what takes place and what makes the place what it is. Writing such a description requires taking the time to closely follow the vital experiments taking place in these marginal territories located some distance from the official city. Writing such a description requires listening to the dreamers and builders and seeing everything they build as "good news": clear proof that something—not nothing—is happening. In Calais we met not only hundreds of refugees but also countless volunteers, and we came across some incredibly powerful places and witnessed some amazingly beautiful gestures. These were doubtless signs for the future left by a world we lack the tools to translate, a world we are as yet unable to identify and that we asphyxiate as a result. In Calais, we recorded everything that contradicted violence, and at the same time we intended this text to look forward to the future, echoing the magnificent phrase that was the watchword of constellation.s: "Thinking in the light of what is no longer, and of what is yet to come".

Third, the "decree" urges us to avoid blindly rushing into things, to resist ridiculous political schedules that demand that action be taken far too quickly, and to develop, against all the odds, a long-term vision of what needs to be constructed. In Calais, in Grande-Synthe, and in Paris, spectacularly tragic architectural forms have been used to house containers, modules, and technical solutions used in the framework of social and urban policing. In them, refugees are "encamped" like raggle-taggle vagrants and "sheltered" like potential criminals. With its attendant panoply of officially lauded architectural gestures, hospitality has been offered in exactly the wrong way: by keeping people at a distance and by ruining what human hands have built. Future policy must instead endeavour to bring people together, and it must strive to highlight what the refugees and their supporters have invented. We are currently under threat from the increasingly numerous forms of "housing for all", from the deployment of new "centres" far from our historic town centres, and by the implementation of phony planning initiatives always described as "humanitarian" to mask the fact that they are not, in any way, shape or form, simply "human".

So the "decree" appeals to architects to relinquish their role as "camp designers", to resist the breathless proposals of crisis management experts, and to refuse to build heterotopias where no form of humanity is actually able to live. And it asks the question: can we consider contemporary architecture to be like gardening? And if so, can it cultivate, develop and grow things which, although they are to be found at the heart of the disaster, are not its cause?

S T

the making of informal housing in Cairo, or questions on the relevance of architects

Charlotte Malterre-Barthes architect and urban planner

There was nothing that could not be put right with good design and a broom.
Hassan Fathy

In the French edition of *Architecture for the Poor*, Hassan Fathy dedicates his book to the Egyptian *fellah*[1]. He regrets though that until the time these peasants learn to read and decide for themselves, only the professionals who do so in their place can take advice from his book, listing among them architects designing places for people to live. The picture he paints is dramatic: "God helps those who help themselves, you might say, but these peasants could never do that. Hardly able to afford even reeds to thatch their huts, how could they hope to buy steel bars, timber, or concrete for good houses? How could they pay for builders to put the houses up[2]?" He argues that as neither the private sector nor the State cater to the lower classes left to live in miserable dwellings, it is the architect's task to remedy this. Published in 1976, Fathy's call for architects to act for the housing needs of the poor remains an influential manifesto of his vision as an architect of conscience. And yet, four decades later, the situation has radically changed. Low-income populations have not waited for planners to solve the housing crisis: they have taken the matter into their own hands. Their answer to the shortcomings of political and governmental structures is inventive, resourceful and even ingenious. Architects are excluded from these informal modes of construction and their speculative real-estate spinoffs. Is it that the pace of ongoing urbanisation has been too fast for design professionals? Have designers abandoned a field where little profit is to be made? Would architects rather operate within the corporate sector as elite-serving practitioners, leaving the immense majority of spatial production to the informal sector? Investigating the making of informal housing in Cairo forces us to examine the relevance of the profession both there and within the global context of rapid urbanisation.

Informal housing in Cairo

Home to approximately 60% of the twenty million inhabitants of the Egyptian capital, so-called informal constructions may be up-to-fifteen-story concrete structures with brick infill, built without permits, mostly on former agrarian land. While the phenomenon is not new, the pace of illegal constructions on fertile areas at the capital's fringes has accelerated since the 2011 revolution. In *Understanding Cairo*, urban researcher David Sims claims that "in 1950 there were virtually no informal settlements around Cairo," and that the first developments on agricultural land appeared in the early 1960s following Gamal Abdel Nasser's industrialisation policies[3]. State housing programmes had proved unable to cope with the ensuing rural exodus. A decade later, housing clusters were identified spreading incrementally on privately owned farmland near rural villages just north of Cairo. Illegal urbanisation on the city's edges continued to thrive under the terms of office of Anwar Sadat and Hosni Mubarak, fuelled by market liberalisation policies and remittances from Egyptian male labourers in the Gulf. After the January 2011 events, illegal developments skyrocketed – no doubt due to the power vacuum left by the collapse of the ruling regime. And what with the absence of any form of control, incremental and self-built construction has evolved into a neoliberal speculative scheme. New semi-legal construction firms are currently engaged in the underhand production of a real estate stock to be sold illicitly, but nonetheless in plain sight. This 'for-profit' mode of illegal construction has led to a noticeable change in housing typologies, evolving from self-built low structures to semi-professionally built fifteen-storey towers.

Heart of the Egyptian economy and institutions, Cairo has drawn rural migrants from Upper Egypt and the Nile Valley constantly since the 1970s. While Nasser's welfare state policies backed public housing programmes and rent-control laws, construction of mass housing came to a standstill after the 1967 war with Israel. Soon after, evacuees from the Suez Canal Zone and Egyptian workers from the Gulf amplified the housing demand in Cairo[4].Under Sadat, with limited national expenditure dedicated to public housing, the task of housing the people devolved to private investors, who cared little for the needs of lower income families. For these, the formal market remained inaccessible, and housing in informal areas was the only affordable solution. Informal housing was thus the logical response to the lack of public and private solutions for a large majority of Egyptians. And architects were conspicuously absent from this mass production.

Protocols of urban informality are characterised by 10 patterns:

1. Urban expansion appends to the property lines of the Egyptian *feddan*[5].This narrow strip of farming land 100 to 300 metres long and

6 to 17 metres wide, is framed by irrigation canals, which in time become alleyways and streets as the area is occupied[6].

2. Farmers and landowners subdivide their plots in direct collaboration with local brokers who act as mediators to help minimise bureaucracy and bypass government restrictions. A single *feddan* is subdivided for sale into 24 equal square plots (called *qirat*), which may range in size from 40 to 180 m².

3. Changing land use from agriculture to informal housing generates a 200% profit - a powerful incentive to sell property. Farmers of modest means, urban landlords or urbanised peasants can sell their plots in a single *qirat* parcel.

4. Clients are rural migrants or low-paid workers from the centre of Cairo. They either buy a completed unit or hire a local contractor to build a new structure.

5. Savings, remittances, collective pooling of resources within an extended family and personal loans are the chief sources of financing. Formal financial institutions are rarely involved.

6. The construction process is rapid and while before 2011 several methods were used to conceal construction from government control (e.g. night work, roadblocks, secluding walls, sentinels), it is now done openly and as quickly as one floor per month[7].

7. Buildings are in reinforced concrete poured on site, with red brick infill walls. Foundations are at most 2 meters deep.

8. Pillars on the last floor anticipate further construction. Initially, the buyer might request that a contractor erect a single-story building, one room of which the buyer occupies, while the other rooms are rented to tenants. After saving money for 8 to 10 years, another floor may be added, followed eventually by a third. This practice has evolved: speculative developers or a group of small investors may now build a fifteen-storey tower straight off.

9. Due to the subdivision patterns, the construction unit (the *qirat*) varies from 40 to 180 m². The building occupies the entire plot, save for a 1.5 m-wide strip left for the street, with one street facade and three blind sides. Shafts along facades and in the interiors provide ventilation and daylight.

10. The *qirat* typology replicated *sine fine* along one *feddan* after another, creates an architecturally homogeneous environment, with no public space except for the streets.

Gad Mahmoud: an example

Informal construction, mostly on former agrarian land, involves local actors, whose aim is to produce standardised housing at reduced cost while generating a profit. These operators run the entire process: pooling finance, buying land, sourcing materials and human resources, organising and supervising construction, and connecting to infrastructures. Gad Mahmoud, age 60, resident of Ard-el-Liwa, an informal area of Cairo, is one of them[8].

He hails from Upper Egypt and worked in the Gulf between 1970 and 1990. With his wages, he secured a plot of agrarian land at the edge of the upscale neighborhood of Mohandesseen in Cairo. The land was bought through a *gamaya*, a savings-and-credit association, for two Egyptian pounds per square metre (at the time, about US $5), with a legal subdivision licence[9 10]. The *gamaya* hired engineers to draw a street grid complying with municipal rules (widths of 10 m for main roads, 8 for secondary roads). The average *qirat* covers 150 m², from which the space of the street is deducted, leaving a net surface of 125 m² on which to build. For construction on his 196 m² plot, Mahmoud hired a contractor to erect a multi-storey building. Funds were transferred monthly to a cousin, who paid the contractor

View over the informal area of Ard-el-Lewa, Cairo, Egypt

(Source: Lorenz Bürgi)

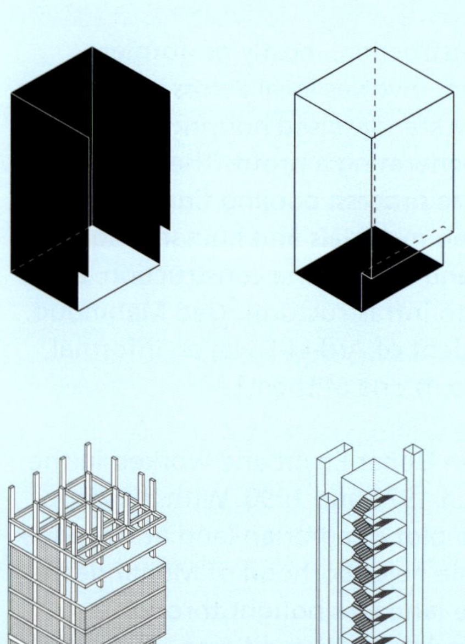

Prototypical characteristics of informal construction: Three blind sides and one street façade, Entire plot (*kirat*) occupation, after deducting space for the street, concrete structure with brick infill, and ventilation shafts and single staircase.

(Source: B.Falcao, G. Dimitriades, S. Terada, in *Housing Cairo: The Informal Response*, eds. Marc Angélil and Charlotte Malterre-Barthes, Berlin: Ruby Press, 2016)

in cash – 16,000 pounds per floor (US $4700)[11]. The building had three 60 m² apartments per floor, each with two bedrooms and a living room. Since there were no official height regulations, Mahmoud decided on a five-story structure, which took eight months to build, foundations plus one concrete slab per month. The fifteen apartments were put to rent for between 7 and 10 pounds a month, respecting the rent-control laws (which apply regardless of the building's legality or tenure status), until Mahmoud moved his family from Upper Egypt into the building, a few years later[12]. At that time, Anwar Sadat instigated the neoliberal policy of *al-Infitah*, steering away from Gamal Nasser's state socialism and post-colonial nationalism, opening the economy to foreign capital, and pivoting politically toward the West[13]. As these changes were implemented, land prices everywhere in Cairo inflated. Speculation and construction emerged as the favoured ways to achieve prosperity, and land became the prime repository for remittances. Between 1974 and 1984, informal construction thrived, encouraged by the permissive attitude of the authorities and fuelled by the oil boom in the Middle East and the ensuing flows of capital into Egypt from Saudi Arabia and the other Gulf states. This period can be considered as a watershed for informal housing, with a change from construction out of need to a profit-oriented approach. Wealthy individuals bought land from farmers and subdivided it on their own, without engineers or licences, and ignoring government regulations. Some agrarian landlords subdivided their farmland to maximise the built-and-sold area, generating smaller street sizes. Instead of buying a net area, purchasers would get the whole plot including the street – paying, for instance, for a 100 square metres plot from which half a street had to be deducted, and thus actually getting only 70 square metres. These practices and the lack of regulation marked the true beginning of informality, the *'ashwa'iyyat*. When Gad Mahmoud returned from the Gulf, he got involved in the budding construction business in informal areas. Today, he defines himself as a developer-contractor. Since he has no permanent staff, he hires employees for specific contracts, purchases the construction materials bulk, and supervises construction. He considers real estate to be the most reliable and stable form of investment in Egypt. His most recent building reflects the shifts in formalisation and capitalisation taking place in the informal construction industry. With three business partners, he purchased two adjacent plots, an area of 500 square metres. He bought the agricultural land for about $200 per square metre. An engineer was hired to calculate the structure, and the building was completed in a year. He holds a permit approving construction on agricultural land, and the building complies with regulations. Authorities reviewed the structural plans and verified the setbacks and the size of the daylight and ventilation shafts. It is a ten-story building with an elevator shaft; the first five stories are reserved for commercial use and the remaining five are for residential flats, with four apartments per floor, two overlooking each street. At about $200 per square metre, the land cost $100,000, a sum split equally among the four business partners, who paid via lump-sum bank transfers. Each partner also contributed $62,500 for construction, which cost in all some $250,000. Each now owns a quarter share of the commercial floors, one residential floor, and a flat; in total, each share is worth $225,000. Prices vary from $150,000 for the commercial spaces, while apartments range from $18,700 for a 90 square metres with 3 bedrooms, a reception room, and a balcony, to $20,000 for 129 square metres, or $22,500 for the largest on the main street. Although Mahmoud will eventually move into this building, guaranteeing by his presence the soundness of the structure to potential buyers, it is evident that his building activity is a speculative process.

Transformation of housing typologies

The changes in the production processes of informal housing, and the shift to a for-profit mode of illegal construction bordering on neoliberal speculation, have led to the transformation of housing typologies, which have evolved from self-built low structures to semi-professionally built fifteen-storey towers. Initially, housing structures followed a simple typology of concrete frames and brick infill, with street patterns registering agrarian subdivisions, generating 'urban canyons'. Urban growth was relatively timid because buildings were placed at a distance from the main road as contractors sought to conceal illegal housing from the authorities' attention. Buildings were, at first, single-house types and multistorey apartment buildings, like Gad Mahmoud's first home, with a typical building footprint varying from 75 to 125 square metres, and one or two small flats per floor. This corresponds to what Sims identifies as the "classic informal", characterised by simple brick-and-concrete construction of one and up to 7 floors – the maximum acceptable height to be reached without a lift[14]. This is still the prevalent typology, and is often a building commissioned by a family, home to the elderly parents with one son per floor. The structure is left open on the roof for further extension. At the other end of the spectrum, speculative one-off towers appeared in the mid-1990s, mainly on the fringes of Cairo. The tower typology has a much larger footprint, from 250 up to 450 m² with several large apartments per floor. Unlike the plain brick-and-concrete aspect of the simple houses, towers are rendered and painted in bright colours to facilitate sale and rental[15]. Buildings go up to 15 floors, and if inhabited, are equipped with lifts. After the January 2011 events and the collapse of the regime, contractors grew more confident and upfront with speculative illegal constructions. High-rise towers with balconies and ornamental facades appeared along Cairo's Ring Road. Units bought as securities on the market within

Gad Mahmoud's latest building, with three upper floors under construction, Ard-el-Lewa, Cairo.

(Source: Leonard Streich, *Housing Cairo: The Informal Response*, eds. Marc Angélil and Charlotte Malterre-Barthes, Berlin: Ruby Press, 2016)

Gad Mahmoud's latest building,
Floor plans, section and elevation,
Ard-el-Lewa, Cairo.

(Source: *Housing Cairo: The Informal Response*, eds. Marc Angélil and Charlotte Malterre-Barthes, Berlin: Ruby Press, 2016)

the framework of a grey economy, these dwelling have owners, yet they often remain unoccupied, betraying their speculative nature. This new typology shows the penetration of market forces making larger investments and operating in neoliberal mode, with contractors and investors engaged in illegally producing real estate stock that is sold openly. Informal construction at this stage of development points to the manner in which the forces of capital and finance have taken over what was formerly a small-scale, owner-builder form of urban production. What emerged in the 1970s as the popular response to public failure to provide affordable housing solutions for the lower classes in Egypt has evolved into a classic market process, tending towards the formal modes of real estate investment, a far cry from Hassan Fathy's observations. While the "classic informal" type still prevails, the "tower" type is the architectural materialisation of market-oriented logic, one that might turn informal construction into a more formal process.

This possible status change of informal housing areas into formal urban districts is not unlikely[16]. New towers materialise, in a more obvious manner then the early, discreet types, the illegal aspect of informal construction. This blatancy might force authorities to take action. While many public policies designed to combat informal construction have been implemented, none has been able to limit its continuous expansion[17]. Legalisation is thus a path that should be explored. Currently, in terms of tenure, buildings in informal areas are not fully registered as built on the municipal cadaster. At the moment of land purchase, a signed change-of-ownership contract is brought to the notary public to be certified. Buildings are thus exempted from land tax. This represents a significant, untapped resource for the national budget, which could be exploited, providing informal areas are legalised and benefit from public services. In short, the emergence of speculative typologies, with an architectural output similar to that of formal markets, points towards a possible dismissal of the current dichotomy between formal and informal. The recognition of these areas as inherently part of the city would *de facto* officially allow architectural practices to engage in their production, from which the profession is at present entirely left out.

Questioning the relevance of architects

Abdullah is a neighbour of Gad Mahmoud. He bought a plot in 2013 and built a 5-storey home for his family. Discussing the construction process, Abdullah explains that although he hired a contractor, he "knows how to mix concrete, and the principles of construction." For the design of the building and the floor plans, the contractor "made the interior division, added 12 columns, (...) showed the drawing," which Abdullah approved[18]. Similarly, when Gad Mahmoud was questioned on the design of his units, he admitted to having the structural drawings checked by an engineer, but never expressed the urge to consult an architect on the plan and interior layout. This is largely because the urban and architectural patterns produced by the protocols of informality are typical and repetitive. Floor plans are optimised and vary little from one building to another; the need for improvement is not obvious. These revealing details show that architects and designers are not considered necessary to the production of living space in informal areas of Cairo. And this is symptomatic of the worldwide situation of the profession when it comes to engaging in informal urbanisation processes. However, in the case of Cairo, some current changes suggest another possible route (other than legalisation) for reengaging architects in the production processes of informal housing. The penetration of market forces with larger investments, the shift to a profitable mode of illegal construction, and the transformation of housing typologies show an increase in available "grey" capital as well as signs of market saturation. These factors may signal an emerging clientele for designers. In fact, when offered alternative designs, Mahmoud showed interest in them, implying a growing need for a more diverse housing offer. This path was explored in the framework of a MAS Urban Design at the ETHZ, with architects undertaking the paradoxical task of designing the informal while respecting the "rules of the game", the economic, social and spatial laws of the informal housing market[19]. Inspired by the existing solidarity among inhabitants of an area, one of the many projects thus developed is named "Solidary City"[20]. Based on the resources-pooling system used by local actors to finance construction, the project proposes to rationalise and save resources by building two houses side-by-side, instead of the single house back-to-back typology built on one *qirat* with three blind facades. By combining two houses on two *qirats*, the new typology makes it feasible to have only one staircase, and the saved area that a second staircase would require is used for a courtyard, which improves ventilation and lighting. Pursuing the sharing logic, new typologies with shared kitchens suggest a more sustainable, communal way of living, inspired by an ancient typology. This housing prototype on the scale of the neighbourhood, would break typological monotony and convert existing social solidarity into spatial reality. Another ambitious project worth mentioning is "Inside Out"[21]. Challenging the informal building archetype of a single open facade facing a narrow street, relying on vertical shafts for cross-ventilation and light, this proposal offers change via a simple recombination of shafts and staircases. Juggling the "classic" elements of informal housing (shafts, circulations, cantilevers, party walls, etc.), the new design implements an inside-out tactic. Staircases and shafts are positioned along exterior walls and facades. If repeated, this new typology would allow joint circulation between adjacent units and generate a new urban morphology. Many projects developed were handed over *gratis* with their plans to local contractors, for them to include parts of the improvements and features in their *modus operandi* of construction.

A single family house typology similar to Abdhullah's, Ard-el-Lewa, Cairo.

(Source: Lorenz Bürgi)

Persistent informal urban growth shows that, while lacking services and public infrastructure, these settlements are nonetheless successful in generating dense and affordable housing for the lower classes. However, the inherent illegal nature of construction of this type has kept architects at bay. Ongoing changes in protocols of informality may reconcile architects with Fathy's plea for the design of habitat for the people. Indeed, designing the city - regardless of legal status - remains the prerogative of architects and planners. And with it comes responsibility for the current state of the world.

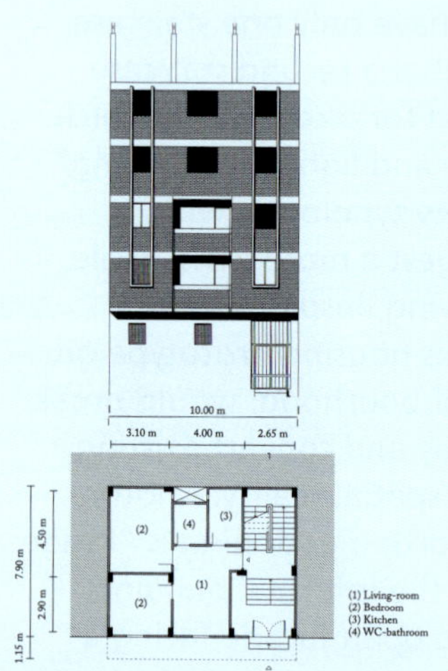

Abdhullah's single family house, elevation and ground floor plan, Ard-el-Lewa, Cairo

(Source: *Housing Cairo: The Informal Response*, eds. Marc Angélil and Charlotte Malterre-Barthes, Berlin: Ruby Press, 2016)

References

Abdullah, M. "Informality Construction Processes." by Charlotte Malterre-Barthes (2015).

Alexandropoulou, Zoi , and Marilena Fotopoulou. "War on Informality: Governmental Policies against 'Ashwa'iyyat ". In *Housing Cairo: The Informal Response*, edited by Marc Angélil and Charlotte Malterre-Barthes. Berlin: Ruby Press, 2016.

Areas, Egyptian-German Participartory Development Programme in Urban. *Cairo's Informal Areas between Urban Challenges and Hidden Potentials: Facts.Voices.Visions*. Cairo, Egypt: GTZ, 2009.

El Kadi, Galila. "L'articulation des deux circuits de la gestion fonciére en Egypte: le cas du Caire." In *Housing Africa's Urban Poor*, edited by Philip Amis, Peter Cutt Lloyd and International African Institute, 103-17. Manchester; New York: Manchester University Press for the International African Institute, 1990.

Fathy, Hassan. *Architecture for the Poor : An Experiment in Rural Egypt* [in English]. Chicago: University of Chicago Press, 1976.

———. *Construire Avec le peuple : Histoire d'un village d'Égypte : Gourna* [French edition]. Arles; Paris: Actes Sud ; Sindbad, 1996.

Kouniaki, Dyonisia, and Alice Merche. "Solidary City." In *Housing Cairo*, edited by Marc Angélil and Charlotte Malterre-Barthes. Berlin: Ruby Press, 2016.

Kouvari, Maria, and Heechul Jung. "A New Vernacular. Typology, Construction, and Aesthetics ". In *Housing Cairo: The Informal Response*, edited by Marc Angélil and Charlotte Malterre-Barthes. Berlin: Ruby Press, 2016.

Malterre-Barthes, Charlotte. "A Story of Construction." In *Housing Cairo: The Informal Response*, edited by Marc Angélil and Charlotte Malterre-Barthes. Berlin: Ruby Press, 2016.

Mansour, Salma. "New Law, Old Problems: The Egyptian Rent Control Dilemma." *The Chronicles* 1, no. Spring 2010 (2010): 40-43.

Sabry, Sarah. "An Introduction to Informal Housing in Cairo." In *Housing Cairo: The Informal Response*, edited by Marc Angélil and Charlotte Malterre-Barthes. Berlin: Ruby Press, 2016.

Sims, David. *Understanding Cairo : The Logic of a City out of Control*. Cairo: The American University in Cairo Press, 2010.

Vignal, Leila, and Eric Denis. "Cairo as Regional/Global Economic Capital?". In *Cairo Cosmopolitan: Politics, Culture, and Urban Space in the New Globalized Middle East*, edited by Diane Singerman and Paul Amar. Cairo, New York: American University in Cairo Press, 2006.

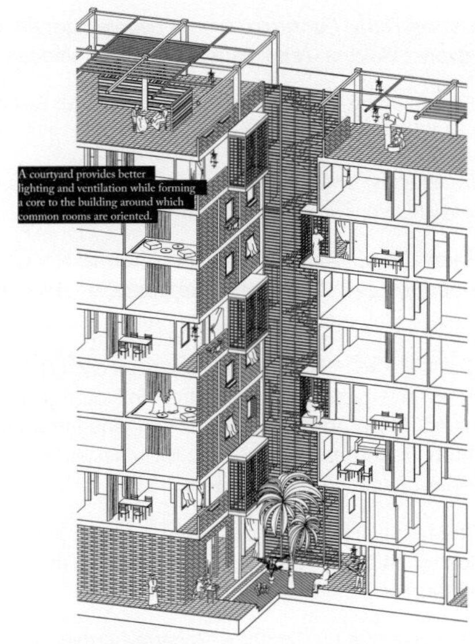

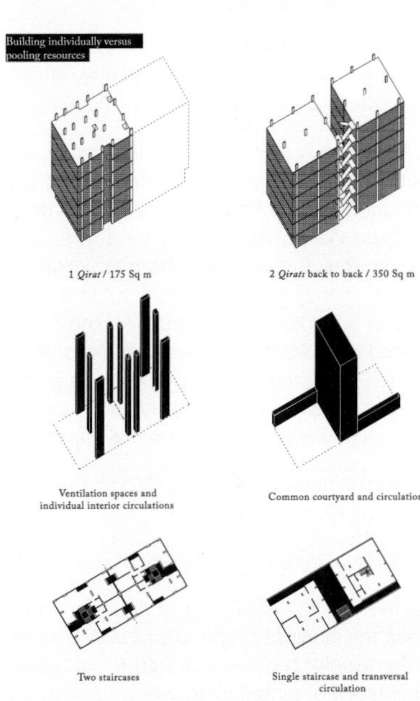

Solidary City, by Dyonisia Kouniaki and Alice Merche, proposes to rationalise and save resources by building two units together, instead of the present-day single unit, the back-to-back typology built on one qirat with three blind facades.

(Source: *Housing Cairo : The Informal Response*, eds. Marc Angélil et Charlotte Malterre-Barthes, Berlin: Ruby Press, 2016).

1. Hassan Fathy, *Construire avec le peuple : histoire d'un village d'Egypte : Gourna* (Arles; Paris: Actes Sud ; Sindbad, 1996).18.

2. Hassan Fathy, *Architecture for the Poor : An Experiment in Rural Egypt* (Chicago: University of Chicago Press, 1976).3.

3. David Sims, *Understanding Cairo : The Logic of a City out of Control* (Cairo: The American University in Cairo Press, 2010).

4. Sarah Sabry, "An Introduction to Informal Housing in Cairo," in *Housing Cairo: The Informal Response*, ed. Marc Angélil and Charlotte Malterre-Barthes (Berlin: Ruby Press, 2016).

5. Galila El Kadi, "L'articulation des deux circuits de la gestion fonciére en Egypte: le cas du Caire," in *Housing Africa's Urban Poor*, ed. Philip Amis, Peter Cutt Lloyd, and International African Institute (Manchester; New York: Manchester University Press for the International African Institute, 1990).

6. The feddan is a unit of area used in Egypt, Sudan and Syria. 1 feddan = 24 qirat = 60 m x 70 m = 4200 sq. m. = 0.42 hectare = 1.038 acre

7. Field research by Charlotte Malterre-Barthes, Mariotiyah, Greater Cairo, April 2013.

8. Charlotte Malterre-Barthes, "A Story of Construction," in *Housing Cairo: The Informal Response*, ed. Marc Angélil and Charlotte Malterre-Barthes (Berlin: Ruby Press, 2016).

9. A *gamaya* is a group saving association, a social mechanism that relies on collecting, each month for one or two years, a fixed amount of money from each member. A group leader collects the fixed shares and holds the fund. The number of members pooling their money ranges from as few as six to as many as 40, and the money collected is paid out as a lump sum in rotation to each member of the group, allowing them to finance major expenditures (land purchases, weddings, education, etc.). Like the ROSCA (rotating savings-and-credit association) the *gamaya* is based on balanced reciprocity and is a popular form of informal finance, in which members are both savers and borrowers.

10. At the time of the survey (2015), the Egyptian pound was worth roughly $0.12.

11. Time of construction (1996), it was worth roughly $0.29.

12. Rent-control laws in Egypt date from the early 20th century, when the landlords' right to evacuate tenants was first abolished. In the socialist Nasser era, a statute was passed allowing the inheritance of rented units, which permitted the continuation of rent-control implications across generations. Laws passed under Sadat allowed tenants to re-rent or exchange the unit they occupied without approval from the landlord. This, combined with the rental inheritance law, marked the near-full elimination of landlords' rights over their property, while still holding them responsible for its maintenance. After maintaining the bulk of the aforementioned laws for over two decades, Mubarak passed Rent Law No. 4,of 1996, which exempts units erected from that date onwards from rent controls. Salma Mansour, "New Law, Old Problems: The Egyptian Rent Control Dilemma," *The Chronicles* 1, no. Spring 2010 (2010).

13. Leila Vignal and Eric Denis, "Cairo as Regional/Global Economic Capital?," in *Cairo Cosmopolitan: Politics, Culture, and Urban Space in the New Globalized Middle East*, ed. Diane Singerman and Paul Amar (Cairo, New York: American University in Cairo Press, 2006).99-152

14. Sims, *Understanding Cairo : The Logic of a City out of Control*.105.

15. Maria Kouvari and Heechul Jung, "A New Vernacular. Typology, Construction, and Aesthetics " in *Housing Cairo: The Informal Response*, ed. Marc Angélil and Charlotte Malterre-Barthes (Berlin: Ruby Press, 2016).

16. Egyptian-German Participatory Development Programme in Urban Areas, *Cairo's Informal Areas between Urban Challenges and Hidden Potentials: Facts.Voices.Visions*. (Cairo, Egypt: GTZ, 2009).

17. Zoi Alexandropoulou and Marilena Fotopoulou, "War on Informality: Governmental Policies against 'Ashwa'iyyat " in *Housing Cairo: The Informal Response*, ed. Marc Angélil and Charlotte Malterre-Barthes (Berlin: Ruby Press, 2016).

18. M. Abdullah, interview by Charlotte Malterre-Barthes, 2015, Ard-el-Lewa, Cairo.

19. The MAS Urban Design cycle (2014-2016) on Egypt at the Chair of Marc Angélil was directed by Charlotte Malterre-Barthes. Outputs of the research and design studio were exhibited at the Shenzhen Urbanism Biennale in 2015, the Egyptian Pavilion of the Architecture Biennale in Venice in 2016 and the constellation.s exhibition in Bordeaux in 2016.

20. Dyonisia Kouniaki and Alice Merche, "Solidary City," in *Housing Cairo*, ed. Marc Angélil and Charlotte Malterre-Barthes (Berlin: Ruby Press, 2016).

21. Bernardo Baillif Sousa Menezes Falcão and Gregorios Dimitriadis, "Inside Out,"in *Housing Cairo*, eds. Marc Angélil and Charlotte Malterre-Barthes (Berlin: Ruby Press, 2016).

the global landscape of cities

Jean Attali philosopher and professor in urban planning

Lecture given as part of **constellations** at arc en rêve centre d'architecture, at the invitation of the École d'Enseignement Supérieur d'Art in Bordeaux

constellation.s invites us to consider the legacy of the exhibition entitled "Mutations" organised by arc en rêve in 2000. To gauge the distance between the two, we have to step back and remember how influential the show was. Rem Koolhaas was the chief curator, five years after the publication of his masterwork *S,M,L,XL*. This book was a compendium of projects carried out by the Office for Metropolitan Architecture (OMA) before 1993, and featured all kinds of written texts (fragments from diaries or autobiographies, poems and nightmares, urban reports, essays and manifestos, a dictionary) produced by the architect/writer. I look back at "Mutations" in the light of the best known of his texts: *Generic City*, written in 1994. This date is important because, the same year, another exhibition was presented at the Pompidou Centre in Paris entitled "The city, art and architecture in Europe, 1870-1993". The curators, Jean Dethier and Alain Guiheux, brought together the plans from a large number of projects forming a historic legacy of modern urban planning. On this occasion, Françoise Choay published a corrosive article entitled "Le règne de l'urbain et la mort de la ville" (The Reign of the Urban and the Death of the City). I say this now: everything I defend here is nothing more nor less than a way of opposing what this title means. Françoise Choay's caustic words instilled into urban thinking the poison of a segretating, purely ideological approach that I entirely reject.

Generic City was seen to be making an observation (if not expressing an illusion): that of the gradual global unification of the landscape of cities. It was thought to be making a statement about the uniform and the undifferentiated. This interpretation is wrong. As is often the case, its pithy title confiscated, to its own benefit, the sophistication of analysis. It is thus necessary to get back to what the text actually said, simply highlighting two or three remarkable hypotheses. The first is that awareness of the global and large-scale nature of urbanisation forces us to reconsider the very definition of the city. What do we call "the city" when we know that half of humanity lives in urban areas in conditions that correspond to city lifestyles? We can see how relevant this question is in the early 21st century. When we say "half", the figures given at the time only represented a global average. In reality, In many countries (in the EU, but also in the other continents), urbanisation figures are well above 80 %. In a way, at such levels, talking about the city or urban conditions means talking about the human condition per se. However it goes without saying that we cannot exclude the other "half" of humanity from the analysis.

Does the way we define and classify cities not pose problems of taxonomy similar to those that fascinated 18th century naturalists? This amounts to saying that the question of the definition of the city should only be asked after attempting to draw up a complete inventory of these modes of existence. This inventory would be a necessary condition for any theory: the vast amount of taxonomic work undertaken by naturalists made the theory of evolution possible. Questions of classification, inspired by nominalist philosophy, open up theoretical perspectives that are historic and structural, in other words dynamic and systematic. At several points Rem Koolhaas' texts discuss cross-fertilisation between different types of architecture: urban forms or ideas spring up somewhere in the world, but they blossom or bear fruit elsewhere. Knowledge of cities can only develop if we observe these many exchanges. In the section of *Generic City* that focuses on urbanism, he writes: "Usually the generic city has been "planned", not in the usual sense of some bureaucratic organization controlling its development, but as if various echoes, spores, tropes, seeds fell on the ground randomly as in nature, took hold—exploiting the natural fertility of the terrain—and now form an ensemble: an arbitrary gene pool that sometimes produces amazing results." This theme of random cross-fertilisation is further developed in "Globalization", another text that appears in *S,M,L,XL*. Globalisation has recognised its precursors in the dissemination of styles and in ostensibly inimitable forms of architecture which, although designed in Europe, could only be built in America or Japan—to mention only examples chosen by Koolhaas (Le Corbusier, Aldo Rossi, etc.) This is thus not about ironing out differences or creating indistinct cityscapes. We are faced with a generalised process of transference, where each part of the global system of cities is affected by all the others. What's left of the city? One could answer this by parodying something Jean-Paul Sartre once said: "a city, made of all cities, worth all of them, and any one of them worth the others". The question is how to square a host of differences with the fact of belonging to a single constantly changing system.

This patently ambitious approach reintroduces the question of definition: what might a "global" definition of the city be when we are attentive to the variety of cities, their number, and the way they are all interconnected? To construct a definition of the city, we have to arm ourselves with concepts and methodology—precisely those that I recognise in Rem Koolhaas' text. In the section on urbanism, he admits three major characteristics. The first is that the generic city accommodates the primordial and the futuristic (and only them, he adds). I wondered for a long time what this rather mysterious expression meant: what does he mean by "the primordial"? The primordial preserves a relationship with origins and foundations, even if it is dressed up in ancient history and its popular throwbacks, while "the futuristic" refers to the tendency towards the possible, the anticipation of the future whatever it may be. Is this tension between being rooted in the immemorial and projecting ourselves towards utopia typically the legacy of European urban history? In other words, the interweaving of urban and cultural questions—what might be described as a combination of a debt to the past and future instalments to be paid. To cut the Gordian knot, Rem Koolhaas introduces the idea of a radical cutoff point in the generic city, according to the most inexorable rule of all (the one that governs all trade): what doesn't work disappears.

Second, Rem Koolhaas states that: "the generic city represents the apotheosis of the concept of multiple choice […]." This is another rather strange statement, which references the basic format of statistical surveys. He says that it's as if all the boxes (of a questionnaire) are ticked. Urban landscapes include very different and highly contrasting forms of development: skyscrapers and rice fields; the CBD and the kampung. These are typical examples that turn our attention towards major urban areas in Asia: is the city of the "multiple choice" concept not in Singapore, Malaysia, Indonesia, Thailand or Hong Kong? Cities which have in many ways, according to Rem Koolhaas himself, after his early experience of the ruins of Rotterdam and far from London and New York, been templates for his own urban culture? So we might sum up, temporarily, as follows: a concept one might describe as European, followed by another defined as Asian; and then a third that proclaims that the best definition of the generic city is *freestyle*. This arose in the United States from the emancipation of forms of dance and music; it's a typically American concept. So the generic city might be the embodiment of this synthesis combining different legacies and trends: vectors of development that are respectively European, Asian and American, each probably attached to a particular conception of time. Consequently, Rem Koolhaas' thesis does not point to a levelling-out of the urban landscape. Instead it introduces an idea of the city that might integrate the different expressions of a polymorphous urban landscape in regions of the world with radically contrasting cultures. Far from suggesting disenchantment, such suggestions express the intuition that a stupendous dynamic exists: one that allows all sorts of urban forms to flourish within their own globalised context.

I think we need something else to form a correct interpretation of *Generic City*. We need to look at the term "generic" and distinguish, hypothetically at least, the explicit and implicit ways in which Rem Koolhaas uses it. I have just given one logical meaning of the word "generic": it refers to the question of classification, in a shifting sense that makes one-sided definition impossible. Are there genres to which European, Asian, African and American cities belong? Does "generic" only refer to the apparent unifying effects of reciprocal influences and cross-fertilisations? Let us leave to one side another meaning of "generic" applied to consumer goods devoid of the intangible attributes that are supposed to increase their value: a drastic reduction in value—or a sense of ordinariness that eradicates the aura of rarity… Rem Koolhaas has made several observations on this subject.

But "generic" has a third possible meaning. At an event three years before "Mutations", Documenta X (1997) in Cassel, Germany, Rem Koolhaas and OMA presented their early work focusing on cities along the Pearl River Delta in China. Their approach was based on several themes, but I would like to focus here on one: *The City of Exacerbated Difference*. The acronym COED is the same as the abbreviation "coed" referring to mixed education in the United States, so it subtly introduces the question of gender into the issue of the status of the city: a transgressive question of differentiation, of polarity, of intensity, and no longer a question of logical belonging or reduction to the minimum. We can see the effects of this very subtle intellectual construction, far from the approximations that have generally been made in order to disseminate or criticise the theme of the Generic City. We discover an intellectual landscape that clearly needs to be described in detail. I think that events as important as "Mutations" in the past and constellation.s today must be considered in the light of the intellectual standpoints that made them possible.

So let's ask ourselves: what about "constellation.s"?

The most remarkable thing is the name chosen for this new exhibition. Constellations are a mental construct. They are artefacts of distance: they symbolically bring together objects that are independent, representing links between bodies located light years apart. Humanity has identified and named figures in the night sky, giving them mythological meanings. But we know that these configurations have no other reality than the one we give them, and that they obey no laws of perspective other than those that arise from our Earth-bound perception of them. We also know the part these celestial models play in navigation and mapmaking. Constellations are a primitive code for humans who walk and sail over long distances.

The word "constellation" leads us to focus on intellectual and symbolic constructs connecting sets of facts whose common denominator is the fact that they belong to the same "map". Humans make maps, creating codes to link signs together and to connect disparate objects. We can hardly ignore the apparently disparate nature of the production, experiments, and presentations brought together in "constellation.s". The fragmented and non-uniform nature of the subjects presented in the different sections of the exhibition is meaningful in itself. When I talk about "artefacts of distance" to interpret the title of "constellation.s", I use the word "distance" deliberately. Jacques Levy and Michel Lussault have republished their *Dictionnaire de la géographie et de l'espace des sociétés* (2013, Belin), a book whose aim is to define the conceptual framework of the geographical sciences. The very subject of geography may precisely be distance: distance in space and in societies. Questions of spatial distance can arise from distances relating to social distinction, separation, or even segregation: distance from all the others. Constellations do not only concern the objects they show as connected figures, but the spaces and chasms that separate them. Distance may be the subject of geography, or one of its subjects; it is also that of "constellation.s".

Another key theme in geography is the concept of movement, so fundamental to the cultural geography of Denis Retaillé. Movement is not mobility. Movement is the action of societies with regard to themselves; it is the manifestation of the propensity of cities for constant change; it is the role of cities as major instruments for the understanding, leadership and planning of displacement territories: "Cities On The Move" was, let us remember, the title of an exhibition by OMA in London in 1999.

More than the disparate nature of facts, cases, expressions and projects, the focus here is on the universal nature of our condition as inhabitants of cities. What kind of universality are we talking about? First of all, the universal nature of forms of habitat: dwelling is a human trait *par excellence*. But the universal experience of dwelling takes forms that are inexhaustibly diverse. The same human preoccupations appear everywhere, concerning shelter, home life, the way we relate to food and rest, etc., but they are deployed via rituals and customs in a very wide range of forms. It is this tension between the universal and the particular that the city embodies in today's cultures: no, "generic" does not mean "undifferentiated".

There are not only relationships between separate subjects or objects. Houses or flats are like rooms apart inside the city; they give shape to the distance between the communal and the private. This tension inhabits the universal. We live in the in-between space: "constellation.s" is a forum for the representation and formulation of the space between images and words. If we only consider pictures, photographs or maps, we miss the world of words. The problem is that there is no connection between them. It's also an in-between space between pictures and concepts! Between the image that shows and the word that denotes, there are syntaxes and grammars that we need to learn to decode. What I am saying is inspired by a text written by Gilles Deleuze and Félix Guattari, which I have constantly referred to over the years: the chapter entitled "Géo-philosophie" in *Qu'est-ce que la philosophie?* The aim of the text is to distinguish the world of figures from the world of concepts, and I echo this here by distinguishing the world of representations (on the "figures" side) from that of formulations (on the "concepts" side). The text says that figures are paradigmatic (but also hierarchical, projective and referential), whereas concepts are syntagmatic (but also vicinal, connective and consistent). Here again, I am not undertaking a literal explanation; I only retain the fact that admitting this opposition between the paradigmatic and the syntagmatic means first of all that there is no model that would make it possible to understand the diverse range of cities. The approach to the global cityscape can no longer be paradigmatic: we only have concatenations of differences and sequences in motion. In the world of architecture, saying: "be careful, the concept is not projective" when architectural culture is constantly fuelled by the idea of a "project" is obviously an intriguing proposition. So what replaces the projective? The answer is the connective, nothing more. The word has assumed its fullest importance today: thoughts and actions take place in networks in connected environments.

All this leads me at last to talk about the subject of this lecture, namely the global atlas of cities. Let me tell you briefly how it all started. After the exhibition entitled *Mutations*, and after I published a book of architectural philosophy, I started working on a book on cities, no doubt carried along by the impetus of the exhibition. I soon realised that it was an impossible task, and that before attempting to write anything about cities, it was necessary to patiently accumulate knowledge on as many cities as possible. I was lucky enough to be asked to head up a research seminar at ENSA Paris-Malaquais; so I undertook to put together an atlas of cities using a collaborative platform (Wiki, then DokuWiki). The tool I used is significant, because our digital platform makes it possible to record and archive the work and to make it easily accessible. My students, my colleagues and I quickly understood that the accumulated data pointed to a number of themes, and that it raised host of questions and thoughts that I am going to say a few words about here.

In quantitative terms, over a period of nine years we gathered 450 contributions (research dissertations counting towards the master's degree). In the formats we encouraged, there are now over 10,000 pages of texts, as well as hundreds of pieces of graphic, cartographic and photographic material. It's a significant collection of data, and we are now looking for the best ways to publish the results of the work. We are naturally delighted whenever we have the opportunity to discuss these subjects, as is the case today at arc en rêve.

Imagine you have to present an encyclopaedia: what page would you choose? I have this problem all the time: how should we enter the atlas? Where should we start? What should we show? The latest productions, or the oldest? Cities we know, or cities we don't know? And so on. If I mentioned, in a polemical way, Françoise Choay's words earlier on, it was to say that we applied a deliberately anti-hierarchical principle to our work: our subject is all cities and the entire city, in all its extensions and all its states. Keeping strictly to this principle is a way of avoiding many oppositions or pairs of notions that actually have little substance, except perhaps from an ideological standpoint: the formal and the non-formal, the central and the peripheral, the well-formed and the formless, etc. There is form everywhere, and cities extend to wherever groups of dwellings and human settlements spring up and multiply all over the world. What has thus been produced with no prior model or methodology, nor even an initial theoretical framework, based on a simple rule each author had to obey (one city, one hypothesis) is a set of themes so varied that it allows a multitude cross-references between both subjects and places. Among these many subjects, I would like to focus on some that we find in constellation.s.

The first subject is pioneering urban fronts: there are cities in all sorts of areas across the world where we hardly expect to find these. The processes of urbanisation are subject to vectors of expansion in space, and they are sometimes projected very far from densely urbanised areas. They are, for example, the pioneering fronts of mineral prospecting and mining areas or regions with extreme climates: in Siberia, northern Canada, Chile, and so on. On the edges of the urbanised world there are forms of urban construction that cannot be ignored. The second theme, or group of themes, is what I call submersible cities: Atlantis, as a final myth, resurfaces in response to the ineluctable rise in water level. In the year 2000, the United Nations World Urbanisation Prospects showed that over half of the world's largest cities (with populations of over 2 million) were at zero altitude: on the edge of maritime basins, oceans, or river estuaries. The risk of submersion, of tsunamis, and of flooding is significant, from New Orleans to Miami, from Phuket to Aceh and Jakarta, and all along the Tōhoku coast. The balance to be restored between major urban settlements and water raises crucial questions. The pictures of floods presented in the main hall as part of constellation.s are anything but anecdotal. And the third theme, to which we still hesitate to give a name, is that of the scattered metropolis: because of the very scale of urban expansion, the metropolis can no longer only be considered in the light of its central functions. The Venetian urban planners Bernardo Secchi and Paola Viganò popularised the concept of the "diffused city". Their concept takes account of the fact that the spatial extension of cities increases spatial and morphological discontinuity and creates conditions that are relatively independent from central attractors. Urban societies try to produce adequate responses to this situation: non-dependence on the centre, or the ability to make distance from the centre a positive thing. The role of intermediate-sized cities and the extension of peripheral urban systems profoundly change the overall structure of areas: behind the largest cities lie a host of secondary cities.

The formulations I suggest here are provisional. They are always an attempt to appropriately name these artefacts of distance I talked about in relation to the word "constellation". Via an accumulation of urban studies, we are drawing a map of the world's cities in the most concrete and the most technical sense. We use an interactive platform to the exclusion of all other media: the work in its entirety can be found on a website. The seminar entitled *Le paysage mondial des villes* gives the publication of the content its collective meaning and its cross-disciplinary dynamic. Social networks provide concrete proof that any production of knowledge presupposes the existence of a working collective, and that all publishing initiatives have a social dimension: for years, our seminar involved discussing the documents we put on line one by one. The atlas ends up producing its own map: each page is an address (URL), and every link from one page to another is a road. It's a bit like a new Peutinger Table in the age of Web 2.0: a sort of fabulous construction that creates numerous links between disparate subjects and objects, as I described them at the beginning.

But from this moment on, the plethora of themes might adversely affect the legibility of the whole, and the internal structure of the atlas might become opaque. It needs an index. More than classifying content, this involves formulating the emerging themes: how do we name not only these cities, these urban realities, but also the links we establish between the different items? The work is expressed largely in cartographic terms. On our platform there are a lot of texts, as I said, and there are photographs and sometimes videos. There are often original drawings—but most of all there are maps. Maps are a special medium that is well suited to the themes I just mentioned.

Patrick Bouchain / Licence to…

A desultory conversation with Patrick Bouchain. In which he talks about family, religion, Africa, the *Fête de l'Humanité*, film, art, anthropology, context, experimentation, education, culture and a number of other things. But he also talks about living and inhabiting – in general and in particular. Patrick Bouchain was interviewed in Paris on 30 January 2017 by Marie Bruneau and Bertrand Genier.

In a recent interview on France Culture, we discovered that you, too, have connections with Africa… Yes, Africa is very important to me. In a way it was Africa that opened my eyes and brought me into the living world. In fact, I was incredibly lucky. Here's the story: at a time when compulsory military service was being called into question, architects, designers and artists were allowed to take part in a cooperation programme (until then only scientists and teachers were allowed to benefit from this exception). I quickly put together an application, which was rejected. The director of my school saw my case as a matter of principle and decided to talk to one of his friends at the *Conseil d'État.* And it worked… I was sent to the French Cultural Centre in Abidjan to look after the film library, with complete freedom of movement. I had high-quality projection equipment, with several projectionists and two lorries to organise film club tours. I could also use the diplomatic bag to bring films over from France. I discovered a continent – Africa – that did not correspond at all to what I'd learned at school. I saw the part Catholicism played in colonisation. I became aware of the importance of economic challenges, and of certain more or less honest aspects of decolonisation. At the time, Côte d'Ivoire was still governed by a two-pronged administration – French civil servants stayed on to help the country embrace its independence. I also discovered the political, economic and cultural life of the country. And I travelled! I travelled with Africans, because the French Embassy, unlike other bodies, mainly employed local staff. The experience made a lasting impression on me. As a member of the army, I had a salary that was the equivalent of the average wage of an African civil servant. One day, my friend Bassiro offered me a deal: *"Patrick, there are six of us on your team: you make seven. And we all agree that we should take it in turns to give one of us, every month, one seventh of our salary so that he can organise a party… Don't you think that's a good idea?"* You agree to forfeit a seventh of your pay, and instead of living in a state of continuous monotony, when it's your turn you suddenly have a lot of money: you're the king! But the rule is that you have to celebrate, invite friends and guests, plan cultural activities, look after the catering… Everything! Suddenly, this new way of looking at wages and our relationship with money showed me a new way of looking at life.

My friends had suddenly become my mentors, and I learned simply by living with them. When my African friends talked among themselves, I heard a beautiful melody. In Bambara dialect, there are all sorts of words that are repeated: the first time, for example, you say the table. But if that's not enough you say it again, going into more detail: the table with four legs, then the white table with four legs, then the white table with four legs you can lay for dinner, and so on. I find this mixture of Republican French and grammatical forms from local dialects enchanting. Why were Africans (why are they still?) mimicked and ridiculed for their way of speaking? *– Tell me, Patrick, it seems that where you live they water the verges. Is that true? – Yes, we do that. – Why? – Well, to tell the truth, I don't really know... So the grass will grow, I suppose... – So you have some sheep? – No... no sheep... – So what do you do with the grass? – Oh, that's simple: we mow it. – You mow it? And where do you put it? – Well, we chop it up... – If I understand you correctly, you water the soil, and it goes green. So you water it for the sake of colour? In that case, you'd be better off painting it!* Gradually, I became interested in the architecture of the areas I visited. I started to take notes, casually and unscientifically. This survey on the traditional habitat led me to observe little details more closely: little by little, I was able to put together a set of drawings and photographs of things that are probably no longer there. At that time, Africans were encouraged to demolish their huts for reasons of hygiene. These campaigns, financed by the Lafarge cement company (which has succeeded, since then, in restoring its image via well-targeted and well-publicised sponsorship), promoted the construction of concrete houses. The State subsidised the purchase of the breezeblock moulds and cement, and people built houses with corrugated iron roofs that were unbearable to live in. The story that follows permanently changed my perspective and probably influenced my future. It took place in northeast Côte d'Ivoire, in the Lobi tribe. In Lobi tradition, when a couple forms, they have to become independent, so they have to be allocated a territory. So the Lobi community looks for a place where the new couple can live without bothering anyone, and where they have sufficient resources to get by. As soon as they find the place, the community begins to build a house – traditonally made of earthen strips 50 centimetres wide. The plot is carefully dug out so that a quarter of the house is below ground level to keep it cool. The first strip of earth is laid, and then the work stops, and they let the couple live for a while with no walls and no roof,

just the beginnings of a house: a kind of life-size plan. Only then does the community come back to finish the house. **These people build by scoping out the plot: what matters to them is context, and the economy of that context.** So they just start by building a low wall. Only after a time does the project take shape: they finish building the walls and they add a flat roof where they can spread millet out to dry. It's so beautiful! Unfortunately, there are very few traditional Lobi houses left. This life-size experimentation process in house-building clearly shows the part played by the family, or rather the community. That's another thing I discovered with the Lobi: community organisation. They practice polygamy, but it's very marginal. Boys are raised by their uncles, not their fathers. And because I was educated by my father and other adults, I know how important this split paternity is because it allows the child to determine his personality by referring to several different people. Maybe that's why psychoanalysis doesn't work in Africa: the complexes we develop with respect to our parents have no reason to exist there. This is primarily because these are matriarchal societies where children spend a lot of time with their mothers as they work, and it's also because the role of the father vis-à-vis the child is tempered by the presence of other men. **That's how I discovered life and vernacular architecture at the same time. And it's how I understood that what matters is really inhabiting a particular place. So my time in Africa corrected everything I'd learned.** I received a Jesuit education and the director of the cultural centre in Abidjan, himself a highly educated Jesuit, was aware of that. During a tour, we stopped at Katiola, a Catholic bishopric, and we were received by the Bishop, who was from Alsace. My boss, who'd got it into his head to demonstrate our host's theological shortcomings, kept trying to wrong-foot him: the Bishop was incapable of responding to his arguments. As soon as we said goodbye, my boss summed up the evening:

– *And that, Patrick, is the Catholic Mission in Africa!*

He'd made his point. In parallel, the eighteen months I spent running the film centre gave me an opportunity to discover the cinema.

At the time I had almost no knowledge of cinema, and now I was to watch films for a year and a half! We got a lot of educational documentaries – on scientific or technical subjects. I remember Alain Resnais' wonderful film *Le Chant du Styrène*, which I'm sure few people remember today: a kind of ballet, an ode to substance and progress. I discovered so many French directors: many weren't very good, but they were connected to the French education system and set out to educate people.
But the most exciting films for me, while I was exploring the realities of Africa, were the ones about anthropology and ethnography. I was able to invite Jean Rouch to present *Les Maîtres Fous* at the film club. Seeing Jean Rouch demonstrate a Voodoo session he'd witnessed and hearing him talking about it is a once in a lifetime experience! My time in Africa also taught me a lot about the army. I was able to meet some remarkable army doctors, who helped me to understand what experimental field medicine is all about. I saw what solidarity is, too... And cars! I loved engines – I wanted to be a mechanic. The Africans dreamed (and still dream?) of being able to afford the things we owned, although they didn't give them the same symbolic value as we did. When someone managed to buy a car – by doing a bit of scheming, borrowing some money, or whatever – it would represent a lifetime's work. Beside himself, he'd drive like crazy until he wrecked it. Then he'd calmly get out of the car and leave it on the roadside. He wouldn't complain, he wouldn't even think about what it was worth: he'd just leave it there. As if he'd experienced all there was to experience in the car, and that was it. And then someone else might pass by and decide to salvage the vehicle to try and repair it...talk about a healthy sense of perspective!
Another lesson, this time about technology: one day, my friend Bassiro, again, wanted to know if a transistor radio with a large number of batteries in it would be able to tune in to more radio stations than a model with fewer batteries. I was stumped: I was unable to explain why that's not how it works: for the first time I found myself talking to an educated person my own age asking me a question for which I had no adequate answer. I'd just realised I was using a device without knowing how it worked.
What I took away from all these experiences was essentially an awareness of the power of life. When I got back to France, what I'd just experienced in Africa had had such an effect on me that I promised myself: *"I'll never build anything"*. Or to be more precise: *"I'll repair things, I'll transform what exists, but I won't build anything from scratch"*.
So in 1968 you weren't in Paris? No, I wasn't in Paris in May '68, and

the news we got distorted what was happening in France. Côte d'Ivoire had only recently gained independence: people were afraid that things might flare up. I went back to Paris in June. Everything was a bit vague; I wasn't really aware of what had happened, and it was hard to realise the nature of the void people found themselves in. I just didn't get it! I took part in demos, went to debates at the School of Decorative Arts, and I met up with friends who were activists. But I was completely lost! I lived in the 15th arrondissement, near the Citroën factory. It was the end of the sit-ins, petrol was becoming available again… I felt like I'd missed out on a step in the proceedings. Then I realised that it was out of the question for me to operate on my own. By saying that I wouldn't build, was I in effect leaving my profession behind? Did it mean I would no longer belong to a community? I couldn't relinquish my social environment – characterised by progressive Catholicism: after all, I had a brother who was a priest and a teacher who, a little like the worker-priests, refused to draw his priest's salary, preferring to live and exercise his calling freely.
I understood that I needed to be organised, and realised I needed a framework. In Africa I had met several enthusiastic teachers who organised film clubs at the University in Abidjan. One was a communist who was very active in the *Peuple et Culture* network and heavily involved in running film clubs. He encouraged me to approach the Communist Party. Back in Paris, I hesitated a little: I was active in non-profit organisations, and was a member of the PSU [*Parti Socialiste Unifié*] for a while. When the *Programme Commun* was signed, people had to make a choice: some went over to the Socialist Party *"to penetrate it"* as the expression went at the time, while others entered the Communist Party (not to penetrate it – it was impenetrable – but to join a powerful and well organised body). So I joined the *Parti Communiste.* I discovered a very high-level academic milieu – architects, philosophers, sociologists, anthropologists, filmmakers, and so on. I realised this was my cultural family. And I realised that my profession – architecture – didn't really interest me. **What fascinated me was the idea of building something that would bring people together in the general interest.** I was politically active in the 6th arrondissement and my "cell", as it was called in those days, would meet at the home of René Hilsum, founder of the *Au Sans Pareil* publishing house. The place was as unassuming as the office where we're sitting now, except you could see first editions of André Breton, Paul Eduard or Max Jacob, and the furniture was designed by Pierre Charreau and Francis Jourdain…

A whole world opened up before me: Louis Daquin, Marina Vlady, Françoise Arnould, Christian Topalov… All these film people whose movies I'd seen in Abidjan (I'd screened *French Cancan, Le Point du Jour,* etc.) were there in the flesh! I still find it amazing that I was able to meet them. I was very open-minded and willing to give people a lot of my time: I quickly became the indispensable *aide de camp* for anyone organising an event or a party… I was with Antoine Vitez, for example, when he opened the Quartiers d'Ivry theatre, and many others. And that's how I ended up at the *Fête de l'*Humanité. **So it really was your vow "never to build" that opened things up for you? As if by saying it you'd made yourself available and shown you were searching for something?** Yes. And if we go even further, saying *"I'll never build"* was also the logical outcome of something I thought at the time and still think today: *"I'm not good enough"*. I still think I'm lacking something. I can disagree with someone and think he's wrong without feeling that I'm on the same level as him. And that's probably why I'm so curious. By stepping back, I put things in another perspective and I tell myself that I'm not on the same level as this model: in fact, I'm not on a level at all. My father taught me that, in a competition, it's pointless to put yourself on the starting grid: you're likely to lose, because a lot of people are better than you. It's better to stay on one side, without a model or a point of comparison. That's why I make myself available to anyone who can teach me something. One day, for example, a dancer told me his knee hurt when he danced on a wooden floor. It suddenly occurred to me that the elasticity of the floor was the essence of the question I had to work on – I didn't give a damn about the light or whatever! Another time, someone came to complain about the cold: so I thought, before thinking about heating, what kind of insulation could be used… And it was in this role as an assistant, listening attentively to questions, that I kept experimenting with things. There's no answer to the question, so there's no profession that meets a need. But if we rephrased the question, maybe the question would disappear? **How to ask a question – that's what it's all about, isn't it?** **Maieutic, perhaps?** Yes [smiles], it's a Jesuit thing! Here I can say that I really have been influenced by my education! I wasn't really at a Jesuit school, it was actually a religious college run by a practically defrocked priest: almost an agnostic. I was eight; my father felt that he'd lost his first son, who'd entered the priesthood, and focused all his love on me. It was all a bit too much for me. The college superior, who realised this, wanted to lighten my burden. He tried to protect me (perhaps excessively) from indoctrination. In any case he made me think for myself. Maybe that's why I'm interested in everything! When a sewage worker tells me that what really disgusts him is changing his baby daughter's nappy, I wonder why that smell bothers him although it's not a problem in his daily work—which might even put him in contact with the same nappy! Does he fell he has a mission – a city can't function without sewers – that helps him get over his revulsion? Just like blood doesn't matter to a surgeon.

If everything interests you, how do you avoid getting lost in it all? Yes, everything interests me, but only from the point when a question is asked. It's not that everything interests me all the time! Or to be more precise, I'm interested in everything, but when I put my little fishing net in, I catch something. And as soon as that thing appears in the bottom of my net, there are a hundred things I no longer see, or whose existence I forget. But it's not that I've "missed" 99 other things: I fished to catch just one – and I let 99 get away. Ultimately, I'm only interested in the one I've caught, and I focus all my strength on that one: that's why I don't get lost! **Everything interests me…when it leads to something to do! I look for ways of starting to do things.** **To get back to what we were saying earlier, your interest in the *Fête de l'Humanité* foreshadowed your later involvement in ephemeral architecture, and many other things after that…** There were other things before the Fête de l'Huma: events for *Rouge*, the *Ligue Communiste Révolutionnaire* newspaper, and charity events at La Villette. The La Villette site, which was partly abandoned, had three halls: the central hall, the Pavillon de Paris and the "sheep hall". The Pavillon de Paris was occupied by some crook who organised non-conformist concerts, and no one was allowed into the "sheep hall". Only the main hall could be used. I had to set it up several times for events – it was the beginning of street theatre, the Festival d'Automne was looking for venues… With a friend who worked at Chaillot, I started to set up temporary facilities, including for rock concerts – in particular for the Rolling Stones in 1992! Little by little I climbed the ladder, so to speak, and finally worked for the Fête de l'Humanité, not on the central stage, which at the time was reserved for Oscar Niemeyer, but inside what was called the *Cité Internationale*, to help representatives of poor struggling countries who couldn't afford to set up a booth: refugees from Chile after the coup, or from Argentina fleeing the dictatorship – often intellectuals or artists. I was there to help them, and that's how I made a lot of friends from the theatre (Alfredo Arias, for example), as well as painters and so on. There was a sense of solidarity and La Courneuve was the focus for it.

The Fête de l'Humanité always coincides with back-to-school time in early September. In August, we'd set up camp in La Courneuve. My children remember: we'd take the bus and pitch our tent. We'd meet people from the Dordogne, from Chile, or other places. We ate together, chatted to each other, watched Leonard Cohen or Joan Baez rehearse on Friday night for the Saturday concert… **The *Fête de l'Humanité* is a perfect example of an encampment or the "tent city" – there were 600,000 people there!** 1968 to 1978 was a major period of collective action and activism for us. And for ten years I myself lived in a communal world where we only thought about communal things. We could never have let anyone sleep rough: we'd have immediately requisitioned a place for him to live. At the time, that's all I did: printing leaflets, occupying an apartment, putting someone up at my place, launching subscriptions, etc. A remember buying Santiago Carrillo's flat in Aubervilliers, at a time when he needed to be housed in France. When I talk about that now, people sometimes find it hard to believe! **It was a period that lived and breathed politics…** Why did it all disappear? That's the problem. I don't think politicians are less good, I think policies were really made to destroy all that. Now you see art galleries in areas workers used to live in. I had friends on the Rue de Savoie and the Rue Saint-André-des-Arts who would set off in their overalls to work at the Paris Mint. In 1974, the coin factory was transferred to Pessac near Bordeaux, and the historic Mint on the Quai de Conti now houses Guy Savoie's restaurant, recently fitted out by Jean-Michel Wilmotte. It's unbelievable! For what higher reason should we push those things away? The dislocation of the social fabric leads to the dislocation of the city itself, in all its diversity.

It was also the time the New Towns were starting to develop…

Yes, remember de Gaulle's famous words: *"Mettez-moi de l'ordre dans tout ce bordel!"* [Sort out this bloody mess for me!] Creating new towns from scratch without taking into account the local area or the environment was part of a strategy to break up the Communist suburbs – what used to be called the Red Belt around Paris. General de Gaulle had appointed an officer in charge of new towns: Paul Delouvrier. The idea was to create towns with no connection with the outside world where everything would be provided: schools, jobs… **But life, like happiness, can't be planned: it has to be experienced.** Later on I had the opportunity to work in some of these towns and I became aware of their positive qualities. People said Sarcelles was an unbearable place to live, and yet Jews and Arabs lived there together, and there were restaurants on the ground floors of the buildings serving African food, Portuguese food and so on. I know Noisiel well because I designed a small theatre there on the banks of the Marne. Since then I've seen the damage that's been done: it's a farming area covered in magnificent rural architecture that, in a way, represented France. Now we have an area where everything revolves around motorways, cut up into an incomprehensible grid that won't let you travel across it. As for the theatre in Noisiel, whereas at the beginning you could just walk in, it's now got decking all around it and has code-protected gates! The rest is just the same: we create ugliness and neglect. There's been a tipping point against which I've fought tooth and nail. And when I'm asked why I'm still so passionate about things, and why I still want to find alternative ways of doing politics, I reply that it simply seems impossible to me to avoid tackling communal issues. **I could never have imagined, in 1974, that one day there'd be a policy to destroy social housing. It's so brutal!** Since everything interested me, I decided I was going to work with other people. It's called participation, but it's more than that. All I knew was that I wouldn't stop. Even in situations of crisis, even in the heart of the worst kinds of conflict—I've been to war-torn countries such as Lebanon—the instinct for survival generates incredible energy. After an earthquake you see all these ruined houses, all these people crying, and then you see two kids who've found a tyre to play with in the rubble. Before anything else, they play! And then people start to get organised. How will they stay clean? How will they find food? You have to be optimistic! **Closer to home, what can we learn from the Jungle in Calais, which gradually developed and created its own social fabric?** What we call a slum is, on the face of it, a sustainable development habitat: it's made by re-using things. We could learn how to re-use what we throw away. We could also help improve the quality of these constructions. Situations of this kind are just going to get worse. There have always been major periods of population movement, but today there are quite a few more of us on the planet. It's something we're going to have to live with. And living with it means not allowing slums, which are ghettos, or camps like the ones we're seeing today, to continue. On the contrary it means looking at how we can integrate the community (which wasn't a ghetto to start with but which became one because people speak the same language, for example, or have the same social background). **Integrating the community doesn't mean losing it but taking it into account – both as a necessity and as a source of strength.**

Calais is a town in decline, a town that's losing its industry and part of its working-class habitat. So why is it that nobody wanted to renovate empty housing or closed-down factories? We could have repaired housing evenly distributed across the area and made it available to these people, who would then have become new residents. In the beginning the "Jungle" was really difficult because there were a lot of poor people there living in very tough conditions. And little by little, as it developed, entire families with children, middle class people, and people with jobs like mine (architects, doctors and so on) came to Calais. Some, from Beirut, had experience of camps. I met one of them, who'd been a teacher in one of the camps for five years. How was it possible to imagine that they were incapable of setting up a real school? It might have been great if a Syrian teacher who'd left Beirut to go to Calais set up a school here, not in the camp but in town, with the support of the Education Ministry. **There was even a democratically elected camp council. Why didn't Calais Town Council ask these elected members to attend council meetings?** Why this contempt? We could have found an intermediate space between Le Channel and the camp, and built a marquee, which would have been a place where people could come. Someone told me they'd built a theatre in the Jungle and that there were fourteen restaurants and lots of little shops… Isn't that what we're not able to do in housing estates – bring life back? We could have had a new district in Calais. **All this demonstrates an unbearably blinkered approach, and we're paying a very high price.** Hosting foreigners is a difficult but exciting issue. And it's a question of survival: if we don't tackle the subject, we'll die.

I have friends who look after the camp at Porte de la Chapelle/Clignancourt, and who'd like to recover the containers used for housing refugees when the Jungle was demolished. It's so complicated legally that it's impossible to give them these shelters. So the camp was demolished because it wasn't part of the town, then they set up specially equipped containers that cost 15 million euros, and now they're going to throw them away!

I came across ten Syrian intellectuals who wanted to stay in France, and I tried to help them. They weren't poor or isolated migrants: their parents were sending them money. I couldn't do a thing – in the end they couldn't stay in Paris and had to go back to Beirut, where they now work for an NGO running a camp. How come nobody found a way of using their skills (some were primary school teachers, others architects) to welcome poor or less well-organised Syrians? We really have to sit round a table and think about these kinds of situations! **All these fragments of cities built from salvaged materials themselves represent an ecological approach.** All that's missing in a sewage system, as in all towns, and it's up to the authorities to look after that, but once you've dealt with the sewage disposal, you can leave people free to build. **Are you just about to set yourself a new challenge?** After ten years working in the Construire architecture firm, from 1995 to 2005, I made up my mind in 2006 to give up architecture in the traditional sense. But it takes a long time to stop: you build up a certain momentum and I didn't want to cause problems for the other partners. So I decided to use this time and make the most of the structure of the firm to do some experiments, starting with social housing. In three projects we tried to do what no architect wanted to do: renovate social housing earmarked for demolition and keeping people in their homes. I wasn't saying that I was better at architecture than others, it was more like "give me some architecture that's scheduled for demolition". We succeeded in running three very different projects, whose common denominator is to involve future residents in the reinvention of their homes: – *Les Bogues du Blat*, in Beaumont in the Ardèche, a project presented in the *Constellation.s* exhibition; – *The 53 houses in the Stephenson* area in Tourcoing, northern France, jointly produced by the future residents who worked on the build in a very hands-on way; – *And 60 houses in Boulogne-sur-Mer*, in the Pas-de-Calais. Of the three projects, the last was the most complicated because the original buildings were emergency housing that should have been demolished after twenty years and which are now thirty-five years old. The consensus was that these buildings should be demolished because the people who lived in them were impossible to live with: burglars, unemployed people, drinkers, rapists…the list goes on. People who were in tragic social situations. I decided to tackle the problem. The mayor of Boulogne-sur-Mer agreed, although he didn't believe I'd succeed. I asked Sophie Ricard – who was 23 and a recent architecture graduate who had done her internship at Construire – to take charge of the project, on the sole condition that she must live in one of the houses. So we chose one of the walled-up houses, and Sophie moved in with her boyfriend. She didn't have much money. We helped her move. There was an underlying question: "can we live here and, by doing so, make others want to live here?" She made the house into a place to live and work, and she showed that this place, which was going to be demolished, could be lived in, even by someone who wasn't from the same background as the other local residents, although nobody thought it would work. It started with the children: they were the first to see an interior that was more pleasant to live in than their own. Sophie even helped kids with their schoolwork when some of them, although they were at school, asked her to help them read and write. And slowly but surely she was able to enter the homes of all the local residents…

So instead of doing a project for 60 houses, she did 60 projects for one house. That's all. What I just said doesn't seem like much, but it's fundamental: she turned the question on its head. She took the time to look at each house in detail and ascertain its condition. And each time it was a house with a name, a resident, a house number, and an address. She even managed the budget – a quarter of the price of demolition and reconstruction for the residents: – What would you like? Do you prefer the big bath, like the one in this magazine? But then we won't be able to put that paint here…and do you want a super-modern kitchen, in which case there won't be a fireplace? And so on. **And after these three experiments in self-production of social housing?** I then decided to focus on the question of the non-brief: "is it possible to tackle questions we have no answer to, simply by turning up, in other words by saying "let's start by occupying the place, the answer will come"? I launched the idea of "architectural presence", which took the gamble of occupying a plot with no predefined aim. We ran three experiments of this kind, and they are now closed or completed.

Last but not least, I've just deposited my archives at the FRAC (Fonds Régional d'Art Contemporain) in Orléans. This FRAC is unusual in that it has set up – on the initiative of Frédéric Migayrou and Marie Ange Brayer – a collection of "manifest architecture" at the frontier of art and architecture.

Abdelkader Damani, the current director, convinced me that it would be interesting to add my archives to this collection, because my work is not always seen as architecture – which is true – but that I have nevertheless built things that have been used. After all, architecture is a service art… So on 18 November 2016, I gave them all my sketchbooks and all the records of my experiments since 1977 (before then, I threw things away). People around me were really worried, they thought I'd get depressed… But curiously enough, it made me feel lighter and younger. I know where my archives are, and I no longer have to look after them! In the meantime at the request of Fleur Pellerin I'd got involved in the *Loi Création, architecture et patrimoine* supported by Patrick Bloche at the National Assembly. A lot of architects and clients had been consulted, but the law

remained very corporatist. My idea was – based on precise examples that could be used – to prove that things get done when people are free to do them **When I worked with Daniel Buren I discovered a fundamental difference between art, which can only be judged retrospectively, and architecture.** As you know, in 1986, following a lawsuit undertaken by the Association de Défense du Palais Royal, the work in the main courtyard we'd started with Daniel Buren was halted by order of the court. I was responsible, as the architect, for having begun the work without a building permit. We were defended by the Conseil d'État, which considered that it was impossible to judge an artwork before it's completely finished, and that the work should thus resume to finish what had been started. This opinion forms a kind of Daniel Buren jurisprudence. That was a non-violent battle. It was a political act that supports the idea that one can engage in debate about art: so today it is accepted that an artwork is a process, and that you can't judge it until it's finished. But it's not the same for architecture, which has objectives to achieve, rules to comply with (relating to disabled access, ecology, history, safety, and so on.) And in this field it's still not acceptable to say: *"We'll judge the architect on what's been done"*. There are too many prior precautions that just hold up the action… It would be better to do things, then observe the outcome: thought modifies the act, and the act modifies thought. Do we ask a film director to show us his film before he starts filming it? No! He can film because he's sold an idea: people trust him, with the risk it might not work. And he films! From that point there's a chemistry that takes place between the sound man, the actors, the set designer, the script writer and so on, and that's what makes the film work (or not). Architecture should be like that.
I worked on one of the very short articles of the *Loi Création, Architecture et Patrimoine*: it runs to ten lines and is entitled permis de faire. These ten lines were then submitted to the legislator and tested by the experts working alongside the legislator. The law was ultimately passed on 17 July 2016, and the "social, economic and cultural experimentation" part had been removed from the ten-line article; what was left was technical experimentation, which is interesting but only from a corporatist point of view. And the decree of implementation, which will be issued soon, is even more restrictive. To take this as far as it would go, I'd asked the Ministry to give me the means to observe seven experimental projects, in the form of a mission entitled *La Preuve Par Sept* (the seven-step proof). Meanwhile, Fleur Pellerin left the minis-

try… so I eased off on this issue until someone suggested I join the Belleville architecture school to carry out the research – which is both applied and fundamental. OK, but in what framework? I'm retired, which means that, for the first time in my life, I got a grant. So it was out of the question that I might occupy a teaching post. I'd give them my time free! Initially, the other teachers were reluctant and suspicious of this idea of volunteer work. For me it's very clear: I get a pension because we're in an organised society. So it's only natural that I should give my time. It's Republican volunteer work. My proposal was finally accepted. So I'm going to work in the Belleville school to set up a teaching chair on the *permis de faire*. People object that you need prior authorisation to set up an academic chair. That's precisely why it's a good idea to apply the *permis de faire*: with no authorisation: we're going to set up the chair for three years, then we'll see if it's proved its worth! I don't want the chair for myself, but I can prepare it so that a doctoral student can take over. The first initiative will be a week of lectures on economic, social and political issues in May. Meanwhile, a bit like someone reading by the fireside, I'm choosing a few books by authors I want to invite to do readings for volunteer students who will then be involved in the May event. And from October, classes relating to this research will be included in the school's syllabus.

The word "chaire" dates back to the Middle Ages – doesn't it refer to an object?

It's a place to speak from! **So ultimately you're carrying on with something that you've always done: passing on knowledge.** That's right! And what's funny is that at the heart of it all I still keep feeling I don't make the grade. I see the lecturers, the classes, the subjects, I attend education committee meetings, I hear things I can't make head or tail of…

And then at a certain point I realise that when I speak, people are intrigued: *"Wait a minute, that actually sounds pretty interesting …"*

Sigrid
Didier
Francine
Hélène
Corinne
Diallo
Aude

Diallo, Corinne, Hélène, Francine and Didier were homeless. Thanks to Gironde Habitat they were housed in the Gleditschia facility in Eysines while they got back on their feet. This living environment that allows its occupants to recover their dignity forms part of an initiative known as "logement passerelle"—bridge housing—developed with the Emmaüs housing department. People live there for an average of six to eight months. As soon as they have recovered their independence, they leave the hostel and move into normal housing.
Also takin part in the round table: Sigrid Monnier, Director of Gironde Habitat, and Aude Boyer, Director of the housing department of Emmaüs Gironde.

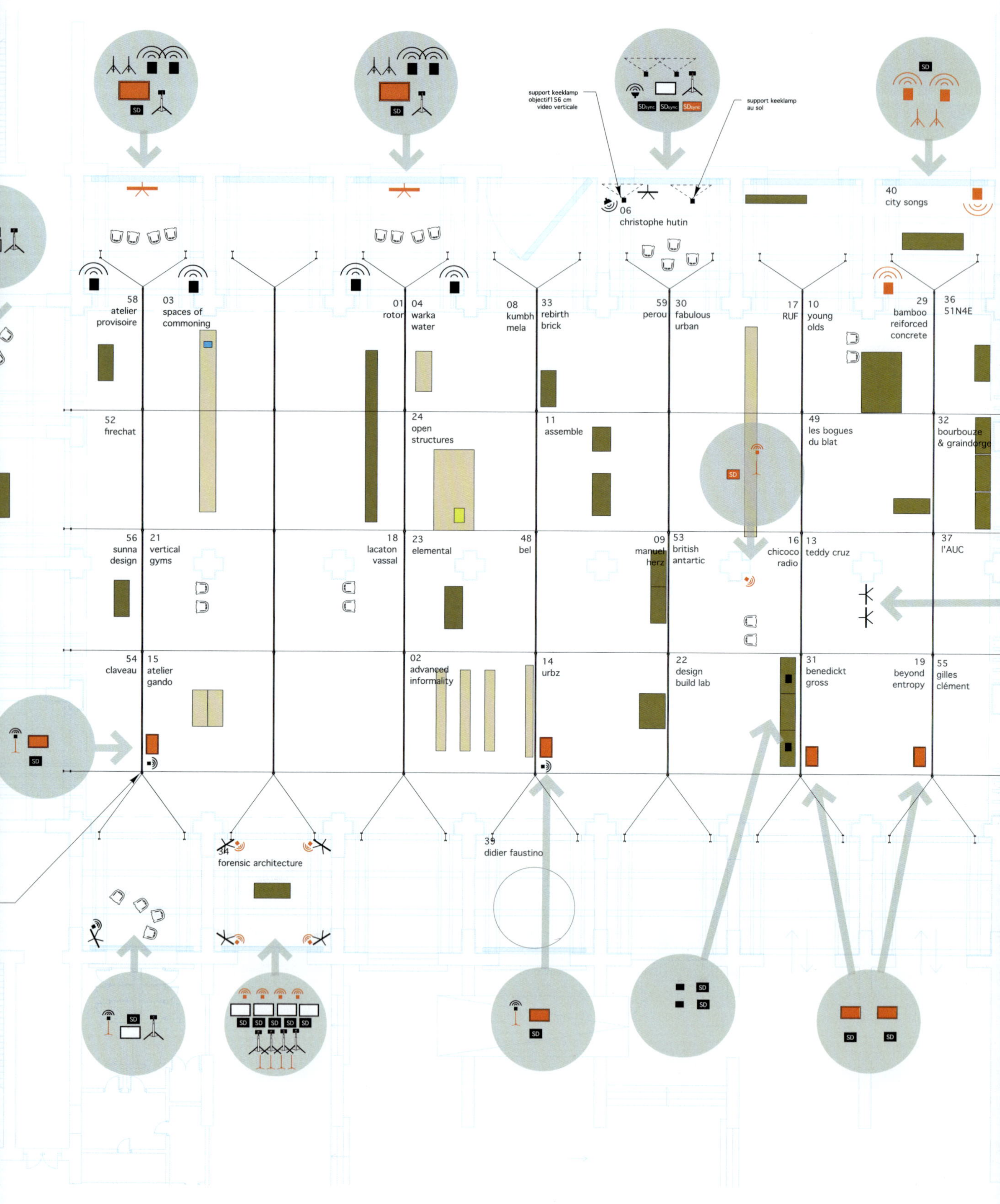

support keeklamp
objectif156 cm
video verticale
support keeklamp
au sol
06
christophe hutin
40
city songs
58
atelier
provisoire
03
spaces of
commoning
01
rotor
04
warka
water
08
kumbh
mela
33
rebirth
brick
59
perou
30
fabulous
urban
17
RUF
10
young
olds
29
bamboo
reiforced
concrete
36
51N4E
52
firechat
24
open
structures
11
assemble
49
les bogues
du blat
32
bourbouze
& graindorge
56
sunna
design
21
vertical
gyms
18
lacaton
vassal
23
elemental
48
bel
09
manuel
herz
53
british
antartic
16
chicoco
radio
13
teddy cruz
37
l'AUC
54
claveau
15
atelier
gando
02
advanced
informality
14
urbz
22
design
build lab
31
benedickt
gross
19
beyond
entropy
55
gilles
clément
34
forensic architecture
39
didier faustino

the exhibition

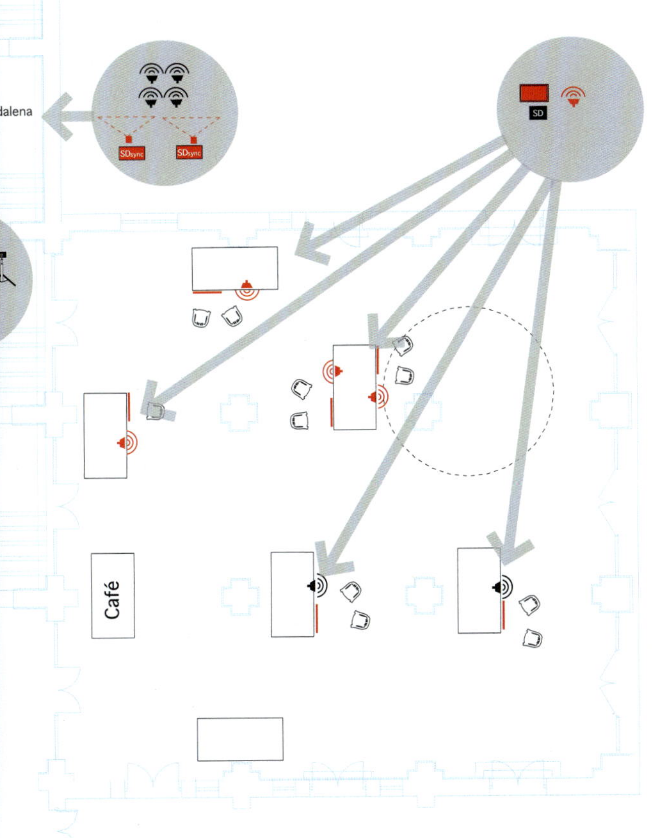

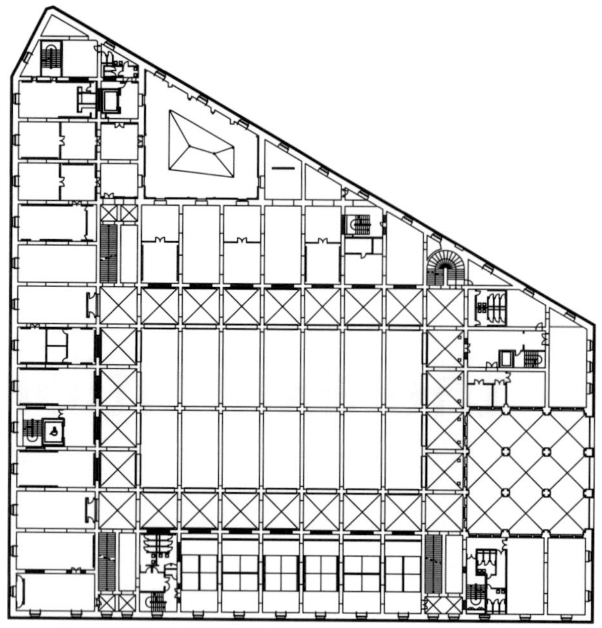

First floor

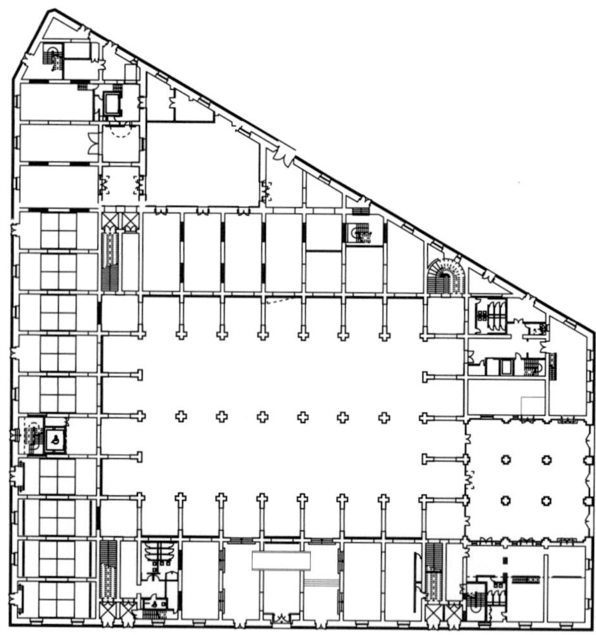

Ground floor

layout

constellation.s takes the form of a public space that visitors can freely walk around.
The exhibition occupies several areas of the Entrepôt including the main hall and the ground floor concourse, the mezzanines, the large gallery, and the white gallery on the first floor.
Once through the reception area, the visitor enters the monumental main hall, which opens out like a public square, in the shade of a series of large hanging visuals.
A selection of forty-two projects, approaches and situations is displayed on large printed canvas panels three metres tall and six metres long, bathed in natural light.
A regular pattern of steel cables supports these panels, which hang just above the visitor's eye-line so that there is a clear view of the entire hall.
On the floor, under the rows of hanging panels, among the display units, are over two hundred "generic" white plastic garden chairs scattered randomly around, where visitors can sit and read, look around them, share impressions, consult documents, or just have a rest. The hall thus also becomes a meeting place that can be explored across its entire length and breadth.
On the edge of the central area, under the mezzanines, in semi-darkness, documentaries, situations, testimonials and objects are presented, all directly linked to the themes explored in the hall.
On the first floor, the areas on the walkways offer visitors the opportunity to watch interviews with intellectuals and excerpts from documentaries, which can also be seen in full in the white gallery.
The walkways are divided into a series of areas equipped with Texaa acoustic padding, Serif viewing screens designed by Ronan & Erwan Bouroullec, and white armchairs.

At first floor level, two further rows of panels run lengthways along the hall. Displaying twenty-five photographic contributions, these large diptychs are designed to be viewed from the mezzanines.
The concourse, which is cool in summer, features a café and a relaxation and meeting area in the middle of a specially designed installation. Last but not least, the large gallery offers a series of installations covering 450 square metres, provided by the exhibition sponsors and focusing on urban innovations reflecting new approaches in the corporate environment, directly linked to the themes explored in **constellation.s**.

Michel Jacques

2 juin > 25 septembre
arc en rêve centre d'architecture
constellation.s
ENT

constellation.s
2 juin > 25 septembre
arc en rêve centre d'architecture
OT.

#09
La contrainte
de la solution, pas
Repensons les
urbaine pour ouvrir
à un monde
la rente et la
the solution, not
We must rethink
the urban economy.

issance
elle met
s et valeurs
ne à voir
net en récit
force.
act, and
values.
ce that
llenges and
our shared

744

746

#09
La contrainte économique fait partie
de la solution, pas du problème.
Repensons les règles de l'économie
urbaine pour ouvrir des alternatives
à un monde souvent façonné par
la rente et la spéculation.
Economic parameters are part of
the solution, not the problem.
We must rethink the rules of
the urban economy, opening up
alternatives to a world all too often
shaped by profit and speculation.

LA VIE DE FAMILLE
ANACHRONIQUE
LE BON SENS

LA VILLE EXPLOSE
MULTICOLORE

café

café
arc en rêve centre d'architecture
station
mollat
Michel Lussault, géographe

751

etc.

constellations

ENTREPÔT

the exhibition

curators
arc en rêve centre d'architecture

Michel Lussault, geographer, president of arc en rêve
Francine Fort, director, chief curator
Michel Jacques, architect, artistic director

research, follow-up and coordination
Wenwen Cai, architect
Éric Dordan, architect

texts
Félix Mulle, architect
Théo Fort-Jacques, geographer

with the entire arc en rêve team and our assistants, interns and volunteers

exhibition design
Cyrille Brisou, designer
Daniel le Hérissé, coordinator
Pauline Kerzerho, architect
Ludovic Gillon, architect
Emmanuelle Maura, graphic designer

production assistants
Éloïse Roch, Sophie Geoffroy, Marina Tolstoukhine

events coordination
Anastassia Mathie Deltcheva

communication
Joëlle Dubois, communication manager
Marie-Christine Mendy, layout designer
Constance Leprêtre, assistant

mediation
Sara Meunier, architect

administration
Adrien Bensignor, general secretary
Frédérique Jacotot, accountant

special team members
Loup Niboyet, graphic designer
Marie Bruneau & Bertrand Genier, graphic designers
Éric Troussicot, architect
Martyn Back, traducteur

occasional team members
Charlotte Bertruc, Jennifer Poirier, logistique
Florence Esnault, Valérie Baran, graphic designers

construction
Christophe Hautemanière, Daniel Avram, Théo Lebleu, Grégoire Laroche-Joubert, Camille Florent, Irwin Marchal, Johann Milh, Bruno Sauvonnet, Jean Michel, Kuba Gorny and pupils from the Lycée des Métiers Léonard-de-Vinci Blanquefort and the Centre de Formation d'Apprentis du Bâtiment et des Travaux Publics Blanquefort

reception, security
Hakima Chahid, Lémy Busato, Massimo Capano, Émilie Fleurot, Margaux Liesenborghs, Lauryann Magar, Isabelle Quintana, Pierre Minard, Hélène Abdelli

interns
Luc Sanciaume, University of Westminster
Pauline Bonnin, Nicolas Féola, ensapBx
Celina Carrier, Émilie Nouvel, Théo Ménivard, Sciences Po Bx
Alice Jean-Jean, ISIC Bx and students from l'Icart
Inès Benais, Lycée Professionnel des Chartrons
Justine Vaillant, sudents studying publishing at IUT Bordeaux Montaigne

volunteers
Christine Bielle, Joffrey Bispo, Laetitia Grucy, Severin Kaling

thanks

institutional
partners

Mairie de Bordeaux

Bordeaux Métropole

Ministère de la Culture
DRAC Nouvelle-Aquitaine

Région Nouvelle-Aquitaine

Groupe Caisse des Dépôts

cultural and educational
partners

ensapBx

EBABx

ICART

Centre de cultures Bordeaux Métropole

Centre de formation d'apprentis du BTP Gironde Blanquefort

UFA Lycée des métiers Léonard-de-Vinci Blanquefort

CNC Centre national du cinéma et de l'image animée

l'Agence VU

sponsors

Nexity

Domofrance

aquitanis

Tollens

Bouygues Immobilier

Vinci Construction France

Samsung

Gironde Habitat

Vilogia

Mazars

Texaa

media partners

Télérama

Le Monde

Mollat Station Ausone

d'a

arcenreve.com

la ville, l'architecture, le paysage, le design, à Bordeaux, dans sa région, dans le monde, tous les jours, toute l'année, avec arc en rêve centre d'architecture, architecture, landscape, design, urban societies, all over the world, every day of the year at arc en rêve centre d'architecture, Bordeaux

a project

arc en rêve is a project. A project that involves building a culture of architecture shared with those who make the city: elected officials, professionals, intellectuals, and residents, both adults and children…
A programme designed to develop a cultural sensitivity to the contemporary forms of planning, architecture, design and landscaping, and to generate a qualitative dynamic in the field of planning and development.
It reflects our eagerness to inform and train people about the processes of production involved, sharing knowledge on new ways of living and new ways of using land.
Our ambition to bring together the points of view of intellectuals, artists, politicians and inhabitants to help us understand our time and think about the future of our societies.
Our commitment to the dissemination of ideas, interfacing with the political, social and economic spheres.
Our goal of organising and running a space for social communication where architects and technicians work in direct contact with the images and stories produced by inhabitants.
Still, as ever, our purpose is to foster a desire for architecture, to encourage creativity, and to open people's eyes to a changing world.

Francine Fort
general director, arc en rêve

arc en rêve centre d'architecture **bordeaux**

index constellation.s
120 contributions

constellation.s the book

editorial team

chief editor **Francine Fort**
artistic director **Michel Jacques**
editorial assistant **Théo Fort-Jacques**
editorial coordinator **Margaux Liesenborghs**

graphic design **Nicolas Etienne**
audio transcripts **Jeanne Richard**
translations **Martyn Back**

additional photos
Collectif Cocktail + ppLab pp.752
Rodolphe Escher pp. 42, 67, 146, 435, 725, 732, 734, 736, 738, 740, 742, 744, 746, 748, 750, 756
Michel Jacques pp. 28
Florent Larronde pp. 329
Margaux Liesenborghs pp. 50, 82, 90, 112, 126, 138, 147, 156, 166, 211, 218, 226, 242, 254, 279, 284, 306, 358, 382, 392, 414, 544
Yvan Mathie p. 754
Emmanuelle Maura p. 388
Eloïse Roch pp. 384
Luc Sanciaume p. 386

Published by
arc en rêve centre d'architecture
7 rue Ferrère
33000 Bordeaux
T. +33 5 56 48 45 20
www.arcenreve.com

Printed in Spain
by Ulzama,
Pol. Ind. Areta, calle A-35
31620 Huarte
www.ulzama.com

Distributor:
Actes Sud
www.actes-sud.fr

Legal deposit: October 2017

ISBN: 978-2-330-08927-6

October 2017

This book has received financial support from the Bordeaux City Council, Bordeaux Métropole and the Ministry of Culture.
Its price reflects this, making it accessible to a broad readership.